THE ESSENTIAL

Vancouver Island Outdoor Recreation Guide

THE ESSENTIAL

Vancouver Island Outdoor Recreation Guide

BY JOHN KIMANTAS

whitecap

Edited by Elaine Jones
Proofread by Joan E. Templeton
Cover and interior design by Diane Yee,
    Enthusiastic Elephant Illustration & Design
Photography and maps by John Kimantas **www.thewildcoast.ca**

Printed in Canada by Friesens

Library and Archives Canada Cataloguing in Publication

Kimantas, John
    The essential Vancouver Island outdoor recreation guide /
John Kimantas.

Includes index.
ISBN 978-1-55285-920-9

    1. Outdoor recreation—British Columbia—Vancouver Island—
Guidebooks. 2. Vancouver Island (B.C.)—Guidebooks. I. Title.

GV191.46.B7K45 2008   796.509711'2   C2007-905171-5

The publisher acknowledges the financial support of the Government of Canada through the Book Publishing Industry Development Program (BPIDP) and the Province of British Columbia through the Book Publishing Tax Credit.

To my father, Frank, who has quietly but enthusiastically supported all my oddball projects and misadventures over the years. And to my mother, Valerie, who passed away May 21, 2005, just days before I had a chance to show her my first book. Thanks for everything, to both of you.

Kennedy Lake, Clayoquot Sound.

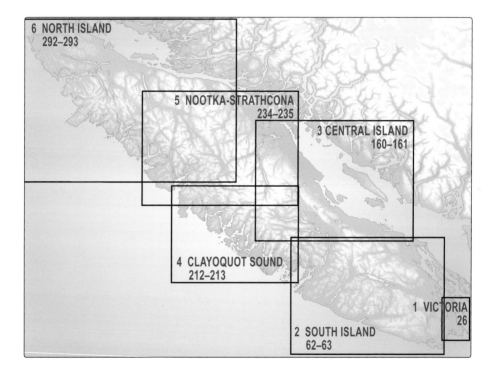

6 NORTH ISLAND
292–293

5 NOOTKA-STRATHCONA
234–235

3 CENTRAL ISLAND
160–161

4 CLAYOQUOT SOUND
212–213

1 VICTORIA
26

2 SOUTH ISLAND
62–63

Contents

Preface

This book is written for people who love Vancouver Island. It's not for those who love to *use* Vancouver Island.

Lovers of Vancouver Island will visit an area—sometimes taking great pains to reach it—for the simple appreciation of the time and place. They will experience it by soaking in the beauty, then depart. The wilderness will suffer no more than the fleeting impact of footprints along a trail or the impression of a tent.

Those who love to *use* Vancouver Island see it as a commodity and look for what the area has to offer and how it can be exploited. All too often the wilderness is abused and discarded in the process—akin to a visit to an outdoors motel, with Mother Nature left as the housekeeper to return order in the aftermath. Unfortunately this type of housekeeping can take decades. Sometimes the damage can't be repaired.

Vancouver Island is under pressure like never before. Readers of this book will notice an undercurrent of frustration with the extent of logging and encroaching development. Vancouver Island is essentially a tree farm for a handful of logging companies. Outside a few protected pockets of parkland, everything—the wildlife, the scenic vistas, the recreational potential—has been handed to these companies to destroy at their whim. For us as a society it seems sufficient that trees can grow back, as if the island is unharmed in the process.

Occasionally pockets are saved, but these cases are few and far between amid the wholesale slaughter of complete valleys. While I am under no illusion that Vancouver Island should be turned into a museum for tree lovers, there must be a balance. Currently it is tipped so heavily in favour of the logging companies that it *should* be criminal; it's hard to think of another word when you look over a formerly scenic vista and see nothing but scarred hillsides. At the very least this level of exploitation is a sad commentary on our generation. We can applaud the employment; we can benefit from the tax revenue; we can be thankful for the wood. But we cannot be proud of the devastation we are leaving behind. Yes, I know—trees grow back, ecologies recover. But the forests are never the same. And

I wonder how many jewels like the Vanishing River (page 311) have been lost forever.

Residential development is equally out of control. As this book is being written the island is going through a phenomenal growth phase, and it's difficult to read a day's newspaper without hearing about another new major development being proposed. I find it ironic that high-rises gain the most opposition. It is urban sprawl that will kill the character of Vancouver Island, not high-density development within cities. Consider that southeast Vancouver Island is almost entirely private property, much of it owned by logging companies that can flip properties for development once the trees are gone. Increasingly, municipalities are being hamstrung by a popular option from developers: allow us a high-density, urban-style development in exchange for some parkland or we'll develop the whole thing, as we are entitled to do. And so in exchange for what was once a sprawling forest we get a pocket park, often on land that could never be developed. We shrug it off as the price of private ownership, as progress, as a necessity for the newcomers that need somewhere to live, even as an economic boost. The result will soon be non-stop housing developments from Victoria to Campbell River—a Mississauga in paradise (with apologies to Mississauga, but the metropolitan urban sprawl it represents will be a travesty on Vancouver Island).

While this is grim enough, it will have an increasingly adverse effect on the few remaining wilderness areas. More and more recreation is being pushed into the few accessible pristine areas left, and too many people do not understand the impact of their visits in these locations. The results are often tragic. I don't want to dwell on the leftover garbage, the degradation by unthinking visitors in four-wheel-drive vehicles, the proliferation of firepits in unsuitable locations, the unregulated use of ATVs and dirt bikes that tear up the landscape, the endless noise of powerboats on lakes. Obviously, some people don't understand how to treat the wilderness beyond their own immediate needs. Worse yet, they don't care. It seems if someone can benefit from the recreation—whether beach bonfire booze-ups or an ATV along a creek bed—the noise, pollution and leftover garbage is of no consequence. For many, these destructive activities define a wilderness experience. And thus I fear for the future of many of the most attractive places on Vancouver Island.

Sharing information about Vancouver Island's few remaining wilderness locations in this book comes with a risk—one of which I am painfully aware. In no case does a wilderness area improve once it is discovered. Visitors should know that no-trace camping is a myth. No matter how light the footprint you leave, when it is repeated a thousand times it has the potential to destroy the area— through trampling, through garbage, through erosion, through driving away wildlife. In other words, your most simple visit to these places could be helping ruin the very thing that made it so attractive.

Please, be a lover of Vancouver Island, not a user. Tread lightly. Take nothing but the memories. Leave nothing but your appreciation. Leave the motors as far away as possible. Enjoy the exercise, fresh air and natural beauty without leaving a trail of carbon monoxide and tire prints.

And if you truly love Vancouver Island, help make it better. On the return leg of a backpacking trip, for instance, instead of stepping over a bit of garbage and cursing the person who left it, pick it up. Fill the space left by your depleted food with things you can carry out. It's a small step, but done a thousand times it will make a huge difference.

Also, fight for the protection of the areas you love the most. Help ecological campaigns and land purchase fundraisers to buy choice parcels for future parks and wilderness reserves.

I know it's a cliché, but with a little thought you can leave the island better than you found it.

Acknowledgements

I am once again grateful for the assistance provided by BC Parks, Parks Canada, Ministry of Energy, Mines and Petroleum Resources, Ministry of Agriculture and Lands Integrated Land Management Bureau and various municipalities across Vancouver Island from Sooke to Mount Waddington. I would also like to thank organizations such as the Freshwater Fisheries Society of BC, BC Hydro, Caving Canada (**www.cancaver.ca**) and the Canadian Mountain Encyclopedia (**www.bivouac.com**).

There are also the many people along the way—the tourist bureau workers, fellow travelers, loggers and government employees—who always helped point me in the right direction. Thanks to them all.

Introduction

A few years back I was in my office in Ontario looking at a map of Canada to find two communities: Truro, Nova Scotia, and Nanaimo, British Columbia. I was in line for a promotion and could have ended up at either location. A few weeks later I was strolling to work along Nanaimo's seawall on my way to my new office when I stopped to watch a seal playing in the picture-perfect harbour, with two nearby islands framed by the breathtaking white-capped mainland mountains in a scene of brilliant blue ocean dotted with dozens of boats at anchor. I can't speak for what Truro might have been like, but I felt like I had won a lottery coming here.

A few weeks later I was offered a promotional helicopter ride to the top of Mount Cokely near Mount Arrowsmith. Our group was dropped off with a picnic lunch and a bottle of wine on the mountaintop, with a chance to walk along the alpine bluffs to search for viewpoints. During the helicopter portion of the trip we circled many of the major mountains of Strathcona, and the pilot listed off names of peaks that meant nothing then, but now each has its distinctive personality and individual appeal in my mind—from benign alpine hiking to difficult climbing ascents.

Sunny summer weekends became a chance to more widely explore the island, and not long after that helicopter trip I was back on the peaks at Mount Arrowsmith, this time the hard way. It felt better arriving by personal effort, because I knew this was the way the island should be explored—in tune with its grace and beauty. A formula was soon established. The longer and more difficult the trip, the greater the feeling of accomplishment, the more enjoyable the experience and generally the better the scenery once you arrived.

My attention eventually turned to the water, and for several years I explored the BC coast by kayak. For anyone interested in visiting the shores of Vancouver Island, whether by motorized boat or paddle (though my bias to paddles is obvious), consider the *Wild Coast* series of guidebooks. Three volumes cover the entire British Columbia coast: *Volume 1* focuses on the island's north and west coast, *Volume 3* on the island's south and east coast and *Volume 2* on the north and central BC coast to the Alaskan border.

This book looks at Vancouver Island from a terrestrial perspective, though water remains an intrinsic part of exploring the island—whether canoeing Great Central Lake to reach magnificent Della Falls or tackling the whitewater of Puntledge River. The book covers most of the inland water features of the island, as well as the coastal communities and ocean areas that can be reached by foot. So expect a bit of overlap into the *Wild Coast* series, though not into the marine features. For everything beyond the land, consult volumes 1, 2 and 3 of *The Wild Coast.*

The format for *The Essential Vancouver Island Outdoor Recreation Guide* gelled about the time I picked up a road map to try and pinpoint a feature mid-island. I found, to my dismay, that beyond the road to Youbou the map had no roads and no features for the inland of southern Vancouver Island. It was an empty land mass. I imagine a good majority of people who visit and even live on the island have the same impression—that recreation is limited mainly to the established corridors; everywhere else is an obscure, remote, featureless and almost inaccessible wilderness.

The polar opposite also exists. Diehard crag climbers, for instance, have named just about every obscure rock face on the island. Whitewater paddlers have chronicled the bends and rapids on every river, no matter how remote. Mountain bikers have multitudes of trails through entire regions, each lovingly named and rated for its features and difficulties. And hiking trails can be found just about anywhere. In the end every hill and mountain is a potential ascent. Every river is a potential whitewater route. Every lake is a potential paddle. And every forest has a potential trail. The problem is the quality and access vary considerably.

This begs the question of what sort of information should be in a general-interest wilderness/outdoors guide covering an area of about 31,000 square kilometres. Naturally, this book can't include the technical details of every individual sport. That's the topic for a half-dozen books, not one. Nor is it necessary to list every obscure option when several dozen (and sometimes hundreds) of better options exist.

So this book evolved into a juggling act of what to include and what to leave out. It is essentially a tribute to the land, with an outline of the range of adventures available for exploring it.

Many locations are remote, so a great deal of information is provided to get you to these places. There is a huge difference between a squiggle on a map indicating a logging road and actually finding your way through a maze of unnamed logging spurs. Route maps, text descriptions and GPS waypoints are all offered as ways to get you to your destination quickly and safely.

MAP KEY

⊞ REST AREA: The picnic table icon denotes locations ideal for a break but where camping is restricted or unsuitable.

⊿ ESTABLISHED CAMPSITE: The blue tent indicates wilderness or hike-in-only campsites with a developed camping area. Expect these sites to be free.

⊿ UNDEVELOPED CAMPSITE: The red tent icon is for possible camping areas that have not yet been developed, or are under-developed with no official sanction or protection beyond being located on Crown land.

⊿ FEE CAMPING: The green tent indicates formal walk-in campsites that require fees, usually in provincial parks.

⊿ VEHICLE-ACCESSIBLE CAMPSITE: This icon indicates sites with vehicle access, possibly in combination with tent-only campsites. Only provincial, regional or municipal sites are listed. Private sites are not, unless strategically significant.

⊜ BOAT LAUNCH SITE: This icon indicates locations suitable for launching trailer-carried boats, cartop boats or kayaks. The list is not exhaustive for coastal launch sites; see the *BC Coastal Recreation Kayaking and Small Boat Atlas* series (Whitecap, 2007) for a full listing of marine features.

⊙ CANOE LAUNCH: This indicates places suitable for launching canoes or other cartop boats. They invariably have no official status.

⊙ LIGHTHOUSE: This symbol is used for manned lighthouses or previously manned light stations where the buildings are still in evidence. It does not include lighted buoys or navigation lights.

⊙ PRIVATE MARINA: This icon shows the general location of a private marina. The list is not exhaustive; for a more detailed listing of Vancouver Island marinas, see the *BC Coastal Recreation Kayaking and Small Boat Atlas* series (Whitecap, 2007).

⋰ TRAIL: Dotted lines indicate recognized hiking routes. Most coastal routes are not maintained and may be overgrown. In some locations the maps were too congested to indicate complete trail systems.

⊛ FIRST NATIONS HERITAGE SITE: This stylized eagle head is used to indicate significant former village sites or traditional-use sites. It is not comprehensive.

▨ PARKLAND: Orange land indicates provincial, federal or regional parks. Marine areas and some terrestrial areas protected as parkland are indicated by a hatched orange outline. The two can be used interchangeably. The reason is practical: in some cases shaded areas can obscure details, in others the hatched outlines can be difficult to see.

FIRST NATION LAND: Pink land indicates specific First Nations land as allotted (in most cases) in the 1880s. It is not comprehensive, as most reserves are too small on the map scales used in this book to be of use.

MUNICIPAL BOUNDARY: Purple hatched lines indicate boundaries of towns, villages or cities. In areas of southern Vancouver Island where urban development is heavy, no boundaries are offered.

MILITARY PROPERTY: Light orange property indicates Department of National Defence lands.

ICON KEY

CAMPING

GROUP CAMPSITES

CAMPING AND RVING

PICNIC AREAS AND DAY USE

SHORT WALKS

HIKING

CYCLING

MOUNTAIN BIKING

SWIMMING

HORSEBACK RIDING

CANOE LAUNCH

WHITEWATER PADDLING

KAYAKING OR CANOEING

FISHING

SPELUNKING

ROCK CLIMBING

SIGHTSEEING / VIEWING POINT

BIRD WATCHING

BOAT LAUNCH

POWER BOATING / WATERSKIING

RESTAURANT

JOHN'S RECOMMENDATION

GPS WAYPOINT (LISTED ON P. 341)

INTERNET RESOURCE

Giving you the 👍 thumbs up

Guide writers always face the horrific—having to write about places they would rather not visit. These places may be plain, repetitive, difficult to reach for minimal rewards, crowded or otherwise uninspiring. However, a professional detachment is required, as obviously people have differing tastes. Otherwise, why would people pack their RVs into a line at campsites when just the thought has me running for cover?

I've thrown away my professional detachment by sharing with you the places I deem the best on Vancouver Island, those worth seeking out above all others. Look for the thumbs-up icon 👍 on the title line (along with the other icons I hope are useful). Places without a 👍 are not necessarily bad. They simply aren't the best of the best—in my mind. And the worst? Well, that's a matter of personal taste, isn't it?

What's with all the ● dots?

As you read through this book you'll notice a good number of RED DOTS ● scattered throughout the text. These indicate that the point described is matched with a GPS waypoint in the appendix (page 341). The waypoints are provided as a backup for the text and map descriptions. Things are often vastly different when trying to reach a location as opposed to reading directions (particularly due to the changing nature of logging roads), but a GPS waypoint will never change. It can be used as a last resort or simply a routine part of navigation. In writing this book I used them many times and was glad to have them. They are particularly useful for driving down long, meandering logging roads where there are no ready references for your location. Occasionally, I've checked and found I was driving away from my destination instead of toward it.

To find a waypoint in the appendix, simply cross-reference the page number of the dot with the page number listed in the appendix. You will notice capitalized words beside each dot; these are repeated in the appendix to help you further, as several waypoints may appear on one page.

WAYS TO ENJOY THE OUTDOORS

Ⓐ Camping

Camping opportunities vary wildly across Vancouver Island, from RV-style parking lots to wilderness sites that are simply flat, clear areas in the middle of nowhere.

The most widely accessible option is provincial, federal or regional park campgrounds that have designated vehicle-accessible campsites. These can be popular areas requiring reservations, and they have a range of facilities that can include electricity, flush toilets and showers. Most, however, will have simply picnic tables and pit toilets.

Occasionally, provincial parks have walk-in or cycle-in campsites. They tend to be more remote and will be preferred by those seeking a wilderness experience. Designated wilderness camping within easy access of vehicles is rare. Look for this at Koksilah River Provincial Park, for instance (page 108).

Backcountry camping is another matter. Along multi-day trails, campsites are often designated, though there is little stopping anyone from camping anywhere along a route in a provincial park. Where campsites aren't designated, sites often evolve at key locations, such as scenic bluffs or level areas alongside accessible creeks. Naturally, no-trace camping is encouraged in these circumstances. In the case of sensitive alpine areas, many camping locations are designated with strict restrictions on where to camp, where to walk and even where to dispose of waste (grey) water. This is the case in Forbidden Plateau. In alpine areas without restrictions, hikers should be aware of proper no-trace practices. Please, do not use the lack of restrictions to act any differently from where controls are in place.

Because of the nature of Crown (public) land, where unrestricted public recreational use is the general rule of thumb, wilderness camping is possible almost anywhere. The exception is forestry land: most Crown land is held by forestry companies through Tree Forest Licenses (TFL), granting them essentially the same control of the land as private ownership of the land, with the ability to build roads and log up to the restrictions of the forest license. These licenses

Reserving a provincial park campsite

Many provincial park campgrounds take reservations through a central BC Parks reservation system. Most of the popular and accessible campsites are booked solid during summer, making early reservations a good idea, assuming you know when you're going to be at a location no matter the weather. The need for a reservation diminishes depending on the time of week and time of year. For any campground, expect to book early for the July 1 (Canada Day) long weekend, for instance, or at busy parks like Rathtrevor Beach Provincial Park all summer long from June 21, when school is out, to the September long weekend.

Most parks with reservations keep a portion of campsites aside as first-come, first-served. Naturally, these disappear quickly, so don't expect to get a site when arriving on a Saturday afternoon. Your chances are much better earlier on a Friday afternoon, however. Many parks provide overflow camping during peak periods, such as the Karst Creek day-use area for the Ralph River campground in Strathcona Provincial Park over the Canada Day long weekend; these are last resort options and probably won't be the camping experience you were expecting, as they sometimes consist of nothing more than a grassy area next to a parking lot.

To reserve a campsite, call 1-800-689-9025 or visit **www.env.gov.bc.ca/bcparks/ reserve/camp.html**.

Wonderful scenery off the Adam Main in the Upper Adam Valley.

also stipulate the holder must encourage public access, which is reflected in the creation of the many forest recreation sites covered in this book. These designated campsites can be among the best on the island. They are generally remote, scenic, well kept and quite often free, sometimes including firewood. Unfortunately these sites can also be unmonitored, and it is common to have many of the best sites taken over for the entire summer by RVs. Other recreation sites, especially those near urban centres, have gained reputations as party locations and can be noisy, with rampant alcohol consumption, especially on summer weekends. Provincial parks, which are usually quite well monitored, tend not to have this problem. Hosted forest service campsites also monitor guests for noise—worth the extra fee, if you've ever camped at a free site and been kept awake by an all-night party.

(As a footnote, my worst experience was at Clayoquot Arm, where a neighbouring camping group did not just bring a guitar for some campfire songs but brought an electric guitar, an amplifier and a drum set. They wound up at about 1 a.m. Another campfire group with an acoustic guitar, a lot of alcohol and no consideration for their noise wrapped up their night at 5:30 a.m., just as my day began.)

Commercial campsites are generally not covered here except in special circumstances. This is due to the constantly changing nature of private enterprises. Most tend to be RV and family oriented with some form of tenting area. A few can be exceptional; most tend to be little more than glorified parking lots for RVs. For commercial listings visit the Internet resource listed for the closest tourist office or chamber of commerce website.

🚶 Hiking

Expect two types of trails on Vancouver Island. The best known are the sanctioned and maintained trails, most of which run through parks and protected areas. The others—by far more numerous—are created by clubs or the general public and run mostly through forestry or Crown (public) land.

Sanctioned trails have the advantage (in most cases) of being groomed and marked with the possibility of parking at the trailhead and designated camping along multi-day trails. Most sanctioned trails across Vancouver Island are covered in this guide.

Because provincial parks and significant regional parks are more likely to be sought out for hikes, these are generally described in detail without taking into account the appeal. For the best parks and trails, look for the thumbs up 👍.

Casual trails are dealt with rather more selectively in this book. Only a few casual trails have evolved to the point they can be considered established. In a few cases, like the Kludahk Trail on San Juan Ridge, they are created with the cooperation of BC Forest Services. This gives the trail a semi-official status. Even though it is not within parkland, it's likely to exist even if future logging cuts through a portion.

In other cases trails evolve solely by the work of the users, such as the Lomas Lake Trail north of Lake Cowichan. These trails have the greatest potential for problems over time. If not in parkland, they will invariably cross forestry land and quite often private land, which means the trail may be altered or disappear altogether as logging changes the landscape. (Some designated trails even have this problem, such as the Trans Canada Trail near Nanaimo, where active logging keeps changing the route.) Access restrictions may be put in place. When a logging road is closed it can be gated and ditched, making access difficult. In the case of the Lomas Lake trail, a Notice of Trespass sign suddenly appeared in spring 2007 at the road access. While you can take your chances and ignore these signs, be aware that forestry companies can and do tow cars if parked where they can impede logging. This is not the type of surprise you want at the end of a week-long hiking trip. Naturally, this book cannot recommend trails or routes that oppose the wishes of landowners, no matter how established the trails may be.

Development increasingly impacts wilderness trails on the south island. I recently returned to an old favourite at the base of Mount Benson only to find a large housing development where the trailhead used to be.

Another problem is that without regular maintenance a rainforest trail is doomed. Teams maintain the West Coast Trail year-round; the Clayoquot Valley

In the alpine terrain of the Comox Glacier Trail in late August.

Witness Trail, meanwhile, received very little maintenance after its creation and quickly became impassable.

Neighbourhood trails dot the island. Few undeveloped rural properties near residential areas are without a local trail of some sort. Because these trails change over time, they are not usually detailed in this guide.

In almost all cases, trails that trespass are omitted completely.

ⓘ For a good listing of island and BC clubs, vist **www.clubtread.com** and click on the "Clubs" tab.

⊛ ⊛ Mountain biking and cycling

Mountain biking is a fairly specialized sport. Those with a genuine interest will be familiar with biking clubs and resources to learn about biking areas. Most major mountain biking areas are covered in this guide; casual visitors will find the necessary information on how to get there and where to ride. Look to the listed Internet resources for additional information, including detailed trail maps and ratings.

Cycling is a far more accessible activity. Trail riding is a great way to see the countryside, covering more distance and often requiring less energy than hiking. However, many parks do not allow bikes.

Cycling on deactivated logging roads is another option. This allows access deep into areas that even four-wheel-drive vehicles can't reach.

CYCLING VANCOUVER ISLAND: Every year a few dozen hardy cyclists make the trip from Victoria to Port Hardy by bicycle. The route is invariably the Island Highway. While some portions have the necessary wide, paved shoulders, the traffic is incessant and potentially dangerous. While still in its infancy, the Trans Canada Trail is an alternative for the southern portion. Almost never done is a route combining trails and logging roads, avoiding the Island Highway for much (or all) of the length. It's a long-time dream of a few enthusiasts to create a multi-use backbone corridor along Vancouver Island. Unfortunately it's still decades away.

ⓘ South Island Mountain Biking Society, **www.simbs.com/html/links.html**; Arrowsmith Mountain Bike Club, **www.arrowsmithmtbclub.com**; Nanaimo Mountain Bike Club, **www.nanaimomountainbikeclub.com**; Cycling BC, **www.cycling.bc.ca**; Comox Valley Cycling Club, **www.cvcc.ca**.

⊛ Whitewater and flatwater paddling

My first three guidebooks focused on ocean kayaking, and for those who share that passion, the *Wild Coast* series covers paddling the open ocean around Vancouver Island and along the rest of the BC coast. I've attempted to duplicate as little of the information as possible in this guide by sticking to shoreline attractions and the freshwater component of paddling only.

Two types of freshwater paddling opportunities exist: flatwater and whitewater. Flatwater paddling is far more accessible to the general public. Canoeing and kayaking on lakes and a few choice rivers can be a relaxing way to spend a day— or a few days, if you pick the more ambitious routes. The main bugbear is wind. Keep one simple general rule in mind and you should do okay: the wind tends to be lowest in the morning and rises through the day to peak in the early to mid afternoon. If you keep your paddling to the morning you will avoid the worst winds. A common mistake is heading somewhere in the morning for a casual paddle, then finding the return journey an epic battle against the wind.

Calm water at Nahmint Lake.

Whitewater paddling is a specialty sport, and enthusiasts are likely to know the clubs and resources necessary to get the technical details required of a route. Such information is beyond the realm of a general book like this, so instead I've simply mentioned the best and most accessible whitewater routes. Many Vancouver Island routes are extreme, with 10 m drops over waterfalls common. Enthusiasts generally enjoy the best conditions in winter or after heavy rainfalls. Casual attempts to run rapids without intimate local knowledge is foolhardy.

Every year people die or require rescuing on Vancouver Island lakes and rivers. Here are some considerations.

- Water temperatures can be frigid year-round and it's not unusual for the shock of sudden immersion in cold water to cause cardiac arrest. A casual canoe trip can be fatal within moments of capsizing. Often people believe they don't need a personal flotation device because they're close to shore, but when submerged they're quickly overcome by cold and disappear under water, resulting in a fatality when a rescue would have been possible.

- Water levels are variable. Rivers that are placid one day could become rapids after rainfall. In addition, some rivers are dammed and water may be released, potentially endangering those using the river. Know the nature of a river before trusting your life to it.

- Whitewater paddlers should attempt rivers only with intimate knowledge of local conditions. A walk-by is strongly encouraged, as log-jams can develop at the bottom of drops or conditions can change, including the formation of deadly rapids. In 2007 the danger was brought home when a highly experienced kayaker died on Harris Creek. Novices interested in this sport should have the proper training and team support before attempting any run.

As an avid paddler I'm always shocked by the poor decisions paddlers make that lead to fatalities. These incidences are tracked and analyzed on my website at **www.thewildcoast.ca/fatalities**. It's sobering reading, and three lessons quickly become obvious: wear proper clothing, wear a personal flotation device and do your homework on the weather before setting out.

ⓘ Vancouver Island Whitewater Paddling Society, **www.surfkayak.org.**

🌏 Mountain climbing

This can be a specialized sport requiring equipment, expertise and a demanding level of physical fitness. Or it can be a day outing, with perhaps a rock scramble or two to reach a peak. Many of Vancouver Island's mountains are easily accessible, while others have reputations as some of the most challenging climbs anywhere. Not every mountaineering opportunity is listed here—just the best, the most common and the most accessible. Day-trippers be warned: if you see the word "technical" used in the text, the climb will likely require ropes and gear, or at least a high degree of skill. If in doubt, find an easier trail. For those looking for more information about mountain climbs, a good guide is *Island Alpine* by Philip Stone (Wild Isle Publications, 2003). As with many forms of recreation, the changing status of access roads is a constant consideration. Fortunately many of the island's major peaks are protected within Strathcona Provincial Park. Other key mountains are covered in each region, but casual explorers are strongly urged to go to the established trails throughout Strathcona Provincial Park. There is a peak for all fitness levels.

🌏 Spelunking

Vancouver Island's caves are generally a well-kept secret, with the locations of many of the best and largest caves exchanged only on a need-to-know basis within spelunking circles. However, recreational caves do abound, such as Coral Caves north of Tahsis and Horne Lake Caves near Qualicum Beach. The latter is perhaps the best example of how to manage a cave system: limited controlled access gives a good mix of conservation and public recreation. But it's a sad lesson that the access to Horne Lake Caves was controlled only after much vandalism and, as a last straw, after someone spray-painted inside the remarkable Riverbend Cave. Access is currently unregulated at the two main Horne Lake caves only because all sensitive features have long been destroyed.

Exploring a deep coastal cave near Bamfield.

Hopefully this is not what's in store for the rest of Vancouver Island's caves, all of which are currently unregulated. Many of the finest caves in Canada are here, and they're completely open to public recreation and thus the potential for misuse and abuse. For that reason the information given on caves in this guide is somewhat circumspect.

Vandalism is the most obvious problem, but even benign interest can kill a cave. The most interesting geological features grow over millennia. Simply touching features such as flowstone may leave skin oils that destroy the process, essentially killing the rock.

So while the opportunity exists to enjoy many of Vancouver Island's caves without restriction (for now, at least), visitors should be aware of their impact. Walk with a light footstep and do not touch any of the sensitive or unusual features.

Spelunking in many caves requires a high degree of skill, knowledge and equipment, and most caves are not conducive to casual visits. For those interested in simply exploring a cave as a day-trip, the Horne Lake Caves system is ideal, and highly recommended. Casual explorations of larger caves is not recommended; in many cases it would be downright foolhardy. If you have an interest, though, cave tours are offered by specialized companies. Look to the Internet resources for a current listing of tour providers.

ⓘ **www.cancaver.ca**.

⊜ Fishing

For decades sport fishing has dominated the Vancouver Island countryside, with ardent fishermen creating many of the trails, filling the forest recreation campsites and dotting lakes with boats when these areas would otherwise be deserted. The prizes are as varied as those fishing and their techniques. In addition to the natural bounty, hundreds of lakes are stocked with fish each year, so there are too many fishing options to list completely in a general-interest guide. Only the top or most accessible fishing locations are outlined in this book.

Note that every lake and river has particular restrictions, from catch-and-release only to restrictions on barbs and the number of hooks. Seasonal restrictions also apply. A license is mandatory. Be sure of the rules before you cast.

ⓘ **www.gofishbc.com**; government angling regulations at **www.env.gov.bc.ca/ fw/home/guide**.

Motorized sports

A small but active segment of the population has combined engines and wilderness into its own particular form of recreation. Dirt bike and ATV trails dot the island, usually near urban areas. Trail erosion and degradation, noise and the difficulty in safely sharing trail use with other non-motorized users make this an annoying form of recreation to all but the vehicle operators. Dirt paths tend to develop muddy ruts when used by motorized vehicles, making portions difficult for hikers to pass. Developed trails run by clubs do exist, and I urge people to leave wilderness areas to less destructive recreational uses. I imagine that's wishful thinking, however: for many the outdoors means using motorized wheels. In this book I offer no tips for where to use motorized vehicles. For those who wish to avoid dirt bikes and ATVs while hiking, steer clear of casual rural trails on the outskirts of urban centres.

USING THE INTERNET

Things have changed dramatically since I first started writing guides. Information that once meant knocking on doors and begging harried government employees is now available free at home. So while it is possible to plan a trip entirely by the Internet these days, it's not as simple as it sounds. The Internet can raise the frustration meter and give misleading advice. Many self-interested travel and tourism Internet marketers tend to be more concerned with advertising fees than providing comprehensive information, and give more attention to doing well on search engine results than making sure they're helpful to the user. Then there are the well-meaning sites that provide limited information. Outdated information is another hazard, reflected, for instance, in references to the forestry lands of MacMillan Bloedel—a company that hasn't existed since the early 1990s. In all, it can mean wading through hours of garbage to pick out a nugget or two.

Two features should help to keep the information in this guide current. First is a list of Internet resources. These are my picks for the most helpful official websites, current as of 2008. They can be used for additional information, such as detailed maps, or updated information, such as current schedules. Many of these website names are long and nitpicky to type into your web browser's address bar, so, to save the trouble, the sites are all duplicated on **www.thewildcoast.ca/ websites**. Simply cross-reference the page number in this book with the link on the website, and click the link—no typing is necessary. These links will also be updated to keep them current and useful. So while the book may remain static, the website will help ensure the information in this book is never outdated. Also, watch **www.thewildcoast.ca** for additional updates under the "Exploring Vancouver Island" heading.

ABOUT LOGGING ROADS

Because highways and paved roads are limited to a few major routes on Vancouver Island, logging roads are the gateway to the vast majority of wilderness areas on Vancouver Island. This means relying on logging companies for access, and in many cases they restrict recreational traffic. Consider three basic scenarios: private logging roads across private land, a situation that dominates southeast Vancouver Island; private logging roads on Crown land, a situation that dominates the north and west sides of Vancouver Island; and forest service roads, maintained by the government for mixed public and industrial use. The latter are the least frequent but are found along the major corridors, such as to communities like Zeballos and Tahsis. So while they are the least common, they are probably the most likely type of logging road you will use. These are the best bet for unimpeded public use and are generally wide and well maintained.

This is also generally true for the mains—the major roads used by logging companies for hauling wood—on both private and Crown forestry land.

Main lines most often follow river or lake valleys, providing the most level route through a region, and are usually named for the dominant water feature. Mains are often the only routes into regions, such as the Walbran and Carmanah valleys. They are subject to active logging and industrial traffic and may involve restrictions on public access, even on Crown land. Occasionally the restrictions are indicated by signs; look for a red stop sign symbol and a small-print explanation restricting the hours of public use, usually Monday to Friday from 6 a.m. to 6 p.m. Other mains simply have warnings to watch for industrial logging truck traffic. Others don't have signs; take your chances.

The state of mains varies considerably. Many are wide and well maintained and safe for travel even with heavy logging traffic. Others are narrow, twisting and in poor condition, creating a white-knuckle experience for drivers facing the possibility of logging traffic at every blind corner.

Meeting a logging truck on a questionable road is never fun. For this reason I strongly urge people to travel active logging roads in the evening when industrial traffic dies off. Many signs warn of potential industrial traffic 24 hours a day, 7 days a week, but this rarely occurs. Most mains are quiet after about 4:30 p.m., though some continue to see industrial traffic until about 7 p.m. Logging roads that make an anxious driving experience during daytime hours become a pleasant meander at night. At the very least you avoid the dust trails of passing logging trucks.

Logging spurs (also called branches) tend to branch off the mains to reach higher elevations. Spurs are generally dead ends that may be useful for reaching remote areas, particularly alpine climbs, but these roads can be steep, narrow, rutted and may not have a suitable turning area for the return trip. Expect the need for four-wheel drive along many of these routes.

Deactivated roads are a continual problem for recreational access to areas, particularly alpine regions. Deactivated roads are those no longer needed by logging companies and retired—that is, no longer maintained. They tend to have a life cycle. For a few years they are useful for vehicle travel. Occasionally they are ditched—that is, a ditch is cut across the road to stop a culvert from becoming blocked, reducing the possibility of a flood. Most often the ditches are shallow and can be crossed by four-wheel-drive and some two-wheel-drive vehicles, but occasionally they bar travel completely.

After a few years, decommissioned roads will suffer washouts. Even if the road is in good condition, vegetation can encroach until it impedes vehicle travel. The first trees to grow are usually alder, and when alder takes root in mid-road, you can be sure the road is in its final stages of life. It can be used for a few years as a walking path, but if not cut back the alder and scrub will fill in, obstructing even foot traffic. Eventually a young forest will materialize. For a few years at least the area is lost to recreation unless the undergrowth is cut back (a major undertaking), then the maturing forest will be logged and the process can begin again.

This life cycle for decommissioned roads can play havoc with established recreational areas and is the bane of this book, as many areas I would love to recommend will be inaccessible or nearly so in a few years. As logging companies are under no obligation to keep access open, vast regions are falling off the map for public use. This is unfortunate, as new trails aren't being created nearly quickly enough to replace the ones being lost. Worse yet, other established recreation areas are falling victim to new logging, with spurs, cutblocks and impassable slash replacing old trails or access routes into regions. Lastly, many trails and recreation areas were established with good intentions and a lot of hard work but without forethought to maintaining them.

Considering all this, the recreational vibrancy of Vancouver Island is very much at risk.

Private logging roads dominate the southeast of Vancouver Island around locations such as Sooke, Lake Cowichan, Nanaimo, Parksville, Comox and south of Campbell River. These roads can have many more restrictions than private logging roads on Crown land. Nanaimo Lakes is an example where the entrance is manned, fees apply and a gate is locked at night. (While this may seem draconian, users should be reminded that access was once unrestricted but vandalism to logging equipment prompted the gates and fees to cover insurance costs. Dumping is another problem along many logging roads near urban centres and recreational fires are a constant irritant. I doubt many people inconvenienced by restrictions would act any more charitably to visitors if the land was theirs.)

For all active logging roads, traveling in the evening helps avoid industrial traffic. Beyond that one simple tip, here are a few others to consider when using these roads.

- If intimidated, wait at the entrance for a logging vehicle to enter, then follow it to your destination. Company vehicles are in radio contact with one another and will know when to pull aside to let a logging truck pass. You can simply wait behind them, though following a dust cloud can make this a dubious way to travel.

- Bring a mountain bike. If your destination is blocked by a decommissioned road in poor shape, a mountain bike is a great way to travel across country. It may not be fast, however, as the roads can be steep, rutted and rocky, requiring a lot of pushing the bike. But my experience is biking is generally faster, and a cross-country biking experience can be part of the attraction.

- Carry a full-size spare tire and check it before setting out. Should you spring a leak on a remote stretch of logging road, the mini spares found in most smaller cars won't last five minutes on the island's rougher logging roads.

Who to contact—getting logging road info

Wouldn't it be nice if at some point in the future logging companies created websites where maps of their logging routes had point-and-click information on access restrictions and current logging conditions? At present, though, don't expect a great deal of information to be volunteered publicly. With a few exceptions, forest companies tend not to share information and have no formal facility for answering queries on access restrictions. During the writing of this book, formal requests to the companies for current restrictions were ignored, as were requests for contact information.

A good bet is phoning the regional logging office and hoping someone can answer your query. Logging road maps of sometimes dubious helpfulness are generally available at regional offices of logging companies, tourist information centres and a few other select locations. (A Western Forest Products forester told me the company doesn't even have the current information themselves: "Our

"Turn right at the Kenquot Main"

If you are hoping a description like the one above will lead you somewhere on Vancouver Island, think again. Most logging road mains aren't signed. So how do you know where you are?

I've driven enough logging roads on Vancouver Island to know how easy it is to get lost. In some areas the signs are fantastic. Western Forest Products tends to have great signs, and getting around the logging roads near Port Alice, for instance, is simple. But elsewhere there is often just an array of roads, and the more remote the area the greater the number of nameless intersections and the less complete even the official logging road maps suddenly appear. New logging spurs will change the landscape, and deactivated roads prominent on maps can disappear behind alders and overgrowth. Don't plan on taking the second left as shown on the official maps; it may be the first left or it may be the fourth.

Knowing that getting to the starting point is likely to be the most confounding part of any trip, I've taken several steps to assist you. First, access descriptions are offered for every point of interest. All directions start from a major transportation route. All major transportation routes are discussed in the section on transportation that begins each chapter. So if you're wondering what the Head Bay Forest Service Road is, for instance, while reading about the Malaspina Lake recreation site, just flip to the start of the chapter and look for the heading on the Head Bay Forest Service Road. (Isolating the major routes means less duplication in giving directions.)

Wherever possible distances are given so you can reset your trip odometer. But experience tells me trip odometers are a flawed form of travel security that work only as long as you reset the odometer. Fly past an intersection without resetting it, and you have the option of driving back over a rough logging road to try again or giving it your best guess. And with unmarked logging roads, guessing is not a good strategy.

My solution has been to navigate by GPS. In many a worst-case scenario I have looked at the shape of the route tracked on the GPS as I drive, compared the bends and turns on my GPS-tracked route to the bends and turns on my logging road maps and matched them to find which logging road I'm on. Many times I've found myself heading in the right direction but on the wrong main in the wrong valley. The price of GPS units is so low right now and the headaches that I've avoided so numerous that I can't say enough good things about this technology. Don't head off into the wilderness without it.

GPS waypoints for major logging road intersections have been added to help you along as well. You can generally find where you are if you know the location of the nearest major intersection, so I strongly advise punching in the key waypoints for your trip before heading out—particularly your destination. Logging roads will change. The GPS location of a destination will not.

"Turn right at the Kenquot Main" (continued)

Observant readers will note that a few points of interest don't have directions in this book. Directions aren't offered when access is not allowed (such as some ecological reserves) or possible (such as isolated provincial parks). I have also taken the liberty of not describing access to some ecological reserves or sensitive areas (such as Arch Cave). Please go elsewhere or go by guided tour.

Maps in this book illustrate the main logging routes as accurately as possible, using a combination of official logging road documents and personal experience (including GPS tracking). While the mains and spurs of interest are illustrated on the maps, due to the scale all spurs are not marked. So please, do not navigate by taking the second left, as might be indicated on the maps. A half-dozen unmarked spurs might lie in between.

rolled-up digital information is six to twelve months behind reality and doesn't include road access.")

Only a few companies hold Tree Farm Licenses on Vancouver Island. TimberWest is the largest, with TFL 44 in Carmanah and Port Alberni, TFL 19 in the Gold River region and TFL 6 in northern Vancouver Island (Quatsino Sound). Western Forest Products holds TFL 39, which includes the area around Sayward, blocks near Port McNeill and portions of the Sunshine Coast. Teal-Jones Group holds TFL 46 near Jordan River (Honeymoon Bay) and TFL 37 in the area near Port McNeill. (Knowing the TFL numbers can help differentiate logging companies, logging styles and the amount of logging activity, as well as who to contact for current access restrictions. If you're interested in the boundaries, visit **www.for.gov.bc.ca/hth/timten/provincial-map.htm**. Iisaak Forest Resources holds TFL 57, which includes most of the logging land remaining in Clayoquot Sound. Western Forest Products holds TFL 25, which includes forest lands near Sayward and Jordan River; much of the land around Jordan River was recently removed from the TFL, reverting it to private ownership (and ultimately development). International Forest Products holds TFL 54, which includes several smaller parcels of land around Clayoquot and Nootka sounds. TFL Forest Limited holds TFL 47 in the Nimpkish region.

Note that in the early 2000s the province cut back the size of TFLs by 10 percent to introduce a market-based auction system for setting stumpage fees (the taxes paid for logging publicly owned trees). This means many maps indicating logging lands will be out of date.

Ownership of private logging land on southeast Vancouver Island varies wildly. See the corresponding text of a region for particular instances.

The following is limited contact information for the various companies holding Tree Farm Licenses, though there is no warranty that companies will respond to queries. Former Vancouver Island logging companies are listed in the event outdated information is provided elsewhere.

- CASCADIA: This company was purchased by Western Forest Products.

- IISAAK FOREST RESOURCES: **www.iisaak.com**. Call 250-726-2446.

- INTERNATIONAL FOREST PRODUCTS: **www.ifpcorp.com**.

- ISLAND TIMBERLANDS: **www.islandtimberlands.com**. This company controls huge tracts of private land near Duncan, Nanaimo, Port Alberni, Courtenay and Campbell River. Call 250-755-3540. It's a new company, so don't expect many references in traditional Vancouver Island information sources.

- MACMILLAN BLOEDEL: This BC-based forestry company was the largest in the province for many decades, controlling vast portions of the forests on Vancouver Island until the sale of its operations to Weyerhaeuser in the mid 1990s. Many references and signs indicate MacMillan Bloedel still exists, though the company does not. Western Forest Products now manages most of the former MacMillan Bloedel land.

- PACIFIC FOREST PRODUCTS: This company was purchased by TimberWest in 1997.

- TEAL-JONES GROUP/TEAL FOREST PRODUCTS: **www.tealjones.com**. Contact the Cedar Shake Mill in Port McNeill at 250-956-3851 or the Honeymoon Bay timber harvesting operation for TFL 46 at 250-749-4510.

- TFL FOREST LIMITED: This is a TimberWest related company and affiliate.

- TIMBERWEST: **www.timberwest.com**. For south island operations, contact 250-287-9181. For central island operations, contact 250-729-3700.

- WESTERN FOREST PRODUCTS: **www.westernforest.com**. Regional offices are located in Holberg, Port Alice, Port McNeill, Woss, Campbell River, Gold River, Port Alberni, Jordan River and Kerry.

- WEYERHAEUSER: This American-based forestry conglomerate purchased MacMillan Bloedel's BC operations in the mid 1990s, then divested them in the early 2000s. References may still exist for Weyerhaeuser lands. Western Forest Products is the new owner of most of their former lands.

ABOUT SAFETY

This is an outdoor guide to Vancouver Island, not a guide on how to manage wilderness trips, so safety information is included only if it is unique to the area being visited.

Many of the activities indicated require exceptional skill and training. People with an interest in sports such as whitewater paddling or rock climbing should have training and expertise that goes well beyond the information provided in this guide.

Any travel into the wilderness involves risks, and it is incumbent upon the individuals entering the wilderness to be aware of those risks, to plan for them, to carry the proper safety gear, to have the skills necessary to deal with those risks and to have a plan in place in the event of accident. However, here are a few basic safety considerations unique to Vancouver Island worth mentioning.

- RAIN: Most of Vancouver Island is coastal rainforest. This means wet, slippery conditions on rocks, wood, boardwalks and exposed roots. Hiking boots with exceptional traction are essential. Calk boots can be handy as well. Always carry raingear. Weather can turn quickly.

- CELL PHONES: These are considered by many to be safety equipment, but coverage in rural areas is sporadic on Vancouver Island and can be intermittent even when close to urban areas.

- GPS DEVICES: Another potential safety device, these have limitations in heavily forested or mountainous areas where signals to and from satellites can be blocked. Do not rely on GPS tracking in a heavily forested area or under the cover of tall mountain ranges.

- SNOW: Some alpine and even subalpine trails can have snow late in the summer—not just pockets, but deep blankets covering possible tenting areas and trail routes. Snow can melt from underneath as rocks become warm, creating pockets into which it is easy to fall. Extra caution and experience is required in areas where the ground is covered by snow. Be aware that the alpine hiking season generally begins in August. Hike earlier and accept the risks.

TRAVEL NOTES: I have solo kayaked extensively across British Columbia, and I'm completely at ease with my knowledge of the conditions and my safety equipment, which includes flares and a marine radio. I'm not nearly so at ease hiking solo, as a twisted ankle can render a person immobile without easy communication to the outside world. Solo hiking is strongly discouraged, as is going off an established trail. Leave a detailed itinerary at home with someone you trust and stray from it at your peril. Even a small diversion could make a search and rescue next to impossible. And I reiterate, as I believe it to be the single most important safety consideration: don't leave the trail!

Protect your belongings

Here's an awful scenario that happens all too often. You're packed up for a two-week trip across the island. You stop for a half-day hike at a provincial park or at the trailhead off a logging road. When you return, you find a broken car window and all your belongings gone.

While there is nothing you can do to stop a window from being smashed, you can take steps to protect your gear from being stolen. The best strategy is to pack only what you expect to carry for that outing—meaning pack wisely and pack light. Unfortunately this is easier said than done, especially if you're planning a holiday of relaxed camping, and simply want to take a quick side trip up a hillside to a viewpoint. I have no doubt several people on Vancouver Island augment their income quite nicely off people in just that situation. Busy provincial parks and even Pacific Rim National Park are popular locations for thieves, so official parking lots are no protection.

Let's assume you are car-camping and simply cannot carry all your belongings on a hike. My favourite solution is to make a day trip from a campsite. Modest valuables can be left inside the closed tent. While it's still a risk, most thieves tend to target a car because it's easy-in, easy-out: they can smash, grab and drive away. A tent, on the other hand, could have an occupant. It also requires more work on the part of thieves, who are far less likely to walk into a camping area than drive up to a car.

Watch for parking areas that are ideal for car thieves. The Cape Beale Trail parking lot near Bamfield is a perfect example. The parking is 400 m from the trailhead and about 1 km from the Bamfield Road intersection, giving thieves a good advance look at anyone who might be coming along. They can smash, grab and be on their way even as you exit the trailhead. All you'll see is the vehicle disappearing.

One possible solution is to stash your belongings in the bush, possibly wrapping your gear in a green tarp and finding a hidden location well off the trail. Is this safer than your trunk? I suppose it depends on how well it's stashed. Having it visible from the trail or parking lot will encourage people to take a look. And whatever you do, don't try to stash food.

TRAVEL NOTES: My partner, Leanne, had the misfortune of hearing her car window being smashed near a trailhead at Nanaimo River. She returned to the parking lot to see the car with the offenders driving away. She flagged down a passing logging truck and had the driver radio ahead to another truck to get the license plate. The license plate was passed on to police, but the car owner said he lent the car to a friend and no charges resulted. She ended up footing the bill for the damage, even though the car was identified. It's a sad commentary on the fact that as soon as you leave your car, you are vulnerable.

A bear delays us from reaching the North Coast Trail trailhead at Shushartie Bay. Eventually a bear banger was needed to prompt it to keep its distance. Photo by Leanne Chetcuti.

ABOUT WILDLIFE

Vancouver Island is home to black bears, cougars and wolves. While incidents are rare—statistically you're far more likely to be killed in a car accident on your way to a wilderness area than to be mauled by a wild animal once you arrive—a risk certainly exists.

Most problems with black bears result from learned behaviour, that is, associating humans with a food supply. In 2006 the situation was highlighted by a black bear on the Juan de Fuca Marine Trail that developed a taste for backpacks and became quite bold about snatching packs away from hikers—even hikers just stopping for a quick break.

The solution is never to give bears the chance to learn that a human means food. That means stashing food and being bear-wise in your habits. A good defense is a bear banger, a cap that can be ignited to create a loud bang to scare the bear before it has a chance to consider its options. I recommend this over bear spray—a device useful only as a final measure in a close confrontation with a bear.

There is no grizzly bear population on Vancouver Island, and those who have spent time around bears know the black bear is a different beast altogether. It prefers berries to confrontation, and most encounters will likely be the good old "triple b"—a bounding bear butt as it disappears into the forest.

You'll be lucky if you ever get a chance to spot a cougar, but in a dozen or so documented cougar attacks on Vancouver Island in the last century, a high number have been aimed at children. Pets also tend to make easy targets and could be snatched away before you have a chance to react. While the odds are low, be extra wary if you are with small children or dogs on a wilderness trail.

Wolves also tend to learn by experience, and the most useful way to avoid conflict is to carefully stash belongings. Wolves have been known to ransack campsites, but people have also been known to hand-feed wolves, so it's questionable which behaviour comes first. Don't be the one to begin this unfortunate habit.

CHAPTER ONE

Greater Victoria

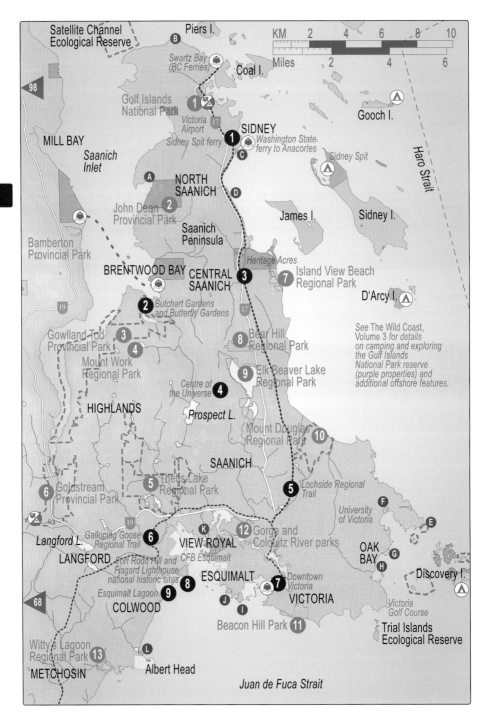

GREATER VICTORIA

Satellite Channel
Ecological Reserve

Piers I.

Swartz Bay
(BC Ferries)

Coal I.

B

KM 2 4 6 8 10

Miles 2 4 6

98

Golf Islands
National Park

1

Gooch I.

Victoria
Airport

Sidney Spit ferry

17

SIDNEY

1

Washington State
ferry to Anacortes

C

Sidney Spit

Haro Strait

MILL BAY

Saanich
Inlet

A

NORTH
SAANICH

D

James I.

Sidney I.

Saanich
Peninsula

John Dean
Provincial Park

2

Bamberton
Provincial Park

BRENTWOOD BAY

CENTRAL
SAANICH

3

Heritage Acres

7

Island View Beach
Regional Park

D'Arcy I.

19

2

Butchart Gardens
and Butterfly Gardens

17

Bear Hill
Regional Park

8

See The Wild Coast,
Volume 3 for details
on camping and exploring
the Gulf Islands
National Park reserve
(purple properties) and
additional offshore features.

Gowlland Tod
Provincial Park

3

4

Mount Work
Regional Park

Elk Beaver Lake
Regional Park

9

HIGHLANDS

Centre of
the Universe

4

Prospect L.

Mount Douglas
Regional Park

10

SAANICH

Thetis Lake
Regional Park

5

Lochside Regional
Trail

5

Goldstream
Provincial Park

6

University
of Victoria

F

Galloping Goose
Regional Trail

19

6

K

VIEW ROYAL

12

Gorge and
Colquitz River parks

OAK
BAY

E

G

Langford L.

LANGFORD

Fort Rodd Hill and
Fisgard Lighthouse
national historic sites

CFB Esquimalt

H

Discovery I.

68

8

ESQUIMALT

7

Downtown
Victoria

Esquimalt Lagoon

9

COLWOOD

J

I

VICTORIA

Victoria
Golf Course

Beacon Hill Park

11

Trial Islands
Ecological Reserve

Witty's Lagoon
Regional Park

13

L

Albert Head

METCHOSIN

Juan de Fuca Strait

James Bay, downtown Victoria.

Victoria is widely accepted as one of Canada's most beautiful cities, famous for its year-round mild climate, picturesque waterfront and harbour, stately Victorian architecture and laid-back West Coast atmosphere. About a million visitors a year flock to the downtown to shop the boutiques, sip lattés at sidewalk cafés and stroll the waterfront promenade. There are a thousand ways to be parted from your money, whether it's a ride on a horse-drawn carriage in front of the stately legislature building, high tea at the Empress Hotel or a walk through the ornate flowerbeds of Butchart Gardens. In the larger picture, however, Victoria is suffering the same pains of most other major cities: growing residential urban sprawl, rush-hour traffic gridlock and endless cookie-cutter strip malls designed for automobiles. Most people will likely see it as a place to escape rather than to seek out wilderness. However, it wasn't long ago that Greater Victoria was a forest of huge Douglas-fir trees and meadows filled with twisted Garry oak. Vestiges of this former glorious wilderness still exist, with large tracts of the best remaining examples now protected as regional or provincial parks, such as Gowlland Tod or John Dean. Locals looking for a quick outing or tourists with only a short time to spend in the city will find no lack of places to stretch the legs, as an extensive corridor of green areas crosses Saanich Peninsula. Cyclists will find extra reason to love Victoria, whether it's commuting along the Galloping Goose Regional Trail or hitting the mountain bike trails at Mount Work Regional Park.

ⓘ The Capital Regional District provides a regional government perspective for Greater Victoria's 13 municipalities, including the regional parks. Visit **www.crd.bc.ca**. Follow the regional parks link for detailed park and trail information. For service information including accommodation, visit **www.tourismvictoria.com** or **www.victoriachamber.ca**.

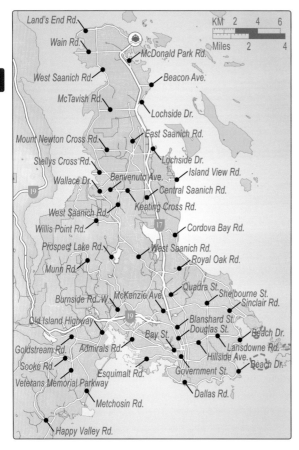

TRANSPORTATION
By vehicle

Two major highways connect most areas in this region. The Island Highway (also known as Highway 19, Highway 1 and the Trans-Canada Highway), connects downtown Victoria at Douglas Street with the up-island communities such as Duncan, Nanaimo and Campbell River. Highway 17, also called the Patricia Bay Highway or Pat Bay Highway, leads from downtown Victoria at Blanshard Street up the Saanich Peninsula to the BC Ferries terminal at Swartz Bay.

Driving in Victoria can be confusing, in part because of road name changes. Quadra Road becomes Saanich Road; Helmcken Road becomes Wilkinson Road; Hillside Avenue becomes Lansdowne Road; McKenzie Avenue becomes Sinclair Road; and the main road skirting the waterfront along Greater Victoria changes from Dallas Road to Beach Drive to Cadboro Bay Road to Arbutus Road to Ferndale Road to Ash Road to Cordova Bay Road, with several other names along the way for good measure. The latter is the scenic route through the region, and the gateway to many of Saanich Peninsula's eastern shoreline parks.

When directions are given, they always start with one of the main routes shown on the accompanying map. Once you know these roads, getting anywhere is quite simple—by Victoria standards at least.

By ferry

Unless you're flying in, visiting Victoria requires a boat ride. Fortunately, ferry service is generally fast and efficient from both the BC mainland and Washington State, with a number of options available. The main service is provided by BC Ferries, with service to the mainland available at the Swartz Bay terminal on the north end of Saanich Peninsula at the end of Highway 17. Ferry service to the main Gulf Islands is also available from here. For visits from Washington State, a ferry runs from Anacortes, Washington, to Sidney on the northeast end of Saanich Peninsula just off Highway 17. Vehicle and foot passenger services are offered.

Another option for those arriving from Washington is MV *Coho*, which operates between Victoria's Inner Harbour and Port Angeles, offering both foot and vehicle passenger service. The passenger-only catamaran *Victoria Clipper* operates from the Inner Harbour in Victoria to downtown Seattle.

ⓘ For BC Ferries, visit **www.bcferries.com**. For the Washington state ferry, visit **www.wsdot.wa.gov/ferries**. For the MV *Coho*, visit **www.cohoferry.com**. For the *Victoria Clipper*, visit **www.victoriaclipper.com**.

COMMUNITIES

The Greater Victoria region can be a confusing one for visitors, as Victoria itself is actually quite small. Surrounding it are numerous other independent municipalities: Esquimalt, Colwood, Langford, Metchosin, Sooke, View Royal, Oak Bay, Highlands, Saanich, Central Saanich, North Saanich and Sidney. Most are residential in nature and the borders largely indistinguishable until you reach rural areas such as the Highlands and Metchosin. While downtown Victoria is rich in character, most suburban centres follow the typical North American pattern of urban sprawl: subdivisions and strip malls. Pockets do retain some character, however, with some of the best outlined below.

Saanich

Saanich, Central Saanich and North Saanich cut Saanich Peninsula into three separate municipalities, all essentially bedroom communities for Victoria. The Swartz Bay ferry terminal for BC Ferries and the Victoria Airport are both located at the peninsula's north end. Wilderness highlights are the large parks, such as Mount Work and Gowlland Tod, with much of the rest remaining as farmland; the Highland region near Goldstream also remains largely rural.

The three Saanich municipalities operate over 200 parks, most of which are playgrounds, ball fields and green spaces, plus dozens of beach accesses without parks. A few choice beach areas are listed separately at the end of this chapter.

CYCLING: Great strides have been made for cyclists in this region in recent years, including the creation of several regional trails and routes. Saanich offers a bicycle tour route around the municipality that follows portions of the Galloping Goose

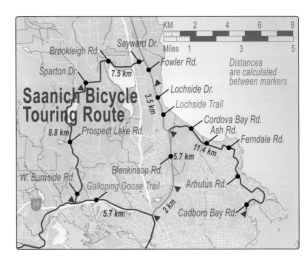

and Lochside trails plus some rural or residential roads, becoming particularly rural in the western portion of the route.

ⓘ **www.gov.saanich.bc.ca**; **www.centralsaanich.ca**; **www.northsaanich.ca**.

Sidney

This small seaside residential community of about 11,000 has a pleasantly laid-back atmosphere, with pedestrians and cyclists as common as cars. Most stores and businesses are clustered near Beacon Avenue, accessible off Highway 17, which ends in a wharf and the ferry terminal for foot passengers bound for Sidney Spit, part of Gulf Islands National Park on nearby Sidney Island. Just to the south of Beacon Avenue is the Washington State ferry terminal to Anacortes. The sea is definitely Sidney's key focus, with numerous beach accesses and a pleasant oceanfront boardwalk. A recent change is the number of large waterfront condo developments clustered near Beacon Avenue.

The beautiful waterfront at downtown Sidney.

ⓘ **www.sidney.ca**.

Brentwood Bay

This sleepy little community on the shore of Saanich Inlet is notable for being one terminus for the Brentwood Bay to Mill Bay ferry, plus being home to tourist attractions Butchart Gardens and Butterfly Gardens. A pair of small waterfront parks offers a chance to enjoy the bay, while nearby Tod Inlet can be visited as part of Gowlland Tod Provincial Park.

Oak Bay

This upscale suburban community is probably best enjoyed by a drive or cycle along the scenic oceanfront route beginning at Victoria's Beacon Hill Park (Dallas Road/Cadboro Bay Road) and ending at Mount Douglas Regional Park. Between the two is a mainly residential stretch of stately homes, picturesque gardens and manicured boulevards with the occasional waterfront park or marina. The commercial centre tends to cluster around Oak Bay Avenue, featuring a number of galleries and studios.

🛈 **www.oakbaybc.org**.

Victoria

As capital of British Columbia, Victoria is home to the province's legislature, and the granite legislative building is a landmark on the waterfront of Victoria's picturesque James Bay and Inner Harbour. The waterfront is the heart of the city, and a wide boardwalk around the harbour is perfect for strolling and watching the busy water activity. The surrounding few blocks are also the commercial heart of the city, a square roughly bordered by Belleville Street, Blanshard Street, Hillside Avenue and the harbour. Visitors will find an array of shops, pubs, restaurants and cafés within this area, including Chinatown. Also clustered here are many of the city's tourist attractions, which range from Miniature World to a wax museum. The best picks are listed separately below.

🛈 **www.victoria.ca**.

POINTS OF INTEREST

❶ Sidney Spit ferry *(map p. 26)*

Sidney Spit is the only island within the Gulf Islands National Park reserve that has foot-passenger ferry service directly to the park. The spit is an ecological wonder of tidal flats, salt marshes and sandy intertidal beaches that attract a huge number of birds, from herons to migrating shorebirds. The park offers trails, a dock for visiting vessels, mooring buoys, drinking water, washrooms, picnic areas and individual and group camping areas. It even has a bit of history in the remnants of a brick factory and a war-era bomb shelter hidden in a field in the park's interior. Ferry service runs seasonally from the wharf at the end of Beacon Avenue, the main street in the village of Sidney. For a schedule call 1-877-559-2115. For more information on Sidney Island and the nearby water features, see *The Wild Coast, Volume 3*.

❷ Butchart Gardens and Butterfly Gardens *(map p. 26)*

Butchart Gardens is the site of an incredible transformation—a worked-out quarry remade into 22 hectares of flowerbeds and gardens. The quarry was originally worked for the Portland Cement Company, the few remnants of which are protected within Gowlland Tod Provincial Park (page 41). While the cement plant and the townsite have long since vanished, the garden and Butchart homestead both live on as one of BC's most popular tourist attractions.

The Butchart family moved to this seaside home near Brentwood Bay in 1904. Jennie Butchart decided the eyesore of the quarry could be brought to life again with flowers, and the resulting sunken garden was expanded over the years to include a Japanese garden, Italian garden and rose garden. Today over a million plants ensure constant bloom from March to October and it remains a family business. The gardens take on a festive atmosphere with lights and seasonal displays over the Christmas season. A popular summer attraction is the weekly fireworks, while the original homestead is now the Dining Room Restaurant.

An island of gardens

While Butchart Gardens is the best known of Vancouver Island's gardens, it is just one of a rich assortment of gardens and sanctuaries that can form a trail of sorts from Victoria to Cape Scott. Here are a few main choices.

- **Glendale Gardens and Woodlands:** This 40-hectare nature conservancy is a demonstration garden open year-round. Expect rhododendrons, plants of the Pacific Northwest and the Takata Japanese garden. It is located north of Victoria on Quayle Road. From West Saanich Road take Beaver Road; it turns into Quayle Road. Visit **www.hcp .bc.ca**.

- **Finnerty Gardens:** A Lake Cowichan estate provided the many rhododendrons, magnolias and perennials in 1974 that today compose this 4-hectare garden on the University of Victoria (UVic) campus. Admission is free and the gardens are open daily. The garden is on Finnerty Road, convenient to UVic's parking lot 6 on the southwest corner of Ring Road. The major road into the area is Sinclair Road; Ring Road is to the south. Visit **www.external.uvic.ca/gardens**.

- **Abkhazi Garden:** A heritage home created by Georgian Prince and Princess Abkhazi in 1946, the garden is now operated by The Land Conservancy of BC. Along with a tea room and gift shop, expect views, Garry oaks, rhododendrons and a select choice of West Coast plants. It is located on Fairfield Road. From Douglas Avenue take Burdett Avenue, which turns into Fairfield. Visit **www.external.uvic.ca/gardens**.

- **Hatley Park National Historic Site:** This garden dates back to 1912 when the Dunsmuir coal baron family had the property developed into a classic Edwardian park. It eventually changed hands to become the Royal Roads Military College, then finally Royal Roads University. Today the grounds still showcase the Japanese, Rose and Italian gardens. It is located on Sooke Road (the Old Island Highway). Visit **www.hatleypark.ca**.

- **Providence Farm:** This 72-hectare working farm providing therapy, vocational training and rehabilitation is operated by the Sisters of St. Ann near Mount Tzouhalem in the Cowichan Valley. A store, an arts program, hanging baskets and events such as plant sales, craft fairs and even a hoedown help finance the program. It is located on Tzouhalem Road in Duncan. Visit **www.providence.bc.ca**.

- **Mayo Creek Gardens:** This 2-hectare property in the Cowichan Valley combines native and cultivated plants to keep the grounds in harmony with the natural environment. Expect workshops, tours, teas and a variety of other programs. From Highway 18 take Skutz Falls Road, then an immediate left onto Cowichan Lake Road, then right onto Mayo Road and left onto McLean Road. Visit **www.mayocreekgardens.ca**.

- **Milner Gardens and Woodland:** This property combines 24 hectares of Douglas-fir woodland with 4 hectares of manicured garden at the site of the Milner homestead built in 1937; in 1996 it was acquired by Nanaimo's Malaspina University-College. It is located at 2179 West Island Highway (Highway 19A) at Qualicum Beach. Visit **www.mala.ca/milnergardens**.

- **Tofino Botanical Gardens:** Paths and boardwalks lead across 5 hectares of gardens, including a Frog Pond, Children's Garden and pocket forest gardens that showcase plants native to the area's coastal temperate rainforest. It is located in Tofino at 1084 Pacific Rim Highway. Visit **www.tbgf.org**.

- **Kitty Coleman Woodland Gardens:** This 10-hectare property features trails through about 3,000 varieties of rhododendrons as well as native plants and wildflowers. It is located at 6183 Whittaker Road in Courtenay; from Highway 19A take Coleman Road to Left Road to Whittaker Road. Visit **www.woodlandgardens.ca**.

- **Filberg Heritage Lodge and Park:** See page 197

- **Shephards' Garden:** This 1.6-hectare garden started in 1991 features bulbs and perennials in a setting along the Nimpkish River. A trail leads to the river through the rhododendron garden and into a forest with a few old-growth trees. It is located near Port McNeill; west of the Nimpkish River bridge on the Island Highway turn south onto Nimpkish Heights Road then east onto Nicholson Road. Visit **www.shephardsgarden.ca**.

- **Ronning's Garden:** See page 333

In 2004 the gardens were named a National Historic Site of Canada.

Its neighbour, Butterfly Gardens, is a popular tourist destination with an array of butterflies housed in exotic tropical gardens. Birds, fish and a learning centre round out the attractions.

ACCESS: From Highway 17, take Keating Cross Road west through four sets of traffic lights as it changes to Benvenuto Avenue and leads straight to the gardens. Butterfly Gardens is adjacent.

ⓘ **www.butchartgardens.com** and **www.butterflygardens.com**.

❸ Heritage Acres *(map p. 26)*

Heritage Acres, a museum run by the Saanich Historical Artifacts Society, features the largest collection of working steam engines, tractors and agricultural machines in western Canada. Trails wind through the grounds linking historic buildings and picnic areas. Among the buildings are a blacksmith shop, a boathouse with marine artifacts and a working 1917 sawmill.

ACCESS: From Highway 17 turn east onto Island View Road, then north onto Lochside Drive.

ⓘ **www.horizon.bc.ca**.

❹ Centre of the Universe ● *(map p. 26)*

This is the whimsical name for the public portion of the Dominion Astrophysical Observatory, a landmark set on Little Saanich Mountain. The observatory specializes in research involving ultraviolet, optical and infrared wavelengths. The Centre of the Universe offers an introduction to astronomy through interactive exhibits, the Starlab Planetarium and tours of the 1.8 m Plaskett telescope. The telescope was built in 1918; new technology makes it 10,000 times more sensitive than the original.

(🚶) SHORT WALKS: The parking lot at the top of Little Saanich Mountain provides a good viewpoint toward the Malahat. A short trail links two levels of the observatory buildings.

ACCESS: From Highway 17 take the Royal Oak exit west to West Saanich Road (the first major intersection). Take West Saanich Road north 3.2 km to Observatory Road, which winds its way up Little Saanich Mountain.

ⓘ **www.hia-iha.nrc-cnrc.gc.ca**.

GREATER VICTORIA

❺ Lochside Regional Trail *(map p. 26)*

For the southern portion in detail, see map page 56.

The Lochside Regional Trail runs 29 km along the entire length of the Saanich Peninsula on a former railway bed. From Swartz Bay it connects with the Galloping Goose Regional Trail at Switch Bridge, a crossing of the Island Highway. The result is a path for non-motorized traffic running from Swartz Bay to Sooke.

From the starting point at Switch Bridge the trail goes northwest, skirting Swan Lake Nature Sanctuary. Much of the southern portion is heavily developed and near major roads, but urban encroachment begins to melt away once north of McKenzie Avenue. The trail generally follows Lochside Drive, a road that disappears and reappears between McKenzie Avenue and the village of Sidney. At Island View Road the trail parallels Highway 17 until Newton Cross Road. At this point you can turn right off the highway and continue northward onto Lochside Drive along the waterfront into Sidney. At Sidney the trail again links with Highway 17 until McDonald Park Road. It passes the federal park campground before relinking with the highway and the trail's only hill at the Land's End Road overpass just before the ferry terminal.

Visitors from the mainland can cycle directly off the ferry from Vancouver onto the trail, which also connects with the Washington State ferry terminal in Sidney for those arriving from Anacortes. For those who wish to cover the trail or a portion in one direction only, BC Transit bus #70 is equipped with a bike rack and makes frequent stops between Victoria and Swartz Bay at points along the trail.

The trail has numerous potential side trips, particularly into Elk/Beaver Lake Regional Park and Mount Douglas Regional Park. Camping along the route is possible at McDonald Campground.

ⓘ **www.crd.bc.ca/parks/lochside/index.htm**. For a bus schedule, visit **www.busonline.ca/regions/vic**.

❻ Galloping Goose Regional Trail (east portion) *(map p. 26)*

Portions of the trail are detailed on the maps on page 30 and on page 56, with the trail start on page 36.

This non-motorized-vehicle and pedestrian route covers 55 km from downtown Victoria to Sooke. By combining the 29 km Lochside Trail, it's possible to ride the length of southern Vancouver Island from Sooke to Swartz Bay. Eventual plans are to connect the Galloping Goose Trail with the Trans Canada Trail running through Cowichan Valley (page 100) to Nanaimo (page 151).

The trail begins at the east side of the Johnson Street bridge, then heads north along the harbour to the wooden Selkirk Trestle, a 300 m span across Selkirk Water (off the southern end of The Gorge waterway). The trail then follows several urban roadways to the Switch Bridge, the junction for the start of the Lochside Trail. The Galloping Goose leg turns west and parallels the busy Island Highway for 5 km until crossing the highway and coming out at the parking lot at Atkins Avenue. This is a popular commuting route. At Atkins Avenue the asphalt ends and the trail begins to follow a former railway right-of-way. Mountain bikers may want a diversion by following Six Mile Road to the trails at Thetis Lake Regional Park (page 45).

Details of the trail west of Atkins Avenue are covered on page 69.

TRAVEL NOTES: Plans are underway to create a new green corridor from the Johnson Street bridge and the Galloping Goose Trail to Goldstream Provincial Park near Sooke Lake Road using the E&N Rail corridor. The $12-million E&N Rail Trail project is expected to be completed in time for the 2010 Olympics.

ⓘ **www.crd.bc.ca/parks/galloping-goose/index.htm** and **www.crd.bc.ca/parks/e_n_railtrail.htm**.

❼ Downtown Victoria
(map p. 26) ⓘ

All the best commercial features of Victoria tend to be focused in a fairly small area adjacent to Victoria Harbour. A wide seawalk borders the harbour, providing a chance to stroll between the busy marinas and landmarks such as the provincial legislative buildings and the stately Empress Hotel. Here are a few suggestions for those who love the outdoors but are caught in the city.

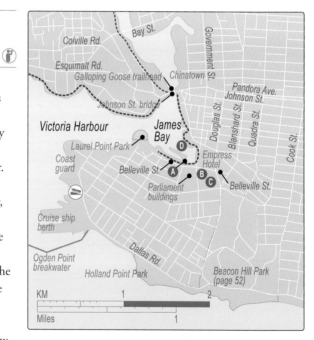

Ⓐ UNDERSEA GARDENS: Get an up-close look at life under the sea from the comfort of an underwater gallery. About 5,000 creatures inhabit the aquariums located in James Bay. Visit **www.pacificunderseagardens.com**.

British Columbia's legislative building looks out over busy James Bay.

B ROYAL BRITISH COLUMBIA MUSEUM: The permanent galleries here focus on natural history, modern history and First Nations, with the latter offering a detailed look at the history and lives of the people who lived here before European contact. The museum also features traveling exhibits, which in the past have included artifacts from Leonardo da Vinci. An adjunct to the museum is the large-screen Imax theatre. Visit **www.royalbcmuseum.bc.ca**.

C EMILY CARR HOUSE: One of Canada's greatest artists and personalities, Emily Carr is revered for her works depicting landscapes and First Nations villages. Her home, built in 1863, has been preserved as a museum portraying Carr's Victorian-era lifestyle. It also features a gallery that alternates between local works and original Emily Carr paintings. Visit **www.emilycarr.com**.

D WATER TOURS: Boats leave regularly from the docks at James Bay to head into Haro Strait for glimpses of killer whales. For a current listing of operators, visit the Tourism Victoria website at **www.tourismvictoria.com** and click on "Whale Watching/Wildlife/Cultural Tours" in the business directory. Campers may want to hire a water taxi for trips to Discovery Island, a beautiful provincial park off Oak Bay. For full information on Discovery Island, see *The Wild Coast, Volume 3*.

---

❽ Fort Rodd Hill and Fisgard Lighthouse national historic sites *(map p. 26)*

British Columbia's first lighthouse is preserved as a National Historic Site.

Fort Rodd Hill was a coastal artillery fort built in the 1890s, and part of a wider military presence on the south coast of Vancouver Island that covers about 4,000 hectares and includes Canadian Forces Base Esquimalt and Canadian Forces Ammunition Depot Rocky Point near Sooke. Fort Rodd Hill, on the western entrance to Esquimalt Harbour, is now a National Historic Site and its historic facilities, such as gun batteries, underground magazines, guardhouses, barracks and searchlight emplacements, are open to the public. The park also protects the 1860 Fisgard Lighthouse, another National Historic Site and the first permanent lighthouse on Canada's west coast. An added bonus is a pleasant beachfront picnic area. Visit **www.pc.gc.ca**.

❾ Esquimalt Lagoon (map p. 26)

Bird enthusiasts will be drawn to this lagoon, and beach lovers will enjoy the spit for a stroll. Protected by Coburg Peninsula, the lagoon has no special status as a park, but it is a migratory bird sanctuary and an ecological standout on a number of fronts. Fifteen hectares of eelgrass provide habitat for a rich mix of species, including cutthroat trout, coho and chinook salmon. The south end of the lagoon attracts waterfowl, including swans drawn to the combination of fresh and salt water. Marshes on the edge of the lagoon provide nesting habitat and food. Bivalves such as mussels and clams thrive in the gravel bars at the lagoon entrance, providing nourishment for migratory birds at low tide. And the peninsula supports an array of dune plants and grasses. Not all is perfect within the lagoon, however, as pollution and human encroachment—including a new 660-home development on the lagoon's south end—take their toll. Visit **www .crd.bc.ca/watersheds/elsi**.

MAJOR PARKS

❶ Gulf Islands National Park (map p. 26)

Created in 2003, the Gulf Islands National Park reserve adds federal protection to a large portion of the southern Gulf Islands off southeast Vancouver Island, particularly Saturna and the Pender islands. Those islands can be reached by ferry from Swartz Bay, while many of the smaller islands within the park reserve can only be reached by boat. Because of the marine nature of the park, the park is covered in much greater detail in *The Wild Coast, Volume 3*. The only portion of the park on Vancouver Island is McDonald Campground. Convenient as a base for exploring the region, it also features a few trails that connect to neighbouring local Blue Heron Park, off the southeast end of the campground. That park has playing fields, picnic tables and a trail that in turn connects to Lillian Hoffar park on the east side of McDonald Park Road behind Kiwanis Village. A trail through the park leads to the beach.

Ⓐ CAMPING: Vehicle-accessible camping is located on North Pender Island at the Prior Centennial campground and on Saanich Peninsula at the MCDONALD CAMPGROUND ●. The McDonald site has 50 drive-in sites plus 6 walk-in or cycle-in sites and is open March 15 to October 31. Marine camping is possible at Portland, Rum, D'Arcy, Sidney and Prevost islands. Walk-in camping is possible at Beaumont on South Pender Island, though the route is a strenuous one across Mount Maxwell.

ACCESS: McDonald Campground is easily accessible from Highway 17 just 2.4 km south of the Swartz Bay ferry terminal, with a left-turn lane off Highway 17 onto McDonald Park Road for those arriving from the ferry terminal. Follow McDonald Park Road past the schools to the park entrance.

ⓘ **www.pc.gc.ca/pn-np/bc/gulf**.

② John Dean Provincial Park ● *(map p. 26)*

This park protects a sizeable portion of old-growth Douglas-fir forest, the largest remaining on the Saanich Peninsula, as well as many of the at-risk native plant species unique to southern Vancouver Island, including wildflowers such as camas, lilies, shooting stars and Indian paintbrushes. Expect a colourful show if you visit here in May.

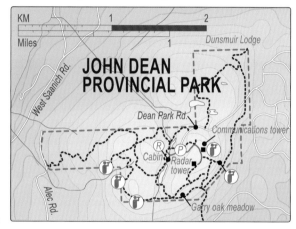

The park is on Mount Newton (306 m) providing viewpoints across Saanich Peninsula. Note that the main official viewpoint next to the communications tower is mostly obscured by trees.

The park has a long history of settlement; a historic remnant is the stone foundation of the cabin of the park's namesake, John Dean. Dean donated the original property for the park in 1921, which has expanded many times since to its current size of 173 hectares.

🎋 PICNIC AREAS AND DAY USE: The park has a day use area, parking lot and pit toilets.

🚶 SHORT WALKS: Several easy loop trails are accessible from the parking lot. A gated road allows walks to the viewing platform (with a marginal view only) and the radar tower.

🚶 HIKING: About 6 km of trails cross the park, with several steep and difficult portions. Trail map kiosks are located throughout the park.

ACCESS: From Highway 17, take McTavish Road west, then East Saanich Road south to Dean Park Road, which leads into the park. The main gate is closed dusk to 8 a.m. in the summer and closed completely November to March each year.

③ Gowlland Tod Provincial Park (map p. 26)

This park protects a large wilderness area on the border of Saanich Inlet's Squally Reach and the smaller anchorage of Tod Inlet. The main geographic feature is the Gowlland Range, low mountains that run along the park and reach an elevation of 430 m. About 150 species, ranging from hawks and mink to the rare phantom orchid, have been recorded in the dry coastal Douglas-fir ecosystem.

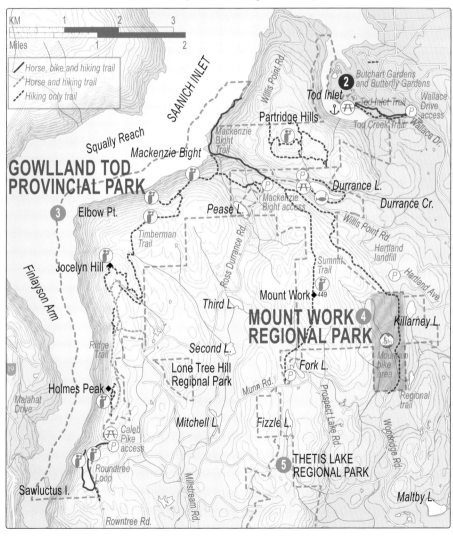

Two First Nations village sites used more than 1,500 years ago are among the six archaeological sites within the park. Another is the industrial town created by the Vancouver Portland Cement Company on the east shore of Tod Inlet. It operated from 1904 until the 1920s. Hiking trails use the town's roads and railroad right-of-way. Another historic reminder is a pioneer copper mine; near it is the Caleb Pike homestead.

Gowlland Range offers views along the length of Saanich Inlet.

The marine features of this park and Saanich Inlet are covered in *The Wild Coast, Volume 3*. The park protects 1,219 hectares and was created in 1995.

HORSEBACK RIDING: Gowlland Tod is one of the few provincial parks that allow horseback riding, thanks to horse trails created by the Garden City Horse Club that predate the park. Many of the original routes follow old logging roads.

CYCLING: Bicycles are allowed on the Tod Inlet Trail, the Mackenzie Bight Trail and the Roundtree Loop.

PICNIC AREAS AND DAY USE: Gowlland Tod has day-use facilities at Tod Inlet, Mackenzie Bight and Caleb Pike. Picnic tables are at Tod Inlet and Caleb Pike; the tables at Caleb Pike are convenient to the parking lot.

SHORT WALKS: The simplest trails in the park are located off Wallace Drive and lead to Tod Inlet. The trails pass through the former Portland Cement Company townsite and end at the picnic area at Tod Inlet.

HIKING: About 25 km of trails criss-cross the park; popular destinations are Partridge Hills viewpoints and the waterfront at Mackenzie Bight. The trails at Partridge Hills are not marked or maintained. A shorter and less demanding loop from the Caleb Pike entrance offers viewpoints. More grueling trips offer viewpoints from Jocelyn Hill and Holmes Peak. A trail connects with Mount Work Regional Park, while an extended hike is possible to Goldstream Provincial Park and Mount Finlayson via Rountree Road and Finlayson Arm Road. See page 46 for details on those trails.

ACCESS: Three major road access points lead into the park. The Wallace Drive parking lot is convenient to Tod Inlet and is immediately off Wallace Road. The MACKENZIE BIGHT PARKING LOT ● is off Willis Point Road at Ross Durrance

Road. Willis Point Road connects with Wallace Drive near the intersection with West Saanich Road; signs are marginal, so keep an eye open. The Caleb Pike access is off Caleb Point Road, accessible via Millstream Road, which runs north-south and connects with the Island Highway. Alternative access is possible from Mount Work Regional Park or the south end of the park via Rowntree Road off Finlayson Arm Road.

❹ **Mount Work Regional Park** *(map p. 26)*

Detailed map page 41

Mount Work Regional Park is one of the largest in the Capital Regional District, dominated by the namesake peak that reaches 449 m. As well as a selection of trails, it offers the opportunity for recreation and fishing in Durrance Lake and a designated mountain biking area—the only official one on Vancouver Island.

MOUNTAIN BIKING: The designated mountain bike area is located off the Hartland Avenue entrance where parking, toilets and a bike-washing facility are available. Mountain bikers can use the park trails or the Hartland Surplus Lands designated for bike use to the north of the parking lot. Established trails are augmented with user-created trails, most of which require technical skills involving roots, rocks and drops. Cyclists are urged to stay on designated trails to reduce erosion. The South Island Mountain Bike Society is making trail maps available; visit **www.simbs.com**.

PICNIC AREAS AND DAY USE: Durrance Lake offers picnicking and swimming.

FISHING: Fly-fishing is possible in Durrance Lake for smallmouth bass and cutthroat trout.

SHORT WALKS: A pleasant forested trail meanders around Durrance Lake.

HIKING: A good, moderately difficult trail leads to the viewpoint atop Mount Work. The trail is accessible from two ends. From the parking lot at Ross-Durrance Road it is 2.5 km to the peak; from the Munn Road parking lot it is 1.8 km to the peak.

ACCESS: The two entrances to the north end of the park off Willis Point Road are convenient to Mackenzie Bight and Durrance Lake. From West Saanich Road take Wallace Road, then Willis Point Road. Most mountain bikers will use the Hartland Avenue access, which is directly off West Saanich Road. Fork Lake at the park's south end can be reached from Munn Road. From the Island Highway take Burnside Road north, then Prospect Lake Road to Munns Road. An access is also being built from a new subdivision at the end of Woodridge Road into the designated mountain biking area of the park. The trail was under construction in 2007.

ⓘ **www.crd.bc.ca/parks/mountwork/index.htm**.

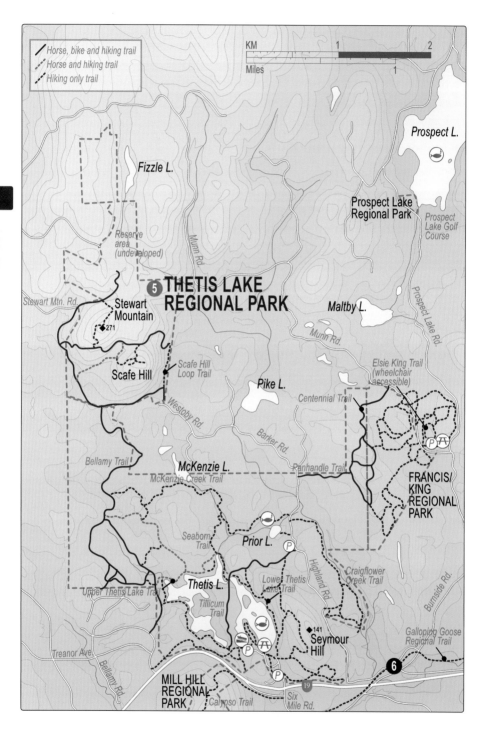

GREATER VICTORIA

Horse, bike and hiking trail
Horse and hiking trail
Hiking only trail

KM
Miles

Fizzle L.

Prospect L.

Prospect Lake
Regional Park

Prospect
Lake Golf
Course

Reserve
area
(undeveloped)

Munn Rd.

⑤ THETIS LAKE
REGIONAL PARK

Maltby L.

Stewart Mtn. Rd.

Stewart
Mountain

♦271

Munn Rd.

Scafe Hill
Loop Trail

Scafe Hill

Elsie King Trail
(wheelchair
accessible)

Pike L.

Centennial Trail

Westoby Rd.

P 🏕

Bellamy Trail

Barker Rd.

McKenzie L.

Panhandle Trail

FRANCIS/
KING
REGIONAL
PARK

McKenzie Creek Trail

Seaborn
Trail

Prior L.

P

Craigflower
Creek Trail

Burnside Rd.

Upper Thetis Lake Tr.

Thetis L.

Lower Thetis
Lake Trail

Highland Rd.

Tillicum
Trail

Seymour
Hill

♦141

Galloping Goose
Regional Trail

Treanor Ave.

P 🏕

⑥

Bellamy Rd.

MILL HILL
REGIONAL
PARK

P

Calypso Trail

19

Six
Mile Rd.

Detailed map page 44

This park was Canada's first nature sanctuary in 1958; it continues a mandate for the conservation of its 831 hectares while allowing recreation ranging from trails to fishing. It connects with 107-hectare Francis/King Regional Park, a wilderness setting of trails through 500-year-old Douglas-firs. Francis/King features a nature centre and meeting room with brochures, displays and volunteer naturalists to answer questions.

HORSEBACK RIDING: Mixed-use trails throughout the park allow horses on the Tillicum Trail, Bellamy Trail, Scafe Hill Loop Trail and Stewart Mountain Trail.

PICNIC AREAS AND DAY USE: The beach area at Thetis Lake is a popular picnic location; the lake is suitable for swimming or canoeing. Picnic areas are also located in adjacent Francis/King and Mill Hill regional parks.

FISHING: Bass can be found in Thetis Lake, plus it is stocked with rainbow trout.

SHORT WALKS: Upper and Lower Thetis Lake trails offer short, scenic routes along groomed paths. Neighbouring Francis/King Regional Park has numerous short routes among its 11 km of trails, including the Elsie King Trail, a short wheelchair-accessible loop on a cedar boardwalk.

HIKING: Moderately challenging trails lead to Stewart Mountain and Scafe Hill in the park's north end.

RESTRICTIONS: The park is open sunrise to sunset, with pay parking in season (May to October). Electric motors are allowed only on Thetis Lake, but not gasoline-powered boats. No boating is allowed on Prior Lake.

ACCESS: The main park entrance and parking lot for Thetis Lake Regional Park is on the south end of Thetis Lake off Six Mile Road near the Island Highway. For Francis/King, the entrance and parking lot is located near the junction of Munn and Prospect Lake roads. Prospect Lake Road connects to Burnside Road and eventually the Island Highway.

ℹ www.crd.bc.ca/parks/thetis/index.htm.

GREATER VICTORIA

6 Goldstream Provincial Park *(map p. 26)*

Goldstream Provincial Park is a fantastic wilderness area at the head of Saanich Inlet. It protects the estuary of Goldstream River along with an old-growth Douglas-fir forest in the picturesque setting of a hanging valley complete with a 47 m waterfall.

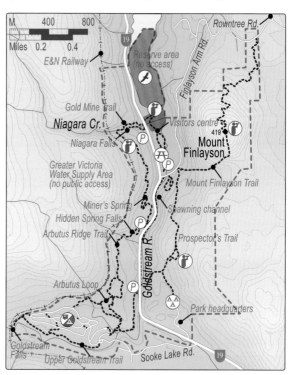

An annual attraction is the chum and coho salmon run, when as many as 25,000 salmon attempt to beat the currents of Goldstream River to reach the spawning beds. The park is an excellent observation point for watching the salmon, along with the many eagles drawn to the feast, in late October and November.

A prospector named Peter Leech first called the river Gold Creek in 1858. Despite a minor gold rush, very little gold was actually found. The last evidence is some small workings near the Gold Mine Trail.

⊞ PICNIC AREAS AND DAY USE: The day-use area off the north parking lot features sheltered picnic areas, fire rings, washrooms and the year-round Freeman King Visitor Centre and its interpretive programs. Some of the park's river pools are suitable for swimming, particularly near the campground's gatehouse. Note the water may be frigid.

🚶 SHORT WALKS: A trail leads along a boardwalk to an observation platform overlooking the Goldstream River estuary near the visitor centre. Another trail, the Arbutus Loop, is located near the campground, as is a trail to Goldstream Falls. Portions of the shorter trails are wheelchair-accessible.

🚶 HIKING: The park features 16 km of trails of varying degrees of difficulty. The Arbutus Ridge Trail links the campground to the visitor centre, about 6 km return. A far more difficult route is a clamber to the alpine-like peak

GREATER VICTORIA

of Mount Finlayson. The ascent from the south begins just off the visitor centre parking lot across the bridge over Goldstream River. Portions are steep, rocky and quite difficult. The north route from Finlayson Arm Road is less demanding but also less scenic. A recent change is heavy development of the entire area bordering the park, including a golf course, homes, condominiums

Goldstream River, a major salmon waterway, meanders through Goldstream Provincial Park.

and apartment towers. This has affected the trail's wilderness appeal, as it once looked out only over forest.

Ⓐ CAMPING: Vehicle-accessible camping is located at the south entrance of the park. Facilities include campfires, showers, water, a sani-station and amphitheatre. Group camping is located off the park headquarters on the south end of the park. Reservations are taken May to September 4.

RESTRICTIONS: Access to some areas on the west border of the park is prohibited. Bicycles are only allowed along the visitor centre trail. Public access, including boat use, is banned at the estuary.

ACCESS: The main parking lot at the visitor centre is located immediately east of the Island Highway at the southern end of the Malahat Drive (see map page 98), where there is a hazardous section of twists and hills. Extreme caution is necessary when making left-hand turns out of the parking lot to return to Victoria or when making left-hand turns into the park when approaching from the north. Note that at many times during the year the main parking lot can fill quickly, causing congestion and forcing parking along the highway north or south of the parking lot turnoff. Other small parking areas are located alongside the Island Highway at points

Old-growth trees line the trails at Goldstream Provincial Park.

shown on the map. Note they are only safely accessed by southbound traffic. The campground is reached by turning off the Island Highway south of the park onto Sooke Lake Road. It also requires a potentially difficult left-hand turn if leaving Sooke Lake Road to head north on the Island Highway.

TRAVEL NOTES: This portion of the Island Highway is being reworked and the Sooke Lake Road intersection will likely be rerouted south to Amy Road.

⑦ Island View Beach Regional Park *(map p. 26)*

While not a particularly large park, at just 42 hectares, Island View Beach Regional Park does offer one of the largest oceanfront recreation areas on the Saanich Peninsula. It also protects a rare sand dune ecosystem. On the berm, look for American searocket, orache and gumweed. In the dunes, look for silver sandbur, beach knotweed and bonsai-like Pacific crabapple. Rare species include yellow sand verbena, contorted-pod evening primrose and fleshy jaumea.

A good time to visit is the spring or fall when migratory birds use the eelgrass beach at low tide for feeding. The park is split into two portions; the south end is most popular as a boat launch.

PICNIC AREAS AND DAY USE: The park features a wheelchair-accessible group picnic shelter.

SHORT WALKS: Stroll along the beach or through the park trails along the salt marsh and sand dunes.

RESTRICTIONS: No camping; the park is open daylight hours only. Care should be taken when walking the sand dunes to protect rare plants. Pets should be under control when migratory birds are using the beach.

ACCESS: From Highway 17, follow Island View Road east to the waterfront. Homathko Road leads to the north portion of the park.

⑧ Bear Hill Regional Park *(map p. 26)*

Detailed map page 49

At 49 hectares, Bear Hill offers woodland trails through Douglas-fir stands and spring wildflower displays. Watch for rare camas, chocolate lily and fawn lily

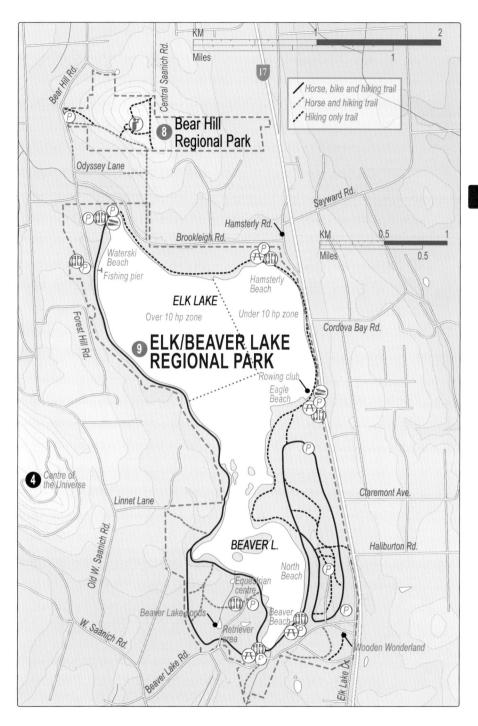

KM ⎯ 1 ⎯ 2
Miles ⎯ 1

17

/ Horse, bike and hiking trail
— Horse and hiking trail
··· Hiking only trail

Bear Hill Rd.

Central Saanich Rd.

P

ℹ️

8 **Bear Hill Regional Park**

Odyssey Lane

Sayward Rd.

P P 🎋🚻

Hamsterly Rd.

Brookleigh Rd.

KM 0.5 1
Miles 0.5

🚻 P
Waterski Beach
Fishing pier

P 🎋🚻

ELK LAKE
Over 10 hp zone

Hamsterly Beach

Under 10 hp zone

Forest Hill Rd.

Cordova Bay Rd.

9 **ELK/BEAVER LAKE REGIONAL PARK**

Rowing club
Eagle Beach

🎋🚻
🎋 P
🚻

4 **Centre of the Universe**

P

Linnet Lane

Claremont Ave.

Old W. Saanich Rd.

BEAVER L.

North Beach

Haliburton Rd.

Equestrian centre

P

Beaver Lake ponds

🚻 P

Beaver Beach

Retriever area

🎋 P
🚻

🎋🚻 P

Wooden Wonderland

W. Saanich Rd.

Beaver Lake Rd.

Elk Lake Dr.

GREATER VICTORIA

in bloom if you visit in May. Other rare or endangered plants to watch for are white-top aster, farewell-to-spring, Howell's violet and yellow montane violet. You may also catch a glimpse of the rare propertius duskywing butterfly (*Erynnis propertius*).

SHORT WALKS: Bear Hill offers an easy viewpoint over Saanich Peninsula at 220 m elevation, as well as other less strenuous trails.

HIKING: Bear Hill is part of a trail network to Elk/Beaver Lake Regional Park. Horses are allowed on the multi-use trail.

ACCESS: Roundabout access from Highway 17 involves several turns. Just north of Elk Lake turn west onto Sayward Road, south onto Hamsterley Road, west onto Brookleigh Road, north onto Oldfield Road, then east onto Bear Hill Road to the park entrance.

9 Elk/Beaver Lake Regional Park (map p. 26)

Detailed map page 49

Elk/Beaver Lake Regional Park is one of Victoria's most popular recreation areas, combining interests ranging from powerboats and jet skis to competitive rowing and horseback riding. It even has an area for retriever training and trial events at the Beaver Lands ponds in the park's south end, under the auspices of the Vancouver Island Retriever Club. The 443-hectare park was established in 1966.

POWER BOATING: Waterskiing, jet skiing and other motorized boating enthusiasts will want to launch from the north end of Elk Lake at Waterski Beach. The northwest end of the lake is open to boats over 10 hp; white and orange buoys mark the boundary. A constant hazard is submerged stumps. Use extra caution when water levels are low.

EQUESTRIAN: An equestrian centre in the park's south end is operated by the Elk/Beaver Lake Equestrian Society, which is mandated to provide public access. Member clubs include the Peninsula Reining Club, Lower Island Equestrian Club, Vancouver Island Appaloosa Club, Vancouver Island Arabian Horse Association and Victoria-Saanich CADORA. Visit **www.ebles.org**.

PADDLING: The Victoria Rowing Society runs the boathouse at Elk Lake and enforces safety and flow pattern rules for the lake. The society's members include the national and provincial rowing teams. Each member hosts its own programs, with those like the Victoria City Rowing Club offering accessible activities such as training programs, camps and private coaching. Each summer the lake is used for regattas and races including triathlons. Visit **www.vcrc.bc.ca**.

GREATER VICTORIA

CYCLING: Most of the trails in the park are open to cyclists, though not along the entire length of the main trail that leads around the park.

FISHING: Elk Lake is stocked with rainbow trout.

PICNIC AREAS AND DAY USE: Beaver Beach, on the south end of Beaver Lake, is a popular swimming hole and picnic area complete with a shallow and sandy beach. Eagle Beach on the east side of Elk Lake has a covered group picnic shelter and change rooms. Hamsterly Beach, on the north end of Elk Lake, has a beach area, playground and change rooms.

SHORT WALKS: Good short walks lead from the parking areas at North Beach or Beaver Beach. Many of the trails are multi-use; for quiet walks, pick pedestrian-only trails.

HIKING: The main loop trail around Beaver and Elk lakes is 10 km, with the north and east portions open to hikers only. An adjunct continues north on a regional trail through to Bear Hill Regional Park.

RESTRICTIONS: Power vessels are prohibited sunset to 11 a.m. Events such as regattas and derbies can cause additional prohibitions on boat use. Change rooms are open in the summer only.

ACCESS: For the Elk Lake entrance, take Sayward Road west from Highway 17, then left on Hamsterly Road and right on Brookleigh Road. For Beaver Lake from Highway 17, turn west onto Royal Oak Drive, then north onto Elk Lake Drive to Beaver Lake Road.

ℹ **www.crd.bc.ca/parks/ elkbeaver/index.htm**.

⑩ **Mount Douglas Regional Park** ●

This 181-hectare park protects the namesake mountain overlooking Cordova Bay. In 1942 artist Emily Carr painted her last works here, and it's easy to understand why she

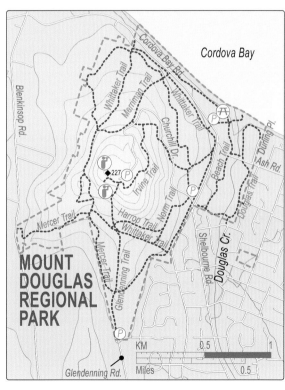

chose this location. The peak offers sweeping panoramic views—the best, in my opinion, in Victoria—over a large and healthy Garry oak meadow (one of the finest examples remaining in Greater Victoria). Churchill Drive offers direct access to a good viewpoint, with even better viewpoints a short walk away to two summits.

Views from atop Mount Douglas are 360 degrees, with this view over Cormorant Point and Haro Strait to the US San Juan Islands.

🏕 PICNIC AREAS AND DAY USE: Washrooms, a picnic site and an information kiosk are located at the parking lot off Cordova Bay Road. Nearby is a sandy beach area. The park also has a ball field.

🚶 SHORT WALKS: A good selection of low-elevation, short trails is located off the Cordova Bay Road parking area. Beach Trail and Douglas Trail offer a scenic low-elevation loop. Parking at the end of Churchill Drive offers an easy ascent to the summit viewpoints.

🚶 HIKING: Trails criss-cross the entire park. The Whittaker Trail offers a circle around the park, while the Irvine Trail is a demanding hike starting from near the Cordova Bay Road parking lot. It twists its way toward the Mount Douglas summit. The Mercer Trail connects to Blenkinsop Road and eventually to the Lochside Regional Trail.

ACCESS: The Glendenning Trail is reached from Glendenning Road. From Cedar Hill Road take Mount Douglas Cross Road west to Glendenning. Other accesses are off Churchill Road, reached from Shelbourne Street near the Cedar Hill Road intersection. Beach access is off Cordova Bay Road. Note that the beach access is easy to miss; drive slowly near the Ash Road and Shelbourne Street intersection.

---

11 Beacon Hill Park (map p. 26)

Detailed map page 53

This park, located just minutes from downtown Victoria, has a pleasant mix of landscaping and wilderness in an area rich in history. First reserved as a park in the 1850s, it has been owned by the City of Victoria since 1882. It was first landscaped for a park by noted Scottish gardener and landscape architect John Blair—one of the reasons for the English-garden style that graces much of the park to this day.

- A Songhees fortified village was located at Finlayson Point at about 950 AD, and was occupied on and off for the next 500 years. House platforms can still be seen, though much of it, including a defensive trench, has been destroyed by development. Another defensive site was located at Holland Point.

- A graveyard located on Beacon Hill was named Meeachan, meaning "fat man lying on his back." Over the years, including as late as the 1970s, the cairns were removed by park staff to make it easier to mow the grass. Four of the burial cairns were reconstructed in 1986 by arranging scattered boulders.

- Beacon Hill was equipped with navigation beacons in the 1840s. The intent was to warn mariners of the dangers around Brochie Ledge, located just offshore.

- As early as 1858 Beacon Hill was being used for horse racing; the track is now Circle Drive. Cricket was the other common sport of the day at the park; the cricket ground remains.

- Threat of war with Russia prompted the military to use the hill in the 1870s. Batteries were constructed at Finlayson Point, Holland Point and Beacon Hill in 1878. Two 64-pound guns were kept in service at Finlayson Point until 1892.

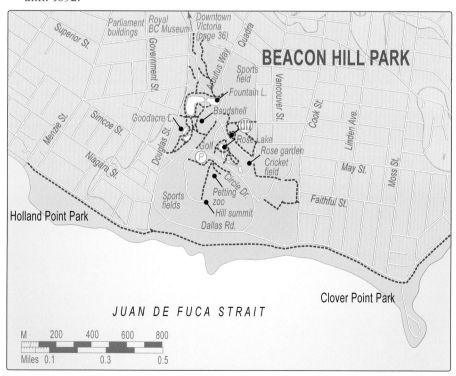

One small portion of the extensive gardens at Beacon Hill.

- Former Prime Minister Pierre Trudeau launched his leadership campaign at the park in 1967, landing in the park by helicopter.

- Marilyn Bell started her successful and historic swim across Juan de Fuca Strait at Beacon Hill Park.

SPECIAL FEATURES:

- Beacon Hill is Mile Zero of the 8,000 km Trans-Canada Highway. The Mile 0 marker is a classic starting or ending point for trips across Canada.

- Great blue herons nest at Point Roberts, one of 23 known colonies of the birds on Vancouver Island. You can view the nests live online at **www .heroncam.com.** A renegade bald eagle, dubbed Birdzilla, devastated the nests in 2007.

- The Cameron Bandshell is a stage for outdoor performances, hosting free dance, theatre, band and choral performances each summer.

- The sloping grasslands of the park feature introduced European grasses, though a number of native plant species can still be found, such as camas, Easter lily and western buttercup. Human impact, however, is taking its toll, and golden paintbrush and prairie lupin have disappeared from the park.

- Windsurfing is popular on the waterfront off Beacon Hill Park, but if you're passing by and see what appear to be kites moving back and forth over the water, take a closer look. Chances are they're attached to people on wakeboards. Power kiting (or kite boarding) is a growing sport, with the kites generally outnumbering windsurfers now.

- ⊕ PICNIC AREAS AND DAY USE: Playgrounds, tennis courts, benches, a petting zoo—there are a multitude of ways to while away a day here.

SHORT WALKS: The rose garden, Rose Lake and Fountain Lake make ideal places for a picturesque stroll. The waterfront linked by Holland, Beacon Hill and Clover Point parks offers views and fresh ocean air. Steep stairwells offer access to the rough beach.

ACCESS: The park is within walking distance of many of the major downtown hotels and the downtown core shopping area, and visitors will also find ample parking space along Dallas Road and within the park. A good route to the park for visitors unfamiliar with Victoria is to continue through the downtown south along the Island Highway and then Douglas Street. You can either turn into the park or continue to a parking spot on the waterfront.

ⓘ **www.victoria.ca/visitors/leisure_parksbcn.shtml**.

⑫ Gorge and Colquitz River parks *(map p. 26)*

Detailed map page 56

Several trails and greenways connect some of the larger parks and notable geographic features just north of downtown Victoria. A highlight is The Gorge, a tidal river that connects Portage Inlet with Victoria Harbour. The rapids at Tillicum Narrows can be viewed from the pretty walkways that parallel the waterfront at Gorge and Kinsman Gorge parks. From there you can cycle or walk along Dysart Road to Cuthbert Holmes Park, which protects the mouth of Colquitz River in the setting of a mature forest.

Cuthbert Holmes Park is the beginning of a linear trail system that follows Colquitz River through Hyacinth and Panama Hill parks. A few street connections are necessary to complete the link that includes Copley, Brydon, Layritz and Quick's Bottom parks.

Walkways extend along much of The Gorge's pretty waterfront.

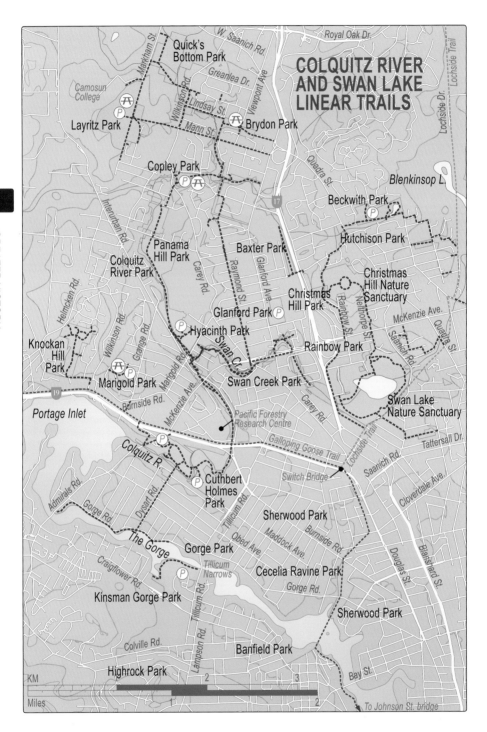

COLQUITZ RIVER
AND SWAN LAKE
LINEAR TRAILS

Royal Oak Dr.

Lochside Trail

Lochside Dr.

Quick's
Bottom Park

W. Saanich Rd.

Greanlea Dr.

Markham St.

Wilkinson Rd.

Lindsay St.

Viewmont Ave

Blenkinsop L.

Camosun
College

Layritz Park

Mann St.

Brydon Park

Quadra St.

Beckwith Park

Copley Park

17

Hutchison Park

Panama
Hill Park

Baxter Park

Christmas
Hill Nature
Sanctuary

Interurban Rd.

Colquitz
River Park

Carey Rd.

Glanford Ave.

Raymond St.

Christmas
Hill Park

Nelthorpe St.

McKenzie Ave.

Helmcken Rd.

Glanford Park

Rainbow St.

Saanich Rd.

Quadra St.

Hyacinth Park

Swan Cr.

Knockan
Hill
Park

Wilkinson Rd.

Grange Rd.

Marigold Rd.

Rainbow Park

Swan Creek Park

Swan Lake
Nature Sanctuary

Marigold Park

19

McKenzie Ave.

Burnside Rd.

Pacific Forestry
Research Centre

Carey Rd.

Galloping Goose Trail

Lochside Trail

Tattersall Dr.

Portage Inlet

Saanich Rd.

Cloverdale Ave.

Colquitz R.

Switch Bridge

Admirals Rd.

Gorge Rd.

Dysart Rd.

Cuthbert
Holmes
Park

Tillicum Rd.

Sherwood Park

Burnside Rd.

Blanshard St.

Douglas St.

The Gorge

Gorge Park

Obed Ave.

Maddock Ave.

Cecelia Ravine Park

Craigflower Rd.

Tillicum
Narrows

Gorge Rd.

Sherwood Park

Kinsman Gorge Park

Tillicum Rd.

Lampson Rd.

Colville Rd.

Banfield Park

Bay St.

Highrock Park

KM

Miles

2

3

2

To Johnson St. bridge

Another option is to follow the series of park connectors that lead to Swan Lake Nature Sanctuary. A 2 km trail surrounds the lake. The Swan Lake sanctuary is run in conjunction with the Christmas Hill Nature Sanctuary about a kilometre to the north. Both sanctuaries can be enjoyed via a circle walk using Nelthorpe and Rainbow streets, though Rainbow Street has the advantage of a pedestrian overpass across busy McKenzie Avenue. The 122 m peak at Christmas Hill offers views over the area.

A longer option, about 8 km in total, is a circuit of Swan Lake, Christmas Hill and Beckwith Park to the north. Beckwith offers trails through a Garry oak forest plus a popular water park during the summer. Lochside Regional Trail closes the loop. Lochside is covered in greater detail on page 35 though both it and Galloping Goose Regional Trail pass through this area, connecting at Switch Bridge near Swan Lake.

PICNIC AREAS AND DAY USE: Picnic areas are offered at parks marked with a picnic table icon. Parks vary from undeveloped green spaces and wilderness to sports fields and playgrounds, so be sure to pick a park that mirrors your interests.

SHORT WALKS: While various options exist, my recommendation is the boardwalks along The Gorge waterway or the trails around Swan Lake. The ascent of Christmas Hill is also a fairly simple climb.

HIKING: The best route for an extended walk is probably along the Colquitz River and Swan Creek parks.

CYCLING: With the Galloping Goose and Lochside regional trails running through this area, it's possible to use either or both to make loops of the most interesting areas. Just be prepared for some urban stretches and road portions.

ACCESS: Parks with parking lots are indicated on the trail map. Limited street parking exists on the neighbouring roadways of most parks. Be sure to watch for parking restrictions before leaving your car.

⑬ Witty's Lagoon Regional Park *(map p. 26)*

Detailed map page 58

This wildlife gem in Metchosin offers trails over volcanic cliffs, a scenic waterfall and sandy areas perfect for a day at the beach. Naturalists will be particularly thrilled with the wide range of birds and intertidal life found in the park.

HORSEBACK RIDING: Horses are allowed on the outer north trails of the main portion of the park, while the Tower Point area is a designated equestrian zone.

PICNIC AREAS AND DAY USE: The park has three official picnic areas, plus access to an extensive beach west of the park. The sandy spit and beach areas are popular with families, while the southwest beach outside the park is a traditional clothing-optional beach (an obstructive tree separates the nudists from the park's beach users). A nature centre at the park entrance has brochures, interpretive displays and volunteer naturalists. Hours are limited and seasonal.

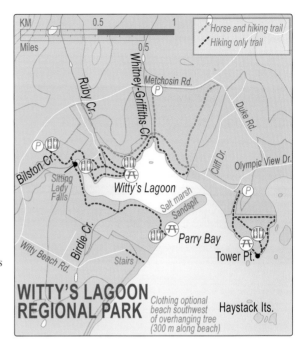

SHORT WALKS:

The visual highlight of the park is Sitting Lady Falls, which cascades from Bilston Creek into the lagoon. The salt marsh offers a chance to view bird life drawn to the rich intertidal environment. About 160 bird species have been identified within the park, making it a prime birdwatching area. Tidal pools at Tower Point also make for interesting exploration.

ACCESS: Three parking lots are accessible from Metchosin Road, 18 km from Victoria. The Tower Point parking lot is open only seasonally.

ⓘ **www.crd.bc.ca/parks/wittys/index.htm**.

OCEAN STROLLS

See the map on page 26 to locate these recreation sites

The residential nature of Saanich Peninsula and the waterfront around Greater Victoria allow numerous beach accesses. Not all beaches are suitable for long walks, however, and a few rocky and/or steep areas prevent any sort of walk at all. Here are a few choice locations for reaching the water. While directions are given, it is recommended to have a street map, which may mark additional beach entrances and features.

Ⓐ COLES BAY REGIONAL PARK: On the shore of Saanich Inlet, this park has a picnic area plus washrooms with wheelchair access, a short selection of trails and a beach area suitable for swimming.

ⓑ LAND'S END: There are no parks and not much beach on the northern tip of Saanich Peninsula, but the intertidal rock pools and views toward Satellite Channel and Saltspring Island make it a good place to visit nonetheless. Land's End Road skirts the north end of the peninsula; beach accesses can be found at the ends of Moses Point Road, Seabreeze Road, Junco Road and Shearwater Terrace (off Dawson Way). An access is directly off Land's End Road just west of West Saanich Road opposite Woodcreek Park. Note some accesses are steep.

ⓒ SIDNEY: Numerous waterfront accesses can be found in Sidney at the ends of residential streets. One small waterfront park is just north of the Washington State ferry terminal. The major waterfront park in the town is Tulista, a popular boat launch area with a playground and parking just south of Beacon Avenue, Sidney's main thoroughfare. A waterfront walkway leads into downtown Sidney.

ⓓ CY HAMPSON PARK: Located south of Sidney off Lochside Drive, Cy Hampson offers wheelchair-accessible oceanfront, a viewing area and picnic tables.

ⓔ MAYNARD COVE: This picture-perfect little circular cove with a pleasant beach makes a great family outing for those with young children. To get here, take Tudor Road from Cadboro Bay Road, then McAnally Road to the cove. Note the roads can be tricky in this area, as they are short, narrow and the street names change often.

ⓕ CADBORO GYRO PARK: This family park offers a beach, washrooms, tennis courts, a playground and picnic tables. It is off Cadboro Bay Road at Sinclair Road.

ⓖ UPLANDS PARK: This park has a loop road with two boat ramps and an otherwise rocky headland off Beach Drive with a large upland portion.

ⓗ WILLOWS PARK: A small family park with a nice beach off Beach Drive south of Uplands Park.

ⓘ MACAULAY POINT PARK: Located in Esquimalt on the ocean between Victoria Harbour and Esquimalt Harbour, it is next to Fleming Park, a popular boat launch. Macaulay Point Park is Department of National Defence land leased to the municipality. Gun emplacements and bunkers add to the waterfront views over Juan de Fuca Strait.

ⓙ SAXE POINT PARK: Trails lead through gardens, a forest and picnic tables to a sheltered beach. From Esquimalt Road follow Fraser Street to the end.

ⓚ PORTAGE REGIONAL PARK: Located on Thetis Cove, it is the only local park fronting Esquimalt Lagoon. Trails lead through the park and to the waterfront, not far from the Galloping Goose Trail. To get here, find your way onto the Old Island Highway. The park is adjacent to the railway.

L ALBERT HEAD LAGOON REGIONAL PARK: This is a small park (7.1 hectares) that protects a lagoon and a cobble beach. From Metchosin Road take Farhill Road to Park Drive, then Delgada Road to the park entrance. A trail leads across the spit fronting the lagoon. Look for migratory birds, geese and ducks that frequent the lagoon.

Vineyard tours

Saanich Peninsula has established a reputation as one of British Columbia's top wine-producing areas. Along with the Cowichan Valley, the region creates an opportunity to tour wine country. Given the rural nature of the region, it would be possible to plan a cycling wine tour (keeping in mind that being impaired on a bicycle is also an offence). Most vineyards are open for wine tasting and lunches during the summer, but often with limited hours off the peak season. Many are also amenable to visits by appointment at other times.

- **Chalet Estate Vineyard:** 11195 Chalet Road, North Saanich. It has limited hours but will open by appointment. The vineyard patio is available for lunches and there is also a banquet room. Call 250-656-2552 or visit **www.chaletestatevineyard.ca**.

- **Church and State Wines:** 1445 Benvenuto Avenue, Brentwood Bay. Limited hours are offered for tours, tastings, lunches and private events. Call 250-652-2671 or visit **www.churchandstatewines.com**.

- **Marley Farm Winery:** 1831-D Mt. Newton X Road, Saanichton. This is a family winery in a farm setting in the Mount Newton valley. Open daily May to September with limited off-season hours. Call 250-652-8667 or visit **www.marleyfarm.ca**.

- **Sea Cider Vintage Cidery:** 2487 Mt. St. Michael Road, Saanichton. Traditional hard ciders are served at the family farm by the sea. Open weekends and by appointment. Call 250-544-4824 or visit **www.seacider.ca**.

- **Starling Lane Winery:** 5271 Old West Saanich Road, Victoria. A small tasting room with limited hours is located on a heritage farm. Call 250-881-7422 or visit **www.starlinglanewinery.com**.

- **Tugwell Creek Honey Farm and Meadery:** 8750 West Coast Road, Sooke. This honey producer was licensed as BRITISH COLUMBIA's first meadery in 2003, producing vintage mead, metheglin and honey wines. The gift shop and tasting room has limited hours. Call 250-642-1956 or visit **www.tugwellcreekfarm.com**.

- **Winchester Cellars:** 6170 Old West Saanich Road, Victoria. A tasting room for their perennial award-winning wines is open weekends and by appointment. Call 250-544-8217 or **visit www.winchestercellars.com**.

i The Wine Islands Vintners Association details vineyard locations, including those in the Cowichan Valley. Visit **www.wineislands.ca**.

CHAPTER TWO

The South Island

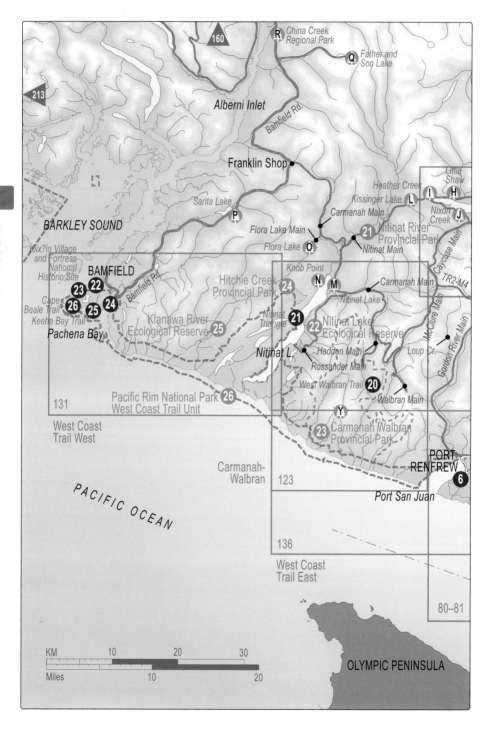

160

213

China Creek
Regional Park R

Q Father and
Son Lake

Alberni Inlet

Bamfield Rd.

Franklin Shop

Heather Creek

Little
Shaw

Kissinger Lake   L   I   H

Sarita Lake

Carmanah Main

Nixon
Creek   J

P

BARKLEY SOUND

Flora Lake Main

21

Nitinat River
Provincial Park

Cayuuse Main

Flora Lake   O

Nitinat Main

Knob Point

Kíix?in Village
and Fortress
National
Historic Site

Hitchie Creek
Provincial Park

24

N   M

Carmanah Main

TR2-M4

BAMFIELD   22

23

Bamfield Rd.

Nitinat Lake

Cape
Beale Trail   26   25   24

Klanawa River
Ecological Reserve   25

Nitinat
Triangle

21

22

Nitinat Lake
Ecological Reserve

McClure Main

Keeha Bay Trail
Pachena Bay

Haddon Main

Loup Cr.

Gordon River Main

Nitinat L.

Rossander Main

West Walbran Trail

20

131

Pacific Rim National Park
West Coast Trail Unit   26

Walbran Main

West Coast
Trail West

Y

23

Carmanah Walbran
Provincial Park

PORT
RENFREW

6

Carmanah-
Walbran   123

Port San Juan

PACIFIC OCEAN

136

West Coast
Trail East

80–81

KM   10   20   30

Miles   10   20

OLYMPIC PENINSULA

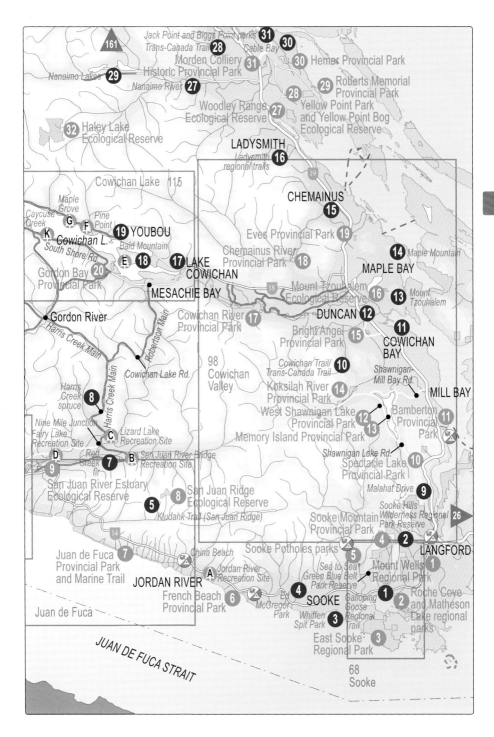

161

Jack Point and Biggs Point parks **31**
Trans-Canada Trail **28**   Cable Bay **30**

Morden Colliery **31**   **30** Hemer Provincial Park
Historic Provincial Park
Nanaimo River **27**   **28**   **29** Roberts Memorial
                                            Provincial Park
Nanaimo Lakes **29**   Yellow Point Park
                        Woodley Range **27**   and Yellow Point Bog
                        Ecological Reserve   Ecological Reserve

32 Haley Lake
Ecological Reserve

LADYSMITH
Ladysmith **16**
regional trails
                                    CHEMAINUS

Cowichan Lake 115   **15**

Maple
Grove
Caycuse   Pine   Eves Provincial Park **19**
Creek   **G**   Point
K   **F**   **19** YOUBOU   **14** Maple Mountain
Cowichan L. Bald Mountain   Chemainus River
South Shore Rd.   Provincial Park **18**   MAPLE BAY
E   **18**   **17** LAKE
Gordon Bay **20**   COWICHAN   Mount Tzouhalem **16**   **13** Mount
Provincial Park   Ecological Reserve   Tzouhalem
        MESACHIE BAY   **18**
Gordon River   Mount Tzouhalem   DUNCAN **12**
                    Cowichan River   **11**
Harris Creek Main   Provincial Park **17**   Bright Angel
                            Provincial Park   COWICHAN
                        15   BAY
            98   Cowichan Trail/ **10**
            Cowichan   Trans-Canada Trail   Shawnigan-
            Valley   Mill Bay Rd.
Harris   Cowichan Lake Rd.   Koksilah River   **14**   MILL BAY
Creek   Provincial Park
spruce   **8**   West Shawnigan Lake   Bamberton
                        Provincial Park **12**   Provincial
Nine Mile Junction   **C** Lizard Lake   Memory Island Provincial Park **13**   Park **11**
Fairy Lake   Recreation Site
Recreation Site   San Juan River Bridge   Shawnigan Lake Rd.
D   **B** Recreation Site
Red   **7**   San Juan River Estuary   Spectacle Lake   **10**
9 Creek   Ecological Reserve   Provincial Park
fir   Malahat Drive   **9**
            5   **8** San Juan Ridge   Sooke Hills   **26**
            Ecological Reserve   Wilderness Regional
        Kludahk Trail (San Juan Ridge)   Park Reserve
                    Sooke Mountain
            14   Provincial Park
Juan de Fuca   **7**   Sooke Potholes parks   **4**   **2**
Provincial Park   China Beach   **5**   LANGFORD
and Marine Trail   Jordan River   Sea to Sea   Mount Wells **1**
    JORDAN RIVER   **A** Recreation Site   Green Blue Belt   Regional Park
                    Park Reserve   **1** **2** Roche Cove
French Beach   **6**   **4** SOOKE   Galloping   and Matheson
Juan de Fuca   Provincial Park   McGregor   Goose   Lake regional
            Park   Whiffen **3** Regional   parks
        Spit Park   Trail   **3**
        East Sooke
        Regional Park
JUAN DE FUCA STRAIT   68
                Sooke

Rapids and calm pools alternate along the canyons that form Sooke Potholes.

Vancouver Island's south coast combines two very different worlds: the urban corridor of southeast Vancouver Island that is dotted with small parks, and the southwest coast with its unbroken wilderness corridors.

This creates an enviable range of options for outdoors enthusiasts. You can windsurf on Nitinat Lake, mountain bike Mount Tzouhalem, tube down the Cowichan River, relax on a beach on Cowichan Lake and hike—well, take your pick of a short scenic walk to a waterfall near Ladysmith or an epic week-long hike combining the Juan de Fuca Marine Trail and the San Juan Ridge.

A huge factor limiting where you can go on the south island is the vast amount of private land. Put the blame on a deal that goes back about 125 years now. In 1884, in exchange for building the Esquimalt and Nanaimo (E&N) Railway from Victoria to Nanaimo, coal baron Robert Dunsmuir was granted about one-quarter the land mass of Vancouver Island—essentially everything east of Campbell River in the north to Jordan River in the south. As a result of this so-called E&N land grant, Vancouver Island is divided between two distinct sections: the private lands to the island's southeast and the Crown land that composes the majority of the rest of the island.

Private land doesn't necessarily mean developed, fortunately, but it does affect the ability to freely move about in places like Jordan River, Sooke, the Malahat, Koksilah River, Cowichan Lake, Chemainus River and Nanaimo Lakes, to mention just a few. This also tends to funnel recreational traffic to the few most accessible locations. TimberWest has done this around Cowichan Lake, creating a good number of camping sites on the lakeside while barring entry to many of the surrounding private logging roads. At Nanaimo Lakes it has gated the access, requiring a fee and limiting hours but still offering camping at key locations.

Public access is further restricted to protect water supplies. For Victoria this affects access to watershed areas in the Sooke Hills; in Nanaimo it affects the Nanaimo Lakes and Jump Lake area.

There are seven relatively distinct regions covered in this chapter: Sooke, Juan de Fuca, Cowichan Valley, Cowichan Lake, Carmanah-Walbran, the West Coast Trail and Yellow Point–Cedar. The range of attractions in each region is vast, but the general rule applies: the farther you go, the greater the rewards, and few rewards are as great as time spent, for instance, in the Carmanah and Walbran valleys.

TRANSPORTATION

Three major paved highways are the gateway to most areas covered in this chapter, with transportation outside the major urban centres limited essentially to logging roads. The Island Highway—also referred to as Highway 19, Highway 1 and the Trans-Canada Highway—leads up the east coast of Vancouver Island, linking Victoria to Duncan and points north. Highway 14 leads down the southwest coast from Langford to Port Renfrew. West of Sooke it becomes a twisting, hilly stretch of road that can be treacherous in poor conditions. Fortunately work to straighten the most dangerous curves was underway in 2008. Even so, several bridges are still single-lane. The third main route is Highway 18, leading from north of Duncan to Lake Cowichan.

Most of the major logging mains in this region are in exceptionally good condition, though all mains can be busy with industrial traffic. For peace of mind, travel on weekends or evenings. The major logging road routes generally have unrestricted access, but restrictions can occur at any time, usually for active logging or during dry, hot periods when the fire risk is high.

The major logging mains are detailed below.

HARRIS AND ROBERTSON MAINS: These are the two major logging roads that connect to link Cowichan Lake and Port Renfrew. The route is wide and in good condition, with the 13 km closest to Port Renfrew paved. It is linked from Highway 18 by Deering Road at Port Renfrew (turn north at the Port Renfrew visitor information centre). Deering Road crosses the San Juan River by a single-lane bridge to the Pacheedaht reserve and the West Coast Trail trailhead. Bypass the trailhead by keeping to the main paved road skirting east of the reserve and continue north across the Gordon River to the GORDON RIVER JUNCTION ●. Here you have a choice: turn left (west) and take the Gordon Main or head right (east) and take the Harris Main, which is paved until NINE MILE JUNCTION ●. The route is clearly marked in both directions, with the route continuing about 37 km north of Nine Mile Junction to SOUTH SHORE ROAD AT MESACHIE BAY ●.

SOUTH SHORE ROAD: This route skirts the south end of the village of Lake Cowichan, and is paved as far west as Honeymoon Bay (at Gordon River Provincial Park). It links up with North Shore Road on the west side of Cowichan Lake.

NORTH SHORE ROAD: This skirts the north side of Cowichan Lake, and is paved until just past Youbou. This is the best route for continuing west across the island to Bamfield, Nitinat or Carmanah.

BAMFIELD ROAD: This is a major route, wide and in good condition, linking Bamfield and Port Alberni. The best access from Highway 4 through Port Alberni is to turn left at the information centre at the east entrance to Port Alberni, then follow the signs through a convoluted series of local roads to the gravel logging road at the end of SHIP CREEK ROAD ●. Signs are generally few and easy to miss. A good bypass is to turn onto the Cameron Main Connector just west of the Alberni summit on Highway 4 (see page 163) and take the Cameron Main west to the Ship Creek Road intersection. From there Bamfield Road continues as a wide, gravel and dirt logging road for 37 km to the intersection with the Carmanah Main at the FRANKLIN SHOP ●. Carmanah Main links Bamfield Road with Nitinat, Carmanah and Cowichan Lake. Bamfield Road continues another 42 km or so past the Franklin Shop to Bamfield, with only the last few kilometres near Bamfield paved.

CARMANAH MAIN: This route begins at Bamfield Road at the FRANKLIN SHOP ●, then continues south and east, first to Nitinat, then to a junction with the HADDON ● and WALBRAN ● mains. Together these tend to create one continuous route, with the various mains dying off in deactivated branches. In conjunction with the McClure, Haddon and Walbran mains, this route provides an indirect link to Cowichan Lake from Bamfield or Port Alberni by passing through the Upper Walbran Valley. Oddly, the Carmanah Main is paved from the Franklin Shop to near Nitinat. There is no reasonable explanation for this phenomenon. After the Haddon junction the Carmanah Main dips southwest to peter out within the north end of Carmanah Walbran Provincial Park, where access into the park is restricted.

WALBRAN MAIN: This route runs from the Haddon Main through the Upper Walbran Valley, connecting with the MCLURE MAIN ●, then continues south to end in the Lower Walbran Valley and the border of Carmanah Walbran Provincial Park. Note that at the McLure Main junction the Walbran Main turns on a tight switchback that can be easily missed. You might find yourself well up the McLure Main before you realize you've missed the Walbran Main turn.

MCLURE/CAYCUSE MAIN: This route links Cowichan Lake at SOUTH SHORE ROAD NEAR CAYCUSE ● with the Walbran Main, and provides the quickest route across Vancouver Island into the Walbran Valley. It is called the McLure Main to the south and Caycuse Main to the north.

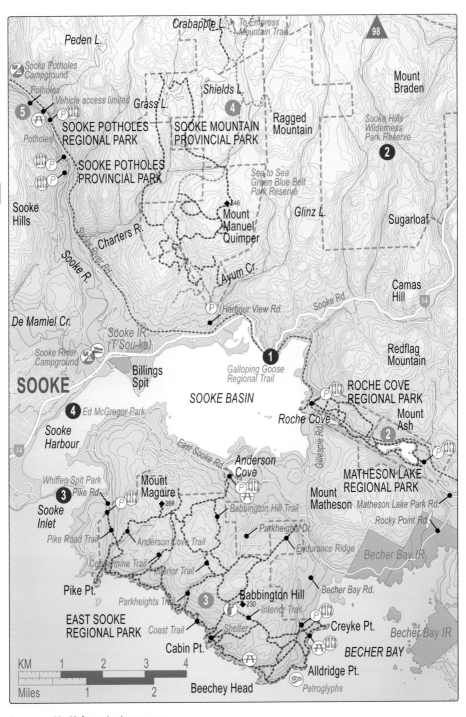

Crabapple L.

To Empress
Mountain Trail

98

Peden L.

Mount
Braden

Sooke Potholes
Campground

Potholes

5

Vehicle access limited

Shields L.

4

Grass L.

Sooke Hills
Wilderness
Park Reserve

Ragged
Mountain

2

SOOKE POTHOLES
REGIONAL PARK

SOOKE MOUNTAIN
PROVINCIAL PARK

Potholes

SOOKE POTHOLES
PROVINCIAL PARK

Sea to Sea
Green Blue Belt
Park Reserve

Sugarloaf

Sooke
Hills

546

Charters R.

Mount
Manuel
Quimper

Glinz L.

Sooke River Rd.

Sooke R.

Ayum Cr.

Camas
Hill

14

De Mamiel Cr.

Harbour View Rd.

Sooke Rd.

Redflag
Mountain

Sooke River
Campground

Sooke IR
(T'Sou-ke)

1

Galloping Goose
Regional Trail

ROCHE COVE
REGIONAL PARK

SOOKE

Billings
Spit

SOOKE BASIN

Roche Cove

Mount
Ash

4

Ed McGregor Park

2

Sooke
Harbour

Gillespie Rd.

MATHESON LAKE
REGIONAL PARK

14

East Sooke Rd.

Anderson
Cove

Mount
Matheson

Matheson Lake Park Rd.

3

Pike Rd.

Mount
Maguire

Rocky Point Rd.

Sooke
Inlet

268

Babbington Hill Trail

Pike Road Trail

Anderson Cove Trail

Parkheights Dr.

Becher Bay IR

Coppermine Trail

Interior Trail

Endurance Ridge

Pike Pt.

Parkheights Trl.

230

Babbington Hill

Becher Bay Rd.

EAST SOOKE
REGIONAL PARK

Coast Trail

Interior Trail

3

Shelter

Creyke Pt.

Becher Bay IR

Cabin Pt.

BECHER BAY

Beechey Head

Alldridge Pt.

Petroglyphs

KM   1   2   3   4

Miles   1   2

See pages 62–63 for main chapter map.

GORDON RIVER MAIN: This is an alternative to Harris and Robertson mains to get between Cowichan Lake and Port Renfrew. From Port Renfrew cross the Gordon River, and at the T-junction turn left (west) rather than east onto the Harris Main. It is a narrower, rougher option but with some scenic advantages, particularly the views of the Gordon River along the way. It is the most direct route between Port Renfrew and points west, such as Bamfield, Carmanah, Walbran and Nitinat. It joins with SOUTH SHORE ROAD AT HONEYMOON BAY ●. Note that rather than continuing north to Cowichan Lake to get to Walbran and Nitinat, the route can be shortened by crossing TR2-M4 (Truck Route 2, MacLure 4). It is a steeper, rougher option but generally passable by front-wheel drive. The east junction is just south of the Gordon River logging station.

NITINAT MAIN: This is part of a major route from Cowichan Lake to Bamfield or Carmanah. The east junction is at the end of North Shore Road. Simply drive along the north end of Cowichan Lake and continue west to the CARMANAH-NITINAT JUNCTION ● just north of Nitinat Lake. From here you can head northwest to link with Bamfield Road or head south to Nitinat Lake and the Carmanah and Walbran valleys. The link is surprisingly short—about 20 km. Note that some logging maps may indicate the main connecting at South Shore Road. This older route is now gated.

Sooke region

The seaside community of Sooke has the best of both worlds: a west coast feel without the isolation of the smaller northern communities. Most activity focuses on Sooke Inlet, while properties around Sooke Basin tend to be quite rural. A good smattering of parks in the area is a bonus, particularly since many make use of scenic waterfront locations. It is a full-service community with marinas and some interesting bed and breakfast locations.

POINTS OF INTEREST

❶ Galloping Goose Regional Trail (west portion) *(map p. 63)*

See page 68 for the westernmost portion. The Metchosin to Sooke portion is described but not illustrated.

West of the Atkins Avenue parking lot (see page 35 for the eastern portion) the Galloping Goose trail must cross numerous roads, including Sooke and Jacklin roads, both major arteries. It then parallels Happy Valley Road for about 7 km through Metchosin before turning on a route skirting Rocky Point Road toward Sooke. Despite the prospect of crossing some traffic, this is a fairly rural stretch through a great deal of farmland along a former railroad bed. Because it isn't paved it's best suited for mountain bikes or horses.

The route then travels through Matheson Lake and Roche Cove parks (page 72) before heading around the north end of Sooke Basin to the Sooke River and its many potholes (page 74). At Todd Creek adjacent to Sooke Potholes Provincial Park the original iron and wood trestle remains for foot and cycle traffic. While the trail bypasses Sooke Potholes Provincial Park, it does intersect with the regional park to the north, making cycling an ideal way to visit the area.

North of Todd Creek the trail gains elevation for the next 12 km to end at Leechtown, a former mining town that's now inaccessible private property.

Given the length of the trail, portions tend to make ideal day trips; popular options are the stretches between Roche Cove and Sooke potholes or from the Atkins Avenue parking lot to Roche Cove. BC Transit offers the opportunity to get a lift back thanks to bike racks on its buses. Visit **www.bctransit.com**.

🐎 HORSEBACK RIDING: Horses are not allowed on the paved portions of the trail within Victoria, Saanich and View Royal, but the trail west of Atkins Avenue is unpaved and suitable for horses. The Luxton Fairgrounds is a common starting point for those using a horse trailer. It is found off the south side of Sooke Road just west of the Happy Valley Road intersection.

ℹ️ **www.crd.bc.ca/parks/galloping-goose/index.htm**.

❷ Sooke Hills Wilderness Regional Park Reserve (map p. 68)

This huge wilderness reserve protects a vast portion of the Sooke Hills between Saanich Inlet and Sooke Basin. It is a true wilderness park: no access is allowed, as it is a buffer for the Greater Victoria water supply. The reserve protects 4,103 hectares and is the largest park in the region.

❸ Whiffen Spit Park (map p. 68)

This is a great little strolling park along the spit at the entrance to Sooke Harbour, and a great place to watch marine birds attracted by the tidal currents and shallow sandbar. A trail runs the length of the spit. The spit itself has been reinforced to protect the harbour.

ACCESS: Whiffen Spit is located off Highway 14 at the end of Whiffen Spit Road. A parking lot is located at the park entrance.

❹ Ed McGregor Park (map p. 68)

This recent (2001) addition to Sooke is a former 1.2-hectare homestead site featuring ornamental gardens, sculptures, public art and an access to Sooke Harbour with a pier, trails down to the waterfront and a boardwalk—essentially Sooke's equivalent of Beacon Hill Park. An amphitheatre is offered for community events. Pillars at the park entrance are the only remaining feature of the Sooke Harbour/Belvedere Hotel, which burned down in 1934. The pillars were moved to the park in 2002.

The well-manicured grounds of Ed McGregor Park.

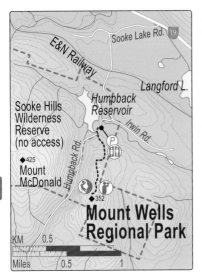

Rock bluffs, meadows and dwarf pine at the summit of Mount Wells make for an outstanding viewpoint overlooking Sooke Lake.

ACCESS: The park is off Highway 14 in Sooke with a parking lot about 75 m north of the park entrance. The park is 2 km south of the visitor centre.

MAJOR PARKS

1 Mount Wells Regional Park (map p. 63)

This 123-hectare park is known for its spring wildflower displays and a few unusual residents, such as alligator lizards, which you may see sunning on the rocks on a warm day. The main feature is a steep but short (20-minute) 1.3 km trail leading from the PARKING LOT ● to the SUMMIT ● of Mount Wells (352 m). It crosses through Douglas-fir and arbutus forests to a scenic viewpoint atop the rock bluff and meadow summit. Other casual trails criss-cross the area. Rock climbing is possible on the mount's west face. Access: From the Island Highway, take Sooke Lake Road (the Goldstream Provincial Park entrance road), then Humpback Road south to the mount wells parking lot just south of the Irwin Road intersection. As with Goldstream Provincial Park, expect the Sooke Lake Road intersection to be rerouted from Highway 1 to Amy Road to the south.

2 Roche Cove and Matheson Lake regional parks (map p. 68)

Two regional parks are located side by side to the east of Sooke Basin. Roche Cove Regional Park protects the namesake cove and the surrounding upland; Matheson Lake Regional Park, to the southeast, protects the lake and the surrounding forested hills.

PICNIC AREAS AND DAY USE: Matheson Lake is a popular swimming hole and recreation area on the lake's sandy beach.

SHORT WALKS: Roche Cove park has 7 km of trails that border the cove, circle the surrounding forest, follow Matheson Creek and include Galloping Goose Regional Trail. The trails connect to Matheson Lake park, which features a trail around the lake.

ACCESS: For Roche Cove, take Gillespie Road south to the park entrance from Highway 14. Matheson Lake is more complicated to reach. From Highway 14 near Victoria your best bet is Happy Valley Road to Rocky Point Road, then Matheson Lake Park Road to the park entrance.

ⓘ **www.crd.bc.ca/parks/matheson/index.htm; www.crd.bc.ca/parks/ rochecove/index.htm**.

③ **East Sooke Regional Park** *(map p. 68)*

This 1,400-hectare park protects most of the 7 km of waterfront between Becher Bay and Sooke Inlet and two notable hills: Mount Maguire and Babbington Hill. The park ranges from groomed picnic grounds to wilderness and marsh areas. A highlight is petroglyphs carved into the rock shoreline near Alldridge Point.

🏕 PICNIC AREAS AND DAY USE: A short trail from the east parking lot at the end of Becher Bay Road leads to a beach; it runs through what was formerly the Aylard farm, with reminders in the old apple orchard and meadow.

🚶 SHORT WALKS: East Sooke Regional Park features some carefully groomed and simple trails, but many are lengthy and require either ascents or navigating difficult portions. The best bet for simple strolls is from the Aylard farm parking lot or the Pike Road Trail to an ocean viewpoint at Pike Point or to Iron Mine Bay.

SOOKE REGION

Bluff shoreline at East Sooke Regional Park.

(🚶) HIKING: Over 50 km of trails link various features of the park. Moderate hikes from the Anderson Cove parking lot lead to the Babbington Hill and Mount Maguire trails. A favourite challenge is the Coast Trail, which runs 10 km along the oceanfront. Portions are difficult.

ACCESS: All three main park entrances can be reached easily from East Sooke Road. From Highway 14, take Gillespie Road south to East Sooke Road, then enter the park by either Becher Bay Road, the Anderson Cove parking lot on the south side of East Sooke Road or the parking lot at Pike Road.

(ℹ) **www.crd.bc.ca/parks/eastsooke/index.htm**.

④ **Sooke Mountain Provincial Park** (map p. 68)

This is an undeveloped park and one of the earliest created on Vancouver Island in 1928. It is located west of the Sooke Hills Regional Wilderness Park and is part of a sizeable wilderness corridor through the Sooke area. It has rocky hills, forests, lakes and potential for recreation, including hiking, fishing and horseback riding, but with no maintained facilities. Mountain bikers, who can use the multitude of trails in the neighbouring Sea to Sea Green Blue Belt Regional Park Reserve, are drawn to the area. Oddly, mountain bikes are officially prohibited within the provincial park, though mountain bike trails criss-cross the adjacent reserve. The main route is a road gated at the parking lot at the end of Harbour View Road. From this numerous trails branch, offering a chance to reach the top of Mount Manuel Quimper, Ragged Mountain and remote Grass and Shields lakes. The most challenging trip would be to follow the access road to Crabapple Lake, from which a trail leads to the top of Empress Mountain (located just north of the Sooke region map).

(△) CAMPING: Backcountry wilderness camping is permitted year-round within the provincial park.

ACCESS: There is no road access into Sooke Mountain Provincial Park. The provincial park is best entered via the Sea to Sea Green Blue Belt Regional Park Reserve. From Highway 14 turn onto Harbour View Road and follow it to the end. You'll find a PARKING LOT ● with trails leading off into the reserve.

⑤ **Sooke Potholes parks** (map p. 68)

Two neighbouring parks under different jurisdictions offer access to the unique sandstone formations known as the Sooke Potholes, carved by moving boulders trapped in the swirling Sooke River. Sooke Potholes Provincial Park is the smaller of the two parks, with 7.3 hectares of undeveloped land. The only facility is a toilet at the PARKING LOT ●. It offers river access, but not at a particularly scenic location. Most of the best views are outside the provincial park in Sooke Potholes Regional Park, which protects 55 hectares along the Sooke River north of the provincial park. A popular time to visit is during the fall salmon run. Day-use parking fees apply at both parks.

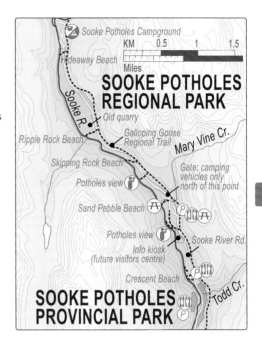

🏕 PICNIC AREAS AND DAY USE: The Sooke River is a well-used swimming area, with pocket beaches at various points along the regional park. The majority of the regional park is not accessible by day-use vehicle, as the access road is gated and only vehicles used by registered campers are allowed beyond it. But as there is no roadside parking at the day-use locations, even campers must walk to places like Hideaway Beach, Ripple Rock Beach and Skipping Rock Beach. The actual beaches are usually quite small and could potentially fill quickly.

SOOKE REGION

🅰 CAMPING: The Sooke Potholes Campground, located just to the north of the regional park, is owned and operated by the Land Conservancy of British Columbia. It is open May to September. Some sites are suited for walk-in or cycle-in camping, but most are quite open and best suited for RVs, with many reserved for RVs only. Reservations are accepted, while some sites are set aside as first-come, first-served. Call 1-888-738-0533.

🚶 SHORT WALKS: Several short trails lead from the roadway to pothole viewpoints or to beach areas. All day-use visitors will be required to walk north of the gate to see Hideaway, Ripple Rock and Skipping Rock beaches, plus other viewpoints. For this reason bicycles make a great way to see this area.

🚶🚴 HIKING AND CYCLING: The Galloping Goose Regional Trail traverses the length of the two parks and continues north to Leechtown, providing a recreational travel corridor through the region along the Sooke River. (See page 68.) Cyclists will have an easier time getting to the regional park than the provincial park, as the trail crosses Sooke River Road inside the regional park. To get to the provincial park directly, cyclists have to leave the trail and take the road to the park entrance.

🎣 FISHING: Catch-and-release angling is possible in Sooke River Provincial Park.

ACCESS: Take Sooke River Road north from Highway 14.

ⓘ www.conservancy.bc.ca/potholescamping; www.crd.bc.ca/parks/ sookepotholes/index.htm

A father and son take a morning stroll on French Beach.

6 **French Beach Provincial Park** *(map p. 63)*

French Beach is the first leg of a long stretch of the Juan de Fuca coastline that's protected almost continuously as a provincial park. The main attraction is a 1.6 km shoreline of sand and pebbles, with some old second-growth Douglas-fir forest in the upland portion.

ECOLOGY: A rare (blue-listed) species found within the park is nodding semaphore grass.

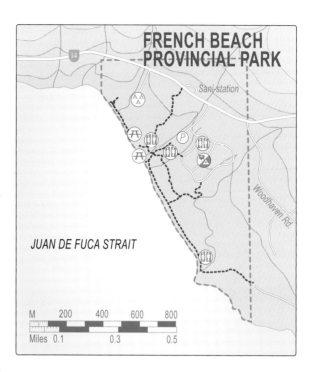

A CAMPING: The vehicle-accessible campsite and separate group campsite at French Beach are both open year-round. Reservations are accepted, with some first-come, first-served sites available.

⟨A⟩ PICNIC AREAS AND DAY USE: A large, grassy picnic site between the campground and the beach has picnic tables, fire rings, water, toilets and a playground. Day use parking fees apply.

⟨⟩ SHORT WALKS: The park has about 2 km of walking trails through Douglas-fir forest and some marsh areas, plus the beach to stroll. Some of the trails are wheelchair-accessible.

ACCESS: French Beach is located 20 km west of Sooke directly off Highway 14.

Juan de Fuca

Juan de Fuca Strait actually begins at Discovery Island north of Victoria, but anyone familiar with the strait will know its real character begins just west of Jordan River. What follows is miles of rugged and generally inhospitable shoreline dotted with occasional beaches perfect for sunning or surfing. Wind is a constant reality here; so are fog and rain. While most visitors stay near the coast, a few notable features are found inland, the newest being the Kludahk Trail, a wonderful wilderness experience atop the San Juan Ridge.

A view toward East Sombrio Beach from near Sombrio Point on the Juan de Fuca Marine Trail.

MAJOR PARKS

Juan de Fuca Provincial Park

(map pp. 62–63)

Detailed map pages 80–81

This is the south end of a belt of oceanfront parkland that continues almost unbroken to the entrance of Nootka Sound. It offers a pleasant mixture of day-use areas and rugged wilderness trails along Juan de Fuca Strait; the highlight is the challenging Juan de Fuca Marine Trail that runs 47 km along the length of the park. Numerous attractions, including waterfalls, old-growth forests and a rugged, rocky shoreline, make this a compelling rival to the more famous West Coast Trail, but there are several distinctions between the two. In particular, the Juan de Fuca trail doesn't require reservations, has no quota limiting the number of hikers and has considerably more access points to break the trail into shorter excursions. Vehicle-accessible camping at China Beach makes this park a good base for exploring the southwest shore of Vancouver Island, while regular access points along the Juan de Fuca Marine Trail make day trips or overnight hikes possible to otherwise remote regions. Day or overnight surf trips to Sombrio Beach are among the most popular uses of the park.

ACCESS: All entry points into the park are located off Highway 14 west of Jordan River. Most are well marked from the roadside, with the exception of the Bear Beach trail, a casual and unmarked route. The Botanical Beach, Botany Bay and Mill Bay trailheads are reached by driving through Port Renfrew.

Juan de Fuca Marine Trail *(map pp. 80–81)*

This 47 km trail begins at China Beach and generally follows the coast of Vancouver Island, ending at Botanical Beach near Port Renfrew. While close geographically to the West Coast Trail, it differs substantially in scenery and difficulty. The Juan de Fuca Marine Trail tends to be more of a forest hike than the West Coast Trail. Beach travel is limited to a few key areas, with long stretches inland from a generally rough and inaccessible shoreline. The Juan de Fuca trail also requires fewer trail aids, such as boardwalks and ladders, making it a less difficult hike in a more natural setting. Its main attraction is some beautiful, open and mature forest reached by a wide, clean trail, with regular visits to an occasionally spectacular oceanfront.

Here are a few key considerations before setting out.

- WHEN TO VISIT: The trail is open year-round, and naturally is more popular in the summer months. It requires no reservations or expensive park use permits, just regular BC Parks parking and backcountry camping fees. Despite the lack of restrictions it sees a fraction of the hikers that use the West

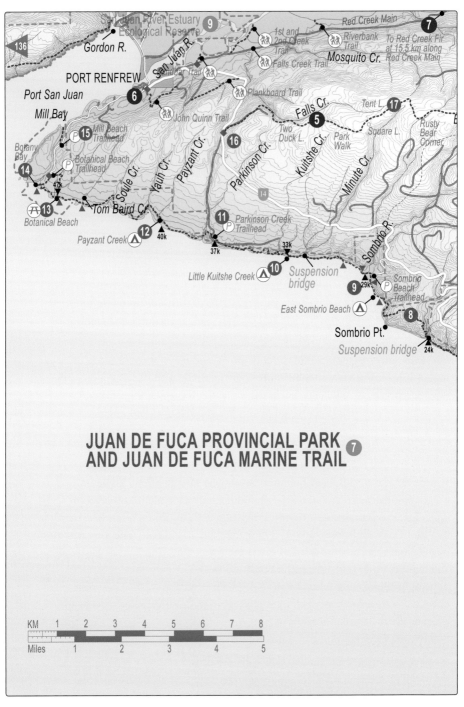

JUAN DE FUCA

San Juan River Estuary Ecological Reserve **9**

Gordon R.

136

San Juan R.

Red Creek Main

1st and 2nd Creek Trail

Riverbank Trail

To Red Creek Fir at 15.5 km along Red Creek Main

7

Mosquito Cr.

Falls Creek Trail

Plankboard Trail

Falls Cr.

Tent L. **17**

PORT RENFREW

Port San Juan

Mill Bay

6

Sandbar Trail

John Quinn Trail

5

Square L.

Rusty Bear Corner

Two Duck L.

Park Walk

Mill Beach Trailhead

15 P

16

Payzant Cr.

Parkinson Cr.

Kuitshe Cr.

Minute Cr.

Botany Bay

Botanical Beach Trailhead

P

Soule Cr.

Yauh Cr.

14

Sombrio R.

14

47k

13

Tom Baird Cr.

11 P

Parkinson Creek Trailhead

10

Sombrio Beach Trailhead

P

8

Botanical Beach

Payzant Creek **12**

40k

37k

33k

Little Kuitshe Creek **10**

Suspension bridge

9 29k

P

East Sombrio Beach

Sombrio Pt.

Suspension bridge 24k

JUAN DE FUCA PROVINCIAL PARK AND JUAN DE FUCA MARINE TRAIL **7**

KM 1 2 3 4 5 6 7 8

Miles 1 2 3 4 5

See pages 62–63 for main chapter map.

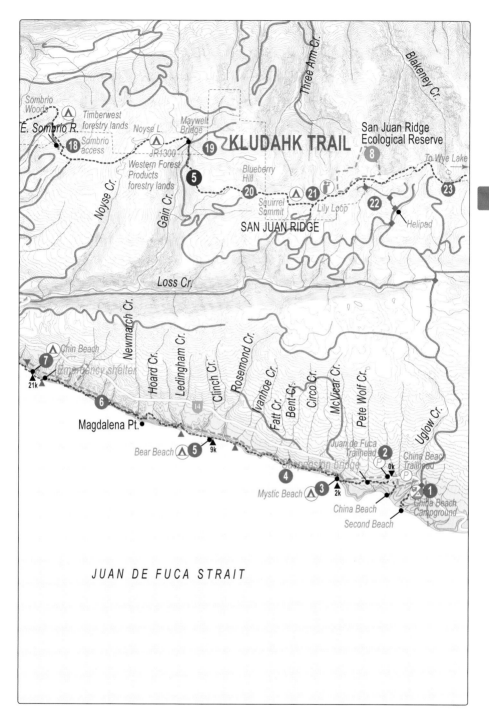

Sombrio
Woods
Timberwest
forestry lands
E. Sombrio R.
18 Sombrio
access
Noyse L.
JR1300
Maywelt
Bridge
19
KLUDAHK TRAIL
San Juan Ridge
Ecological Reserve
8
To Wye Lake
Western Forest
Products
forestry lands
5
Blueberry
Hill
20
21
Lily Loop
22
23
Squirrel
Summit
SAN JUAN RIDGE
Helipad
Three Arm Cr.
Blakeney Cr.
Noyse Cr.
Gain Cr.
Loss Cr.
Newmarch Cr.
Chin Beach
7
Emergency shelter
21k
6
Magdalena Pt.
Bear Beach 5
9k
4
Mystic Beach 3
2k
China Beach
Second Beach
Hoard Cr.
Ledingham Cr.
Clinch Cr.
14
Rosemond Cr.
Ivanhoe Cr.
Fatt Cr.
Bent Cr.
Circo Cr.
McVicar Cr.
Pete Wolf Cr.
Uglow Cr.
Juan de Fuca
Trailhead
2
China Beach
Trailhead
0k
1
2
China Beach
Campground
Ascension Bridge

JUAN DE FUCA STRAIT

Coast Trail, though day-trippers and surfers keep portions busy, particularly China Beach, Sombrio Beach and Botanical Beach.

- HOW LONG IT WILL TAKE: Expect three or possibly four days to comfortably complete the entire 47 km trail. A fit group traveling light could finish it in two days; a group setting out to enjoy the trail won't be disappointed by taking a five-day excursion. Several exit points allow the possibility of cutting the hike short, or ending the hike at a specified time regardless of the distance completed.

- WHICH DIRECTION TO HIKE: If you have two vehicles and drop off one at each end of the trail, it won't make much difference what direction you choose. Assuming only one vehicle, Port Renfrew has the advantage of the West Coast Trail Express or shuttle services back to your vehicle, though the disadvantage is a lengthy walk from the trailhead into Port Renfrew. Thumbing a lift is a popular way to link up to a distant vehicle, or you can wave down the West Coast Trail Express as it passes on Highway 14. Visit **www.trailbus.com/wctrailbus.htm**.

- IN THE EVENT OF INJURY: The Juan de Fuca Marine Trail is a wilderness trail, but with one major advantage over most others on Vancouver Island—it is one of the few with cell phone coverage (though it is likely through US cell towers, so expect roaming charges). Emergency response is possible by calling 911. A small cabin at 20.5 km is available for emergency use.

- WILDERNESS CAMPING: The designated campsites along the Juan de Fuca Marine Trail have the advantage of outhouses, bear caches and established tent areas. They are also located at some of the trail's best scenery, usually (but not all) along beaches. Given the undulating nature of the topography, opportunities for casual campsites in the forest are slim. This means your best bet is to design your schedule to accommodate ending your day at the established sites. Caching food is a necessity, as bears are common along the trail, giving further incentive for finishing your day at a designated spot.

- BEACH CROSSINGS: Some beach areas can be crossed only during lower tides. Tide tables are posted at numerous information kiosks along the trail, but it is still advisable to carry your own. Use the Port Renfrew tide table. You can get them in *Volume 6* of the *Canadian Tide and Current Tables* or from **www.waterlevels.gc.ca**. Note that times listed in the printed chart tables are in standard time and must have an hour added for daylight savings (PDT), if applicable. The electronic Internet version usually has times converted; look for the "PDT" on the tide predictions to confirm this. Orange balls tied in trees mark beach accesses and exits. These can often be difficult to see. Beware of false trail accesses—trails leading from the beach that go nowhere. Most true beach accesses have an information kiosk.

Mystic Beach on an overcast but pleasant November outing.

Here are some of the major features within the park.

1 CHINA BEACH CAMPGROUND: Vehicle-accessible camping is available at China Beach in a forest setting at the east end of Juan de Fuca Provincial Park. Reservations are accepted. Short hikes are possible from the campground to the beach area, which includes China Beach and Second Beach.

2 CHINA BEACH TRAILHEAD: A PARKING AREA ● is located just west of the China Beach campground entrance. From here the Juan de Fuca Marine Trail begins as the 0 km marker and heads over easy terrain for 2 km to Mystic Beach.

Typical shoreline between Mystic and Bear beaches.

3 MYSTIC BEACH, 2 KM: This pleasant beach is easily accessible from the China Beach trailhead, making for a relaxed day outing. Camping is possible here, with a few sites stretched along the beach area. A waterfall is on the east end of the beach.

4 MYSTIC TO BEAR BEACHES, 2–9 KM: This portion of the trail leads through moderately rolling terrain along good trail in mature and old-growth forest, making Bear Beach a possible extended day hike for fit and determined hikers.

5 BEAR BEACH, 9–10 KM: This portion of the trail requires the first extensive beach walk, with portions accessible only at tides 3 m or lower. The beach walk begins at the unnamed creek immediately east of ROSEMOND CREEK ● and exits at LEDINGHAM CREEK ●, a distance of about 2 km. Camping is split among three possible locations: an area around Rosemond Creek, near Clinch Creek and just east of Ledingham Creek at an area known as Rock-on-a-Pillar. An unofficial trail from Highway 14 provides direct access to Bear Beach, making it a possible destination for day trips.

6 LEDINGHAM CREEK TO CHIN BEACH, 10–21 KM: This section features climbs and descents that make it one of the most physically demanding portions of the Juan de Fuca Marine Trail, a fact compensated for by good trail through mature and old-growth forest. Don't expect much in the way of level ground—

Rock shoreline at Chin Beach.

you'll be uphill or downhill the entire way, with the trail usually ascending 100 m or so before dipping to the next ocean-level creek bed. Beach access is slim to non-existent until Chin Beach. There are no campsites between Bear and Chin beaches and little in the way of level ground to create your own, so hikers should be prepared to finish this challenging portion in one day.

7 CHIN BEACH, 21 KM: Chin Beach is a designated CAMPING AREA ●, with about 1 km of beach hiking and a choice of camping locations along the way. An emergency cabin is located at the beach's east entrance. An east portion, at 20.6 km, and a west portion, at 21.3 km, are both passable only at tides below 2.75 m.

8 CHIN BEACH TO EAST SOMBRIO BEACH, 21–27 KM: This is arguably the most grueling stretch of the Juan de Fuca Marine Trail; even though the inclines are shorter than the portion to the east, the trail still tends to be either

BC Parks rates the area around the 24 km marker difficult, but it is mostly good trail with steep portions.

uphill or downhill, with rougher and more frequent muddy sections. The most difficult part is between Sombrio Point and EAST SOMBRIO BEACH ●, where it follows the shoreline cliff on a rough path requiring handholds. A highlight is the suspension bridge over Loss Creek.

❾ SOMBRIO BEACH, 27–29 KM: Past the challenge of Sombrio Point the trail follows the beach for 2 km, with a slight diversion. The portion of beachfront directly east of Sombrio River is private property. As a result the trail extends behind this section, where it meets up with the parking lot. A suspension bridge crosses the Sombrio River, which can

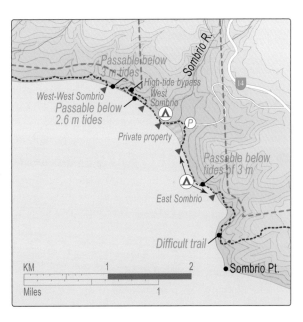

also be crossed at the mouth at lower tides. Camping is popular on the stretch between the east beach access and Sombrio River. Expect large numbers of surfers here, as this is considered one of Vancouver Island's top surfing beaches. The beach becomes rock and boulder west of Sombrio River, limiting camping to the upland portion on the west side of the river where there is a designated tent area. A trail bypass of the beach is necessary at WEST SOMBRIO BEACH ●, at 29.6 km, for tides above 2.6 m. An east portion, at 28 km, and a far west extent, at 30.2 km, are both passable only at tides below 3 m.

Expect more boardwalks and other trail aids west of Little Kuitsche Creek.

10 LITTLE KUITSCHE CREEK, 33 KM: West of Sombrio Beach the trail tends to level out but it becomes rougher, with more mud sections, making it challenging and slow going. A designated CAMPSITE ● is located at Little Kuitsche Creek in the forest above a steep and inaccessible portion of the shoreline. A highlight is the suspension bridge over Minute Creek.

11 PARKINSON CREEK, 37 KM: This portion around Parkinson Creek represents some of the easiest trail, particularly near the Parkinson Creek TRAILHEAD ● where it follows a clear and level old logging road. Otherwise, expect frequent muddy portions through mainly immature forest recovering from 1980s logging. Trail aids such as boardwalks become more frequent west of Parkinson Creek, and numerous interpretive signs dot the trail. Parkinson Creek can be reached by road from Highway 14, making day or overnight trips possible to Payzant or Little Kuitsche creeks.

Ocean view from near Payzant Creek.

⑫ PAYZANT CREEK, 40 KM: This is the westernmost designated CAMPING AREA ● on the trail, set in a nicely forested section west of the creek well away from the ocean. West of the campsite is the easiest portion of the Juan de Fuca Marine Trail, with mostly level sections aided by boardwalks to Botanical Beach.

⑬ BOTANICAL BEACH, 47 KM: This is the west TRAILHEAD ● for the Juan de Fuca Marine Trail. From the parking lot a 1 km trail down a gravel service road leads to a picnic area and a beach access. Tidal pools in the rock platforms provide glimpses of the beach's rich intertidal ecosystem, best viewed at tides below 1.2 m. Note that the intertidal pools are vulnerable and prone to human impact. A no-touch policy on all life forms is in place to avoid adding human oils to the pools. The wealth of marine life captured the attention of the University of Minnesota, which in 1901 created the first marine research centre in the Pacific Northwest here. It has been used extensively for research since.

⑭ BOTANY BAY: This is an easy 1 km walk to the waterfront and a chance to picnic or peek into tidal pools in an alternative to nearby Botanical Beach. Visitors can loop between Botany Bay and Botanical Beach by walking the waterfront.

⑮ MILL BAY TRAIL: This short but steep and potentially demanding trail begins from a parking lot just northeast of the main parking area for the Botanical Beach trail. It leads to a small pebble and shell beach.

⑧ San Juan Ridge Ecological Reserve (map p. 81)

Patches of white glacier lily are common along the Kludahk Trail.

This property on the top of San Juan Ridge was created in 1977 primarily to protect a rare population of white glacier lilies, a flower that is found only in subalpine areas in British Columbia, and in only two locations on Vancouver Island. The ridge tends to attract subalpine vegetation at a lower-than-average elevation, particularly along the sun-shielded north face, due to the high winds and deep snowfall. Another rare denizen is snowbed lichen (*Siphula ceratites*). Access to the reserve is allowed for low-impact visits, though the proliferation of the lilies in the area means you can easily see them from the Kludahk Trail (page 91), avoiding disturbing the reserve.

⑨ San Juan River Ecological Reserve (map p. 80)

This reserve protects a small patch of tooth-leaved monkey-flower, a discovery that stopped the floodplain from being clear-cut and led to the creation of the reserve back in 1996. This is the only place the flower is found in Canada. The 79-hectare

The San Juan River estuary.

reserve protects part of the largest river delta on the southwest coast of Vancouver Island, as well as many rare plant species, such as paintbrush owl-clover, Smith's fairybells, angled bitter-cress and nodding semaphore grass. The delta is also a black bear feeding area during the fall salmon run, and potential habitat for Roosevelt elk. The reserve is open to low-impact visits. Cycling is ideal.

SHORT WALKS: A number of local trails skirt the shores at the mouth of the San Juan River near the reserve. SANDBAR TRAIL ● leads 0.8 km to the edge of the reserve at a delta sandbar. First and Second Creek Trail is located about 1 km farther east. The trail is a 3.2 km round trip leading to a gravel bar along the river. The route is known for pink fawn lilies in spring. Another 0.5 km along the Red Creek Main is the Falls Creek Trail. It and Riverbank Trail are short (400 m) walks to the river. Riverbank Trail begins about 6.5 km farther along. Any of these hikes works well in conjunction with a visit to Red Creek Fir (page 96).

ACCESS: Access to all is off the Red Creek Main, accessible off Highway 4 and marked as Parkinson Road at the curve in the highway just east of the "Welcome to Port Renfrew" sign. Note that portions of the road are narrow and overgrown, and parking is limited at the trailheads.

The Kludahk Outdoor Club cabin at Tent Lake.

JUAN DE FUCA

POINTS OF INTEREST

⑤ Kludahk Trail (San Juan Ridge) *(map pp. 80–81)*

This is one of Vancouver Island's newest trails, created in the early 1990s by a group of interested people in Sooke calling themselves the Kludahk Outdoors Club (KOC). The club deserves a great deal of credit for the amount of work involved in developing the 40 km trail, which surpasses most provincial park trails for quality. A great feature is metal grates over many bog areas, a far more durable and less slippery option than wooden boardwalks. Donations have made a few notable features possible, including metal bridges over Gain Creek and East Sombrio River, as well as a few key wooden boardwalks. A downside is much of the KOC's work is strictly for the benefit of KOC members; public use appears to be discouraged, particularly when it comes to signs at access points. Cabins built along the route are for KOC members only. It's understandable the KOC doesn't want the trail to become as popular as the Juan de Fuca Marine Trail; however, given the many attractions along the trail and the exceptional hiking, its transition from obscurity to one of Vancouver Island's top trails is inevitable.

The trail generally follows the San Juan Ridge from just outside Port Renfrew to Wye Lake through an unusual alpine ecosystem (see page 89).

The trail's position inland of the Juan de Fuca Marine Trail makes it ideal for creating a loop route. A good circle route of both trails would be to exit or enter the Juan de Fuca trail at Parkinson Creek, Jordan River or China Beach and cross to or from the Kludahk Trail. Hikers could finish the Juan de Fuca trail by exiting at Botanical Beach, but this adds considerably to the roadside distance of the loop, so an early exit at Parkinson Creek is recommended.

- HOW LONG IT WILL TAKE: The Kludahk Trail is in good condition with moderate elevation gains, making for an easy two-day hike, with a third recommended for explorations involving Wye Lake. A circuit of both the Kludahk and Juan de Fuca trails is best planned as a six- or seven-day outing.

- LEVEL OF DIFFICULTY: Most elevation gains and losses are moderate, with a few steep areas near major river and creek crossings. Bogs are common in the subalpine meadows, so expect mud and the possibility of wet feet. For the most part the trail is well marked, with the notable exception of logging road access points. This adds considerably to the prospect of getting lost mid-trail. See the notes below for details.

- WHICH DIRECTION TO HIKE: The west access is the easiest to find and enter (requiring no use of restricted logging roads), making a west-to-east traverse the simplest to start. As the Jordan River logging road has restricted access, expect a 10 km hike from the trailhead to the highway. As this is not a particularly scenic hike, with a constant elevation gain toward the ridge, it

JUAN DE FUCA

Lichen on trees, moss on the ground and a stunted pine forest form the subalpine flora on San Juan Ridge.

will be a far more pleasant hike out than a walk in (and quicker, too). Naturally, off-hours travel could mean driving to the trailhead, or dropping off cars at both trailheads, taking away the headache of the long hike out along the logging road. This assumes the gate at the entrance is open, which won't necessarily be the case.

(A) WILDERNESS CAMPING: While camping is technically possible anywhere, level ground outside bogs is rare, so suitable areas are in short supply. Options will be greater in later summer as the spongy, mossy areas dry out.

Here are a few main features. See map pages 80–81.

(16) PARKINSON CREEK ACCESS: The west end of the Kludahk Trail can be reached from Highway 4 by a deactivated LOGGING ROAD ● immediately across from the Parkinson Creek turnoff for the Juan de Fuca Marine Trail. You can park at the logging road entrance, or at several two-wheel-drive accessible pullouts along the logging road. Four-wheel drives can get much closer to the trailhead. Or park at the Parkinson Creek parking lot in Juan de Fuca Provincial Park (which requires a lengthy walk out). The first indication of the trail is a Kludahk Trail marker about a half-kilometre up the logging road. At the first logging road junction keep left, then watch for the small ROCK CAIRN ● on your left. The trail is almost invisible as it winds through clear-cut slash to a creek bed. Miss the cairn and you'll likely never find the trail. Once down the slash and across the creek in the cover of forest the trail becomes exceptionally well marked.

(17) TENT LAKE: From Parkinson Creek the trail rises fairly steadily in elevation to about 800 m and the first subalpine bogs. A KOC cabin is located at one of the prettiest subalpine spots at Tent Lake. Dry and level tenting areas are at a premium here; look to one clear spot just east of the cabin along the trail.

(18) SOMBRIO RIVER: The trail descends from the Tent Lake area's subalpine meadows to a crossing of the Sombrio River, with a good new metal BRIDGE OVER EAST SOMBRIO ●. The descent from the west is through Sombrio Woods, an area of wonderful old-growth forest hard hit by the 2006 winter windstorms. Expect some steep and potentially difficult areas. East of the river and a boardwalk is the SOMBRIO ACCESS ●, a muddy route to the logging road entry point. East of the access the trail rises to another subalpine area and a KOC cabin at NOYSE LAKE ●. The forested areas on either side of the Sombrio River arms have some of the best potential wilderness camping areas.

(19) MAYWELL BRIDGE: A new metal bridge, flown in by helicopter in 2003, crosses Gain Creek. East of the bridge the trail ascends through clear-cut slash to a logging road, at which point all trail markers disappear. This makes it a likely point to get lost. For those traveling east, the trail exits onto JR1300, joining the JORDAN RIVER MAIN ● after about a half a kilometre. It would seem intuitive to head east to look for the trail continuation. Instead head south, following the trail for about 1.2 km past the JR1300 junction just past GILBERT CREEK ●. Don't expect any roadside markers. For those traveling west, simply head north from Gilbert Creek on the logging road and continue north past the junction on JR1300. Follow JR1300 to the end.

JUAN DE FUCA

20 BLUEBERRY HILL: East of Gilbert Creek the trail ascends steadily past Gilbert Lake to the subalpine area at Blueberry Hill, a scenic highlight at about 1 km elevation. A KOC cabin and TENT PAD ● are located here. While very pretty, expect insects. To escape them, or if the tent pad is in use, a clear area can be found in the forest at SQUIRREL SUMMIT ● to the east. Expect snow into July in some areas near here.

21 LILY LOOP: East of Squirrel Summit is COLD LAKE ●, a potential camping area, and the ELK LAKE ACCESS ●. A loop trail, the Lily Loop Trail, leads from the Elk Lake trailhead, providing a moderate circuit of the area—an ideal day trip for those hoping to see white glacier lilies. A good time to visit is June when the lilies are in bloom. The trail loops out to a viewpoint north, where a KOC CABIN● is under construction (2007).

22 JORDAN RIVER ACCESS: This is the sensible east entrance or exit for a traverse of the trail, particularly if it is being looped with the Juan de Fuca Marine Trail, as it is close to the China Beach trailhead (well, relatively close—it is still a 10.5 km roadside hike to link the two ends). Note that the logging road has restricted access during weekdays. The trailhead is also unmarked and invisible from the roadside, meaning the odds of casually finding it are almost zero. For this reason it's highly recommended that you use the GPS coordinates in the appendix. Here are the detailed directions. From Highway 4 take the LOGGING ROAD ● (restricted access) directly across from the entrance to the China Beach campground. It is potentially gated at about 2 km. After about 7 km you will cross the LOSS CREEK BRIDGE ●. Take the right after the bridge. In about another 2 km you will cross ANOTHER BRIDGE ●. Take the right road after the bridge. After about 0.5 km you should see a helipad sign. Take the left at the junction near the HELIPAD SIGN ●. After about another 0.5 km a SPUR will head NORTH ●. Take the spur. It will continue north then turn east. A few hundred metres after the turn west the road will pass a creek with a potential parking area on the south side (four-wheel access is recommended, though front-wheel drive could probably make the trip). Just east of the creek is the KLUDAHK TRAILHEAD ●. It is invisible as it passes over roadside boulders and through overgrown scrub into the forest. Only once you're in the forest and on the trail will you see the Kludahk marker and trail signs.

23 WYE LAKE: East of the Jordan River access the trail passes the south side of the San Juan Ridge Ecological Reserve, allowing trailside views of the white glacier lily. The abundance in the area means you do not have to access the reserve to see the lilies, which tend to do well in open areas and consequently flourish along the trailside. The trail continues east to the Hans Roemer Meadow, Jordan Meadow and Wye Lake. This makes the Jordan River access a good entry point for day trips or short overnight trips.

TRAVEL NOTES: I hiked the trail west to east, walking out via the 10-plus km of logging roads from the Jordan River access to the China Beach campground. Lower portions of the logging roads were quite busy with industrial traffic, meaning less than ideal hiking. Fortunately the slope worked in my favour, making it much easier than hiking in. Even so, it was a four-hour walk (with breaks). I then hitched a lift back to Parkinson Creek and my car. I give the Kludahk Trail a slight edge over the Juan de Fuca Marine Trail for the range of scenery. A loop of both, however, puts the circuit into a new genre combining oceanfront to subalpine hiking. My traverse of the Kludahk Trail took three days, but only because I lost a half-day hiking the logging roads around JR1300 looking for the unmarked trailhead.

❻ Port Renfrew (map p. 80)

This sleepy little community at the end of Highway 14 wakes up for a few weeks every summer when it caters to outdoors enthusiasts, thanks to its place at trailheads for both the West Coast and Juan de Fuca Marine trails. Expect a modest smattering of outdoor supply stores, gift shops, hostels, cafés, restaurants, bed and breakfasts and transportation services. An INFORMATION CENTRE ● is located at the community centre at the entrance to the village, with most services farther south along the main road. A few more, such as a small store, can be found on the Pacheedaht reserve on the north side of the bridge across the San Juan River. As well as the major park trails, a number of local trails dot the area.

HARRISON'S PLANKBOARD TRAIL: This 1.5 km trail follows a 1940s plank logging road and leads through a mature hillside forest. Access is off Highway 14, 4 km outside of Port Renfrew.

JOHN QUINN TRAIL: Park at the Port Renfrew Recreation Centre for the easiest access to this 4 km trail. It follows an old logging road through second-growth forest and past a beaver dam to Highway 4 just across from the Parkinson Road junction.

CAMPING: The Pacheedaht First Nation has its main community on the north shore of Port San Juan adjacent to Gordon River. The band runs the Pacheedaht Campground, which has camping along 3 km of sandy beachfront facing the port. Beach fires are permitted. The community also has a number of other services, including a small store, an espresso stand, watershed canoe tours and a sightseeing charter service.

FISHING: Smelt is often caught at the port, and freshwater fishing in the Gordon and San Juan rivers offers steelhead, rainbow trout and cutthroat. An option is ocean charters for salmon, halibut, groundfish and rockfish.

❼ Red Creek fir *(map p. 80)*

The largest recorded Douglas-fir—the world champion, in fact—is Red Creek Fir, with a height of 74 m, a spread of 22.9 m and a volume of 349 square metres of wood. It is estimated to be near 1,000 years old.

ECOLOGY: The Douglas-fir is not really a fir tree, but was named before this was discovered (thus the hyphen). Scottish botanist David Douglas first identified the tree in 1826 and introduced many of British Columbia's conifers to Europe.

ACCESS: The tree is at the end of a short trail along Red Creek Main, which is in poor condition. If you can make it to the trailhead parking lot, the hike is less than an hour. Because of the poor road condition this makes an ideal cycling trip from whatever point you no longer feel comfortable driving—potentially 16 km one way from Highway 14 if you do not have four-wheel drive. Even so, this is an ideal day trip in combination with some of the other nearby trails.

❽ Harris Creek spruce ● *(map p. 63)*

A short interpretive trail leads to a large Sitka spruce. Fenced off and protected, it is not among British Columbia's largest; for that you'll have to visit the San Juan River (Bridge) recreation site (page 97). It is alongside Harris Creek, which may make for a refreshing, if not cold, dip during a visit.

ACCESS: The trailhead is located along the Harris Creek Main on the main route between Lake Cowichan and Port Renfrew, about 11 km north of Nine Mile Junction.

FOREST RECREATION SITES

See the map on pages 62–63 to locate these recreation sites.

Ⓐ Jordan River Recreation Site

This TimberWest recreation site is set on the eastern point of the mouth of Jordan River. It is a wide spit surrounded by beach, with a parking area and RV sites facing directly over the beach to Juan de Fuca Strait. The west extent is a day-use area with a boat launch into Jordan River. The spit makes a good place for a short stroll—or, for the particularly hardy, a cold ocean dip.

Ⓐ CAMPING: The RV parking is open parking-lot style with the advantage of directly facing Juan de Fuca Strait for an exceptional ocean view. Attractive tent sites can be found in the second-growth forest immediately west of the RV sites.

ACCESS: The recreation site is located just off Highway 14 at Jordan River, 36 km west of Sooke.

JUAN DE FUCA

TRAVEL NOTES: TimberWest put 1,800 hectares of land at Jordan River up for sale in late 2007, including the recreation site. This has put the future of this site and the neighbouring coastline in doubt.

B San Juan River (Bridge) Recreation Site ●

This BC Forest Service campground is set on the San Juan River with a pebble beach, a giant Sitka spruce and a large maple. The Sitka is considered Canada's largest spruce, with a circumference of 11.66 m and a height of 62.5 m. The site has five campsites with a few picnic tables and firepits.

ACCESS: Take Harris Main for 14 km from Port Renfrew to Nine Mile Junction. Take the east road (signed). At the "Triangle" logging road junction take the right option and stick with it until it crosses the San Juan River. The recreation site is to the immediate left.

C Lizard Lake Recreation Site ●

This forest service campground gives access to a small recreation lake complete with a long dock for swimming, fishing or launching small boats. No motors are allowed on the lake. The lake's sandy beach is a popular summer day-use area. Picnic tables are set in the forest adjacent to the beach.

FISHING: Rainbow trout fishing is possible from April to June and in October.

CAMPING: This is a managed campground with 28 sites, a few of them walk-in near the lakeside, with picnic tables and toilets. Fees apply May to October.

SHORT WALKS: An easy 1.5 km trail circles the lake.

ACCESS: From Highway 14 follow the route to Cowichan Lake along the Harris Creek Main from Port Renfrew for 18 km. The day-use area is slightly north of the campground entrance.

D Fairy Lake Recreation Site

This managed forest service site northeast of Port Renfrew has a popular beach area alongside the namesake lake with a boat launch, picnic tables and toilets. Trout fishing is popular here. A short nature trail runs from the logging road west of Fairy Creek.

PADDLING: It is possible to canoe from Fairy Lake to the mouth of San Juan River, a 15 km trip. Log-jams may create portages. During fall it makes an ideal way to witness the salmon run.

CAMPING: There are 36 sites with fees payable May to October.

ACCESS: From Port Renfrew head north, taking the Cowichan Lake Road east for about 4 km just past Fairy Creek.

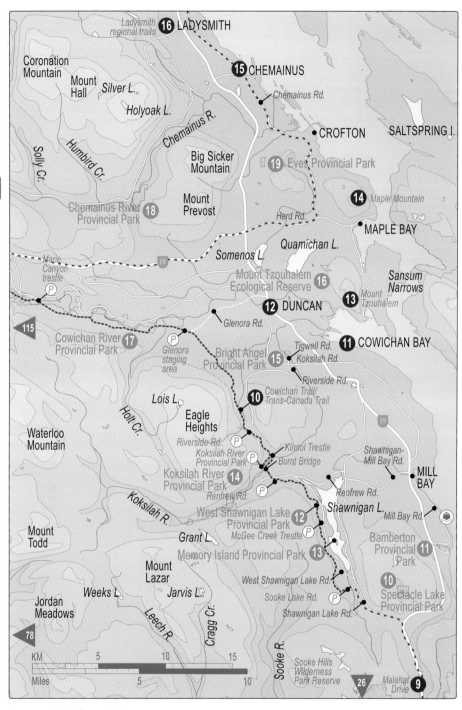

Ladysmith regional trails **16** LADYSMITH

15 CHEMAINUS

Coronation Mountain

Mount Hall

Silver L.

Holyoak L.

Chemainus Rd.

CROFTON

SALTSPRING I.

Solly Cr.

Humbird Cr.

Chemainus R.

Big Sicker Mountain

19 Eves Provincial Park

14 Maple Mountain

Chemainus River Provincial Park **18**

Mount Prevost

Herd Rd.

MAPLE BAY

Marie Canyon trestle **P**

18

Somenos L.

Quamichan L.

Sansum Narrows

Mount Tzouhalem Ecological Reserve **16**

13 Mount Tzouhalem

115

Cowichan River Provincial Park **17**

P Glenora staging area

Glenora Rd.

12 DUNCAN

11 COWICHAN BAY

Bright Angel Provincial Park

15 Tigwell Rd.
Koksilah Rd.

Lois L.

Eagle Heights

Riverside Rd.

10 Cowichan Trail/
Trans-Canada Trail

Riverside Rd.

Holt Cr.

Waterloo Mountain

Riverside Rd. **P**

Kinsol Trestle

Koksilah River Provincial Park **P**

Burnt Bridge

19

Shawnigan-Mill Bay Rd.

MILL BAY

14

Renfrew Rd.

Renfrew Rd.

Koksilah R.

West Shawnigan Lake Provincial Park

12

Shawnigan L.

Mill Bay Rd.

Mount Todd

Grant L.

McGee Creek Trestle **P**

Bamberton Provincial Park **11**

Mount Lazar

Memory Island Provincial Park **13**

10 Spectacle Lake Provincial Park

Weeks L.

Jarvis L.

West Shawnigan Lake Rd.

Jordan Meadows

Sooke Lake Rd. **P**

Shawnigan Lake Rd.

Leech R.

Cragg Cr.

Sooke R.

Sooke Hills Wilderness Park Reserve

26 Malahat Drive **9**

78

KM 5 10 15

Miles 5 10

See pages 62–63 for main chapter map.

The Kinsol Trestle prior to planned renovations.

Cowichan Valley region

The Cowichan Valley is by and large a residential, commercial and industrial corridor extending the length of the Island Highway between the Malahat and Chemainus. Logging remains the economic backbone of the region, bolstered by the private forestry lands to the west of the farming and residential corridor. Some areas are intensely industrial. Crofton and Chemainus are busy pulp mill towns; Cowichan Bay is a major shipping centre. The rest, however, tends toward a rural tranquility dotted with vineyards and sheep farms. Because almost all the land is privately owned, recreation is most often compressed into a few areas of fairly intense use. Shawnigan Lake is a key cottage area for the region, while Cowichan River is arguably the most popular park for camping and water-based activities. Pockets of wilderness dot the area, though very little remains in a natural state.

ⓘ For municipal information visit **www.cvrd.bc.ca**. For tourist information and links to current businesses and services, visit **www.cowichan.bc.ca** or **www.vancouverisland.travel**.

POINTS OF INTEREST

❾ **Malahat Drive** *(map p. 98)*

This portion of the Island Highway leads about 25 km over the Malahat Ridge, a mountainous area on the west side of Saanich Inlet. It is a scenic connector linking Victoria with up-island communities like Duncan and Nanaimo, and the only paved link. It passes through Goldstream Provincial Park plus has three scenic viewpoints over Saanich Inlet at roadside rest areas for northbound vehicles only. Malahat means "place of bait." While it's a beautiful stretch to travel, it's also notoriously dangerous during heavy rain at night or when it's snowing. There are various amenities along the route, including gas and the upscale Aerie Resort. A bypass is the Mill Bay–Brentwood Bay ferry. A scenic driving loop from Victoria includes the Malahat, Mill Bay Road, the Mill Bay–Brentwood Bay ferry and whatever other features you want to add from the Cowichan Valley and Saanich Peninsula.

❿ **Cowichan Trail/Trans Canada Trail** *(map p. 98)*

The Cowichan Rail Trail follows 47 km of Canadian Pacific Railway's former Galloping Goose Rail Line from Shawnigan Lake to Lake Cowichan; it runs 140 km in its entirety if you include the adjacent road routes.

The portion from Shawnigan Lake to the Koksilah River is easy to travel, with negligible grades. It should cross the Kiksilah River at the KINSOL TRESTLE ●, but the historic trestle has fallen into disrepair and requires a bypass. There are plans to restore the trestle, which is the largest wooden rail bridge in the British Commonwealth; seven other historic trestles have already been restored for the trail. Until it is rebuilt, a detour turns west through Koksilah River Provincial Park to cross at Burnt Bridge. Note that portions of the trail through the Koksilah River park can be muddy. Once reconnected to the Kinsol Trestle, the route continues north to the Cowichan River and through Cowichan River Provincial Park to end at Sayward Park on Lake Cowichan.

The trail continues, on paper at least, from Lake Cowichan to Ladysmith using roads—the Cowichan Valley Highway, Herd Road, then Chemainus Road. From there it can conceivably link with the Nanaimo portion of the Trans Canada Trail (page 151). Plans for the south end include linking the Cowichan Trail to Victoria's Galloping Goose Regional Trail (which came a step closer with the announcement of the E&N Rail Trail—see page 36). Naturally, road portions are all potentially busy routes not particularly well suited to cycling.

The Cowichan Trail is open to non-motorized wheels, feet and horseback riding.

ACCESS: Parking areas with washrooms and information kiosks are located at Sooke Lake Road, the McGee Creek Trestle, Renfrew Road, Koksilah River Provincial Park, Riverside Road, the Glenora staging area, Marie Canyon and the Lake Cowichan trailhead.

ⓘ www.cvrd.bc.ca/parks/html/featureparks/trans_can.html.

⑪ Cowichan Bay *(map p. 98)*

This fishing, logging and shipping community is finding new life as a recreational marine centre and tourist destination. Beyond the marinas, cafés and trendy shops, a key attraction is the Cowichan Bay Maritime Centre, a museum offering boatbuilding and restoration projects along a historic wood wharf. Visit **http:// classicboats.org**.

⑫ Duncan *(map p. 98)*

This is the commercial centre for the region, unfortunately best known to most visitors as a string of traffic lights and strip malls along the otherwise fast-moving Island Highway. It's called the City of Totems for its array of 80 traditional First Nations carvings, including the Cedarman, billed as the world's largest totem pole. Guided walking tours of the totems are available in season, while self-guided tours are possible with a booklet available at the visitor centre and city bookstores.

- BIRDS OF PREY VISITOR CENTRE: Owls, hawks, falcons and eagles are on display at this stop just north of Duncan, which offers a self-guided tour, interpretive centre and gift shop. Key attractions are the daily flying demonstrations featuring the talents of falcons and "hawk walks" for an up-close view. Visit **www.pnwraptors.com**.

- BC FOREST DISCOVERY CENTRE: The history of logging comes to life here through a sawmill, an operating steam engine, a logging camp, a ranger station and a lookout tower. Visit **www.bcforestmuseum.com**.

- QUW'UTSUN' CUTURAL CENTRE: Operated by the Cowichan First Nation, the centre offers interpretive tours, traditional art and First Nations cuisine in a café setting along the Cowichan River. Demonstrations include carvers and knitters making the famous Cowichan sweaters. Visit **www.quwutsun.ca**.

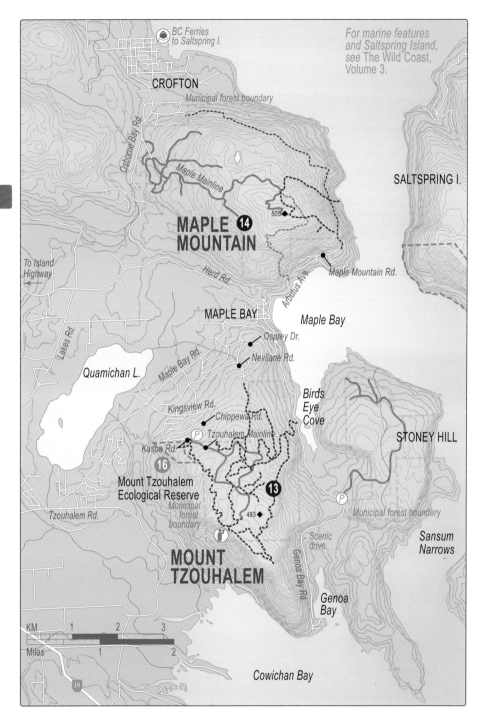

BC Ferries
to Saltspring I.

*For marine features
and Saltspring Island,
see* The Wild Coast,
Volume 3.

CROFTON

Municipal forest boundary

SALTSPRING I.

Osborne Bay Rd.

Maple Mainline

505◆

MAPLE 14
MOUNTAIN

To Island
Highway

Herd Rd.

Arbutus Ave.

Maple Mountain Rd.

MAPLE BAY

Maple Bay

Lakes Rd.

Osprey Dr.

Maple Bay Rd.

Nevilane Rd.

Quamichan L.

*Birds
Eye
Cove*

Kingsview Rd.

Chippewa Rd.

STONEY HILL

P *Tzouhalem Mainline*

Kaspa Rd.

16

Mount Tzouhalem
Ecological Reserve
*Municipal
forest
boundary*

483◆

P

Municipal forest boundary

13

*Sansum
Narrows*

i

*Scenic
drive*

**MOUNT
TZOUHALEM**

Genoa Bay Rd.

*Genoa
Bay*

KM 1 2 3

Miles 1 2

Cowichan Bay

19

The view from a Mount Tzouhalem ridge.

⑬ **Mount Tzouhalem** (map p. 98)

Detailed map page 102

This mountain is a municipal forest reserve crossed by 4.5 km of active and inactive logging roads. The area is notable for its Garry oak stands and wildflower meadows.

🚲 MOUNTAIN BIKING: Tzouhalem is synonymous with mountain biking. The north slope features a multitude of criss-crossing trails that range in difficulty from casual to technical.

🚶 HIKING is also popular, usually along the logging road to the escarpment with multiple views over Cowichan Bay and inland Vancouver Island along the length of the ridge. Be sure to look for the historic cross atop the bluff. Note that many of the biking trails are meant for mountain bike challenges and tend to meander and double back, and are not well suited for hiking.

ACCESS: From the Island Highway in south Duncan, taking Trunk Avenue/ Tzouhalem Road east, then Maple Bay Road northeast to Kingsview Road at a new subdivision. Take Chippewa Road south to Kaspa Road, following it to the end where you'll find a parking lot and the main entry point to the trails.

ⓘ South Island Mountain Biking Society at **www.simbs.com/html/wer2ride/ zoohal.htm**, with links to detailed trail maps.

⓮ Maple Mountain *(map p. 98)*

Detailed map page 102

This mountain in North Cowichan near the small community of Maple Bay is working forestry land crossed by trails. At 505 m it is not particularly high but is remarkable for its rock bluffs and intermittent views over Sansum Narrows toward Saltspring Island.

HIKING: The mountain has 14 km of designated trails in four routes marked by coloured tags, which are reflected on the map on page 102. The yellow and blue trails are the simplest; the orange and purple trails snake toward the peak. Other user-created routes also exist.

ACCESS: The Maple Mainline is an active logging road that winds close to the peak. It is reached from Osborne Bay Road. The north trailheads can be reached from Chilco Road in Crofton, with the turnoff also from Osborne Bay Road. The south orange trailhead is off Arbutus Avenue in Maple Bay. The south blue trailhead is at the end of Maple Mountain Road.

⓯ Chemainus *(map p. 98)*

This community is remarkable for reinventing itself after a downturn in the fortunes of the logging industry by painting murals on the town's buildings. The result was a hit with tourists in a formula since copied worldwide. Twenty years later it maintains a modestly vibrant array of specialty shops and its centrepiece, a professional theatre company. Visit **www.chemainustheatrefestival.ca**. Meanwhile, the town is still an active logging community with a mill dominating much of the waterfront.

ⓘ **www.northcowichan.bc.ca**, then follow "Visitors/Chemainus murals."

This small community of about 7,200 overlooks Ladysmith Harbour and augments its old-time downtown charm each year with a dazzling Christmas light display. While much of the harbour is industrial, Transfer Beach, just off the Island Highway, offers an oceanfront green space and beach plus an adventure playground, kayak rentals, food and a swimming area in season.

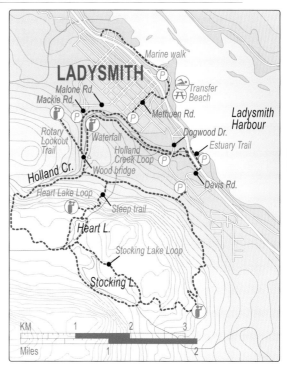

🏃 🚶 SHORT WALKS AND HIKING: Ladysmith maintains an above-average trail network starting at the estuary and running along Holland Creek, ending high in the neighbouring hillsides at remote Heart Lake and Stocking Lake. The most accessible and scenic route follows Holland Creek adjacent to the village. The north trail can be used by wheelchairs. The south trail is significantly more difficult, with several steep portions but a great viewpoint of Crystal Falls. From the Dogwood Drive parking lot to the wood bridge and looping back is an energetic two-hour walk. A possible side trip from near the wood bridge is the Rotary Lookout Trail, which leads along a hydro right-of-way to a viewpoint. Or from the bridge you can continue south to longer trails: the Heart Lake Loop or the 10 km Stocking Lake Loop. The north end of Heart Lake is occasionally used as a campsite. A recommended hike is from Dogwood Drive to Heart Lake via the steep central trail, then back. This offers the best scenery for the distance and avoids some stretches of logging road necessary on the extended trails.

ACCESS: Parking is available at a parking lot off DOGWOOD DRIVE ●. From the main set of traffic lights on the south end of Ladysmith take Davis Road west, then turn right on Dogwood and follow it to just before the bridge. The parking lot is in the woods to the left. Other parking spots are at Transfer Beach, at the end of Methuen Street and off Mackie Road—a short road off Malone Road.

COWICHAN VALLEY REGION

⑩ Spectacle Lake Provincial Park ● *(map p. 98)*

At this small (67-hectare) day-use park at the lakeside, a short trail leads from the parking lot to a gravel beach and picnic area. From there a 2 km trail circles the spring-fed lake. During the winter it tends to freeze over, making it a popular skating site. Trails lead off from the area, but invariably cross into private property.

FISHING: Spectacle Lake is the only place on Vancouver Island where you can fish for eastern brook trout. It's also stocked with cutthroat trout.

ACCESS: Take Whittaker Road northwest from the Island Highway near the Malahat Drive summit just north of the Shawnigan Lake turnoff. There is a left-turn lane for those heading from Victoria.

⑪ Bamberton Provincial Park *(map p. 98)*

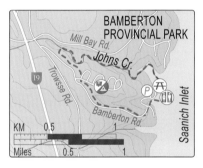

This park near Mill Bay is popular for salmon fishing and its 250 m sandy beach on Saanich Inlet. The shallow water makes it a particularly rich location to see intertidal life in the eelgrass at lower tides. The park is 28 hectares and was created in 1960 as a donation by the Bamberton Cement Works.

PICNIC AREAS AND DAY USE: The waterfront features a parking lot, picnic tables, flush toilets, fresh water and a grassy picnic area. Day parking fees apply. Most areas are wheelchair accessible, though trail portions can be steep.

SHORT WALKS: A 1.5 km trail connects the campsites to the waterfront. Portions are steep.

CAMPING: The park has 50 vehicle-accessible campsites. Reservations are accepted and recommended during peak season.

ACCESS: Turnoff the Island Highway at Mill Bay Road north of the Malahat Drive, then onto Trowsse Road, then Bamberton Road into the park.

⑫ West Shawnigan Lake Provincial Park ● *(map p. 98)*

This small (9-hectare) park features a large grassy clearing in front of a designated swimming area on Shawnigan Lake, a large lake used for fishing, paddling, boating, waterskiing, swimming and cottages. A short trail from the parking lot to the beach runs through some pleasant mature forest. Look for one particularly large dogwood tree in the day-use area.

Across the lake from the provincial park is the municipal Old Mill Park on the site of the Shawnigan Lake Lumber Company, which operated 1881 to 1945. It's now a well-utilized day-use area off Recreation Road.

PICNIC AREAS AND DAY USE: A large grass area adjacent to the lake offers picnic tables, toilets and a change house. Floats indicate the designated swim area.

FISHING: The lake is stocked with rainbow trout.

WATER SPORTS: Windsurfing, paddling, boating and waterskiing are all possible in Shawnigan Lake, though motors are allowed only outside park boundaries. The park doesn't have a boat launch. One can be found at the end of Clearihue Road immediately north of the park off West Shawnigan Lake Road.

ACCESS: From the Island Highway north of the Malahat Drive take Shawnigan Lake Road west, then West Shawnigan Lake Road to the park entrance. This is the quickest route from Victoria. From the Island Highway south of Duncan take Shawnigan–Mill Bay Road, following it west then around the north end of Shawnigan Lake via Shawnigan Lake Road and Renfrew Road to West Shawnigan Lake Road. Follow it south to the park entrance.

⑬ Memory Island Provincial Park *(map p. 98)*

This park is the only island in a freshwater lake protected in the British Columbia park system. It is also one of the smallest parks, at just a hair under 1 hectare. The park provides a day-trip opportunity for boaters on Shawnigan Lake. On it you'll find a trail skirting the island, picnic tables, toilets, a garbage can and a memorial plaque from the family that donated the park for two men killed in the Second World War. Watch for the resident breeding birds, including merganser, belted kingfisher and common snipe. Camping is prohibited. Access, naturally, is by boat only. Note that the other islands in the lake are private and generally developed with cottages.

This is a rough wilderness park split into two segments along the Koksilah River. A number of trails cross it, a major one being a temporary bypass for the Trans Canada Trail around the Kinsol Trestle (see page 100).

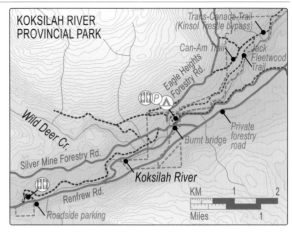

Ⓐ CAMPING: Koksilah River offers front-country camping—that is, designated camping without direct vehicle access near the park entrance. Tent pads are located near a PARKING AREA ● set alongside a partially cleared gravel area slowly recovering from past use. The pads are open year-round, with no fee for winter camping. They appear to be rarely used.

🚶 HIKING: Undeveloped routes lead through the park and the surrounding area. Sections can be muddy and difficult, especially when heavy rain causes flooding.

🚲 CYCLING: The Kinsol Trestle bypass of the Trans Canada Trail leads through Koksilah River park and crosses Burnt bridge. Portions can flood and be muddy, and may be unsuitable for bikes. Improvements are pending. Other trails through the park are popular for mountain biking.

ACCESS: The park is west of Shawnigan Lake. For the south portion, including the walk-in camping, take Shawnigan-Mill Bay Road west to Shawnigan Lake, then pass Shawnigan Lake via Shawnigan Lake Road to Renfrew Road. From Victoria take Shawnigan Lake Road, then West Shawnigan Lake Road and finally Renfrew Road for 7 km to the park. The north portion of Koksilah River Provincial Park can be reached by taking Koksilah Road west from the Island Highway. Immediately west of the single-lane bridge take Riverside Road south.

⑮ Bright Angel Provincial Park ● *(map p. 98)*

This provincial park alongside the Koksilah River is operated by the Cowichan Valley Regional District as a multi-use recreation park. You'll find everything from sports fields to riverside trails. A water swing is a well-used summer feature. A donation by Jack and Mabel Fleetwood in 1958 made the park possible; the name is a nod to Jack's belief in guardian angels.

🏕 PICNIC AREAS AND DAY USE: The park has group barbecue shelters, river swimming, volleyball, baseball and a playground.

🚶 SHORT WALKS: Trails lead through Douglas-fir and western red cedar forests to a suspension bridge over the Koksilah River.

ACCESS: From the Island Highway 3 km north of Cowichan Bay Road take Koksilah Road west, then Tigwell Road north to the park entrance.

⑯ Mount Tzouhalem Ecological Reserve *(map p. 98)*

Detailed map page 102

This reserve was created in 1984 to protect 18 hectares of Mount Tzouhalem's large Garry oak forest and spring wildflower meadows. The reserve's south-facing slopes feature Garry oak groves interspersed with meadows, Douglas-fir and arbutus stands. About 150 plant species have been recorded in the park, plus 30 bird species, including California quail, northern flicker, western bluebird, hermit thrush and warbler. The park is open to low-impact access. Mountain bikers should be aware of the reserve boundary and stay outside. See page 103 for info on mountain biking on Mount Tzouhalem. A residential development hugs the north border of the reserve.

🚶 SHORT WALKS: An easy 10-minute trail leads to the ecological reserve from a parking area.

ACCESS: From the Island Highway in Duncan take Trunk Road–Tzouhalem Road east, then Maple Bay Road northeast to Kingsview Road, then Chippewa road to Kaspa Road.

COWICHAN VALLEY REGION

⑰ Cowichan River Provincial Park

(map p. 98)

Detailed map page 111

Cowichan River is a recreation oasis with a pick of camping, fishing, swimming, paddling, hiking, cycling or simply relaxing in the outdoors. The range is matched by the choice of venues: a half-dozen waterfront access points along the 27 km of protected riverside. In the fall spawning salmon can be viewed at the Skutz Falls and Marie Canyon areas. The park protects 1,414 hectares and was created in 1995.

ECOLOGY: The Garry oak in the park is believed to be the most westerly stand found in Canada. Rare wildflowers found here include the cup-clover near Skutz Falls, blue-eyed-Mary and fawn lily.

PICNIC AREAS AND DAY USE: Day-use areas are located at Skutz Falls, 66 Mile Trestle, Marie Canyon and at SANDY POOL REGIONAL DISTRICT PARK ●. All have picnic areas, parking and toilets. STOLTZ POOL ● is wheelchair accessible. At Stoltz Pool is the Burma Star Memorial Cairn, a half-size replica of the Kohima Monument in Myamar (Burma)—a commemoration of Duncan's Victoria Cross recipient Major Charles Ferguson. Note that some of the north access points, such as Marie Canyon, are isolated from the footpath that runs along the south side of the park and therefore do not connect with other points within the park by trail.

CAMPING: There are three campgrounds in the park. The Stoltz Pool campground has 39 vehicle-accessible sites and 4 walk-in sites. It is open year-round and reservations are accepted with some first-come, first-served sites. The Skutz Falls campground has 33 sites and is closed during the winter; there are no reservations. Group campsites are located at the Stoltz Pool and Horseshoe Bend sites, and can be reserved.

SHORT WALKS: The shortest loop trail is the Stoltz Pool Loop, reached from the Stoltz Pool day-use area. It follows the river, then turns back inland through the forest to return to the campsite. The Skutz/66-Mile Loop Trail is an 8 km outing along both sides of the river using the Skutz Falls forest service bridge and the 66-Mile Trestle to cross the river. Other short loops are possible from the Holt Creek Trailhead. For those considering walking a portion of the Cowichan River Footpath, scenic viewpoints are at the 66-Mile and Holt Creek trestles, while a short trail leads from the Marie Canyon parking lot to the waterfront.

HIKING: The Cowichan River Footpath travels 20 km along the Cowichan River from Skutz Falls to Glenora. BC Parks recommends 6.5 hours to complete the trail. A nearby trail north of the park heads up Mount Prevost.

COWICHAN VALLEY REGION

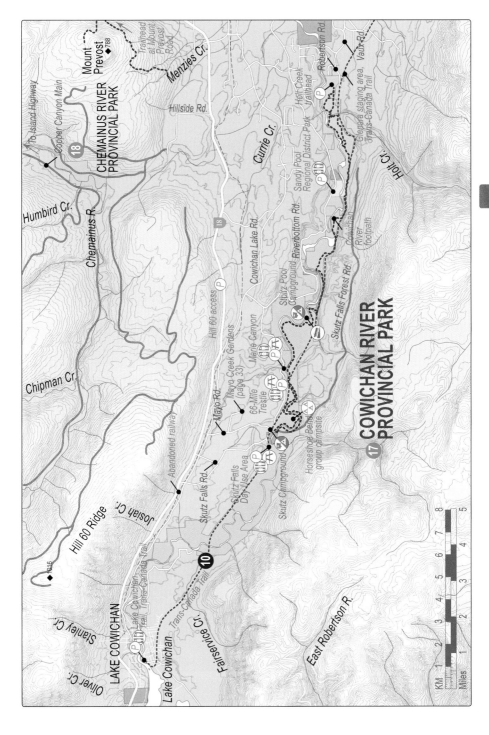

COWICHAN RIVER PROVINCIAL PARK (17)

Mount Prevost ◆ 788

Trailhead at Mount Prevost Road

Menzies Cr.

CHEMAINUS RIVER PROVINCIAL PARK

Copper Canyon Main

To Island Highway

18

Hillside Rd.

Currie Cr.

Robertson Rd.

Vaux Rd.

Holt Creek Trailhead

Glepara staging area, Trans-Canada Trail

Humbird Cr.

Chemainus R.

18

Sandy Pool Regional District Park

Campground Riverbottom Rd.

Skutz Pool Campground

Holt Cr.

Cowichan River footpath

Chipman Cr.

Cowichan Lake Rd.

Hill 60 access

P

Marie Canyon

Mayo Creek Gardens (page 33)

Skutz Falls Forest Rd.

Mayo Rd.

66-Mile Trestle

COWICHAN RIVER PROVINCIAL PARK

17

Abandoned railway

Skutz Falls Rd.

Skutz Falls Day Use Area

Skutz Campground

Horseshoe Bend group campsite

Hill 60 Ridge ◆ 616

Josiah Cr.

10

East Robertson R.

Stanley Cr.

Oliver Cr.

LAKE COWICHAN

Lake Cowichan Trail, Trans-Canada Trail

Fairservice Cr.

Trans-Canada Trail

Lake Cowichan

KM

Miles

COWICHAN VALLEY REGION

Rapids on the Cowichan River.

The trailhead is off Mount Prevost Road. From the Island Highway take Highway 18 west for 1.3 km, then turn north onto Somenos Road. Mount Prevost Road is the first left. Hiking Hill 60, north of Cowichan River Provincial Park, is possible; ongoing logging is always a problem for casual trails here.

CYCLING: The Trans Canada Trail starts in the village of Lake Cowichan at Saywell Park and runs parallel to the Cowichan River, crossing it several times. See page 100 for additional details. Note that it is generally away from the river, runs through immature forest and has few viewpoints, making it far less scenic than foot trails within the park, where bikes are prohibited.

PADDLING: Canoeing and kayaking the Cowichan River are both popular, with whitewater rapids between Skutz Falls and Marie Canyon. A river pullout is located at the Skutz Falls day-use area and a boat launch for non-motorized vehicle launches at the Stoltz Pool day-use area. A more benign option, particularly for casual recreational tubers, is to begin at Marie Canyon and pull out at Sandy Pool. It's about an hour down-river, with some strong currents, particularly at the Marie Canyon put-in.

FISHING: Cowichan River is known for its coho, chinook and chum salmon, as well as for rainbow, brown and cutthroat trout; it's one of just two Vancouver Island rivers with brown trout. Fishing is closed October to mid-December, with other possible fishing restrictions posted at the park.

ACCESS: The park has entry points to the north and east sides.

- SKUTZ FALLS: From Highway 18, take the Highway 18 Connector south to Riverbottom Road; the turn is well-marked from the highway. This is the entry for the Skutz Falls campground and day-use area, the Horseshoe Bend group campsite and the Marie Canyon day-use area. Or take Cowichan Lake Road, then Riverbottom Road for Sandy Pool Regional District Park and the Stoltz Pool Campground.

- GLENORA TRAILHEAD: From south Duncan take Miller Road west to Glenora Road, to Vaux Road, then onto Robertson Road.

⑱ Chemainus River Provincial Park *(map p. 98)*

This small (103-hectare) park protects part of the Chemainus River and a few key recreational spots popular for swimming, fishing and viewing the summer steelhead and coho runs. Steelhead are found in the deep pools above Copper Canyon. Historically, Roosevelt elk used the area; it's hoped they may return to the riverfront as the forest matures. Casual trails follow the river but can peter out quickly, while old access roads provide level walking. Dirt bike trails criss-cross the area.

COWICHAN VALLEY REGION

🅿️ PICNIC AREAS AND DAY USE: The park is undeveloped, but the riverbanks and calm swimming holes make the river a popular summer destination. While there is no designated camping, clear areas near the river are established camping spots. Note the park gate is closed at night.

🎣 FISHING: Spring and summer steelhead runs attract anglers. Other freshwater species also live in the river.

ACCESS: From the Island Highway, take Highway 4 west toward Lake Cowichan but turn north onto Hillside Road. The gravel road is quite rough in portions. This provides access to the SOUTH SIDE ● of the park. Only a small portion of the park is north of the river, but it is an extremely pleasant beach location. You can reach it by fording the river or taking Chemainus River Road, a private industrial logging road with gated access, from just north of the main Chemainus turnoff from the Island Highway. Casual trails from the roadside lead to the river.

⑲ Eves Provincial Park *(map p. 98)*

This small (47-hectare) park was created in 1962 and has been set aside by the North Cowichan Regional District as an ecological reserve to protect its environmental values. Although it's a provincial park the regional district runs it, providing an onsite caretaker. An information kiosk at the parking lot offers a map of the park's features. An odd attraction is the small mining exploratory tunnel, called a "cave," at the roadside marker. Watch for it off the park access road near the rock bluff.

🅿️ PICNIC AREAS AND DAY USE: A large picnic area with a shelter and nature centre is located down a short trail from the main parking lot.

🚶 SHORT WALKS: Trails criss-cross the area; they include strolls over rocky bluffs (with limited viewpoints), through an arbutus grove, to a pond, along a stream, along an old Mount Sicker Railway roadbed and through an old-growth forest.

ACCESS: Eves park is a well-kept secret. Don't expect much in the way of signs. From the Island Highway south of Chemainus take Mount Sicker Road east. At Westholme Road turn south. Follow it 0.7 km. Just past Bonsall Creek you'll see a dirt road intersection for Nimmo and Little Mountain roads. Take Little Mountain Road to the park ENTRANCE ●.

Cowichan Lake region

Cowichan Lake extends 31 km from tip to tip, with numerous arms and island clusters. Roads skirt both the north and south sides of the lake, making its beaches easily accessible for camping or day use. Some particularly good locations are available as formal recreation sites. Gordon Bay, the sole provincial park on

The Cowichan Lake waterfront from Pine Point.

the lake, has a popular beach area. This is emerging cottage country, with many new developments along its length, particularly at Youbou. A scenic highlight is Bald Mountain, a dramatically bluffy peninsula that divides the two arms at the east end of the lake. A trail along the peninsula's summit is a great area to explore. Trout fishing is a large draw in Cowichan Lake; expect rainbow, cutthroat and Dolly Varden.

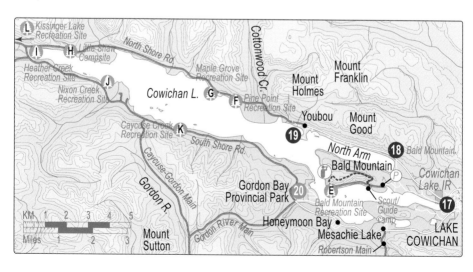

TimberWest, the largest landholder in the area, seems intent on channeling recreation traffic to the lakeshore only. Expect most other spurs extending from North and South Shore roads to have No-trespassing signs on them. This applies to the access roads for both Heather Mountain and Lomas Lake, two established recreation areas, the latter being the traditional base for trips to El Capitan and neighbouring peaks. As these were seemingly arbitrary restrictions introduced in 2007 it's hoped that they are only temporary.

TRAVEL NOTES: Visitors should expect rolling hills with large clear-cut patches from heavy logging to form the scenic backdrop along much of the lake's length. Beaches and recreation sites tend to be busy during the summer, and powerboats and waterskiers are major users of the lake, so don't expect a quiet outing here on key summer weekends. Those seeking a true wilderness getaway can head west to Nitinat Lake.

MAJOR PARKS

20 Gordon Bay Provincial Park ●
(map p. 115)

This is an ideal family getaway location, featuring camping plus a wonderful day-use swimming and beach area. A launch ramp makes it a key access point for boating activities in Cowichan Lake, from fishing to windsurfing. Parking fees apply. The park is 49 hectares and was created in 1969. Immediately adjacent to the park is 7.5-hectare Honeymoon Bay Ecological Reserve, created in 1984 to protect an unusually high number of pink fawn lilies. The pink fawn lily is rare in British Columbia, though commonly found on western Vancouver Island. The park is important for preservation of the fawn lily as it takes four to six years to mature to a blooming state. The plants are vulnerable, as the corms will die if the leaves are picked. The reserve is open for low-impact visits.

CAMPING: Gordon Bay offers a large vehicle-accessible campground with 126 sites and a group camping area. Reservations are accepted. Facilities include showers and flush toilets.

PICNIC AREAS AND DAY USE: The large day-use area has a beach, picnic tables, parking, a playground, an amphitheatre and wheelchair-accessible toilets. It is a popular swimming spot in the summer, with a log boom dividing swimmers from the lake's motorized boat traffic.

ACCESS: The park is off South Shore Road. Turnoff South Shore Road at Honeymoon Bay, just past the March Meadows Golf Course, onto Walton Road; follow Walton to the park entrance at the road's end.

Gordon Bay looking toward Bald Mountain.

FOREST RECREATION SITES
See the map on page 115 to locate these recreation sites.

The vast majority of land in the Cowichan Lake area is privately owned and camping options are limited to designated areas, with a number of campgrounds offered and managed by TimberWest (Caycuse, Heather, Kissinger and Little Shaw). The hosted sites tend to be family oriented and monitored for noise. Take your chances elsewhere. Hosted sites have picnic tables, firepits and outhouses. Fees apply. Because they are in a prime recreation area close to major centres, expect them to be busy during the summer.

(E) Bald Mountain •

This tiny recreation site is part of the larger Bald Mountain hiking area. It's located on a good beach on the southeast end of the Bald Mountain peninsula. There are clear areas behind the beach suitable for camping (potentially about four sites), a picnic table and an outhouse, as well as the west trailhead to the Bald Mountain summit (page 120). Access is walk-in or boat-in only.

(F) Pine Point •

This is a popular family-oriented campground just west of Youbou on the north end of Cowichan Lake. Small beach areas and a boat launch make it an ideal gateway for activities on the lake, from swimming to boating. Thirty-five campsites are spread across the recreation site, with the most popular spots facing the lake. It's supervised by a park host and fees apply May to October. The site is off North Shore Road about 3.5 km west of Youbou.

⑥ Maple Grove ●

Similar to Pine Point, facilities here include a boat launch, tables and toilets. It has 40 sites; those nearest North Shore Road are prone to dust from the traffic. Fees are charged May to October, with a park host in place. Access is off North Shore Road about 2 km west of Pine Point Recreation Site.

⑪ Little Shaw ●

This is a rough, unregulated site just off North Shore Road near the northwest end of Cowichan Lake. There is no formal parking lot, just roadside access. Tent-only camping spots are scattered throughout the area adjacent to the lake. The beach is a popular day-use area, and is potentially rowdy for camping.

⑫ Heather Creek ●

This is a large TimberWest campsite located on the west end of Cowichan Lake just south of the junction of North Shore Road and the Nitinat Main. It's a family-oriented site that is hosted during the summer, with campsites scattered along the loop access road. The most popular sites are alongside the lake, with a number best suited for walk-in tent camping. The boat launch is south of the campground entrance. An extensive beach makes this an ideal lakefront getaway. Nearby, to the north, is Heather Mountain (1,338 m). This is an occasional hiking destination, but TimberWest has closed the access road (Branch R) to the public.

⑬ Nixon Creek ●

This is a pretty, hosted recreation site with an extensive sand and gravel beach. It's located on the south side of Cowichan Lake off South Shore Road west of the McClure Main junction. An unusual feature is a plastic-wrapped building for use as an emergency shelter.

⑭ Caycuse Creek ●

This is another pretty site, hosted during the summer, with a smaller selection of campsites scattered through a forested area with some prime lakefront sites. The main attraction is the inviting sand and gravel beach, making this a good family-oriented destination. It's set well off South Shore Road and accessible by a narrow road about 10 km west of the Gordon River Main junction.

⑮ Kissinger Lake ●

This hosted site is located just over a kilometre west of the junction of North and South Shore roads on the west end of Cowichan Lake. It features several dozen campsites, a boat launch and swimming area. The lake is noted for its warm water.

Cowichan Lake from Caycuse Creek.

POINTS OF INTEREST

17 **Lake Cowichan** (map p. 115)

This pretty lakefront community of about 3,000 is at the eastern limit of Cowichan Lake (note the reversed word order helps to distinguish the community from the lake). Though most services are available, the commercial sector is minimal; look to Duncan for full service. Lake Cowichan is a growing cottage destination, with March Meadows Golf Club in Honeymoon Bay a popular draw. Saywell Park, located in downtown Lake Cowichan along the lakefront just south of Cowichan River, is the north staging ground for the Cowichan Trail (page 100). You'll find parking, washrooms and picnic facilities. Adjacent to the park is the visitor information centre and the Kaatza Station Museum. Housed in an old 1912 railway station, the museum features displays of the area's logging, forestry, mining and railroading past. In it you'll find recreations of a pioneer home, a mining tunnel and a general store.

 www.cowichanlake.ca/index.php?page=museum.htm.

Bald Mountain occupies the large peninsula extending well into the east side of Cowichan Lake, its prominent rocky south-facing bluffs the visual backdrop for the beach at Gordon Bay Provincial Park and the community of Mesachie Bay. The peninsula is partially private property and there has been extensive logging in recent years, with the prospect of high-density development in the near future (an application was in process as of 2008). The lower portions of the mountain have been bulldozed extensively, providing rough roads through the area. Fortunately the summit trail, a beautiful walk through the forest and along the upper bluffs of Bald Mountain, remains intact. This is probably the best hiking in the Cowichan Lake region, crossing the ridge to the peak at 650 m. (This is particularly appealing now that both Heather Mountain and Lomas Lake have been named off-limits.) About a half-kilometre from the access road along the Marble Bay waterfront is a Scout/Guide camp with a dock and numerous associated buildings. Camping is by permission only. Camping on the outer peninsula is possible at the Bald Mountain Recreation Site (page 117).

- SUMMIT TRAIL: This trail follows the spine of Bald Mountain, with access on the west side at the recreation site and on the east via logging roads. A good way to approach is to follow the main bulldozed road along the south shore to the recreation site, then follow the trail up to the summit and loop back. A few portions along steep rock bluffs are not for the faint of heart. An old logging cable has been thoughtfully anchored for a handhold along the steepest section. The trail then continues along the ridge before ending at a logging road. The route back is not intuitive, as logging roads tend to peter out. Take the road that skirts the north edge of the ridge, not the road along the ridge top (which dead-ends). Signs and markers tend to be poor. Finding the EAST TRAILHEAD ● from the gate without prior knowledge of its location will be almost impossible; use the GPS waypoints.

  Or try this route: from the gate past the Scout/Guide camp follow the main logging road to the FIRST JUNCTION ●, an open area with numerous roads. Take the right (north) option as it makes an S-turn up and around the first ridge. Follow this by staying just north of some false summits until the road starts to head downward from the side of the main summit. At the highest point look for a short portion of road that heads uphill and south to the spine. This will be the farthest you can go by logging road up the spine toward the summit. The east trailhead is off this spur.

HIKING: A circuit of the Bald Mountain peninsula is a good half-day to full-day hike. The lakefront location of the recreation site makes a visit here possible by paddle. By launching at a location such as Gordon Bay you could paddle in and hike to the summit—a rare and worthwhile opportunity for a multi-discipline trip 👍.

ACCESS: From North Shore Road past Lake Cowichan, turn left at Meade Creek Road, then right onto Marble Bay Road. At the end are locked gates; a small PARKING AREA ● is located outside the gates.

⑲ Youbou *(map p. 115)*

Youbou (pronounced yew-bough) is a former mill town; a downturn in the economy resulted in the mill's closure in the mid 1990s. It has rebounded as a cottage community, with numerous new developments springing up along the shoreline, thanks in large part to TimberWest selling 250 hectares adjacent to the town for development. It has minimal services, the main one being a large new pub near the town's west end.

SHORT WALKS: Youbou has a half-dozen small lakefront parks that offer good options for a stroll. Price Park, a series of short trails through a mature maple forest crossing Swordfern Creek, has several gravel pocket beaches along the lakefront. A few picnic tables are located near the lakeshore in the forest. Access is off Highway 4 at either Swordfern Way or the end of Miracle Way, where you'll find a good parking lot. This makes a good lunch stop on a drive to Carmanah.

Carmanah-Walbran

Two major valleys are protected in this region—at least in part. The Carmanah Valley and lower Walbran Valley together form one of the most significant provincial parks in North America, protecting examples of some of the largest trees found in the world. Outside of the park, however, there is significant logging, particularly in the upper Walbran Valley. Extensive logging, few navigable logging roads through the region and a dense under-forest limit hiking to just a few trails through the region. This is unfortunate, as it is an exceptional area to visit—if one accepts the harsh weather to be expected of a coastal rainforest.

CARMANAH-WALBRAN

POINTS OF INTEREST

⑳ **West Walbran Trail** *(map p. 123)*

Though it is part of Carmanah Walbran Provincial Park, the West Walbran Trail is not a recognized park route. Built by the Carmanah Forestry Society, the trail has some excellent boardwalk sections through a magical old-growth forest between two logging road accesses. An adjunct leads through central Walbran to Botley and Auger lakes. It makes a good day hike—either a long one or short one depending on the trail condition. The demise of the Bridge Over Troubled Walbran means a short ford, after which the trail continues north. Volunteers do occasionally hack down the encroaching scrub, but some areas can be overgrown, and blowdown will create delays. Expect a full day of hiking to complete the trail end to end one-way, a distance of about 7 km. Here are some key features of the trail.

Ⓐ CAMPING: While designated camping exists on some maps, the best established campsite is at the south entrance. Beyond that look for open, level spots near old-growth trees in the forest or gravel bars along the West Walbran creekside. Note the availability of the latter depends on water levels. Beware of using a gravel bed during periods of rain, when the creek level can rise.

❶ HADIKIN LAKE: This lake is reached by a short side road from near the end of Haddon Main. There you'll find a clear area suitable for camping, a small dock and a trail leading around the lake and the adjacent old-growth forest. It's historically used as a fishing camp.

❷ NORTH ACCESS: The north entrance to the West Walbran Trail is near the end of the Haddon Main. At the HADDON-WALBRAN JUNCTION ● stay on the Haddon Main heading south, and follow it about 6 km south until you get to the junction with an OLD OVERGROWN SPUR ● leading into a young alder forest. Note it is the second spur to the right—the

The incredible enchanted forest of the West Walbran Trail.

CARMANAH-WALBRAN

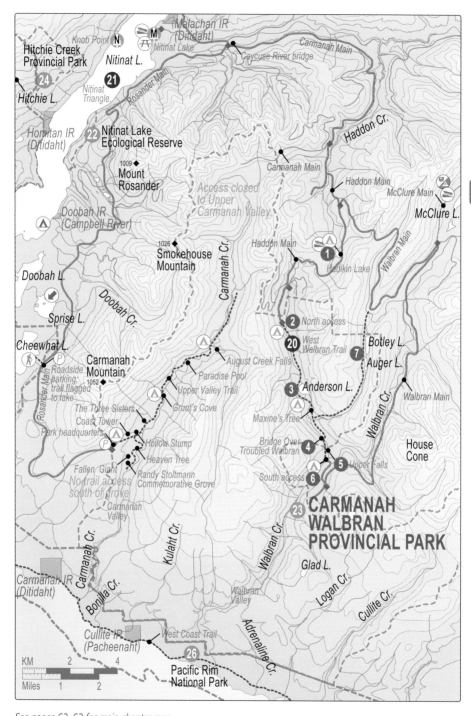

Hitchie Creek
Provincial Park
㉔

Hitchie L.

Knob Point Ⓝ
Ⓜ
Ⓐ Nitinat Lake

Nitinat L.

Malachan IR
(Ditidaht)

Carmanah Main

Caycuse River bridge

㉑

Nitinat
Triangle

Rosander Main

Hornitan IR
(Ditidaht) ㉒

Nitinat Lake
Ecological Reserve

Haddon Cr.

Carmanah Main

Haddon Main

1009 ◆
Mount
Rosander

McClure Main Ⓩ

Access closed
to Upper
Carmanah Valley

McClure L.

Doobah IR
(Campbell River) Ⓐ

1026 ◆
Smokehouse
Mountain

Carmanah Cr.

Haddon Main

Ⓐ ❶
Hadikin Lake

Walbran Main

CARMANAH-WALBRAN

Doobah L.

Doobah Cr.

Sprise L.

Cheewhat L.
Ⓟ
Ⓐ
Roadside
parking;
trail flagged
to lake

Carmanah
Mountain
1052 ◆

Rosander Main

The Three Sisters
Coast Tower
Park headquarters
Ⓟ
Ⓟ

August Creek Falls

Ⓐ
❷ North access
㉔ West
Walbran Trail

Botley L.
❼
Auger L.

Paradise Pool
Upper Valley Trail
Ⓐ
Grunt's Cove

❸ Anderson L.
Ⓐ
Maxine's Tree

Walbran Cr.

Walbran Main

Hollow Stump
Heaven Tree

Fallen Giant
No trail access
south of grove

Randy Stoltmann
Commemorative Grove

Bridge Over
Troubled Walbran ❹
Ⓐ ❺ Upper Falls
South access ❻

House
Cone

Carmanah
Valley

㉓ CARMANAH
WALBRAN
PROVINCIAL PARK

Carmanah Cr.

Kulaht Cr.

Walbran Cr.

Glad L.

Carmanah IR
(Ditidaht)

Bonilla Cr.

Walbran
Valley

Logan Cr.

Cullite Cr.

Cullite IR
(Pacheenaht)

West Coast Trail

Adrenaline Cr.

KM   2   4
Miles 1   2

㉖ Pacific Rim
National Park

See pages 62–63 for main chapter map.

first, about 300 m earlier, is nearly overgrown with scrub. You can park at the entrance of the correct spur or drive the 1.5 km to the trailhead, a route passable by two-wheel drive, which ends with a small spot suitable for parking a vehicle or two. The TRAILHEAD ● begins where the young alder forest ends and is replaced by beautiful old-growth forest. The first major feature is Haddon's Corner, a group of incredibly large spruces, about a half-kilometre into the trail.

❸ ANDERSON LAKE: The mid-point of the trail features good camping opportunities and several unusual features, including an intriguing old burled cedar. To the south is Maxine's Tree, the largest spruce in British Columbia and the second largest in Canada at 80.8 m in height and a circumference of 12.65 m. Note that fishing on Anderson Lake is restricted to protect its rare kokanee trout. No bait or artificial flies are allowed; single barbs only can be used and trout, char and kokanee are catch-and-release only.

❹ BRIDGE OVER TROUBLED WALBRAN ●: Once crossed by a cable car, the route over this arm of the Walbran Creek was replaced by a log bridge, which in turn lies partially submerged along the river's edge. Fortunately, the creek here is quite shallow and placid, making for an easy fording in all but the worst flood conditions.

❺ UPPER FALLS: A scenic highlight, this arm of Walbran Creek cascades down several tiers over bedrock suitable for a scramble to various viewpoints. It is possible but difficult to scale down the bank from the trail to the edge of the waterfall. Note the rock can be slippery. Watch for salamanders sunning themselves on the rock or in small pools.

❻ SOUTH ACCESS: The SOUTH TRAILHEAD ● is just west of the only logging road bridge that crosses Walbran Creek. A trail leads from the end of the bridge north along the creek to the main camping area. You'll find several good campsites scattered along the river's edge plus the trailhead. To get here, follow the Walbran Main for about 14 km past the Haddon Main junction—almost as far as the Walbran Main goes but not quite. Take the LAST RIGHT TURN ● off the main down a deactivated logging road that descends to the old bridge across the Walbran. Both the spur and the bridge are in good shape.

The Upper Falls on the West Walbran Trail.

7 BOTLEY AND AUGER LAKES ROUTE: An arm of the trail extending into what is called the central Walbran Valley gives access to these two lakes. It may be possible, though unlikely, to continue north from Botley and Auger lakes to the Walbran Main.

21 Nitinat Triangle *(map p. 123)*

See also the maps on page 131 (west portion) and page 136 (east portion)

This potential circuit ranks among the most challenging paddles on Vancouver Island, with lengthy and difficult portages across snags and bogs. The generally accepted route is from Nitinat Lake to Hobiton Lake, bypassing Hobiton River, which is closed due to its role as a spawning river. This means a troublesome overland portage without a formal trail.

From Hobiton Lake, there's a 1.6 km portage involving a bog to reach Tsusiat Lake. Another portage is needed to Tsusiat Falls. You then have an option of paddling potentially dangerous open ocean water or portaging to Nitinat Narrows, a treacherous tidal passage with a history of fatalities. An alternative, of course, is simply to paddle Nitinat Lake, which has a variety of camping options generally at the mouths of creeks.

ACCESS: The Knob Point Recreation Site on the northwest side of the lake is no longer vehicle-accessible. Launching is possible from the Nitinat Lake Recreation

Nitinat Lake.

Site or from Nitinat (Malachan 1R), the Ditidaht First Nation reserve at the head of the lake. A park use permit is necessary for the triangle; they can be purchased at the Pachena Bay or Port Renfrew information centre. Call 250-726-7721.

MAJOR PARKS

21 Nitinat River Provincial Park *(map p. 62)*

This small (160-hectare) undeveloped park is set along the scenic Nitinat River in a portion of old-growth forest. The park is split into two portions: Nitinat River Falls and the Nitinat River bridge pool. There are a number of falls and deep pools in the river, which are used by steelhead and salmon. There are no developed campsites within the park, but wilderness camping is allowed.

FISHING: The deep pools in the river canyon are closed to angling, but fishing is possible near the Nitinat River bridge pool.

ACCESS: From Cowichan Lake follow the Nitinat Main west. Nitinat River Falls is located 8 km southwest of Cowichan Lake, while the Nitinat River bridge pool is located 15 km southwest. Local trails lead from the roadside into the park, or you can take an old logging road into the park immediately north of the CARMANAH-NITINAT JUNCTION ● off the Carmanah Main. There are also some good access points to the river outside the park. This is a scenic drive through some beautiful mature forest 👍.

22 Nitinat Lake Ecological Reserve *(map p. 123)*

Another small (79-hectare) reserve, the Nitinat Lake Ecological Reserve was created in 1974 to protect the westernmost Douglas-fir trees found on southern Vancouver Island. The reserve occupies 2.5 km of lakefront and extends about 300 m into largely inaccessible rocky bluffs, where Douglas-firs are dotted along the steep slopes among the Sitka spruce—a rare pairing. While access is allowed, the remote location and steep lakefront make it generally inaccessible.

23 Carmanah Walbran Provincial Park *(map p. 123)*

This provincial park functions more as an ecological reserve than provincial park, as most of the Walbran Valley and much of the Carmanah Valley are essentially inaccessible. The sprawling wilderness area is home to two percent of British Columbia's remaining old-growth forest and to some of the world's largest spruce and cedar trees, some estimated to be over 1,000 years old. This makes the region one of the best examples of the ancient coastal Sitka spruce rainforest ecosystem. Maxine's Tree, on West Walbran Creek, is the largest overall Sitka spruce in British Columbia (in wood volume) and second largest in Canada. The Carmanah Giant on Carmanah Creek's east bank is a Sitka spruce with the distinction of being the tallest known spruce in Canada. Unfortunately, access to this tree and many of the other portions of the park have been blocked by BC Parks due to potentially unsafe conditions.

Though it's not one of the larger trees in Walbran Valley, it is still about the height of a 20-storey building.

The trail at Carmanah Walbran Provincial Park.

The park was created in 1990; additions in 1995 completely protected the Carmanah Creek watershed and added the southern portion of the Walbran Creek watershed.

ECOLOGY: The spruce groves in the park are about twice as dense in biomass—that is, plant weight—as a tropical forest. The old-growth trees support a vibrant ecosystem of about 36 bird species, most notably marbled murrelet, northern goshawk and pygmy owl. The Carmanah Valley was the first place researchers managed to record marbled murrelet nests. Thousands of invertebrates live in the forest canopy, while the forest itself is home to grey wolves, black bears and cougars. Anderson Lake is unique for a fish population that includes kokanee trout. The park is also home to a lichen found only in west coast old-growth forests.

🛆 CAMPING: Several designated wilderness camping areas are located along the Upper Valley Trail. Walk-in camping is possible at the Carmanah Valley trailhead near the park entrance. There are tent pads, picnic tables and fire rings; campfires are allowed at this site only during designated times of the day. Firewood can be purchased. During summer camping is possible on Carmanah

Creek's gravel bars. Short-term vehicle camping is allowed in the parking lot. Backcountry camping fees apply for all locations.

🏕 **PICNIC AREAS AND DAY USE**: Picnic tables are located at the campsite near the parking lot. Cold water taps are located by the park warden's station and at the trailhead; boiling is recommended.

🚶 **SHORT WALKS**: The closest landmark to the parking lot is Coast Tower, 1.2 km from the trailhead. The tower is a Sitka spruce that was 92 m tall until 30 metres fell off during a winter storm in 1997. A viewing platform is located here. A junction 1.3 km from the trailhead allows a choice of two routes; the route south is considerably shorter yet still takes in many of the key features in the park. One of those is Heaven Tree, a Sitka spruce 2 km along the trail that is 77 m tall and has a diameter of 3.5 m, making it one of the broadest spruce trees in the valley. The Randy Stoltmann Commemorative Grove, a stand of Sitka spruce with heights of up to 89 m, is at 2.6 km. Note that the grove is the end of the downstream trail. A continuation to Carmanah Point has been closed.

🏃 **HIKING**: From the junction the Upper Valley Trail continues 7.5 km northward along Carmanah Creek. Here are some things to see along the way.

- 2.5 KM: THREE SISTERS. These three trees are growing from the same spot, and reach a height of 79 m. A viewing platform allows views of the trees. This is also a potential campsite, at the sandbar next to the creek. Pit toilets are located here. Beyond Three Sisters the boardwalks end and the trail becomes rougher.

- 4 KM: GRUNT'S COVE: This is another potential campsite, on the gravel bar next to a stand of old-growth Sitka spruce.

- 5.5 KM: PARADISE POOL. Here a crystal-clear pool is home to cutthroat trout; it is a potential swimming hole, though the water is frigid.

- 7.5 KM: AUGUST CREEK. This creek is the largest that flows into the Carmanah. Camping is possible on the nearby sandbar downstream from the junction. This is also the end of the trail; a former extension to the Carmanah Main is now blocked.

ACCESS: The MAIN PARK ENTRANCE ● is reached via Rosander Main off the Carmanah Main. The Rosander Main meanders 29 km along the slopes adjacent to Nitinat Lake, providing a good VIEWPOINT ● from the roadside near Mount Rosander. A problem in reaching this area is that the Rosander Main deteriorates substantially over the course of the 29 km, becoming increasingly potholed and rocky, requiring a slow and cautious drive.

TRAVEL NOTES: The Wilderness Committee (formerly Western Canada Wilderness Committee) uncovered a few trees destined to be among Canada's largest in an area of the upper Walbran Valley slated to be logged. While Carmanah Walbran Provincial Park is large, it is only a fraction of the size of the area open to logging. It's plain that public policy for this area favours logging over recreational use; indeed, given the poor road conditions to the park, the reduction in the extent of official hiking trails and the request by BC Parks to stay out of Walbran Valley, public access is actively discouraged. This is clearly to the advantage of logging companies, which will have minimal public exposure as the last of the unprotected old-growth forest in the area is liquidated.

㉔ Hitchie Creek Provincial Park *(map p. 123)*

Hitchie Creek on the northwest side of Nitinat Lake is part of a key wildlife corridor used by Roosevelt elk, black bears, cougars and wolves. The old-growth lowland rainforest provides habitat for the endangered marbled murrelet and species such as Keen's long-eared myotis. The park is 226 hectares and was created in 1995.

FISHING: Hitchie Creek is a salmon-bearing stream and also home to anadromous cutthroat trout.

CAMPING: Wilderness camping is possible within the park. There is no fee.

ACCESS: The park has no road access. The BC Parks website suggests hiking in the 1 km along an undeveloped route from Hitchie Lake, from within Pacific Rim National Park; this must be a bit facetious, as Hitchie Lake is not particularly accessible either. This is a trip for experienced backcountry hikers only.

CARMANAH-WALBRAN

FOREST RECREATION SITES

See the map on page 123 to locate these recreation sites.

Nitinat Lake Recreation Site ●

This managed site is a staging ground for boating, canoeing and fishing on Nitinat Lake, though it's used primarily as a base for windsurfing. Amenities are a boat launch, picnic tables and toilets. Fees are charged May to October for the 25 campsites. The winter 2006 windstorms were particularly severe here, turning the heavily forested site into something more resembling a battered clear-cut. If you visit, bring a mountain bike. Trails lead through the nearby area. A map of the trails is on the recreation site kiosk.

Nitinat Lake from the recreation site's beach.

ACCESS: Access is off the Carmanah Main, just south of Nitinat. The main turnoff into Nitinat first passes the boat launch, then enters the community. Continue through the community to reach the recreation site. A south entrance off the Carmanah Main closer to the recreation site passes through an unfortunate roadside dump.

Knob Point Recreation Site

This is primarily a boat camping location with picnic tables and pit toilets. It is well documented as a possible launch site into Nitinat Lake; deterioration of the access road means those days are now over. It is a boat-in site only. There are four campsites and no fees.

TRAVEL NOTES: Most lakes in the area have some form of access, though those near Nitinat Lake have dubious access roads. One well-flagged trail leads from the Rossander Main to Cheewhat Lake; parking is roadside only. A good lakeside campsite is at MCCLURE LAKE ● just north of the junction of Walbran and McClure mains.

The West Coast Trail

The West Coast Trail has established itself as one of the world's premier hiking destinations. It is a 78 km wilderness corridor along an exposed stretch of coast known for its rugged inaccessibility, its storms and its wild rainforests. Improvements to the trail over the years by Parks Canada, such as ladders and boardwalks, have tamed it somewhat, but it continues to be one of the more difficult and challenging routes along the Pacific coast. With limited road access through this region it remains largely a wilderness area, with just Bamfield, Nitinat (above) and Port Renfrew (page 95) providing access points.

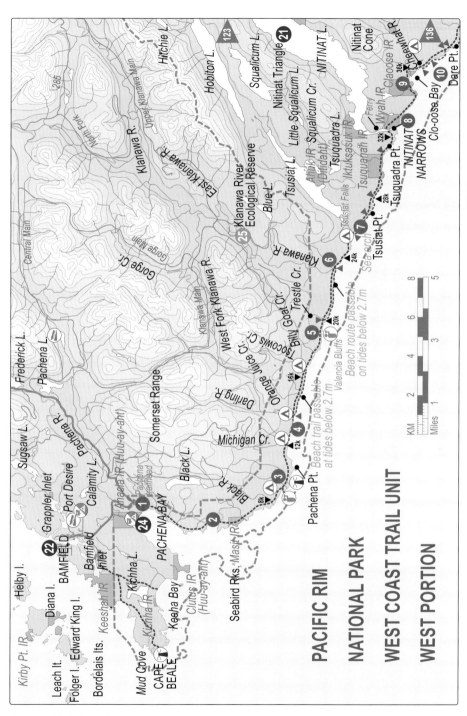

See pages 62–63 for main chapter map.

POINTS OF INTEREST

22 Bamfield (map p. 131)

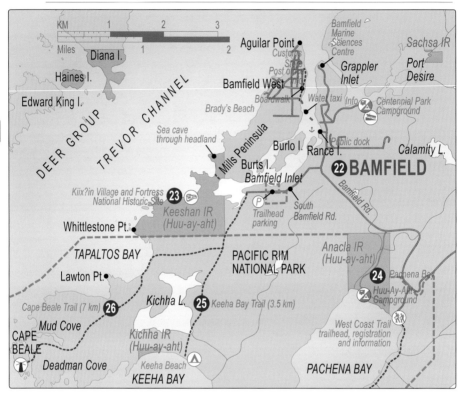

Bamfield Inlet off the south entrance of Barkley Sound divides this quiet fishing and tourism community into two separate areas. Much of the recreational marine traffic bound for Barkley Sound and the Deer Group islands departs from here, as do hikers on their way to the northern trailhead of the West Coast Trail. Expect full services, including bed and breakfasts, cottages, resorts, motels, private and municipal campgrounds, stores, galleries, marinas, water taxis and tour operators. No roads connect Bamfield West to Bamfield, so water taxi is a key form of transportation. Most commercial attractions within Bamfield West are along a wooden boardwalk that runs from the Fisheries dock to the government dock.

- SPECIAL ATTRACTIONS: Bamfield Marine Sciences Centre is located on the northern end of Bamfield at the tip of the peninsula between Bamfield and Grappler inlets. It's housed in what was the Pacific Cable Board cable station, the eastern end of the trans-Pacific telegraph cable that ran the 5,692 km between Bamfield and Fanning Island from 1901 to 1959 (when it became obsolete). Since 1972 the Western Canadian Universities Marine Sciences

Society has operated a marine sciences centre used as a research base by biologists, ecologists and oceanographers. A public education program offers outings for schools, colleges and adults with a focus on marine sciences. For additional information see **www.bms.bc.ca**.

Winter blow-down exposes a large root structure on the way to Pachena Point.

🔺 CAMPING: Centennial Park Campground is a locally run campground located along Grappler Road near Port Desire and the public boat launch. While convenient, it doesn't have the beach presence of the Huu-Ay-Aht Campground at Pachena Bay (see below).

🪑 PICNIC AREAS AND DAY USE: A good place to spend a day is at Brady's Beach on the far end of Bamfield West. It's a highly scenic area, famous for sunsets that often grace calendars and paintings. For Bamfield East, a picnic area is located at Centennial Park.

A gorge at Tsocowis Creek.

ACCESS: Bamfield is at the end of Bamfield Road, about 85 km from Port Alberni. West Bamfield requires crossing Bamfield Inlet by water taxi. An option is walking around Bamfield Inlet. This is possible by leaving the Keeha Bay Trail at a creek bridge on the west end of Bamfield Inlet, then following the shoreline to the village. There is no real trail, however, and as it is mucky it is not recommended.

Boardwalk trail near Nitinat Narrows.

23 Kiix?in Village and Fortress National Historic Site
(map p. 132)

At this site of a former Huu-ay-aht village and fortress some architectural remains are visible, including crumbling longhouses. It was named a National Historic Site in 2002. A notable feature here is the 35 m rock pillar known as Execution Rock, once used as a defensive fortress and lookout. The village was abandoned in the late 1800s in favour of Dodger Cove on nearby Haines Island.

ACCESS: The historic site is on a Huu-ay-aht reserve. While initial plans were to make the site accessible, no current policy is in place; visit **huuayaht.org** for information on guided tours, should they become available. In the meantime the village is hidden within the reserve, and visits to it should not be undertaken without permission from the band.

24 Pachena Bay *(maps pp. 131 and 132)*

This sweeping sand beach is known for its child-friendly surf, making it a good family beach and fun for those lightheartedly playing on surfboards or in kayaks. The beach is divided between Huu-ay-aht First Nations land to the north and the Pacific Rim National Park, where the West Coast Trail's north trailhead office and registration centre is located.

△ CAMPING: The Huu-ay-aht run a large campground adjacent to the bay with some pretty oceanfront sites strung throughout the forested area. Amenities include washrooms, showers, water and some sites with electricity. It makes a good staging ground for West Coast Trail ventures and is a good family destination on its own.

25 Keeha Bay Trail *(map p. 132)*

Keeha Bay is a sweeping arc of beautiful beach located on the northwest corner of Pacific Rim National Park's West Coast Trail Unit, quite separate from the nearby West Coast Trail. The 3.5 km trail leads from the end of South Bamfield Road across generally flat terrain made more difficult by frequent muddy areas. Mud, minimal maintenance and frequent deadfall make this a much more challenging trek than the distance would indicate. The final leg runs along the south end of Kichha Lake and across an unusual floating boardwalk. It then rises to the top of a short ridge and drops toward the bay. There you'll find a bear cache but no outhouse. Camping is popular on the beach, and there are numerous possibilities to help keep multiple groups fairly private. A creek is located on the east end. Near the trailhead is a turnoff for Bamfield West (not recommended due to the muck).

26 Cape Beale Trail
(map p. 132)

A remnant of the old telegraph line.

This trail departs from the Keeha Bay Trail at about 1.7 km and continues 7 km to the Cape Beale lighthouse, a place reached only at tides 1.8 m or lower. It is a potentially muddy and difficult route that can be broken by staying at Tapaltos Bay, 2 km beyond the start of the trail. Because of the difficult nature of the trail, it makes an unlikely day trip; Tapaltos Bay, on the other hand, makes a decent short outing.

MAJOR PARKS

25 Klanawa River Ecological Reserve *(map p. 131)*

Most of the stands of western hemlock, western red cedar and Sitka spruce on Vancouver Island's west coast have been logged, and the Klanawa River Ecological Reserve protects some of the last of the old-growth trees in the area. The reserve is on a forested flood plain about 5 km from the mouth of the Klanawa River.

ECOLOGY: Two endangered plants are within the reserve's boundaries—redwood sorrel and Scouler's corydalis. Redwood sorrel is the most significant, as it is not protected in any other BC park or reserve. The reserve is considered the best site for redwood sorrel in the province. Scouler's corydalis is listed as threatened by the Committee on the Status of Endangered Wildlife in Canada (COSEWIC), and is found in Canada only in the Nitinat and Klanawa river basins and an area west of Cowichan Lake. The Klanawa River is home to coho, chum, chinook salmon, winter-run steelhead, sculpin, Pacific lamprey and cutthroat trout.

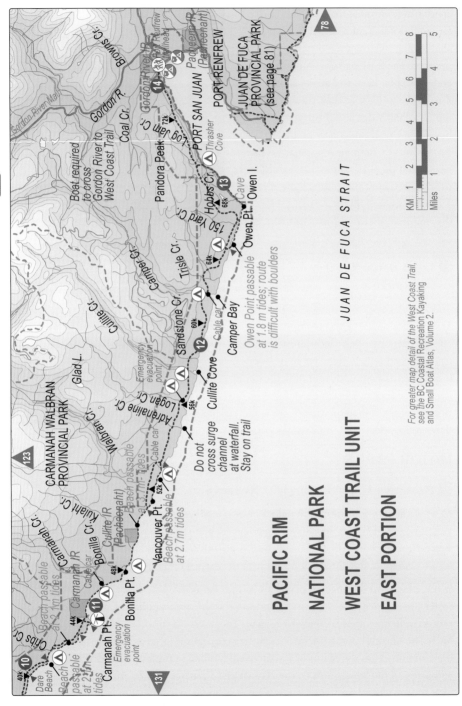

THE WEST COAST TRAIL

CARMANAH WALBRAN PROVINCIAL PARK

PACIFIC RIM

NATIONAL PARK

WEST COAST TRAIL UNIT

EAST PORTION

JUAN DE FUCA STRAIT

PORT SAN JUAN

PORT RENFREW

JUAN DE FUCA PROVINCIAL PARK (see page 81)

Boat required to cross Gordon River to West Coast Trail

Owen Point passable at 1.8 m tides; route is difficult with boulders

Do not cross surge channel at waterfall. Stay on trail

Beach passable at 2.1m tides

Beach passable at 2.1 m tides

Beach passable at 2.7m tides

Beach passable at 2.0m tides

Emergency evacuation point

Emergency evacuation point

Cable car

Thrasher Cove

Owen Pt. Owen I.

Camper Bay

Cullite Cove

Vancouver Pt.

Bonilla Pt.

Carmanah Pt.

Dare Beach

Pandora Peak

Hobbs Cr.

Logan Cr.

Adrenaline Cr.

Sandstone Cr.

Trisle Cr.

Camper Cr.

Cullite Cr.

Logan Cr.

Walbran C.

Cullite IR (Pacheenaht)

Kulaht Cr.

Bonilla Cr.

Carmanah IR

Camaraxby Cr.

Orbs Cr.

Coal Cr.

Gordon R.

Browns Cr.

Gordon River Main

Coal Cr.

Gordon River IR

Port Renfrew

Pacheena IR (Pacheenaht)

150 Yard Cr.

Glad L.

72k
68k
64k
60k
56k
52k
48k
44k
40k

14
13
12
11
10

78
123
131

For greater map detail of the West Coast Trail, see the BC Coastal Recreation Kayaking and Small Boat Atlas, Volume 2.

KM
Miles

See pages 62–63 for main chapter map.

ACCESS: The reserve is 20 km southeast of Bamfield with rough logging road access only along the Klanawa Main. While access is allowed, casual visits are discouraged.

26 Pacific Rim National Park
West Coast Trail Unit *(map pp. 62–63)*

See detailed map page 131 to locate features 1 to 10 and detailed map page 136 to locate features 10 to 14.

This is Vancouver Island's most famous trail, a 75 km route between Bamfield and Port Renfrew. It was begun a century ago as the West Coast Life-saving Trail, created in the aftermath of the sinking of the *Valencia* in 1906 that resulted in the loss of 133 lives, due in large part to the poor link between the rocky coast and the safety of shore. Shortly after, leaps forward in marine safety resources and technology meant the trail saw little of its intended use. It did gain popularity as an adventure hike, though, and by the 1980s became too popular, prompting Parks Canada to limit its use by instituting a reservation system. Trail improvements have made the route far more accessible than was possible in earlier days; sturdy wooden ladders have replaced steep scrambles in and out of creek valleys and there are boardwalks along many of the muddier sections. It still, however, remains very much a strenuous wilderness adventure hike—part endurance test, part obstacle course and part wilderness retreat.

It is a very organized trail, with registration required at the trailheads, along with a mandatory orientation session. Parks Canada also sells a detailed and useful map at the trailheads. The following information is provided to augment the Parks Canada information as well as provide the basics.

Here are a few key topics to keep in mind before starting out.

- TO RESERVE A SPOT: The trail is open May 1 to September 30 each year. A West Coast Trail Overnight Use Permit is required to hike the trail and to cross by boat at Gordon River and Nitinat Narrows. A quota system is in effect from June 15 to September 15, and reservations are highly recommended, though some standby spots are set aside for those who choose to simply

Tidal islets at Bonilla Point.

show up. No reservations are taken outside the summer season. Look up "park use permit" at **www.pc.gc .ca/pn-np/bc/pacificrim/** for full details, or call 1-800-435-5622 in Canada or the US or 250-387-1642 internationally. Day use of the trail from Pachena Bay does not require a park use permit.

Carmanah Point.

- WHEN TO VISIT: The best weather is during the peak season, but because the trail is within a temperate coastal rainforest, rain is a factor any time of year. The shoulder season sees many fewer visitors, so no reservations are required, and May and early June have the advantage of longer days and a fresher trail before the mud is churned by summer traffic. Late summer has the advantage that the trail may be dry; the downside is a summer of use means the trail is degraded; it generally recovers during the winter and is fresher in the spring and early summer.

- WHICH DIRECTION TO HIKE: Hikers can enter the trail via Port Renfrew (Gordon River) or Bamfield (Pachena Bay). Nitinat Lake is also an option; see page 130 for more information. While transportation is often the key factor in deciding which point to start from, there are other considerations. For instance, parking is free at the trailhead at Pachena Bay, whereas no parking lot is offered at Port Renfrew; this means paying for a private parking service. The trail is considerably easier at the Pachena Bay end, giving hikers an opportunity to "warm up" along an easy section while the packs are heavier with food. Leaving from Gordon River means traveling some of the most difficult sections while most heavily loaded. However, the exit across Gordon River at Port Renfrew requires a boat crossing with limited hours (9 a.m. to 5:15 p.m.), so you could be stranded on the trail for an extra day if you miss that window when hiking out. Leaving from Gordon River does have the advantage of getting the toughest sections over early, perhaps while you're less tired, leaving many of the most scenic sections to be enjoyed with the worst trouble spots behind you.

- HOW TO GET THERE: Because the trail is a linear route between two disconnected communities, transportation is often a hurdle. A popular choice is taking two vehicles, leaving a car at one trailhead and driving to the other. Shuttle services and express buses are available for those flying into the area. Lastly, there is always the option of thumbing a lift.

- HOW LONG IT WILL TAKE: While this depends on abilities and preference, most hikers walking for 8 to 10 hours a day can expect to finish the trail in 5 days. Progress will be slower during or shortly after extended or heavy rainfall. Missing boat crossings can prolong the trip a day, as can adverse tide levels at some key locations.

- TIDE INFORMATION: In several portions of the trail beaches can only be traveled at lower tides. Tide levels given in Parks Canada information guides are for the Tofino tide station, not Port Renfrew or Bamfield. Tide predictions can be downloaded at **www.waterlevels.gc.ca/english/Canada.shtml**.

- CHANGES TO THE TRAIL: Purists are critical of the West Coast Trail because of the many trail aids, such as ladders and boardwalks, that have tamed it, making it accessible to a far greater range of hiking skills than previously possible. But don't be fooled into thinking this is an easy outing. Many portions remain unaltered and the ladder climbs are sometimes several hundred feet and can be strenuous. Beach portions are perhaps better now than in past decades due to access restrictions and more stringent monitoring of trail use—in particular, less garbage. Boardwalks and ladders not only aid hikers but also protect areas prone to erosion or trampling. The present mix of developed and wilderness trail seems to be a good compromise by Parks Canada.

- IN THE EVENT OF INJURY: Parks Canada offers an emergency evacuation system, which is detailed at the orientation. The bottom line: this is a wilderness trail and if injured you can expect to spend several hours—as long as overnight—before being evacuated. If you're simply not able to complete the trail, you can bow out at Nitinat Narrows by arranging boat transportation. It's also possible to make arrangements for boat pickup (at a reasonable cost) at the Pachena Point lighthouse, the Carmanah Point lighthouse and at Parks Canada cabins at Tsocowis Creek, Logan Creek, Cullite Cove, Camper Bay and Thrasher Cove. If you're seriously injured and a helicopter evacuation is required, the cost is not covered by BC Medical Services.

- HOW TO RIDE A CABLE CAR: There are five cable cars on the trail at Camper Creek, Cullite Creek, Walbran Creek, Carmanah Creek and Klanawa Creek (the latter washed out in 2007 and is due to be replaced). These can be intimidating at first. They are all reached by platforms, usually about 10 m or more above ground. As the cars are suspended by a single cable and maneuvered by pulling a tow rope, they tend to sink and move outward as you step into them, enlarging the gap between the car and the platform. The best strategy

The cable car at Carmanah Creek.

is to grip the tow rope and pull it toward you as you enter while your partner holds the car in place. You can then hold the tow rope and the platform while your partner enters. Once properly seated simply let go of the tow rope. Do not attempt to hold the rope as you descend; you could burn your hands. Just enjoy the free ride. (Also make sure you are not leaning against the tow rope.) Once your free ride runs out, pull on the tow rope to the opposite platform. Gloves are recommended. Have the strongest person sitting facing the arrival platform, as pulling the tow rope (tug-of-war style) is easier than pushing it away from you. Two can fit in the cable car, but it is a tight squeeze with packs. I find keeping the backpack on is simpler, as room in front of your feet is limited to stash your pack separately.

The beach near Walbran Creek.

- FOOTWEAR: Good, solid hiking boots are recommended, but be prepared for traversing wet bogs and wading rivers. This can mean multiple days of sodden feet if your boots become wet, increasing the likelihood of blisters and other foot damage. A good strategy is to have a second set of footwear, such as good hiking sandals, for wet portions, though you run the risk of damaging exposed toes. Wet shoes are another option. Because the many boardwalks or root supports can be wet and slippery, calk boots will decrease the odds of slipping.

Ⓐ CAMPING: Camping is possible at both trailheads at the Pachena Bay campground (page 134) or at the Port Renfrew trailhead (page 95). These are good staging areas for hiking the trail and recommended for those hoping for standby slots during peak season. Both campsites are within easy walking distance of the trailheads. Designated and casual campsites dot the trail; most are within easy hiking distance of each other to create a convenient network for completing the trail.

Trail markers are oriented with the 0 km marker at the Pachena Bay trailhead and the 75 km marker at Gordon River. The following is a selection of features you will encounter along the trail.

❶ PACHENA TRAILHEAD ●, 0 KM: This is the west entry point to the trail, located just off Bamfield Road at the start of the paved section of the road in the approach to Bamfield. A short gravel road leads to a parking lot and the Parks Canada office where registration and orientation sessions take place. The office is open 9 a.m. to 5 p.m. The first orientation session is usually 9:30 a.m., and hikers can expect to begin the trail no earlier than 10:30 a.m. after the session. Camping is not allowed within 1 km of the trailhead on the West Coast Trail; pay camping is available at the Pachena Bay campground (see above).

❷ PACHENA TRAILHEAD TO PACHENA POINT, 0 TO 10 KM: This is the simplest portion of the West Coast Trail, with just a few ladders and slopes to contend with. Portions were heavily hit by the windstorms of late 2006, toppling numerous old trees. A good VIEWPOINT ● of some rugged coast and a sea lion haulout is at 9.5 km; a photo from this location was used

Sea lions at the haulout near Pachena Point.

on the cover of *The Wild Coast, Volume 1*. For those planning to complete the trail that day but who fall short, an open area just west of the lighthouse can serve as a campsite.

③ PACHENA POINT LIGHTHOUSE ●, 10 KM: This lighthouse was built in 1907 after the sinking of the *Valencia* nearby. It is the oldest original wood frame lighthouse on the BC coast, but it is no longer in use. The current, much smaller light is in front of the old lighthouse. The station is manned and the grounds are open to the public. Drinks and cookies are available by request. Be sure to sign the guest book.

④ MICHIGAN CREEK TO TSOCOWIS CREEK, 12 TO 16.5 KM: The trail follows the beach from Michigan Creek to Darling River; a beach route continuing from Darling River to Tsocowis Creek is passable at tides below 2.7 m. This area has numerous wonderful camping opportunities, with the most established campsites at MICHIGAN CREEK ● and Darling River. Other casual campsites are located along this stretch of beach with a nice spot at ORANGE JUICE CREEK ●. An unusual opportunity along the way is a cave campsite. The small site at TSOCOWIS CREEK ● is located just east of a Parks Canada staff cabin.

⑤ VALENCIA BLUFFS, 16.5 TO 20 KM: Here the trail goes overland above tall bluffs providing views over the rocks where the 76 m steamer *Valencia* foundered and sank over a three-day period in a storm in January 1906. Watch for the rusting century-old trail-building equipment alongside the trail.

⑥ TRESTLE CREEK TO TSUSIAT FALLS, 20 TO 25 KM: Between Trestle Creek and Klanawa River is a beach route passable at tides below 2.7 m. The cable car at Klanawa River was knocked out in the winter storms of 2006 but will be replaced. In the meantime a boat crossing is offered. The river is fordable at low tides. Between Klanawa River and Tsusiat Falls is an overland route. A bridge crosses Tsusiat River above the falls.

⑦ TSUSIAT FALLS TO TSUQUADRA POINT, 25 TO 30 KM: TSUSIAT FALLS ● is a scenic highlight of the West Coast Trail, especially in the spring or after a sustained rainfall when the flow is at its highest. This is a popular camping location, with the option of a cave for camping

The shoreline near Michigan Creek.

just east of the falls. The beach trail to the east is the most popular route, which at tides below 2.7 m leads through Hole in the Wall, the largest sea arch on the Vancouver Island coast.

8 NITINAT NARROWS ●, 32.5 KM: This is the middle of an overland stretch of trail between Tsuquadra Point and Cheewhat River. Nitinat Narrows is fast-flowing water between the ocean and intertidal Nitinat Lake. A boat is required to cross the narrows. It operates roughly 9 a.m. to 5 p.m. with service provided from the east side. Hikers on the west side can generally call to attract the attention of the boat operator. Refreshments ranging from canned drinks and beer to crab are available at the boat dock.

9 CLO-OOSE, 35 KM: Clo-oose is the historic name for the chief village of the Ditidaht (now the Claoose Reserve). In the early 19th century an unscrupulous Victoria real estate promoter marketed some adjacent property as a burgeoning community with full services, including a railroad and road access to Victoria. The buyers, many from Europe, arrived to find nothing—not even a dock to unload their belongings. Some tried to eke out an existence, and a few ruins of those days remain. Cheewhat River is blocked by a large sandbar that is part of a second First Nation reserve (often used as a surf camp by the band members). The river itself is brackish and not recommended for drinking. A good but small casual campsite is just east of the reserve at the beach access, at 36.5 km.

Remnants of century-old trail-building machines.

A cave shelter just east of Tsusiat Falls.

Wild shoreline toward Dare Point.

⑩ DARE POINT AND DARE BEACH, 36.5 TO 41 KM: Clo-oose Bay features one of the best sand beaches on the trail, but it turns to rock platform as you walk east. This gives the appearance of a good beach walk from Cheewhat River to Carmanah Point. While it is possible, be warned that beyond the beach access at 37 km the shoreline is rough and rutted intertidal rock ledge. Unless you are comfortable walking and climbing potentially wet and slippery rocks, I recommend the overland route. It features several good viewpoints over the beach. Watch for remnants of the old cable line along the trail between Clo-oose and Carmanah Point. A beach crossing is the only option near Cribs Creek. Other beach portions are passable only at 2.1 m tides or lower.

⑪ CARMANAH POINT TO VANCOUVER POINT, 44 TO 51 KM: This is arguably the most scenic stretch of shoreline on the West Coast Trail. The beach at Carmanah Creek is a wonderful mix of sand, offshore reefs and incredible surf. But don't frolic in the water here—the undertow is considerable. The lighthouse is an emergency evacuation point. Visitors are welcome and the lighthouse can be reached by either the overland or beach trails. East of the lighthouse the trail crosses the headland to come down to the beach at a reserve, famous for MONIQUE'S ●, a restaurant serving a limited but popular menu (hamburgers and beer are top sellers). The menu is a source of conversation between passing hiking groups within miles of the reserve. Carmanah Creek is a popular camping area and is crossed by the longest cable car on the trail. The trail continues along the beach only until near Vancouver Point. Bonilla Point is particularly scenic, with numerous large sea stacks in the intertidal zone. A small casual CAMPSITE ● is located near Bonilla Point. The beach west of Vancouver Point floods at higher tides (+3.7 m).

Keeping the feet dry in the bog means acrobatics.

⓬ THE BOG, 51 TO 62 KM: Welcome to what's probably the most difficult portion of the West Coast Trail. From Vancouver Point to the high point above Camper Creek is almost non-stop bog, with slow progress over roots, rocks and mud. Expect to average as little as 1 km per hour in wet conditions; it will be much faster if you forego the acrobatics involved in walking from dry spot to dry spot and simply wade through the muck. Progress will be slower in and around periods of sustained or heavy rain. During peak rain periods expect flooded sections and fast-flowing creeks with no crossing aids. Hikers with sufficient time may want to wait for a spell of dry weather before crossing this area. Steep ladders are found at the crossings at Walbran, Adrenaline, Logan, Cullite, Sandstone and Camper creeks. Camping is designated at all these creeks except Sandstone. Note that the LOGAN CREEK CAMPSITE ● can flood out; avoid this site during periods of heavy rain and high (+3.7 m) tides. The CULLITE COVE CAMPSITE ● is set off the main trail in an enclosed bay bordered by cliffs and backed by a large cobble (small boulder) beach.

The CAMPER CREEK SITE ● has an expansive beach and tends to be more popular. The Logan Creek suspension bridge is a West Coast Trail landmark. It was washed away during the winter storms of 2006 but was replaced by the time the trail opened in 2007. Camper Creek is the first (or last) cable car hikers will encounter. An interesting feature on the nearby ladder to the west is that during

Mature forest, ladders and log walkways typify the overland route.

periods of rain a waterfall forms behind the ladder; during exceptionally heavy periods of rain the water flows over the ladder and you will have to climb through a waterfall.

13 OWEN POINT TO THRASHER COVE, 65 TO 70 KM: Hikers have an option of two distinctly different trails along this stretch: overland or the beach route. The campsite at THRASHER COVE ● or a small forest site at the junction of the upland and beach trails at 65 km can be used to wait for a favourable tide if you're taking the beach route to Owen Point, passable only at tides 1.8 m or lower. The Owen Point route features rock ledge beach to the point, where caves are a scenic highlight of the trail. North of Owen Point to Thrasher Cove the trail is a difficult scramble over boulders. Expect this short (2.7 km) stretch to take three hours to complete. The overland option is through a light but mature forest more akin to the Juan de Fuca Marine Trail than other portions of the West Coast Trail. Boggy areas are intermittent. It is simpler than the boulder route, though if you intend to camp at Thrasher Cove you will have to descend the difficult 1 km trail from the ridge to the beach. Note that Thrasher Cove will flood at higher (+3.7 m) tides. For those traveling the upland who don't want to double back to Thrasher Cove to camp, there is a pretty but small one- to two-TENT SITE ● alongside a creek at approximately 70.3 km.

14 GORDON RIVER, 70 TO 75 KM: The last (or first) 5 km of the West Coast Trail are along a fairly high ridge overlooking Port San Juan. It is relatively easy hiking with some steep climbs and a few rough sections, but otherwise it is simple and well marked. Watch for old logging equipment along the route. Gordon River must be crossed by boat; it operates 9 a.m to 5:15 p.m. Raising a buoy alerts the ferry operator that a hiker is waiting. Once across the river, the trail use permits must be dropped off at the park office south of the dock. For those beginning the trail, the boat dock is behind a home alongside the Gordon River immediately north of the home-based store. Pay parking is available near the trailhead, as well as shuttle services. The park office, open 9 a.m. to 5 p.m., will have information on current service providers and will even call shuttle operators for you.

FOREST RECREATION SITES
See the map on page 62 to locate these recreation sites.

Flora Lake Recreation Site ●

This site features a selection of dispersed campsites along an access road adjacent to the lake, which is known for fishing, paddling, swimming and hunting. Most sites have lake access. An outhouse is located midway along the access road near the information kiosk (a considerable distance from some camping sites). Trails head off into the woods at various intervals.

ACCESS: Flora Lake is located just north of Nitinat Lake. From the Carmanah Main follow the Flora Lake Main for about 9 km. Note the Flora Lake Main has a sign stating the road is closed due to oversize logging trucks. This is to discourage the use of the Flora Lake Main as a shortcut route between Bamfield and Nitinat but doesn't affect use of the recreation site.

Sarita Lake Recreation Site

This recreation site has two traditional accesses. The north is closed and the sign stating it is a recreation site has been removed. The road leading to the lake is heavily ditched by creeks, making foot access the best option. This is ideal for walk-in campers, who can avoid RV traffic and set up near the fine sandy beach. Sarita Lake is a pretty spot for fishing, paddling and swimming. The south access is about a kilometre farther south at the tip of the lake and is used for camping and picnicking.

ACCESS: The picnic site, boat launch and camping area are located along Bamfield Road just south of the logging road link to Flora Lake.

Father and Son Lake Recreation Site ●

This is the only formal recreation site in an otherwise inaccessible area of Vancouver Island. Logging road access leads deep into a beautiful, canyon-like valley surrounded by steep, mountainous peaks. The lake is partway up the slope of Douglas Peak. Unfortunately this is a busy logging area with restricted weekday access and the potential for a locked gate on the weekend. The recreation area encompasses the namesake lake, with a short formal trail rounding the lake and informal routes leading up the adjacent peaks. Camping is possible at the lake, which is hike-in only.

ACCESS: From Bamfield Road 9 km south of the Port Alberni Junction take the Museum Creek turnoff, then after 3.5 km take the Thistle Mine Main northeast. Follow it for about 7 km just past a bridge, then turn left. The road is ditched and requires either four-wheel drive or feet. Access is limited to off-hours. Should the Museum Creek Main entrance be gated, try the bypass to the south (the Museum Main Connector).

China Creek Regional Park ●

This busy site on the shore of Alberni Inlet mixes boating and camping, with the focus clearly on boating. The China Creek Marina is run by the Port Alberni Port Authority and has moorage for 250 pleasure craft. The adjacent campground has 265 sites, with 170 fully or partially serviced. You'll find a launch ramp, laundry, store, playground, café, washrooms and showers. Access is off Bamfield Road just south of Port Alberni.

ⓘ **www.portalberniportauthority.ca/english/China_Creek.html**.

THE WEST COAST TRAIL

Yellow Point–Cedar

Between Nanaimo and Ladysmith is a rural area known as Cedar, with divisions known as North Oyster, Yellow Point, Timberlands, Cassidy and Cedar-by-the-Sea. Currently it's a largely rural stretch, but some major developments are planned over the next decade. A good selection of parks offer a choice of worthwhile day trips, with the Nanaimo River leading the way as a water recreation playground. Nanaimo Lakes offers camping, fishing and some limited hiking opportunities. A vast majority of land here is private property, which limits exploration of the area to parks and a few wilderness corridors.

POINTS OF INTEREST

27 Nanaimo River *(map p. 63)*

Detailed map below.

Nanaimo River is an exceptionally beautiful area, but it remains woefully unprotected along most of its length, making it easy prey for abuse—garbage, noise and congestion. The majority of access points are through private property—a mix of residential and industrial, the latter being mainly quarries or logging. Expect numerous "no trespassing" signs, many of which are ignored by river-goers, who can fill the main watering holes well beyond capacity on a sunny summer weekend. The best formal access is provided by the Trans Canada Trail, which offers several side trails down to the river. Most of the main recreational areas are farther east and can usually be identified through the roadside parking areas and signs warning of the dangers at the access trails. Many areas of

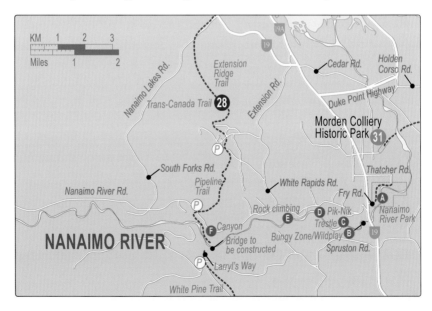

A view of the Nanaimo River at the Pik-Nik access.

established use with access through private property are not identified in this guide; a few key locations are provided where the status may change if private property rights are exercised.

PADDLING: The upper portions of the river may be of interest to hard-core veteran whitewater paddlers, but a good and relatively flatwater paddle runs from the Island Highway bridge to the estuary, a distance of about 7.5 km. People are often tempted to tube the length of the river, but even if you avoid the main rapids, large undercuts in the rocks have the potential to act as traps.

YELLOW POINT–CEDAR

SWIMMING: Nanaimo River is one of the premier swimming and rock-jumping locations in the Nanaimo area. Various popular spots along its length range from good family beaches to youth-oriented party hangouts. While swimming holes can be deep and pleasantly calm, be warned: they are often adjacent to strong currents and rapids. It's easy to be lulled into complacency and then dragged into the current. The result is often several fatalities a year.

A NANAIMO RIVER REGIONAL PARK: This 56-hectare regional park along the Nanaimo River protects some key salmon rearing and spawning habitat. A trail skirts the north shore of the river through the park. Access points are east of the Island Highway just north of the Nanaimo River bridge at either Thatcher or Fry road. A good time to visit is in the fall when the salmon are spawning.

B BUNGY ZONE/WILDPLAY: This is one of the more unusual commercial ventures on Vancouver Island. The oldest feature, the Bungy Zone, offers bungy jumping from a bridge high over the Nanaimo River. Over the years more attractions have been added, including Swing King, a chance to be dropped from the bridge and swing out over the river at speeds up to 140 km per hour. The latest addition is TreeGo, a tree-to-tree obstacle course with zip lines, suspended bridges, scramble nets and swinging logs of increasing difficulty and height. The curious can watch bungy jumping from the Nanaimo River bridge of the Island Highway. Visit **www.wildplayparks.com**.

C THE TRESTLE: This is probably the most popular watering hole for summer sun seekers and rock jumpers. The name refers to a trestle now gone except for the concrete footings. It's located just upriver from the Bungy Zone.

D PIK-NIK: This access point leads to a tiny beach with lots of rock areas to explore. The steep canyon walls make it exceptionally scenic. A short trail offers several viewpoints along the river. Note the trail can be dangerous at points. Access is questionable due to the private property that must be crossed to reach this area.

E ROCK CLIMBING: At the end of the access road for the hydro lines off Nanaimo River Road is a pretty stretch of canyon. The river's north crags are popular climbing routes. About a dozen bolted routes can be found; access is by a steep trail leading west from the ACCESS ROAD ●. For a family swimming area, walk the hydro access road and find the path southeast to a placid section of the river.

F THE CANYON: The Trans Canada Trail offers access to an upland portion of the north side of the Nanaimo River that has been changed in recent years due to a quarry. Access through the quarry may be restricted; if not, look for the gated access road with several distinct boulders. Walk down the main gravel road and it will turn west. It will end with a trail leading to the riverfront with some steep portions along the way. Once there you will find a magical spot where the river has carved its way into the bedrock, leaving sculpted ledges along the length of the canyon, which runs about a kilometre. A trail skirts the north shore, making it possible to walk the canyon then drift back on the current. On the canyon's east end there's a day-use area with some good rock jumps and a small family beach. Expect the ledges to be well used during the summer. An unfortunate development is the area's reputation for being clothing optional.

㉘ Trans Canada Trail, Nanaimo section (map p. 63) 🚶 🚶‍♀️ 🚴

The dream to link one end of Canada to the other by a system of trails is slowly becoming a reality, and an example of that snail-pace speed is the Nanaimo portion. The main victory in recent years has been the completion of the Haslam Creek suspension bridge—a definite highlight of the trail. However, the lack of a bridge over the Nanaimo River, logging diversions and rough portions elsewhere are keeping this section of the trail in its infancy.

The south end begins, fittingly, at a gravel pit at the end of Timberlands Road. The trail skirts the pit, then borders a barbed fence along private property and emerges at the scenic Haslam Creek suspension bridge. The trail then continues along some very rough and steep sections and through several active logging areas for 8.5 km to Spruston Road; cycling is not recommended. At some point in the future the trail may continue across the Nanaimo River. Until that time the only alternative is down Spruston Road to a very busy section of the Island Highway, then returning to the trail via Nanaimo River Road. A pleasant section of trail runs along the Nanaimo River, then jumps across Nanaimo River

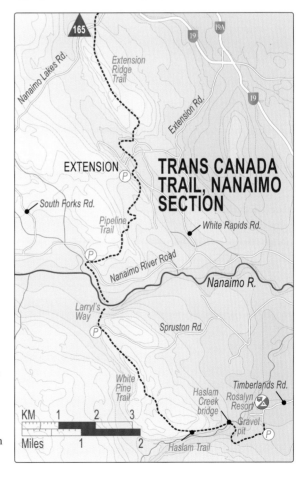

Road to the community of Extension, then crosses a scenic ridge before dropping into Nanaimo near Colliery Dam Park (not to be confused with the Morden Colliery Historic Provincial Park; see page 158 to locate it).

ACCESS: Parking is possible at the end of Timberlands Road, at the trail at Nanaimo River Road, at the end of Extension Road, at Colliery Dam Park and the end of Spruston Road.

㉙ Nanaimo Lakes *(map p. 63)*

Nanaimo Lakes is a potential gateway into the interior of central Vancouver Island, with one major barrier: it is part of TimberWest's holdings of private forest land, and restrictions on access include a staffed entry gate, fees and limited hours in which to pass. Four lakes lie in a line joined by Nanaimo Lakes Road; they are known as First through Fourth lakes, with Third Lake being little more than a small bog.

The main route through the various lakes is generally open to the public on the weekends, but anywhere else can have restricted access, particularly if there is active logging. Nanaimo Lakes is best suited to people who like lakeside camping and recreation, particularly fishing. The area is remarkably bereft of formal trails.

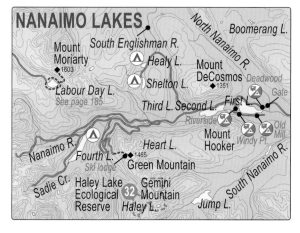

- FIRST LAKE: Four designated campgrounds are located at First Lake. The main campground, OLD MILL CAMPGROUND ● (35 sites) on the lake's south side, has the

An angler tries his luck on Nanaimo River between First and Second lakes.

advantage of a park host. Windy Point (30 sites) and smaller Riverside (4 sites) are located on the lake's west side. Deadwood, located just off the entry gate, has limited water access with 10 sites and an overflow area; the young and rowdy are asked to please camp here. It is unregulated.

The scenic backdrop to Fourth Lake.

- SECOND LAKE: This lake is bordered by cottages along the access road. Access beyond Second Lake is barred Monday to Friday.

- PANTHER AND ECHO LAKES: These two trout fishing lakes have a rough camping and picnic area located between them. Both lakes have launches for small boats. Access is via Dash Main, which departs north from NANAIMO RIVER ROAD ● at the west end of Second Lake. It deteriorates to a four-wheel-drive state near the lakes, where you'll reach an UNMARKED JUNCTION ●. Stay right (north) for Panther Lake access and turn south for the Echo Lake campsite, picnic area and launch. Neither area is particularly attractive, and they're best suited to ardent fishermen only.

- FOURTH LAKE: This is a good trout fishing lake. It is dammed, with access possible to the dam and the waterfall below. A BOAT LAUNCH ● is located at the north end of the lake near the dam. It could double as a campsite near the end of the access road. Another access road farther south is also a potential camping area. Both are best suited to trailers or RVs. Fishing from the dam into the lake is popular. To get here follow Nanaimo River Road past Second Lake, then take the bridge across Nanaimo River at the painted boulder, then take Branch L off the main. Fourth Lake is marked by a sign at the turnoff.

🚶 HIKING: Green Mountain was once a recreational ski hill, and the old deteriorating A-frame ski lodge can still be visited, making for the best hiking option in the Nanaimo Lakes area. Logging can close the access; no access was allowed in 2007. From the main road take Branch K just before the Fourth Lake turnoff. Other hikes are possible up Mount DeCosmos and Mount Hooker but are dependent on logging roads for access. Mount Moriarty can be reached from Labour Day Lake (page 185), though the Nanaimo Lakes logging roads could also potentially be used for access, as logging from this side has reached near the edge of Labour Day Lake.

FISHING: Nanaimo River is home to steelhead and coho salmon plus rainbow and cutthroat trout. There are numerous access points to the river from Nanaimo River Road.

ACCESS: From the Island Highway take Nanaimo River Road west to the gated entrance. It remains paved most of its length through to the various lakes.

30 Cable Bay (map p. 63)

This is a pleasant trail leading from a parking lot to the waterfront at Cedar near Harmac, an industrial pulp mill. During the winter the log boom outside the pulp mill draws potentially hundreds of sea lions, making this a prime viewing location—one of the best from a land-based perspective. The best time to visit is November or early December. As this is private property, be sure not to run afoul of the signs. From where the trail meets the waterfront a path continues across a small bridge then east along the waterfront to Dodd Narrows, one of the fastest tidal channels on the BC coast. It is a dramatic place when the current is at full force. Consult a tidal chart for best viewing times (a hint: plan for a full moon). From Dodds Narrows a trail heads upland to reconnect with the main route back to the parking lot. Note that development is planned for this area, particularly around Dodd Narrows, so the future of the trail is in jeopardy.

ACCESS: From the Island Highway take Cedar Road east at the overpass traffic lights. Follow the road straight after the bridge, then turn right (south) at the stop sign and left (east) onto Holden Corso/Barnes Road. Follow it past the twist to Nicola Road. The parking lot and trailhead are at the end of Nicola Road.

31 Jack Point and Biggs Point parks (map p. 63)

Two adjacent parks (Jack Point and Biggs Point) are indistinguishable as they form one continuous strip of green space running the western length of the peninsula that divides Northumberland Channel and the Nanaimo River estuary. The Duke Point ferry terminal and a variety of industries, including several sawmills, a pulp mill and a deep-sea port, are on the east side of the peninsula. Despite all this the parks make for a scenic stroll over bluffs to a viewpoint at Jack Point at the tip of the peninsula. A few steep stairwells make this a moderately strenuous walk. Shorter trips are possible to a pleasant beach and rock headland about 1 km from the trailhead.

ACCESS: A parking lot on the east side of the Duke Point Highway includes a pedestrian underpass to the park trail. Reaching the lot, however, is convoluted, requiring you to exit the highway and follow industrial Maughan Road, then Jackson Road to the end. A simpler option is parking on the Duke Point Highway shoulder near the First Nations "Welcome to Nanaimo" carving and hopping the concrete barrier to the start of the trail.

MAJOR PARKS

🟡27 **Woodley Range Ecological Reserve** *(map p. 63)*

This reserve protects a meadow and woodland area known for its wide array of resident species, including no less than 15 sensitive ecosystems. In all you can find about 200 species of vascular plants, 27 of which are considered rare, including white-top aster, bog birds-foot trefoil, slimleaf onion, dune bentgrass, western St. John's wort, greensheathed sedge and Nuttall's quillwort. The wildflowers include heavy concentrations of camas. The range is also known for its turkey vulture nests and resident Townsend big-eared bats. An unusual feature is geological: sandstone cuesta-like (cretaceous) formations. The resulting shallow ridge soils have attracted the unusually rich array of plant and animal life.

ACCESS: The range is open to low-impact use, but its proximity to an urban centre has made it an easy target for informal trails along old logging roads that pass through the most sensitive areas. If you're just looking for a casual trail in the area, consider Hemer Provincial Park or Yellow Point Park instead.

🟡28 **Yellow Point Park and Yellow Point Bog Ecological Reserve** *(map p. 63)*

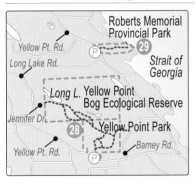

Two connected protected areas offer a rare look at a bog and its associated plant life. Both the park and reserve are open to public access thanks to a network of trails, with low-impact visits possible to the outer edge of the reserve. The reserve is considered to have the highest overall biodiversity of British Columbia's ecological reserves. It was created in 1996 and protects 141 hectares.

ECOLOGY: The area is typical of southern Vancouver Island bogs for its wetland and forest plants with numerous swamps, meadows, shallow lakes and forests in various stages of age. It is home to beaver, otter, small-mouthed bass, pumpkin-seed sunfish, stickleback and cutthroat trout. Rare residents include Vancouver Island beggarticks, slender-spike mannagrass and water marigold.

🪑 PICNIC AREAS AND DAY USE: A small picnic area is located near the parking lot.

🚶 HIKING AND SHORT WALKS: Designated trails cross Yellow Point Park, with a connection to Long Lake in the southwest portion of the reserve; access is prohibited elsewhere in the reserve. The shortest loop in

Yellow Point Park is 1.1 km; the longest loop is 2.2 km. A hike to Long Lake will extend that distance.

ACCESS: From the Island Highway north of Ladysmith, take Cedar Road to Yellow Point Road. The TRAILHEAD ● is at the parking lot 4.2 km along Yellow Point Road. Other trail accesses are at Jennifer and Barney roads.

㉙ Roberts Memorial Provincial Park *(map p. 63)*

This is a small (14-hectare) day-use park on the waterfront overlooking Stewart Channel. It is most remarkable for its sandstone ledges, a feature created from ancient sea beds that is more common among the nearby Gulf Islands than on Vancouver Island. The rocky headlands are ideal for viewing marine wildlife, which commonly includes eagles, great blue herons, seals and sea lions (particularly in winter). A shell midden is a reminder of earlier occupation.

PICNIC AREAS AND DAY USE: An easy 1 km trail leads to the rocky beach where you'll find a pair of picnic tables and an outhouse.

ACCESS: The park is 15 km south of Nanaimo. From the Island Highway take Cedar Road east, then Yellow Point Road.

Sculpted sandstone on the shoreline at Roberts Memorial Provincial Park.

㉚ Hemer Provincial Park *(map p. 63)*

This is a good strolling park located on the edge of Holden Lake through fields and coniferous forests. It includes a working farm currently off-limits to the public due to a life-tenancy agreement with the previous owners of the park. The lake is home to cutthroat trout, steelhead, pea-mouth chub and prickley sculpins and will likely have ducks and perhaps trumpeter swans.

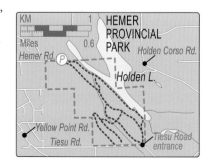

SHORT WALKS: Hemer park has 11 km of trails with benches, trail maps and pit toilets. A regional trail, the Morden Colliery Trail, follows a coal railway right-of-way, starting at

Vancouver Island's last coal tipple at Morden Colliery Historic Provincial Park.

Morden Colliery Historic Park and heading 1 km to the Nanaimo River. A crossing is planned to continue the trail to Hemer Provincial Park, but you can follow the eastern portion separately, which runs 2.4 km along the old railway grade from Hemer Provincial Park to the river.

ACCESS: From the Island Highway south of Nanaimo take Cedar Road to Hemer Road.

⑧ **Morden Colliery Historic Provincial Park** *(map p. 63)*

This park protects a unique part of the region's coal mining history: the only remaining COAL TIPPLE ● on Vancouver Island. The tipple was built in the early 1900s by the Pacific Coal Company to service the Morden Coal Mine, one of many that dotted the Nanaimo area producing fuel for Pacific shipping traffic. The tipple is protected behind a chain-link fence topped with barbed wire that does little for the aesthetic appeal. The small (4-hectare) park is undeveloped, but is alongside a regional trail (see above).

ACCESS: From the Island Highway turn east onto Morden Road 7 km south of Nanaimo. A parking lot is shared with the trailhead for the regional trail.

㉜ **Haley Lake Ecological Reserve** *(map p. 63)*

This 888-hectare reserve was created in 1988 to protect the endangered Vancouver Island marmot, North America's rarest marmot. It is found only in mountainous regions in a small area west of Nanaimo that includes the reserve. Its limited habitat is a contributing factor to its small population; its use of open meadows makes it an easy target for predators. As well as at Haley Lake, the marmots breed in the former ski area of Green Mountain, which has been set aside as a critical wildlife management area. Public entry to the Haley Lake reserve is prohibited.

CHAPTER THREE

The Central Island

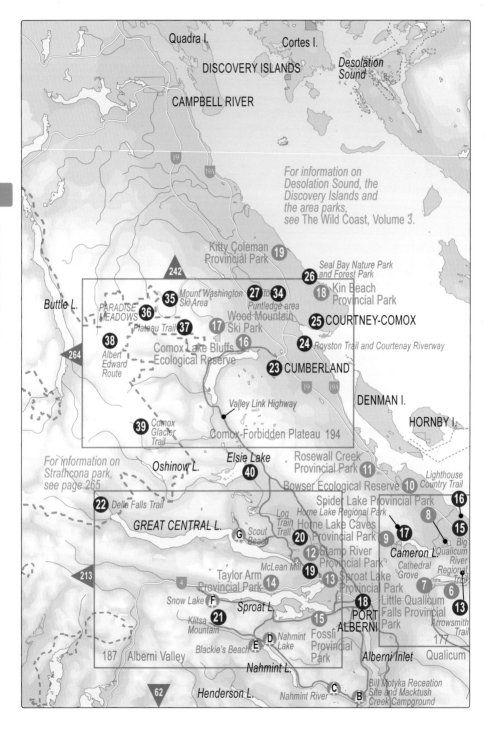

Quadra I.

Cortes I.

DISCOVERY ISLANDS

Desolation
Sound

CAMPBELL RIVER

For information on
Desolation Sound, the
Discovery Islands and
the area parks,
see The Wild Coast, Volume 3.

Kitty Coleman
Provincial Park **19**

Seal Bay Nature Park
and Forest Park

26

18 Kin Beach
Provincial Park

Buttle L.

35 Mount Washington
Ski Area

27 To **34** Puntledge area

PARADISE
MEADOWS **36**

37 Wood Mountain
Ski Park

17

25 COURTNEY-COMOX

38
Albert
Edward
Route

Plateau Trail

Comox Lake Bluffs
Ecological Reserve

16

24 Royston Trail and Courtenay Riverway

23 CUMBERLAND

39 Comox
Glacier
Trail

Valley Link Highway

DENMAN I.

HORNBY I.

Comox-Forbidden Plateau 194

For information on
Strathcona park,
see page 265

Oshinow L.

Elsie Lake
40

Rosewall Creek
Provincial Park **11**

Bowser Ecological Reserve **10**

Lighthouse
Country Trail

22 Della Falls Trail

GREAT CENTRAL L.

G Scout
Beach

Log
Train
Trail

Spider Lake Provincial Park

Horne Lake Regional Park

Horne Lake Caves
20 Provincial Park

16

8

15

Big
Qualicum
River
Regional
Trail

9

17

213

McLean Mill

12 Stamp River
Provincial Park

Cameron L.

Cathedral
Grove

Taylor Arm
Provincial Park **14**

19

13 Sproat Lake
Provincial Park

7

6

Snow Lake **F**

21

Klitsa
Mountain

Sproat L.

18

PORT
ALBERNI

Little Qualicum
Falls Provincial
Park

13

Arrowsmith
Trail

E **D** Nahmint
Lake

15

Fossli
Provincial
Park

Alberni Inlet

Qualicum

177

Blackie's Beach

Alberni Valley

187

Nahmint L.

Henderson L.

62

Nahmint River

C

B

Bill Motyka Receation
Site and Macktush
Creek Campground

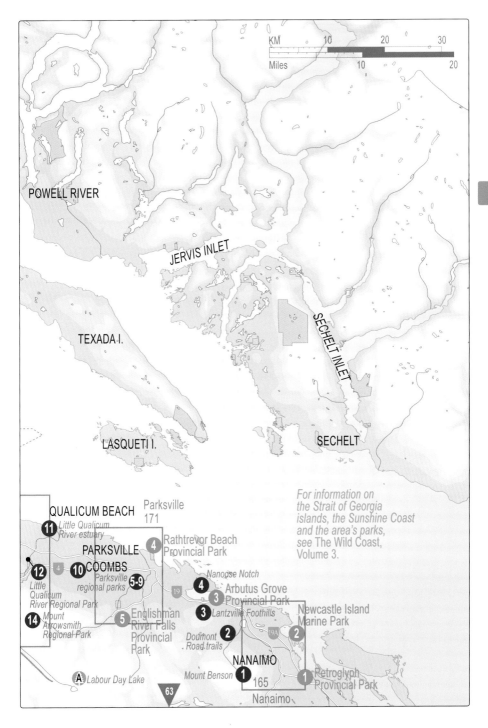

KM
10 20 30
Miles
10 20

POWELL RIVER

JERVIS INLET

TEXADA I.

SECHELT INLET

LASQUETI I.

SECHELT

For information on
the Strait of Georgia
islands, the Sunshine Coast
and the area's parks,
see The Wild Coast,
Volume 3.

QUALICUM BEACH   Parksville
171
11 Little Qualicum
River estuary
Rathtrevor Beach
PARKSVILLE   **4** Provincial Park
10 COOMBS   Nanoose Notch
12   Parksville
Little   regional parks   **5-9**   **4**
Qualicum   Arbutus Grove
River Regional Park   **3** Provincial Park
14 Mount   **3** Lantzville Foothills
Arrowsmith
Regional Park   **5** Englishman   Newcastle Island
River Falls   **3** Lantzville Foothills   Marine Park
Provincial   Doumont   **2**
Park   Road trails
2
NANAIMO
A Labour Day Lake   Mount Benson   **1** 165   **1** Retroglyph
Provincial Park
63
Nanaimo

It's one of those strange quirks of perspective that allows Nanaimo, Parksville, Qualicum and Comox to be considered the central island. Geographically it's off the mark significantly, but in a political sense it's becoming closer to the truth. Nanaimo is poised to surpass Victoria's population, with the region rivaling Greater Victoria. This growth has added greatly to the commercial and residential vibrancy of these communities, but it certainly has done little for the wilderness appeal as new subdivisions and other forms of development overgrow traditional recreation areas.

Development dominates the coastal region in an almost unbroken line of private property, with some rural development but more and more urban-style subdivisions. Protected areas have emerged in small clusters at key locations, but the land is being eaten up at an alarming rate, particularly where logging land is being converted to subdivisions. Inland and away from the coastal communities the island remains almost entirely private logging land (Port Alberni is the largest exception). Public access into these logging areas is generally restricted, which means whole regions can be inaccessible.

The bright spot is that the most scenic areas, such as Mount Arrowsmith, Forbidden Plateau and many of the key lakes and rivers, are now protected as parkland. Lacking in protection are accessible old-growth forests, beyond a few pockets such as Cathedral Grove. These places are sobering reminders of a past long gone. While nearby island communities struggle with how to manage proposals for 20-storey skyscrapers, there's still an occasional glimpse to remind us that the forests once stood even taller.

TRANSPORTATION

Like the south coast, this portion of Vancouver Island is dominated by travel along the Island Highway. There are paved roads in all communities, but once outside the municipal boundaries (with a few notable exceptions) logging roads provide access. Here are the major routes.

THE ISLAND HIGHWAY: This is the main link along east Vancouver Island between Victoria and communities to the north. It has several divisions that may cause confusion:

- HIGHWAY 1: Also known as the Trans-Canada Highway, this is the portion of the Island Highway between Victoria and Nanaimo. It continues through Nanaimo to the ferry terminal at Departure Bay.

- HIGHWAY 19 AND HIGHWAY 19A: Highway 19 (also called the Inland Island Highway) is the portion of the Island Highway from north of Nanaimo to Campbell River. The divided four-lane highway was constructed in the mid 1990s to provide a faster alternative to the oceanside highway between Nanaimo and Campbell River; the old highway has now been renamed Highway 19A (often referred to as the Old Island Highway or the Oceanside Route). The inland route has a much higher speed limit—110 km per hour along most of it—and bypasses communities such as Parksville, Qualicum and Comox except for where it is linked by the connector routes.

- NANAIMO PARKWAY: This divided four-lane highway, part of Highway 19, bypasses Nanaimo, from near Duke Point to past the north end of the city at Lantzville. It is a much faster alternative to Highways 1 and 19A (which go through Nanaimo), giving access to the Departure Bay ferry terminal, the city's downtown area and the many malls at the north end of the city.

Other routes in this section of Vancouver Island include the following.

HIGHWAY 4: This is the major route to Port Alberni and points west. It is also known as the Pacific Rim Highway. The junction with the Island Highway is near Qualicum Beach. Highway 4A, an older route, meets the Island Highway farther south near Parksville and passes west through Coombs before joining Highway 4.

ERRINGTON ROAD: This is a major route through the rural area south of Parksville (known as Errington), with connections to Little Mountain, Englishman River and the Hammerfest mountain bike trails, to name a few features. From the Island Highway take Highway 4A for 3.2 km west to Errington Road.

CAMERON MAIN: This is the major artery for backroad travel in the Mount Arrowsmith–Cameron River area. The HIGHWAY 4 TURNOFF ● is just west of the summit on the pass into Port Alberni. A left-turn lane is a fairly recent and much-needed safety improvement. From this intersection a connector goes downhill to join the CAMERON MAIN ●. The Cameron Main continues southeast from here to connect with PASS MAIN ● for the Mount Arrowsmith routes, or continues in decreasing quality to the Labour Day Lake trailhead. To the southwest, Cameron Main continues on to connect with Bamfield Road, making the Cameron Main route a good bypass of Port Alberni.

BEAVER CREEK ROAD: This key route runs north of Port Alberni between Strathcona Provincial Park and the Beaufort Range. It exits Highway 4 just west of Port Alberni's downtown after the Somass River. It eventually becomes Somers

Road; by turning west at the end of Somers Road you can continue north on the Valley Link Highway to eventually connect with Comox Lake.

COMOX LAKE MAIN: This logging main connects Comox Lake via the Cumberland turnoff of the Island Highway with Port Alberni via Beaver Creek Road in the south. It's a potential gateway to southeast Strathcona Provincial Park, particularly the Comox Glacier. The roads in this region are mainly on private logging land, so restrictions apply, particularly at the north end of Comox Lake, which has restricted access during the weekdays. Portions are steep, narrow and twisting, and roughest in the few kilometres at the south end of Comox Lake. A gate here can be closed at any time, potentially blocking the route (though it is usually open). For the south entrance follow Beaver Creek Road as it curves right and turns into Somers Road; follow it to near the end, watching for the logging road to your left with the sign reading "Comox Main" (it is shortly before the Log Train Trail trailhead). Note the route SPLITS ● about 16.5 km south of the sharp turn at the south end of Comox Lake. The southwest leg, the Ash Main, will take you to Great Central Lake Road; the southeast leg, the Comox Main, will take you to Beaver Creek Road.

SOUTH TAYLOR AND STIRLING ARM MAINS: These are the two main logging roads that skirt the south end of Sproat Lake. South Taylor Main is reached by a sharp turn west of the Taylor River rest area. Portions can be in poor condition, especially toward the Snow Creek Recreation Site. The route continues east to link with Stirling Arm Main and the route to Nahmint Lake. Stirling Arm is reached from Highway 4 west of Port Alberni by turn down McCoy Lake Road until you reach a junction with a wide logging road, ASH MAIN ●. Take Ash Main for a short distance to the Stirling Arm Main junction. Traveling west will take you south of Sproat Lake; heading east will join you with the Macktush Main that heads south along Alberni Inlet's west shore.

STRATHCONA PARKWAY: This is a good paved route to the alpine level at Forbidden Plateau and Mount Washington Ski Resort. Carrying chains is mandatory during the winter, but the road is well maintained and regularly cleared for the skiing traffic, which can be considerable. The route is well marked from the Island Highway north of Comox.

Nanaimo region

Nanaimo is a thriving residential and commercial community of about 80,000 with a rich coal mining history. In the 1850s it became a major waypoint for the Pacific shipping fleet transporting coal from the area's numerous mines. Nanaimo Harbour is still an active place with the bonus of Newcastle Island Marine Park just a short hop across the water (see page 169). The city is blessed with a good amount of parkland that makes the most of the scenic waterfront. Most commercial centres are located along Highway 19A. The ferry terminal at

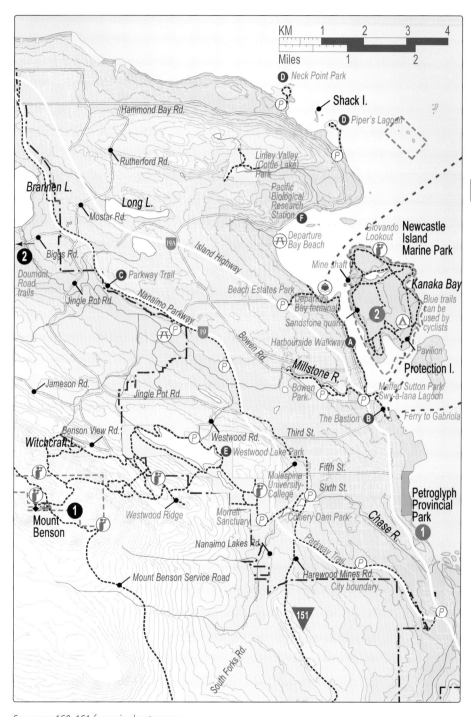

KM 1 2 3 4

Miles 1 2

D Neck Point Park

Shack I.

D Piper's Lagoon

Hammond Bay Rd.

Rutherford Rd.

Linley Valley (Cottle Lake) Park

Pacific Biological Research Station **F**

Brannen L.

Long L.

Mostar Rd.

Departure Bay Beach

Giovando Lookout **Newcastle Island Marine Park**

Mine shaft

2

Biggs Rd.

C Parkway Trail

Doumont Road trails

Jingle Pot Rd.

Island Highway

19A

Nanaimo Parkway

Beach Estates Park

Departure Bay terminal

Sandstone quarry

Harbourside Walkway **A**

Kanaka Bay

Blue trails can be used by cyclists

A

2

Pavilion

Protection I.

19

Bowen Rd.

Millstone R.

Jameson Rd.

Jingle Pot Rd.

Bowen Park

Maffeo Sutton Park/ Swy-a-lana Lagoon

The Bastion **B**

Ferry to Gabriola

Benson View Rd.

Witchcraft L.

Westwood Rd.

Third St.

E Westwood Lake Park

Fifth St.

Malaspina University College

Sixth St.

1

Mount Benson

Westwood Ridge

Morrell Sanctuary

Colliery Dam Park

Chase R.

Petroglyph Provincial Park

1

Nanaimo Lakes Rd.

Parkway Trail

Mount Benson Service Road

Harewood Mines Rd.

City boundary

151

South Forks Rd.

See pages 160–161 for main chapter map.

Departure Bay links central and north island communities with Vancouver and the mainland. Here are a few highlights within the city.

Ⓐ HARBOURSIDE WALKWAY: A wide, paved, multi-use trail runs along the waterfront from downtown to beyond the Departure Bay ferry terminal, passing a downtown park, Swy-a-lana Lagoon and various marinas along Newcastle Island Passage. It links via a trail along the Millstone River with Bowen Park, a large treed park with riverside trails, a pretty rhododendron garden and a fish ladder over a small waterfall. To the north of the ferry terminal the walkway links with Beach Estates Park on Northfield Creek. Here you'll find a fabulous waterfall secluded within a heavily forested area. Eventual plans are to complete the Harbourside Walkway to Departure Bay Beach.

Ⓑ THE BASTION: The last remaining fort of the Hudson's Bay Company is in Nanaimo's downtown on Front Street. The 1853 fort is open to the public during the summer. Visit **www.nanaimomuseum.ca/bastionpage.htm**.

Ⓒ PARKWAY TRAIL: When the Nanaimo bypass was built back in the 1990s some forethought was put into pedestrians and wheels, and the result is the Parkway Trail, a 19 km paved route that meanders alongside the Nanaimo Parkway through trees, fields, forests, Colliery Dam Park and a small section of road near Malaspina University-College. It is multi-use, for feet and non-motorized wheels. It is a good possibility for cyclists transiting this region to avoid vehicle traffic, though ardent cyclists still tend to use the Nanaimo Parkway, which has wide shoulders, fewer hills and fewer pedestrians to navigate past.

Ⓓ WATERFRONT STROLLS: While Nanaimo has numerous parks, two oceanfront parks are particularly notable. Off Hammond Bay Road in the city's north end are Piper's Lagoon and Neck Point Park. Piper's Lagoon has a long spit with a good strolling beach and a trail along the spit to several headlands with good views from the top. Neck Point Park has less climbing on bluffs and even a boardwalk over one rocky area, making it more accessible. Trails meander around the scenic headland, with a few beaches scattered about. For both parks, follow Hammond Bay Road.

Ⓔ WESTWOOD LAKE PARK: Westwood offers a good sandy beach area for swimming, sunbathing and non-motorized boat launching. Fishing is possible in the park; there are cutthroat trout and smallmouth bass, plus the lake is stocked with rainbow trout. A good stroll is the 6.2 km path around the lake, with connections to Westwood Ridge and Mount Benson trails on the far side of the lake across the hydro right-of-way. Westwood's neighbour, Morrell Sanctuary, is also an interesting walk through a variety of forest types with a good viewpoint over the city, a lakeside green area for picnics and interpretive programs. Visit **www.morrell.bc.ca**. A trail connects Westwood and Morrell.

G PACIFIC BIOLOGICAL RESEARCH STATION: Located on the north end of Departure Bay off Hammond Bay Road, the research station is instrumental in stock assessment and research for the Pacific fishery, particularly salmon recovery. It hosts an open house, where it's possible to visit the facilities and talk with researchers—but only once every few years. Visit **www.pac.dfo-mpo.gc.ca**.

ⓘ For municipal information, visit **www.nanaimo.ca**. For tourism information, visit **www.tourismnanaimo.com**.

POINTS OF INTEREST

❶ Mount Benson (map p. 165)

Mount Benson (1,009 m) forms the forested mountain backdrop for Nanaimo, though that is changing somewhat as logging works its way across the

mountainside. It's an established hiking and mountain biking area, with trails criss-crossing the north and east slopes. It lacks the rugged exposed granite bluffs of many other Vancouver Island peaks, but it does have a number of ridges along its length with a few good viewpoints. Most of the south and west face of Mount Benson is owned by TimberWest; Island Timberlands owns much of the south and east slopes and there's a Malaspina University-College (Nanaimo) forestry lot on the north slope near Jameson Road.

Panoramic views from atop Mount Benson.

The SUMMIT● is owned by Cercomm Electronics for a transmission facility. At the eleventh hour there was a reprieve from logging when Mount Benson Regional Park, a 212-hectare parcel on the northeast slope, was created in 2006. It is currently a wilderness park with unofficial trails only.

🚶 HIKING: A popular trip from Westwood Lake or Morrell Sanctuary is across the hydro right-of-way behind the parks and up Westwood Ridge to a viewpoint atop the bluff. Trails continue over the ridge and ultimately up Mount Benson, but it's easy to get confused in the criss-crossing foot and bike trails in the valley on the way to the summit. The most direct route up Mount Benson—and the steepest—is from the WITCHCRAFT LAKE TRAILHEAD ●. Park at the end of Benson View Road off Jameson and Jingle Pot roads, and follow a trail around Witchcraft Lake and across two primitive wooden bridges, then up the slope. Other trails dart off at various intervals, but if you watch for signs and keep gaining elevation you'll find the peak easily enough. It makes an invigorating half-day to full-day return trip. Near the summit the Witchcraft Lake trail meets up with trails originating from Westwood Lake for the final push to the peak. This leads to a wonderful area of dwarf pines and views across Nanaimo and the forest lands behind. A route often used but not recommended is the gravel service road. It is gated at South Forks Road and makes a much longer and less scenic ascent. A few mountain bike trails intermingle with the Mount Benson trails.

ACCESS: For the Westwood Lake access from the Nanaimo Parkway take Jingle Pot Road west, then Westwood Road south to the park entrance. For the Witchcraft Lake trailhead take Jameson Road off Jingle Pot Road, then Benson View Road to the end.

❷ Doumont Road trails (and Ammonite Falls) *(map p. 165)*

This is off-road biking country. Mountain bikers can make use of a spiderweb of trails in the surrounding area featuring everything from twin-width rambles to technical slopes. Weigles Road turns into a logging road from which many of the trails originate (while the access is Weigles Road, it is generally referred to as the Doumont Road trails). Parking is usually near the end of the pavement as the logging road is quite rutted. Hikers may wish to visit Benson Creek Regional Park, off the south end of Weigles Road east of the Wastelands, a motocross track. The Benson Creek park is undeveloped, with informal trails that lead down the steep embankments to a pair of waterfalls. One is picturesque Ammonite Falls, well worth seeing.

ACCESS: Follow Biggs Road to the end of the pavement. From the Jingle Pot–Mostar roads intersection of the Nanaimo Parkway, take Jingle Pot Road west, then Biggs Road to the intersection with Doumont Road where it becomes Weigles Road. Follow it to the end of the pavement, or farther if you are adventurous and have four-wheel drive. Trails to Benson Creek can be found just before the BMX track.

❸ Lantzville Foothills *(map p. 161)*

In the none-too-recent past the Lantzville Foothills were an exceptional hiking and horseback riding trail system, with several wonderful viewpoints atop the knolls over the Strait of Georgia. The property has since been logged and is now being subdivided. When the dust settles, which may take a decade, hopefully the bluff summits will remain accessible. Undoubtedly trails will continue to extend south from the end of the outermost subdivision, particularly along the old logging roads, which are great for off-road cycling. Access from the Island Highway is traditionally off the end of Aulds Road or Phantom Road (off Aulds Road).

❹ Nanoose Notch (map p. 161)

The Nanoose Notch is the local name for a landmark ridge on the Nanoose Peninsula north of Nanoose Harbour. The land surrounding it is either developed with houses or is Department of National Defence land. The peak and viewpoint are reached from either end of a good trail. A second trail goes around part of Enos Lake; the two trail systems are close enough to be combined in one outing.

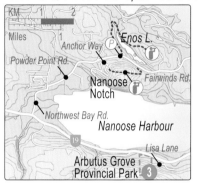

The Enos Lake trail ends at a low lookout on the east side of the lake.

ACCESS: From the Island Highway, take Northwest Bay Road, then Powder Point/Fairwinds Road. The ENOS LAKE TRAILHEAD ● is just past the Florence-Fairwinds intersection stop sign. Access to the notch is at the end of LINK ROAD ●. At the stop sign take Anchor Way south, then Link Road east.

MAJOR PARKS

❶ Petroglyph Provincial Park (map p. 165)

The Nanaimo area, including Gabriola Island, is famous for its number of First Nations petroglyphs, and a particularly high concentration is contained within this tiny (2-hectare) park. The petroglyphs are believed to be more than 1,000 years old, and depict fish, humans and various other creatures. The park has an interpretive centre with plaster castings of the petroglyphs suitable for rubbings.

ACCESS: The park is located at the south end of Nanaimo off Highway 19A just north of the Nanaimo Parkway junction. It is accessible only to northbound traffic.

❷ Newcastle Island Marine Park (map p. 165)

This island is a jewel in Nanaimo Harbour—a protected area of trails, lakes, scenic bluffs and historical landmarks separated from Nanaimo by Newcastle Island Passage, a busy marine traffic route lined with marinas on the Vancouver Island side. Newcastle Island in turn is separated from nearby residential Protection Island to the south by a narrow channel that runs dry at low tide. The resulting intertidal sandbar on south Newcastle Island is a good day-use area, near a dock for foot passenger ferry service, a campground and a pavilion. The pavilion dates back to 1931 when the Canadian Steamship Company ran Newcastle Island as a resort for tourists from Vancouver. The demise of steamship traffic led the company to sell the island to the city for a park in 1955; ownership was transferred to the province in 1961.

Prior to the resort there were two Coast Salish village sites on the island, coal mining, sandstone mining and a Japanese fishing settlement and saltery until 1941. Reminders of all these occupations can still be found around the island.

Ⓐ CAMPING: There are 18 walk-in campsites located near the pavilion, plus a group campsite. Amenities are flush toilets, showers and tap water.

Ⓚ HIKING: Trails surround and cross the island. A highlight is the Giovando Lookout above the bluffs on the island's north end.

Ⓑ CYCLING: Bikes are allowed on the island and on the ferry, but are limited to the Kanaka Bay and Mallard Lake trails only.

ACCESS: The foot passenger ferry leaves Nanaimo from a dock at the edge of Maffeo Sutton Park. Take Highway 19A through the downtown and turn east at the Comox Road–Front Street intersection, then a quick turn north into the parking area for Maffeo Sutton. The dock is along the boardwalk near the playground.

ⓘ Visit **www.newcastleisland.ca**. For a ferry schedule, visit **www .newcastleisland.ca/ferry.php**.

Arbutus trees

The arbutus tree (madrone in the US) is unique as Canada's only native broadleaf evergreen. It is fussy about its terrain, preferring sites near the ocean (not more than 8 km away) in areas low in moisture and out of the shade. In BC, this limits the range of arbutus mainly to rocky bluffs or areas with excellent drainage in the southwestern part of the province. There are two main threats to the survival of arbutus. First, it is shade intolerant and seedlings won't regenerate under a canopy, so it's easily pushed out by other vegetation. Second, it shares its preference for terrain with humans, meaning it's rapidly losing its habitat to development.

③ **Arbutus Grove Provincial Park** (map p. 161)

This small (22-hectare) park between Nanaimo and Parksville protects a stand of arbutus trees, Canada's only broadleaf evergreen tree. The park is on a steep slope facing Nanoose Harbour in an area surrounded by rural residential development. There is no formal development within the park.

ACCESS: The park has no direct road access. Indirect access is at the end of Lisa Lane, which is off the Bayview Park exit of the Island Highway north of Lantzville. There is limited parking at the end of the lane; an old overgrown roadway leads into the park.

Parksville region

Parksville is a relatively quiet residential community of about 11,000 on the shore of the Strait of Georgia in an area known for its extensive beaches at low tide. While much of the community's focus is on the waterfront, including a large community park and busy Rathtrevor Provincial Park, a wonderful development

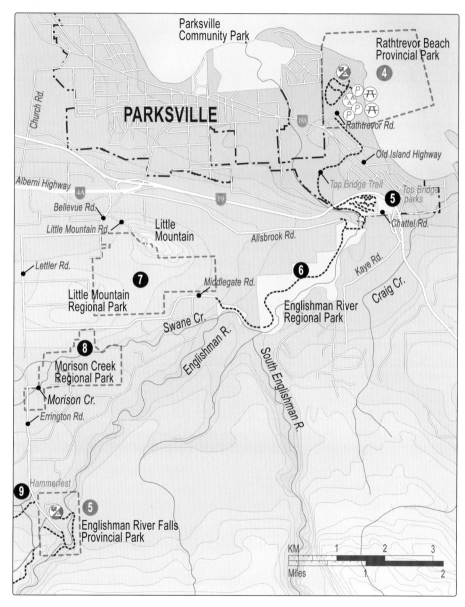

See pages 160–161 for main chapter map.

PARKSVILLE REGION

is an emerging regional trail and green space corridor, with new parks along the Englishman and Little Qualicum rivers. Other parcels are slated to become parks (Morrison Creek and Little Mountain).

POINTS OF INTEREST

5 Top Bridge parks *(map p. 171)*

Four recreational areas are combined under the umbrella name of Top Bridge. The name has roots going back to the early 1900s when Top Bridge was the key transportation route over the Englishman River. The footings of that old bridge can still be seen, but a new recreational bridge has replaced it, linking the Top Bridge parks and trails to Englishman River Regional Park.

HIKING: The Top Bridge Trail leads 5 km from Rathtrevor Provincial Park to Top Bridge.

MOUNTAIN BIKING: The Top Bridge Mountain Bike Park has a number of trails with access off Chattell Road. The trails are maintained by the Arrowsmith Mountain Bike Club.

A view of the Englishman River at the old Top Bridge location before the new bridge was built.

ACCESS: Chattel Road is off Exit 46, the southern entrance into Parksville from the Island Highway. From the Island Highway take Exit 46, then turn south (away from Parksville) past the cloverleaf onto Kaye Road. Chattel Road is a quick right. Follow it past the gun range to a PARKING LOT ● at the end.

❻ Englishman River Regional Park *(map p. 171)*

This new (2003) 177-hectare regional park protects a large portion of the lower Englishman River and its aquatic habitat, as well as a community-operated salmon hatchery. The hatchery is close to the Middlegate Road entrance.

HIKING: The park has a network of informal trails, some along the riverside but most in the adjacent forest. A management plan for the new park is expected to be finalized in 2008, with formal trails to follow. The new bridge at the park's northeast end connects it with the Top Bridge Trail.

ACCESS: There's good access to the existing trails from the gate at the end of Allsbrook or Middlegate road. With the bridge complete it's also possible to begin a visit from the Top Bridge parking lot at the end of Chattel Road.

❼ Little Mountain Regional Park *(map p. 171)*

The land surrounding Little Mountain is Crown land and was promised to the Regional District of Nanaimo as a park by the provincial government in 1995. The promised tenure was too short for the regional district's liking, however, and now the park's status sits in limbo. It remains a recreational highlight of the region due to the distinctive plateau. Communication towers sit at the top of the mountain, where a PARKING AREA ● offers access to the plateau viewpoint. An extensive but informal trail network crosses the south and east slopes of the mountain.

ACCESS: To get to the peak from the Island Highway take the 4A exit to Coombs. Take the first turn south onto Bellevue, then Little Mountain Road.

The sheer cliffs of Little Mountain.

❽ Morison Creek Regional Park *(map p. 171)*

Like Little Mountain, the Morison Creek parcel of Crown land was promised as a regional park to the community in 1995, but a deal has yet to be formalized. It will likely become part of a regional trail through Englishman River Regional Park. It is currently undeveloped with casual trails. An easy-to-find ENTRANCE ● to the park is off Errington Road just south of the bridge at Morison Creek. From there an old access road leads into the forest.

9 Hammerfest *(map p. 171)*

This system of mountain bike trails has a reputation as one of the most difficult on Vancouver Island. The name comes from the annual racing competition hosted by the Arrowsmith Mountain Bike Club. Both downhill and cross-country runs are possible. A loop runs 11 km; running counterclockwise it rises to the top of a logged

area before descending through some technical portions. Unlogged portions can be quite scenic; expect some good views. The trailheads are at Englishman River Falls Provincial Park.

ⓘ **www.arrowsmithmtbclub.com**.

10 Coombs *(map p. 161)*

Coombs, like Chemainus, is an example of how a small town with flair can suddenly develop into a regional attraction. A number of years back a quaint country market decided to create a grass roof complete with resident goats, and the market—particularly the goats—became the focal point of a large tourist-oriented commercial centre. Most of it is seasonal. For braving the possibility of large summertime crowds the reward is a mix of boutiques, craft shops, gift shops, restaurants and, of course, fresh veggies. Another Coombs attraction is Butterfly World and Gardens.

Visit **www.nature-world.com**.

Grazing goats have made Coombs Country Market a hit with tourists.

MAJOR PARKS

❹ **Rathtrevor Beach Provincial Park** *(map p. 171)*

Rathtrevor is one of Vancouver Island's busiest day-use and camping areas, famous for its sandy, shallow beach that dries to a tidal flat extending about a kilometre during low tides. Every March and April the tidal flats attract thousands of migrating Brandt geese. Other visitors are western black turnstone, western grebe, various gulls and numerous other water birds, making Rathtrevor a good place for bird watching.

PICNIC AREAS AND DAY USE: The park is popular for beach strolling and swimming. It has 150 picnic tables, picnic shelters, flush toilets, change rooms and a playground. Parking fees apply.

SHORT WALKS: Top Bridge Trail connects with Englishman River Regional Park. Shorter trails run through the park. Beach strolls are always popular.

CAMPING: The park has 175 drive-in campsites and 25 walk-in or cycle-in campsites located in an open field. Facilities include hot showers, water and a sani-station. Reservations are accepted and are recommended early for peak-season periods.

ACCESS: The park is just off the Island Highway at the east edge of Parksville. It is well signed.

❺ **Englishman River Falls Provincial Park** *(map p. 171)*

This park is located south of Parksville along the namesake river. The highlight is two cascading waterfalls and a deep canyon below.

PICNIC AREAS AND DAY USE: A forested picnic area is located next to the parking lot with viewing platforms over the river. You'll find picnic tables, flush toilets and water.

CAMPING: The 103 campsites are a mixture of vehicle and tent sites. Reservations are accepted and there are some first-come, first-served sites.

SHORT WALKS: Three km of groomed trails follow the riverside and cross at two locations, providing good views of the falls and canyon. Some trails continue beyond the park boundaries. Many of the trails are for the Hammerfest mountain bike circuit.

ACCESS: The park is located at the end of Errington Road where there is a PARKING LOT ●.

PARKSVILLE REGION

Qualicum

Qualicum Beach is a relatively sleepy, mostly retirement community with a plethora of golf courses, a pleasant commercial area and a nice beach for an afternoon stroll and an ice cream cone. Its name is derived from the infamous Qualicum winds that flow from the nearby mountains across the region. Qualicum Beach is also a gateway to Vancouver Island's west coast, with Highway 4 branching west to Tofino and Ucluelet. Along the way you'll pass under the imposing snow-covered peaks of Mount Arrowsmith, which is part of a large recreation area with great hiking opportunities. You'll also pass Cathedral Grove, with ancient Douglas-firs that form one of the most impressive sights on Vancouver Island.

POINTS OF INTEREST

⑪ Little Qualicum River estuary *(map p. 161)*

Three main wilderness areas protect the mouth of the Little Qualicum River. The Little Qualicum River Estuary Regional Conservation Area is a tiny (4.6-hectare) waterfront parcel purchased in 2003. It's located adjacent to the Marshall-Stevenson Wildlife Sanctuary (part of the Qualicum National Wildlife Area) and the Parksville-Qualicum Beach Wildlife Management Area, a provincially managed area on the Strait of Georgia. The estuary is a sandspit ecosystem and key habitat for overwintering and migratory waterfowl. Plans include a boardwalk and viewing platform.

ACCESS: Access is prohibited into the Marshall-Stevenson sanctuary. The beach area of the Qualicum National Wildlife Area can be strolled. A good access point is at the end of Surfside Drive. From Highway 19A north of Qualicum Beach take Kincade north to McFeely Drive, then Surfside, where you'll find a small beachside ACCESS ●.

⑫ Little Qualicum River Regional Park *(map p. 177)*

This new 44-hectare park lies adjacent to Little Qualicum Falls Provincial Park and raises the potential for a riverfront trail corridor. Formal trails are several years away, as the park is going through a management planning process.

ACCESS: Only casual trails exist right now, with old logging roads meandering through the area. One entry point is at the end of MELROSE ROAD ●. From the Island Highway take Highway 4 west for 7 km, then follow Melrose Road to the end. A trail leads to the logging roads. Parking is limited. Follow the development of the park and the creation of formal trails by looking up "parks & trails" at **www.rdn.bc.ca**.

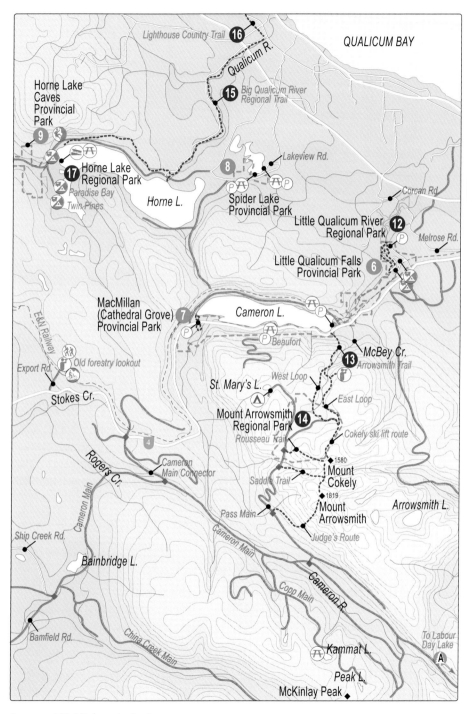

QUALICUM BAY

Lighthouse Country Trail **16**

Qualicum R.

Horne Lake
Caves
Provincial
Park
9

15 Big Qualicum River
Regional Trail

Lakeview Rd.

17 Horne Lake
Regional Park
Paradise Bay
Twin Pines

Horne L.

8

Spider Lake
Provincial Park

Corcan Rd.

Little Qualicum River **12**
Regional Park

Melrose Rd.

Little Qualicum Falls
Provincial Park **6**

MacMillan
(Cathedral Grove)
Provincial Park **7**

Cameron L.

Beaufort

McBey Cr.
13 Arrowsmith Trail

E&N Railway

Old forestry lookout

Export Rd.

Stokes Cr.

West Loop

St. Mary's L.

East Loop

Mount Arrowsmith
Regional Park **14**

Cokely ski lift route

Rousseau Trail

Rogers Cr.

Cameron
Main Connector

Saddle Trail

♦ 1580

Mount
Cokely

Cameron Main

Ship Creek Rd.

Pass Main

♦ 1819

Mount
Arrowsmith

Arrowsmith L.

Bainbridge L.

Judge's Route

Cameron Main

Cameron R.

Copp Main

Bamfield Rd.

China Creek Main

To Labour
Day Lake

A

Kammat L.

Peak L.

McKinlay Peak ♦

See pages 160–161 for main chapter map.

QUALICUM

Looking northwest to the distant peaks of Strathcona from Mount Cokely.

⓭ Arrowsmith Trail *(map p. 177)*

This trail was first constructed in 1912 by the Canadian Pacific Railway and provides a foot route from Cameron Lake to a former ski resort area, as well as a link to other trails on Mount Arrowsmith. From the trailhead across from Cameron Lake the trail follows an old road until a climb up to a bridge over McBey Creek. Atop the ridge after an elevation gain of about 800 m is a choice of routes: the West Loop continues down the old CPR trail along McBey Creek while the East Loop has a short trail leading to a lookout. The main route continues to the old ski hill. The routes connect for a loop or continue up Mount Cokely. Expect a full day of hiking to complete the loop.

ACCESS: Parking is available at the Cameron Lake day-use area of Little Qualicum Falls Provincial Park. The trailhead is on the opposite side of the road.

⓮ Mount Arrowsmith Regional Park *(map p. 177)*

This park protects the Mount Cokely slopes of the Mount Arrowsmith range, a favourite mountain scramble on Vancouver Island and a visual focal point for much of southern BC with its distinctive exposed granite peaks looming over 1,800 m above the nearby ocean. The area was once a ski hill and resort; it is now closed and the access road is maintained only to logging road standards. Several hiking routes lead to both mounts Cokely and Arrowsmith. Due to the elevation, snow is a factor for much of the year. The steep trails can be dangerous in fresh snow. For much of the year an ice pick and crampons are recommended for patches along some steep areas.

A steep portion of the Rosseau Trail.

- THE SADDLE: The most popular route up Mount Arrowsmith is the Saddle, the distinctive shelf that links Cokely and Arrowsmith. The TRAILHEAD ● is just after the 7 km marker on Pass Main at 1,040 m elevation. The trail begins along an overgrown logging road, then heads uphill through a forested area alongside a small creek. There are a few ridge lookouts along the way, a few rock scrambles and the final ascent up the Saddle, which can be tricky on the steep embankment, as the snow can last until August. From the Saddle hikers can scramble up the steep rock to the Mount Cokely summit, or head south to the peaks of Mount Arrowsmith. The initial peak is easily reached, but beyond that the climb becomes technical. The Saddle makes either an energetic half-day or a full day's hike. Camping on the plateau of the Saddle is popular.

- ROUSSEAU TRAIL: This is an alternative route that leads directly up Mount Cokely, bypassing the steep scramble necessary from the Saddle Trail. The TRAILHEAD ● is at the 8 km marker on Pass Main at 1,080 m elevation, and uses an overgrown logging road for about 100 m before turning into the forest.

- JUDGE'S ROUTE: A more difficult ascent, this trail begins at about 750 m elevation and heads almost directly up the southwest face of Mount Arrowsmith. The TRAILHEAD ● is at 2.7 km on the Pass Main just before a creek and culvert. An old logging road is used until about 930 m elevation, after which the trail turns into the forest and heads steeply up the south slope.

ACCESS: All trailheads are off Pass Main, which is reached from Highway 4 via Cameron Main. The main continues to a junction, where a gated decommissioned logging road leads about 5 km to the old ski resort area at about 1,200 m elevation. While rough, the road is passable and provides a quick way to connect to the Cokely ski lift route to the summit. Or from the gate you can stay on the main and continue down the north slope of Mount Arrowsmith to St. Mary's Lake, a recreation area for fishing, limited camping and cross-country skiing. The road is prone to washout, so a hike to the lake may be necessary.

⑮ Big Qualicum River Regional Trail *(map p. 177)*

An agreement between the Regional District of Nanaimo and the Department of Fisheries and Oceans led to the creation of a trail linking the Big Qualicum Salmon Hatchery to Horne Lake, a hike or cycle of about 12 km. The fish hatchery is open for visits during summer season. Much of the trail follows alongside the hatchery service road.

⑯ Lighthouse Country Trail *(map p. 177)*

An unused highway corridor is finding new life as a green path between Qualicum Beach and the tiny community of Bowser to the north. It's in the early stage of development; a bridge to be built in 2008 over Nile Creek will link the two ends of the trail.

⑰ Horne Lake Regional Park *(map p. 177)*

Another recent regional acquisition, this 270-hectare lakefront property adjacent to the provincial park has a campground and boat ramp for access to Horne Lake. Motorized boats are allowed on the lake, making it popular for waterskiing.

⚠ CAMPING: Three distinct campgrounds are located within the park, which is divided by the Qualicum River. The north portion, Northpark, contains a boat ramp, a picnic area and a designated swimming area. The southern two campsites, Paradise Bay and Twin Pines, are reached by driving through the provincial park.

ACCESS: From the Island Highway north of Qualicum Beach follow Horne Lake Road to the provincial park. Take the left at the provincial park and drive through for the second portion of the regional park.

MAJOR PARKS

⑥ Little Qualicum Falls
Provincial Park *(map p. 177)*

This is a gorgeous park set along the waterfalls and canyons of Little Qualicum River and along Cameron Lake at a day-use beach.

QUALICUM

Little Qualicum Falls Provincial Park.

PICNIC AREAS AND DAY USE: The main park has a day-use area with covered picnic shelters at the trail entrances to the lower falls. Swimming has been curtailed within the falls area after two fatalities. A log dam was blasted, which changed the river flow and made the former swimming area unsafe. Swimming along the river within the park is now restricted to a small area at the west end near the campground; see the park kiosk for current information. Lake swimming is always possible in the day-use area at the east end of Cameron Lake. A third day-use area, Beaufort, is slightly farther inland along Highway 4 on the south of the lake. It has two picnic tables, a pit toilet and a small parking area. Windsurfing, waterskiing and paddling are possible on the lake, which is quite scenic thanks to the surrounding mountain bluffs.

FISHING: Cameron Lake and Little Qualicum River are home to brown trout, cutthroat trout, steelhead and rainbow trout.

CAMPING: The park has two distinct campsites—the upper and lower camping areas, all off the main park entrance to the falls; turn left just past the railroad tracks once off Highway 4. Reservations are accepted at most of the 94 sites; a few are available on a first-come, first-served basis. One campsite is specifically wheelchair accessible. The upper site has an adventure playground. This is a great family camping area.

SHORT WALKS: The park has 6 km of trails, most of which meander alongside the falls and gorge, with numerous stunning viewpoints along the way. Several bridges offer a chance to shorten or lengthen the walk. Expect some stairs and a few rocky sections.

THUMBS UP: I've always considered this park one of the most scenic short walks in the region.

ACCESS: The park is just off Highway 4, 9.4 km west of the intersection at Highway 19. The Cameron Lake beach is another 4 km past the campsite turnoff, while Beaufort beach area is another 2 km past the Cameron Lake turnoff.

⑦ MacMillan (Cathedral Grove) Provincial Park *(map p. 177)*

Cathedral Grove is the name for a wonderful old-growth Douglas-fir and western red cedar forest in a small waterside valley near Cameron Lake. A selection of short trails crosses the area, giving access to towering trees believed to be 800 years old (most are 300 to 400 years old) and with circumferences as wide as 9 m. This is the most accessible old-growth forest on Vancouver Island: Highway 4 literally passes through the grove. For this reason it sees about 300,000 visitors a year.

ACCESS: Parking has long been located directly off Highway 4, but congestion and poor visibility prompted the province to plan a new parking lot. Since making it involved cutting into the old-growth forest, environmentalists fought the plan, some camping in trees over a two-year period to halt the construction. The parking lot was eventually scuttled, and new traffic devices are meant to make the area safer by using the existing roadside parking spots.

TRAVEL NOTES: Recent logging of the adjacent old-growth forest has added to the park's susceptibility to blowdown, and the windstorm of 2006 made much of the park inaccessible. The grove is magnificent, though the trampled undergrowth and controlled trails do alter the nature of this old-growth forest; while it's a good example of such a forest, it's not a pristine one.

⑧ Spider Lake Provincial Park (map p. 177)

This small (65-hectare) park protects the south side of Spider Lake, which is noted for its warm water. The small beach at the main park entrance makes it an ideal day-use area. Paddling the convoluted shoreline is possible, but motorboats are prohibited.

🏕 PICNIC AREAS AND DAY USE: The park has two day-use locations. The main area has 16 tables, water, toilets and a beach. It is closed off-season. The smaller day-use area is open year-round. It has two picnic tables and a small parking area. It is better suited for launching small boats.

🎣 FISHING: Spider Lake is home to smallmouth bass and rainbow trout.

ACCESS: Take the Horne Lake Road exit from the Island Highway, then almost immediately take Spider Lake Road south 3.3 km to Lakeview Road. The small day-use area is located just off Lakeview Road. The main park entrance is slightly west.

⑨ Horne Lake Caves Provincial Park (map p. 177)

Cave lovers and the curious will find reason to enjoy Horne Lake Caves Provincial Park, easily the most accessible caves on Vancouver Island. Two large caves are open to the public. Over the years visitors have destroyed notable features, prompting BC Parks to close the largest two caves (Riverbend and Euclataws) and provide access to Riverbend by guided tour only. A family-style 90-minute tour of Riverbend offered during the summer provides a good look at some unusual features within the cave, while a more extreme half-day tour includes rappelling down the seven-storey Rainbarrel to China Shop, the lowest point in the cave. For tour information call 250-248-7829.

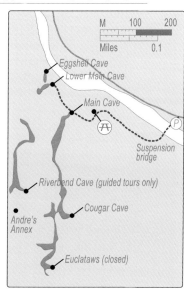

Euclataws Cave has been closed because even experienced climbers could not enter and leave the cave without adversely affecting the fantastic variety of speleothems (cave formations). Features include the Sidewalk, a high concentration of speleothems and chambers called the Dome Room, Stage II, the Attic and the Dining Room. These are filled with translucent soda straw and flowstone draperies referred to as "bacon strips." It ends with impassable connections to the main cave.

Visitors to the two main open caves will find ledges, a waterfall cavern, underwater rivers and numerous side passages. Be sure to bring a backup light source and dress warmly. Portions can be wet and slippery.

Other caves exist but have fewer features of interest to visitors. Andre's Annex is 100 m south of Riverbend Cave on a limestone terrace. It has a number of hazards, such as loose rock and tight passages, that make it unsuitable for visits. Cougar Cave, found on the way to the Riverbend Cave entrance, features a small entrance and a steep drop to two small chambers without features. Eggshell Cave, about 50 m past the Lower Main Cave, is the smallest, at 18 m in length, featuring a narrow and steep opening leading to a chamber not tall enough to stand up in.

SHORT WALKS: A short trail leads from the parking lot over a suspension bridge to the tour operator's cabin and an information kiosk. From there a trail winds its way 1.3 km to the two open caves.

ROCK CLIMBING: The limestone cliffs at Horne Lake have gained a reputation as one of Canada's top climbing destinations. Unfortunately the access is through private property and has been closed in recent years; pay attention to signs for current access restrictions. The climbs are a short hike from a parking area just past the distinctive roadside cliff near the park entrance. Handbooks describing the climbs are available at outdoor retailers in the area.

TRAVEL NOTES: In the Main Cave, just after the narrow entrance, is a ledge. If you climb up to the right there is a narrow side passage that leads to the main shelf. It is easily missed, but a worthwhile diversion for children who will appreciate the adventure of finding an alternate route. A few other smaller openings can be found at the back end of the cave. In all it makes a good family adventure—for those who don't mind the occasional tight squeeze.

ACCESS: The park is easily reached from the Island Highway at the Horne Lake Road turn-off north of Qualicum Beach.

⑩ Bowser Ecological Reserve *(map p. 160)*

Bowser is a little community along the Strait of Georgia between Qualicum Beach and Courtenay. The 116-hectare Bowser Ecological Reserve was created in 1996 to protect a productive forest and wetland. The most obvious feature of the reserve is a Douglas-fir forest that has thrived since a fire 100 years ago and grown to a huge size, with the potential to become record-sized trees in time. Rare residents are some dragonfly species that are only found in peatland marshes, which form some of the swamps and ponds found in the reserve. The park is open to low-impact use.

⑪ Rosewall Creek Provincial Park *(map p. 160)*

This small (54-hectare) park along Rosewall Creek south of Fanny Bay is a day-use park with picnic areas on each side of the creek. The site opposite the parking lot has a small beach that may be of interest to families with children. A wheelchair accessible loop runs along both sides of the creek, though portions have eroded and are now closed on a seemingly permanent basis. A longer trail leads along the north side of the creek under various bridges to a small beach area and a waterfall viewpoint.

ACCESS: From Highway 19A north of Qualicum take Berray Road east to the park entrance.

FOREST RECREATION SITES

See the map on page 161 to locate this recreation site.

Ⓐ Labour Day Lake

This recreation area is tucked under the cover of Mount Moriarty (1,616 m). It features clear areas suitable for camping and a trail around the lake through some mature forest reached by a short trail from a logging road. The bluffs of Mount Moriarty are accessible from here, but don't expect a formal trail to the meadow ridges. Experienced backcountry hikers should have no difficulty reaching the bluffs through the clear forest slopes.

ACCESS: Take Cameron Main to near the end, about 13.3 km past the Pass Main junction at about 930 m elevation. At this point the road will take a sharp left uphill, then end in about 300 m. Don't drive up the final leg! The TRAILHEAD ● is at the corner of the sharp turn next to a culvert and small creek. A wide area for parking is nearby. Note the Cameron Main deteriorates over its course to the point where it's questionable for two-wheel drive. Expect logging in the area.

Alberni Valley

Three major lakes dominate the land here: Great Central Lake, Sproat Lake and Nahmint Lake. Sproat Lake is a recreational playground for boaters, fishermen and cottagers, with most development on the east end and some limited housing on the northwest end. Great Central Lake and Nahmint Lake are both worlds away, however, in areas made remote due to limited access.

POINTS OF INTEREST

🔞 Port Alberni *(map p. 160)*

Port Alberni, a mill town with a population of about 12,000, is situated deep in the heart of Vancouver Island with the advantage of a deep-sea port thanks to Alberni Inlet, which twists northward from Barkley Sound on the west coast. Port Alberni is a waypoint on trips to Tofino, Ucluelet and more than likely Bamfield, plus a gateway for journeys to Sproat Lake, Nahmint, Great Central Lake and the surrounding region. Much of the city's commercial activity is centred along Highway 4, with a vibrant area around Harbour Quay, off Kingsway and Third Avenue. Visitors should have no trouble finding the tourist information centre off Highway 4 at the east entrance to the city. The following are a few key attractions.

- HARBOUR QUAY: This waterfront area is the heart of the city, with a marina, shops, galleries, restaurants, cafés and the clock tower, which allows a view of the surrounding area. Despite the emerging tourist sheen, it's also a working harbour and offers a chance to see a fishing fleet, deep-sea vessels and the logging industry at work.

- MARITIME DISCOVERY CENTRE: The history of the sea is brought to life in this landmark lighthouse refurbished as a museum. The centre is located just south of Harbour Quay; turn onto Harbour Road just before Harbour Quay.

- MV *LADY ROSE*: First launched in 1937, the *Lady Rose* has been a fixture on the BC coast for 70 years now, first with the Union Steamship Company, now as a private cargo, mail and passenger ship servicing Alberni Inlet and Barkley Sound. It's a unique way to see the area, either as a day trip or by staying overnight at Sechart Lodge on the edge of the Broken Group. Visit **www.ladyrosemarine.com**.

- ALBERNI PACIFIC RAILWAY: The railway features a restored 1929 Baldwin steam locomotive that runs between the McLean Mill National Historic Site and Port Alberni in a 70-minute round trip.

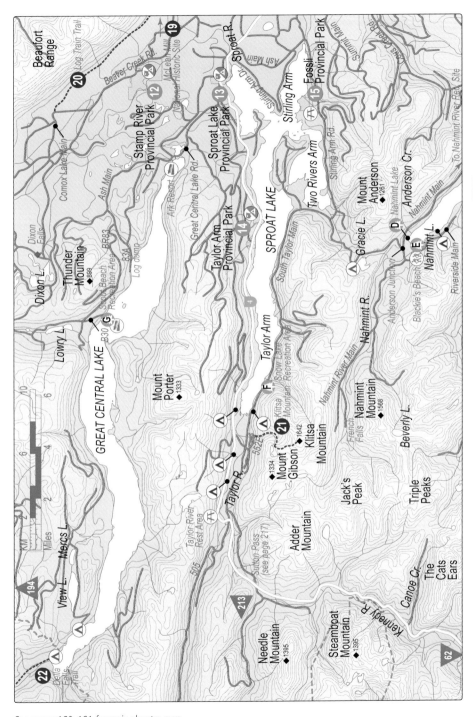

Beaufort Range

Log Train Trail

(20) (19)

Beaver Creek Rd.

McLean Mill National Historic Site

(24)

(12)

Ash Main

Sproat R.

Stamp River Provincial Park

(13)

(74)

Sproat Lake Provincial Park

Stirling Arm

Fossli Provincial Park

(15)

Summit Main

Tofino Creek Rd.

Comox Lake Main

Ash Main

BR83

Air Resort

Great Central Lake Rd.

Log dump

Two Rivers Arm

Stirling Arm Rd.

Anderson Lake

To Nahmint River Rec. Site

Dixon Falls

Taylor Arm Provincial Park

(14)

SPROAT LAKE

South Taylor Main

Gracie L.

Mount Anderson
♦1261

Anderson Cr.

Nahmint Main

ALBERNI VALLEY

Dixon L.

Thunder Mountain
♦899

South Beach Recreation Area

B30 G

Lowry L.

GREAT CENTRAL LAKE

Taylor Arm

Mount Porter
♦1333

Taylor R.

505

552E

Snow Lake Mountain Recreation Area

(A)

(A)

Klitsa Mountain

(21) 1642

Klitsa Mountain

Nahmint River Main

Nahmint R.

Blackie's Beach

(D)

(E)

(A)

Nahmint L.

Riverside Main

Nahmint Mountain
♦1568

Beverly L.

View L.

Mercs L.

(194)

10

6

KM

Miles

6

4

2

1334

(A) Mount Gibson
♦

Jack's Peak

Triple Peaks

French Falls

Canoe Cr.

Taylor River Rest Area

(A)

Sutton Pass
(see page 217)

(213)

Adder Mountain

Needle Mountain
♦1395

Steamboat Mountain
♦1395

Kennedy R.

The Cats Ears

(62)

Bella Falls Trail

(22)

See pages 160–161 for main chapter map.

⑲ McLean Mill National Historic Site *(map p. 187)*

This 1926 steam mill has been restored as a working example of British Columbia's forestry heritage. It offers a look at each step of the milling process as done by an original steam engine through demonstrations, a stage show and guided tours. A restored logging camp is among the 30 historic buildings dotting the 13-hectare property.

ACCESS: From Port Alberni take Beaver Creek Road north to Smith Road, then turn east, following the signs.

⑳ Log Train Trail *(map p. 187)*

This trail running 25 km along the base of the Beaufort Range is suitable for horse, bike or foot. It begins at the information centre at the east entrance to Port Alberni and runs northwest to the outskirts of Strathcona Park past Stamp Falls. The north TRAILHEAD ● is reached via Beaver Creek Road, which becomes Somers Road at the north end. At the end of Somers Road turn right (east). The north trailhead is marked with a small sign and is gated. The trail runs along the base of the Beaufort Range, under the cover of mounts Irwin, Hall and Joan (south to north). While partially logged, the range has good hiking potential, with a SIDE TRAIL ● leaving the Log Train Trail up Mount Hal at Hal Creek at about the mid-point of the trail. The turnoff is marked.

㉑ Klitsa Mountain *(map p. 187)*

This mountain, a more remote and slightly less tall cousin to Mount Arrowsmith (often incorrectly referred to as Mount Klitsa), is a major peak in isolation south of Sproat Lake and a landmark for much of the region. The trail begins at a low elevation, making it a demanding ascent with an elevation gain of 1.6 km. Making it more challenging is the deterioration of the access from South Taylor Main. The old spur leading to the trailhead, 552E, is on its last legs, having suffered several major landslides and overgrowth. Expect to bushwhack and clamber over the landslide gulleys. Once at the trailhead at the end of the logging spur, the trail skirts along a creek to a small lake—just one in a series to be found along the creek—then ascends to the peak.

Ⓐ CAMPING: The west end of Sproat Lake and Taylor River near the highway abound with good casual river or lakeside sites. The most formal CAMPSITE ● is on the northwest corner of the lake down a short access road. Here you can find some sites in the forest, but most are RV-style along the waterfront. This and the launch tend to be busy. A small CAMPSITE ● on the east end of Taylor River is at the end of a short access road with a level area at the roundabout alongside the river, just west of the old Taylor River bridge (which makes a good fishing location). A similar CAMPSITE ● setup is located about 2 km west. The general locations are marked on the map on page 187.

ALBERNI VALLEY

ACCESS: Near the Taylor River rest stop on Highway 4, take the South Taylor Main east for about 4.6 km to an old logging spur that heads south up a hill. Follow this (by foot; it's too rutted now for even 4 × 4s) for about a kilometre to an old SPUR—552E ●. It is not signed, but it should be marked, at least by flagging tape. Alder is encroaching. From there it is about 2.5 km to the creek and the trailhead.

㉒ Della Falls Trail (map p. 187)

Here's a little-known fact: the tallest waterfall in Canada is deep in the heart of Vancouver Island. It's DELLA FALLS ●, set within the southern end of Strathcona Provincial Park but not accessible from the main park entrance at Buttle Lake—well, not accessible without a major undertaking, anyway. The TRAILHEAD ● begins at the north end of Great Central Lake, making the trip a perfect (and rare) opportunity to combine a paddling and hiking adventure. Water taxis are available from Ark Resort at the east end of the lake; a public

launch is also available at the Scout Beach Recreation Site. A campsite is located at the trailhead, but is prone to mosquitoes. Instead consider the lakefront camping area at the point just to the south. The 12 km trail roughly follows Drinkwater Creek, crossing it several times at bridges that may be in disrepair. A main campsite is located near the falls; note that in late summer it can still be snowed in, depending on the amount of snow over the past winter. Keep an eye open for the sawmill ruins along the way. Many vestiges exist, including an old pile of nails fused together by time.

Della Falls.

 THUMBS UP: This is one of the best trails on the island, combining scenic paddling, challenging hiking and mountain and waterfall views. The hiking portion could be done as a day-trip by hardy hikers, but it's best as an overnight trip, or better yet, a three-day trip to fully enjoy the falls and the area. I completed the trail in late August in 1997 after unusually high winter snowfall. Though it was late in summer, the outhouse at the main campsite was still covered; all we could see was the roof. A route supposedly exists to link the Della Falls Trail with the Bedwell Lake area trails, but it is essentially non-existent. A way across is over Mount Septimus, a route called "difficult" by an experienced mountaineer.

MAJOR PARKS

⑫ Stamp River Provincial Park (map p. 187)

This park north of Port Alberni protects a picturesque canyon and waterfall along the Stamp River—one of the most scenic areas in the region.

🍴 PICNIC AREAS AND DAY USE: A picnic area next to the campground is located alongside the river, with picnic tables and pit toilets.

🐟 FISHING: The park is home to one of the richest populations of summer steelhead on Vancouver Island, with spawning, holding and rearing habitat. Chinook salmon, coho salmon, rainbow trout, winter steelhead, cutthroat trout and sockeye salmon populate the river. A fish ladder at the waterfall is an excellent area for watching the salmon runs.

🚶 SHORT WALKS: A trail leads along the riverside 0.5 km to the fish ladder. The trail then continues for a 2 km loop.

🏕 CAMPING: The park has 23 campsites that can be reserved, plus a few first-come, first-served sites.

ACCESS: The park entrance is off Beaver Creek Road, 14 km from Highway 14 with the turnoff west of Port Alberni.

⑬ Sproat Lake Provincial Park (map p. 187)

Sproat Lake has long been a favourite recreation area for the Port Alberni region, popular for fishing, boating, waterskiing and windsurfing. An attraction within the park is a set of petroglyphs named K'ak'awin at the east end of the park. A small pier allows a view of the waterfront petroglyphs.

ALBERNI VALLEY

- PICNIC AREAS AND DAY USE: Three picnic sites are located adjacent to the lower campground, complete with campfire rings, a large grass area, showers and a boat launch.

- SHORT WALKS: A trail leads under Highway 4 to join the upper and lower campgrounds. Another short (0.5 km) trail leads from the day-use parking lot to the petroglyphs.

- CAMPING: Sproat Lake has 58 campsites that can be reserved plus a few first-come, first-served sites in two areas: an upper site away from the lake and a smaller, more congested campground near the lake.

ACCESS: The park is on the north end of Sproat Lake off Highway 4, about 13 km west of Port Alberni. The lakeside portion is directly off Highway 4. The upper campground is off Great Central Lake Road. Both are well signed.

⑭ Taylor Arm Provincial Park *(map p. 187)*

This park is split into two parcels a half-kilometre apart on the north shore of Sproat Lake's west arm. The west portion is a day-use area, while the east portion is a group camping area.

- PICNIC AREAS AND DAY USE: Day-use areas are on the lakefront with facilities limited to pit toilets. Access from the group campsite parking lot is along a trail under Highway 4 to the lake.

- CAMPING: Group camping only is accommodated. Three group campsites are located on the east portion of the park north of Highway 4.

ACCESS: The park is 23 km from Port Alberni along Highway 4.

⑮ Fossli Provincial Park *(map p. 187)*

This is an undeveloped park on the south side of Sproat Lake along Stirling Arm. A 30-minute trail leads through a forest to an old homestead site and pebble beach on Sproat Lake. There you'll find a grassy area, picnic tables and a pit toilet.

ACCESS: Here is the official BC Parks website direction information: "From Port Alberni, take Highway 4 west and after 6.5 km turn south on McCoy Lake Road. After 3 km turn west onto Stirling Arm Road and continue for 0.9 km to the Stirling Arm Mainline junction. Turn right and travel 4 km to a second bridge where a pullout at the bridge entrance serves as a parking lot. Follow the old logging road to the trailhead." Now, I've tried every bridge, possible pullout and open logging road (one had no access allowed) in that area and could find nothing more than a bit of flagging tape and something that may have been a trail for about 5 m. Obviously, this park is much easier to visit by boat. Or maybe you'll have better luck with the BC Parks directions.

Bill Motyka Recreation Site ● and Macktush Creek Campground (map p. 160)

This is a large RV-style recreation area; most sites are in a grassy field. A good beach overlooks Alberni Inlet on the south end of the site. It is a popular staging area for fishing trips, as Macktush Creek supports steelhead, coho, chum and cutthroat. The recreation site also provides access to Alberni Inlet.

ACCESS: From Highway 4 immediately west of Port Alberni take McCoy Lake Road southwest. Turn at the landfill direction sign. Once at the landfill continue south on the Macktush Main to the recreation site.

Ⓒ Nahmint River (map p. 160)

A short trail was developed by MacMillan Bloedel to demonstrate the growth and form of coastal conifers. The trail follows an old logging road nicely overgrown with moss but also, unfortunately, covered by blowdown. Not maintained, the trail quickly dies out, with the weather-beaten interpretive billboards at the trail entrance the most enduring feature.

Ⓓ Nahmint Lake (map p. 187)

Nahmint Lake is a pretty lake surrounded by rolling hills and the occasional bluff. It's a good fishing lake, made accessible by the recreation site on the lake's northeast corner. Nahmint Main skirts the lake's east side, providing a number of good viewpoints, particularly at Grizzly Pass on the south end at the high point between the lake and Alberni Inlet. Pockets of old-growth forest and numerous waterfalls add to the appeal of a lakeside drive. Good viewpoints of a small river canyon can also be found at the bridge crossing of the Nahmint River, known for its many potential swimming pools. Once on the lake, grit and/or gravel pocket beaches dot the shoreline. The best beaches are at the two recreation sites on the north end of the lake and at a good gravel beach slightly south on the west shore. Paddlers may also find rock bluffs suitable for camping. Note that drift logs clog most beaches. Boat access is via a short walk from the recreation site to the beach, making it suitable for cartop boats only. The lake is restricted to 9.9 hp motors maximum. This can be a busy area in season.

FISHING: Nahmint Lake is a popular fishing area, with steelhead found in deep water near the mouth of Nahmint River.

ALBERNI VALLEY

△ CAMPING: A few vehicle-accessible sites can be found within the main recreation site. More walk-in sites are spread along a trail closer to the beach. The number of options was reduced in 2007 by blowdown. There are numerous small clearings on the gravel beach toward Anderson Creek. Boat-in camping is available at Blackie's Beach (see below), and there are several pocket beaches along the lakeshore. The best one is about 1 km south of Blackie's Beach, where a cabin is set back from the lakefront.

ACCESS: The Nahmint Lake recreation site is reached from the Nahmint Main just south of Anderson Junction. A rough, narrow road twists from Nahmint Main to the CAMPING AREA ●.

Ⓔ Nahmint Lake North (Blackie's Beach) *(map p. 187)*

Located on the north end of Nahmint Lake on the southwest side of Nahmint River, this site is adjacent to the Nahmint Lake Recreation Site across the river but is accessible only by foot or boat. As such it makes a good base for boaters exploring the area. A trail leads from the south bank of Nahmint River at the confluence of the lake and river. The river mouth area is a good place to view elk.

ACCESS: A trail leads to the recreation area from Riverside Main. It is off the Nahmint Main south of Sproat Lake. Note the Riverside Main was blocked by blowdown, so walk-in access will be more difficult until the route is cleared.

Ⓕ Snow Lake ● *(map p. 187)*

This site is on the south end of Sproat Lake's Taylor Arm at the mouth of Snow Creek. Access is by the South Taylor Main, only about 10 km east of the Taylor River rest stop, though it's a rough portion of logging road. The site suffered substantial blowdown damage in the winter 2006 storms, and it may be some time before the campsites are completely restored. Expect a handful of sites and a launch at the end of the access road.

Ⓖ Scout Beach ● *(map p. 187)*

This is a managed recreation site popular as a staging area for water-based explorations or fishing trips into Great Central Lake. Sites are spread through a mature forest, with an open gravel beach area suitable for boat launching.

Morning on Great Central Lake.

ACCESS: Take Central Lake Road north from Highway 4. At Ark Resort take Ash Main north, then Branch 83 west, then B30 south to Scout Beach.

ALBERNI VALLEY

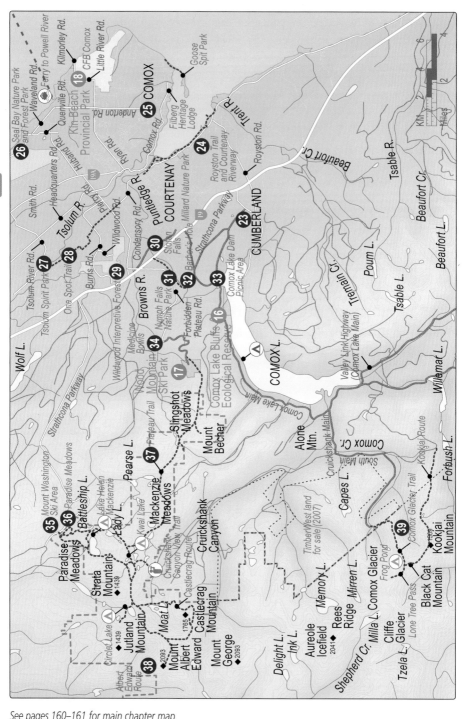

See pages 160–161 for main chapter map.

Comox–Forbidden Plateau

Central Vancouver Island is home to two communities lying side by side (Courtenay and Comox), sandwiched between impressive mountains and the Strait of Georgia, making it a desirable base for a variety of outdoor activities. In fact, it's one of the few locations where you might be able to ski in the morning and kayak in the afternoon. The Courtenay-Comox area is a gateway to numerous attractions, including Strathcona Park's Forbidden Plateau and several incredible features along the Puntledge and Tsolum rivers—probably the best range of river recreation opportunities on Vancouver Island. Outdoor lovers who live in this area are very lucky people.

Comox Lake from near the Cruikshank Main.

POINTS OF INTEREST

㉓ Cumberland *(map p. 194)*

In this small community near Comox Lake, much of the older commercial and residential areas reflect the century of coal mining history in the region.

Ⓐ CAMPING: The community-run Cumberland Lake Campground is located 3 km outside of Cumberland on Comox Lake, offering a large day-use area with a good swimming beach. The campground has 50 sites, electrical hookups and showers. A boat launch is located at the campground entrance. Follow Dunsmuir Road to the west end as it turns into Comox Lake Road, following it to the campsite.

Comox Lake from the Cumberland Lake Campground.

MOUNTAIN BIKING: The community forest to the south of the townsite allows public access to a wide range of trail options that will be popular for hikers and horses, but mountain bikers will get the greatest benefit out of the area. Extensive trails through the area follow the numerous logging roads, with some good cross-country and downhill trails. Good starting points are the BMX trails off Royston Road, the south end of Egremont Road near the downtown or Chinatown Heritage Park off Comox Lake Road. Trail maps are available at the visitor information centre or the local bike shop. Both are on Dunsmuir Road, Cumberland's main street.

- CHINATOWN HERITAGE PARK: History buffs will enjoy this interpretive walk through the former townsite of the Chinese district of Union, the name of Cumberland in its coal mining days back in the 1880s. The park is off Comox Lake Road on the way to Cumberland Lake Campground (see above). This is a good walk in conjunction with the Cumberland Museum on Dunsmuir Road, which features a coal mining exhibit.

㉔ Royston Trail and Courtenay Riverway *(map p. 194)*

The Royston Trail skirts the south shoreline of Comox Harbour, with beach access and a picnic area at the end of Royston Road off Highway 19A. An interesting feature of the shore is the old logging industry pier built with a breakwater of so-called ghost ships, the remains of which are rusting away to the last vestiges. The Royston Trail is part of a larger greenbelt along the harbour that extends to the Courtenay River, a trail popular with cyclists and rollerbladers. At the midpoint is the Millard Nature Park, a 34-hectare reserve with trails through a mature forest and alongside Millard Creek. Good access to the reserve is off Highway 19A at Fraser Road.

A ghost ship at Royston.

㉕ Courtenay-Comox *(map p. 194)*

These largely residential twin communities surround Comox Harbour and spread into the adjacent valleys. CFB Comox, an air force base, is a defining feature of Comox, and military jets on maneuvers can often be seen and heard in the area (a good family visit is the Comox Air Force Museum). These are full-service communities with most commercial business located along or near Highway 19A.

ⓘ **www.comox-valley-tourism.ca**. The Comox Air Force Museum website is **www.comoxairforcemuseum.ca/Home.html**.

- FILBERG HERITAGE LODGE: This property on the north shore of Comox Harbour, an operating lodge since 1929, is now a facility run by a non-profit company as a quasi-municipal park. Trails meander through the grounds and the lodge is now a waterfront tea house. A herb garden on the nearby slope is maintained by the Comox Valley Horticultural Society, offering a chance to see a wide array of unusual plants. In the upper meadow is an animal farm open to the public during the summer for a small fee. An annual event is the Filberg Festival, one of Vancouver Island's premier music festivals. From Highway 19A in Comox follow Comox Road east to Filberg Road. Visit **www.filberg.com**.

- GOOSE SPIT PARK: Comox Harbour dries extensively, with sandbars extending toward Denman Island; one permanent sandbar at the mouth of the harbour is Goose Spit. A good portion is protected as a regional park (the far end is a Comox First Nation reserve). You'll find minimal facilities at the park—just outhouses and picnic tables—but the sandy beach is extensive, continuing well under the steep bluff north of the spit. From Highway 19A in Comox, take Comox Road, then turn north onto Pritchard Road. Turn east again at the next major intersection on Balmoral Avenue. Continue straight as it turns into Hawkins Road, which winds its way down to the spit.

㉖ Seal Bay Nature Park and Seal Bay Forest Park *(map p. 194)*

Two parks are set side by side adjacent to Seal Bay, a waterfront area north of Comox. Bates Road divides the two park portions. The waterfront parcel is 375-hectare Seal Bay Nature Park, with a beach area, a Garry oak glade and some wonderfully groomed trails through a pretty forest, including a wheelchair-accessible loop. Seal Bay Forest Park, a 1,391-hectare forest reserve, was added in 1991. It contains several alder and hardhack marshes. Trails cross the entire park; an outer loop is usable by horses and bikes.

ACCESS: The MAIN ENTRANCE ● is off Bates Road, where a large parking area provides access to the trails. From Highway 19A north of Comox take Coleman Road east; it turns into Bates Road.

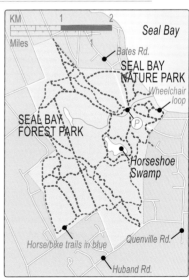

27 Tsolum Spirit Park *(map p. 194)*

This small (7-hectare) park makes use of a former railway right-of-way to give access to a flood plain of the Tsolum River. A short trail leads through the forest area adjacent to the river.

ACCESS: From Highway 19A just north of the bridge over the Courtenay River, take Headquarters Road north to Tsolum River Road to the park ENTRANCE ●.

28 One Spot Trail *(map p. 194)*

This 8 km gravel and dirt trail follows an old Comox Logging and Railway Company right-of-way. The name is a tip of the hat to the first locomotive on the route, the One Spot, a 1909 wood-burning Baldwin engine. It worked the route for 34 years, and the track was removed in 1954. The trail was built in 2005 primarily as a horseback trail, though it can be walked or cycled.

ACCESS: The TRAIL ● begins 0.25 km north of the end of Condensory Road on Bagley Road. There is no parking provided. Condensory Road is off Piercy Road.

29 Wildwood Interpretive Forest *(map p. 194)*

First a provincial interpretive forest, it was handed over to the regional district as a park in 2002. Logging roads and trails cross the 276-hectare property, linking Piercy and Burns roads using an old railway grade, logging roads and trails. Adjacent is the Wildwood Marsh, a 2004 regional park around a marsh, home to swans, ducks and beaver. In the plans is a link to the One Spot Trail.

ACCESS: The simplest access is off Piercy Road. Drive just east of the Forbidden Plateau Road turnoff and watch for a small ENTRANCE ● to the left. Parking is limited. From there the trails are 1 km to the Wildwood Road exit and 3 km to the Burns Road exit.

Listen for the sirens!

The Puntledge River is on a hydroelectric spillway. The release of water from the dam can result in a rapid change in water level. The release is always preceded by a siren. If you are along the Puntledge River and you hear the siren, leave the waterside.

---

30 Stotan Falls *(map p. 194)*

Locals may refer to it as Stokum Falls, but either way it is a scenic marvel. The Puntledge River runs over a broad rock shelf, carving a multitude of potholes of varying size before reaching this wonderful waterfall. Some potholes are large enough to sit in for a very unusual soak. The river is shallow here as it rushes over the broad rock base. The area is a great day-use water hole, with most visitors congregating near the falls and walking from the logging road access along the river. For something different, poke your head behind the waterfall—you should find a shelf suitable for sitting underneath the waterfall.

ACCESS: From the Island Highway take the Piercy Road exit east, then Forbidden Plateau Road south. Just before the road crosses back over the Island Highway take the logging road south to the Puntledge River bridge. PARKING ● is

Stotan Falls.

alongside the bridge. A trail leads down the south shore, but the best river access is actually walking along the river.

③ **Nymph Falls Nature Park** (map p. 194)

This 53-hectare park on the Puntledge River protects Nymph Falls and part of a biking and hiking trail system that runs the length of the river. Watch for the salmon October and November.

WHITEWATER PADDLING: The Puntledge River offers one of the best whitewater kayaking routes on Vancouver Island, if not Canada. The reason: since 2002 BC Hydro has been timing the release of water from the Puntledge River dam to suit kayakers, meaning kayakers have advance notice of when conditions will be best. And when they are good, they are great. The shale bedrock of the river creates a series of pools,

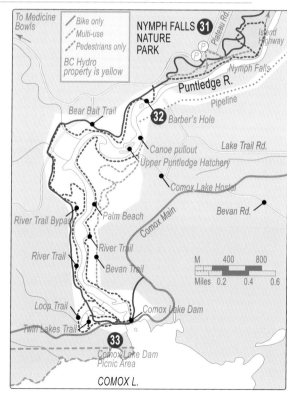

standing waves and holes with the unusual benefit that it is possible to circle back to many of these features—particularly the standing waves—to enjoy them again.

Nymph Falls.

 HIKING AND CYCLING: A system of designated trails runs the length of the park. Red-marked trails are for bikes only; green trails—those along the waterline and the two loop trails—are pedestrian only. The two biking trails on the north end of the park—The Bender and Cog the Log—are for expert bikers only. Other trails extend past the park to the Island Highway and to the Comox Dam Picnic Area.

ACCESS: A PARKING LOT ● is off Forbidden Plateau Road.

32 Barber's Hole (map p. 194)

Just southwest of Nymph Falls Nature Park is a popular spot known as the Barber's Hole. On one side is a high cliff; on the other is a sloping floor of perfectly white clay. Limited space on the rock shelf at the waterline tends to fill quickly with sunseekers during the summer. A popular swinging rope has been removed and the upper rock face fenced to discourage jumping. The hole can be reached from the Nymph Falls Trail or a roadside trailhead off Forbidden Plateau Road just east of the Nymph Falls Regional Park parking lot.

33 Comox Lake Dam Picnic Area (map p. 194)

A pleasant grassy picnic site is located at the west end of Comox Lake and the dam at the head of the Puntledge River. It is also one end of a network of trails along the Puntledge River that connect with Nymph Falls Nature Park on the northwest side of the river, courtesy of BC Hydro, which has opened up its dam lands for recreational use. By crossing the dam you connect with the trails on the river's southeast side for a choice of bike trails, hiking trails and multi-use trails.

PADDLING: It's possible to paddle the Puntledge between the Comox Lake Dam and the Diversion Dam, a distance of about 3.7 km. A pullout is located on the south side of Diversion Dam.

ⓘ www.bchydro.com/recreation/island/island1215.html.

34 Medicine Bowls (map p. 194)

Named for the mythical healing power of the water here, the Medicine Bowls are in a water-carved canyon of the Browns River, where waterfalls drop from

Tiers of pools make up the Medicine Bowls.

pool to pool. A few are suitable for swimming (most near the upper portion). Caution is strongly advised, however, as the area has a history of fatalities, with strong undercurrents, slippery rocks and steep access areas. Duly cautioned, however, the bowls are a stunning area well worth the visit.

ACCESS: Take Forbidden Plateau Road west until just before the pavement ends, 3.5 km past Nymph Falls Regional Park. A decommissioned logging road leads north, deteriorating to wet potholes before ending in a loop. The TRAILHEAD ● is marked by a cairn for two teenagers who drowned here on the same day.

35 Mount Washington Ski Area (map p. 194)

This alpine resort is one of the major recreation areas for Vancouver Island, hosting an array of both summer and winter activities. The winter mainstays are skiing and snowboarding on the resort's 60 runs and 6 chairlifts capable of transporting 12,200 people an hour. Supporting the skiing is a range of accommodations, restaurants, pubs, stores and equipment rentals. The ski hills will appeal to all levels of skill, with some good novice runs, lessons and, for veterans, a whole new selection of black diamond runs on the mountain's east face overlooking the Strait of Georgia. For families there's tobogganing and snow tubing. Accommodation is available either through the resort and its lodges or through private condo and chalet rentals. Most services can be booked online.

Through an arrangement with BC Parks, the resort also grooms cross-country ski trails

The sun almost breaks through over the Mount Washington cross-country ski trails.

into Strathcona Park's Forbidden Plateau area. Backcountry enthusiasts can pay to use the groomed trails for skiing or snowshoeing or simply head off into the Forbidden Plateau area by snowshoe. Overnight camping is possible; parking is at the cross-country skiing area's parking lot. Register at the cross-country skiing lodge and park in the special overnight area.

Mount Washington is also a summer destination offering a scenic chairlift run to the peak for panoramic views over southern BC. Once at the peak you can walk short trails or walk down (walking up is an option as well, of course). Mountain biking is possible, with trails, clinics and races throughout the summer.

TRAVEL NOTES: Snowplows are put to good use on the road to Mount Washington, clearing an average 9 m of snow each year. Some years have more than others, though, and in 1996 I remember driving up the Strathcona Parkway through what seemed to be a snow tunnel, with probably about 10 m of snow at the roadsides. A favourite winter activity is snowshoeing. It's hard work, but it's a good way to break into an undisturbed winter wonderland. As temperatures usually hover near freezing, the cold isn't necessarily hard to deal with. The worst worry is sweating (snowshoeing is hard work), then having the sweat cool when you stop, causing chills. This makes it important to wear layers and plan a lower layer that wicks moisture away from the body.

ⓘ www.mountwashington.ca.

㊱ Paradise Meadows (Forbidden Plateau) *(map p. 194)*

Paradise Meadows is remarkable for being one of the few areas on Vancouver Island where it is possible to reach an alpine area by paved road, making for an excellent opportunity to enjoy a high-altitude environment with a minimum amount of work. The Strathcona Parkway ascends to the 1,100 m level, allowing either a simple walk through alpine meadows, bogs and forest or a chance to go deeper into Strathcona Provincial Park to some of its tallest peaks, particularly Mount Albert Edward, one of the simplest tall-peak ascents on Vancouver Island. During winter the plateau is regulated through the Mount Washington Alpine Resort (see above).

㊙ SHORT WALKS: A system of loop trails extends from the park entrance. A simple trail is the Paradise Meadows Loop Trail, a 2.3 km boardwalk loop through some boggy alpine meadows. A slightly longer option is the Helen Mackenzie Battleship Lake Loop Trail. It meanders 8 km to the edge of Lake Helen Mackenzie and back. An overnight stay at the LAKE HELEN MACKENZIE CAMPSITE ● makes this a relaxed backcountry outing.

㊙ HIKING: A challenging day trip is a loop trail to Kwai Lake 👍. The route continues south from the Lake Helen Mackenzie Loop Trail for 5 km towards

Lake Kwai. The total loop is 14.4 km. An extra 2 km one-way trail leads to a good viewpoint of the Cruickshank Canyon. A campsite at Kwai Lake can break the trip into an overnight excursion. The same route leads to the Plateau and Albert Edward routes.

The Kwai Lake campsite.

 CAMPING: Camping in the near backcountry of Forbidden Plateau is limited to established campsites at Lake Helen Mackenzie and Kwai Lake. The sites feature wooden tent pads and pit toilets. Water is available from the lakes but should be boiled or filtered.

37 **Plateau Trail** *(map p. 194)*

This 12 km trail leads from the Wood Mountain Ski Park to connect with the Kwai Lake route to Paradise Meadows. Transportation is a hurdle unless hikers double back.

38 **Albert Edward Route** *(map p. 194)*

This trail continues west from the Kwai Lake loop to the peak of Albert Edward, elevation 2,093 m. It is the third-highest peak on Vancouver Island with an ominous Tolkien-esque appearance, especially when capped by clouds on an otherwise clear day. Despite the impression it is a relatively easy ascent. A favourite way to climb it is to camp two nights at Circlet Lake, using the middle day to ascend Mount Albert Edward without the need for heavy packs. This makes for a relatively easy three-day outing. The trail ascends rapidly from near Circlet Lake to a rocky ridge with a tough scramble at one point, then follows the curving ridge to the peak with minimal climbing. A side route leads to Castlecrag Mountain to the southeast of Albert Edward. This route loops back to the Circlet Lake area via Moat Lake. For a short side-trip from Circlet Lake follow the trail to Moat Lake without ascending Castlecrag Mountain (this is a very pretty area). Another side trip is possible to Amphitheatre Lake. This

A view to the peak of Mount Albert Edward.

On the ridge towards Castlecrag Mountain.

trail extends around the north shore of Circlet Lake and officially runs 1.3 km, but can be used to reach the backcountry around Jutland Mountain and other features north of Mount Albert Edward. Because of the distances involved, almost any trip to this area will entail an overnight stay.

A route links Forbidden Plateau to the Buttle Lake area of Strathcona Provincial park via Mount Albert Edward. The basic route is from the Albert Edward peak down the peak's west ridge to Ruth Masters Lake and Augerpoint Mountain (see page 268). This is a difficult backcountry route for veteran hikers only.

TRAVEL NOTES: A producer with hopes of a Canadian Survivor-style series took a busload of would-be contestants into the Buttle Lake area and—without proper instruction, equipment or guidance—set them loose on the traverse from Buttle Lake to Forbidden Plateau. Most would-be participants couldn't complete the arduous trip and required a helicopter rescue. As there is no established trail, the traverse is difficult to discern, so hikers can expect to be self-sufficient in every respect when making that hike—or any other backcountry route, for that matter.

👍 THUMBS UP: Mount Albert Edward is a popular first ascent, giving a taste of high-elevation mountain climbing for the least effort. But it is no cakewalk, and effort will reward first-timers with a well-earned sense of achievement and possibly a thirst for other mountain adventures.

🅰 CAMPING: The designated campsite is located at Circlet Lake, 0.6 km from the main trail. It has tent pads and composting toilets.

ACCESS: This is an extension of the Paradise Meadows trails (page 202).

A viewpoint from the Comox Glacier Trail.

㊴ Comox Glacier Trail *(map p. 194)*

This trail was created in about 1967 to create a gateway to the alpine region surrounding the Comox Glacier, as well as the glacier itself—a massive wedge of snow and ice lying between two crags. Its location at the top of the Cruikshank Valley makes it a distinctive landmark from Courtenay and Comox.

The Comox Glacier Trail is well established. It begins with a log crossing of Comox Creek, then winds its way upward, first through meandering switchbacks then into steeper and more demanding grades. The final push to the first ridge is up

The view from atop Mount Kookjai on the Kookjai Trail looking towards Black Cat Mountain.

a difficult rock and dirt scramble to the alpine level and first good VIEWPOINT ●
at about 1,300 m elevation. The trail then continues along up the ridge to
a summit at 1,400 m, where there are panoramic views in all directions,
particularly toward the glacier over the Comox Creek and a few small lakes far
below, especially Century Sam Lake. The viewpoint, known as FROG POND ●,
is often a camping area. It's also a good goal for a day trip, about four hours into
the hike.

From Frog Pond the trail drops down into a ridge crossing toward Comox
Glacier in a mix of alpine terrain and more demanding climbing. A fit hiker
could make it to the glacier and back in about nine hours; for most it will be a
demanding two days. Note that once you reach it, hiking on the glacier can be
hazardous and requires special equipment and expertise.

A second route breaks away from the Comox Glacier Trail near the trailhead
and stays at a lower elevation to head to Century Sam Lake. A third option,
the KOOKJAI ROUTE ●, is a longer alternative that winds its way from near
Cougar Lake across Kookjai and Black Cat mountains to join with the Comox
Glacier Trail.

👍 THUMBS UP: Both the Comox Glacier Trail and the Kookjai Trail provide
valuable routes into an otherwise inaccessible region. A day trip on either trail
offers astonishing views and a look at a wonderful alpine environment, with
the possibility of longer overnight hikes or even week-long technical climbing
trips for advanced hikers. During a late August visit a half-dozen varieties
of alpine flowers were in bloom; the plants had only just been relieved of
their snow cover, allowing them a colourful display in their extremely short
summer season. Day trips to the Kookjai Trail are likely simpler due to fewer
ditches on the approach and no tough scramble at the entry to the alpine
level. Several days would not be time wasted on either trail.

ACCESS: The easiest route is via the Comox Lake Main. Immediately south
of the Cruickshank bridge on the west shore of Comox Lake take the road
west along the Cruikshank River into the scenic Cruikshank Valley. Follow it
about 3 km to a junction, then turn south on the South Fork Main. From there
the trailhead is 10 km, with small yellow signs indicating the directions to the
trailhead. At about 5.5 km turn right (west; continuing south takes you to Cougar
Lake and the Kookjai trailhead). Continue west for 3 km to another junction,
then turn right (north) and continue another 2 km to the TRAILHEAD ●.
Watch for the small yellow marker; the trail heads down from there over the
clear-cut and across Comox Creek. Note the final 5 km is ditched 34 times;
two-wheel-drive vehicles could have difficulty as early as the first ditch but will
be unlikely to make it the final 2 km. The Kookjai trailhead is about 0.5 km
south of Cougar Lake. Park at the sharp turn and look for the trailhead and
a commemorative marker at a small bluff. From there it is well marked.

TRAVEL NOTES: In late 2007 owner TimberWest put the land at the entrance to the Comox Glacier Trail up for sale. It's likely the new owners will be quick to log remaining harvestable timber to recoup the purchase cost. Should the glacier route be blocked, Kookjai is an excellent alternative.

㊵ Elsie Lake region

Elsie and Oshinow lakes are marked on the main chapter map on page 160; Willemar Lake is marked on the regional map on page 194.

Elsie Lake is the largest lake in a region of hills and mountains on the southeast edge of Strathcona Provincial Park north of Great Central Lake. This is all private logging land with restrictions on public use, but should you venture in here, you'll find most lakes have an access of some type, along with a makeshift campsite. Several good sites line WILLEMAR LAKE ●, for instance. Access is off the Comox Lake Main near the south end of Comox Lake where the Comox Lake Main veers east; to get to Willemar Lake, just continue south. Boat access is good here, with a possibility of paddling by a portage into Forbush Lake. The campsite and boat launch at ELSIE LAKE ● are located on the southwest corner of the lake. It is reached by a turnoff from the Ash River Main about 8 km past the junction to Great Central Lake. There's a great VIEWPOINT ● along this route. The lake farthest inland still accessible by the Ash River Main is Oshinow Lake within Strathcona Provincial Park; plans call for an overland route from Oshinow to Della Falls, with no timeline set for the completion.

MAJOR PARKS

⑰ Comox Lakes Bluff Reserve *(map p. 194)*

The bluffs and shallow soil here have helped create an unusual array of plants, several at the limits of their range. The rarest plant to be found is the least moonwort, while an atypical plant association is Douglas-fir, arbutus, manzanita and bearberry.

Ⓐ CAMPING: The Comox Lake Main descends a hill to the west of the reserve, with an ACCESS ROAD ● leading to a small lakefront area. Leading off that into a small forested area is another rough road or trail to a wonderful little beach spit. This is a popular wilderness camping area but be cautioned: it is unregulated and is a party area that is generally poorly treated.

ACCESS: The steep shoreline and limited access along the Comox Lake Main make this a difficult location to visit. The best way to appreciate it may well be by paddle from the vantage of Comox Lake.

17 Wood Mountain Ski Park *(map p. 194)*

This park is an old ski hill named for Clinton S. Wood, the builder of the original Strathcona Park Lodge in 1933 (it was destroyed by fire in 1982). Reminders of the old lodge include the foundations and the ski lift, still mostly intact but sitting idle. The park is one end of the Plateau Trail that connects to Paradise Meadows near Mount Washington in Strathcona Provincial Park (see page 203).

ACCESS: From the Island Highway, take Forbidden Plateau Road to the PARKING AREA ● at the end.

18 Kin Beach Provincial Park *(map p. 194)*

Located near the Comox air force base, this provincial park is run by the community as a hosted recreational park with a playground and campground. Amenities include a store serving food near the parking lot.

PICNIC AREAS AND DAY USE: The large, grassy day-use area has a covered shelter, tables, toilets, firepits, water taps, a playground and a tennis court. It is adjacent to a rocky beach. Low-water tidal pools make a safe place for children to swim.

CAMPING: Kin Beach has 18 vehicle-accessible campsites. Reservations are accepted by calling 250-339-6365.

FISHING: Common targets are salmon, rockfish and shellfish; angling is popular.

ACCESS: From Highway 19 in Comox take Ryan Road east to the entrance to CFB Comox. Turn left onto Little River Road, then right on Kilmorley.

19 Kitty Coleman Provincial Park *(map p. 160)*

This provincial park is managed locally as a popular camping and recreation area. It occupies 900 m of oceanfront at the Kitty Coleman Creek estuary, with some old-growth Douglas-fir estimated to be about 500 years old in the upland area.

A neighbouring attraction on Whittaker Road is the Kitty Coleman Woodland Gardens, a private display of over 3,000 varieties of rhododendrons in a tranquil forest and garden setting. Visit **www.woodlandgardens.ca**.

FISHING: The park's two boat launches give access to the Strait of Georgia and the angling possibilities between Comox and Campbell River. Salmon and rockfish are the most common species.

PICNIC AREAS AND DAY USE: The day-use area has a covered shelter, tables, water and pit toilets.

Winter near Kwai Lake.

Ⓐ CAMPING: The 65 campsites, most strewn along the beach, are all first-come, first-served. The one group campsite is available by reservation at 250-338-1332. Expect it to be a popular RV and fishing base.

ACCESS: The park is 6 km north of Courtenay. From the Island Highway take Left Road, then Whittaker Road into the park.

CHAPTER FOUR

Clayoquot Sound

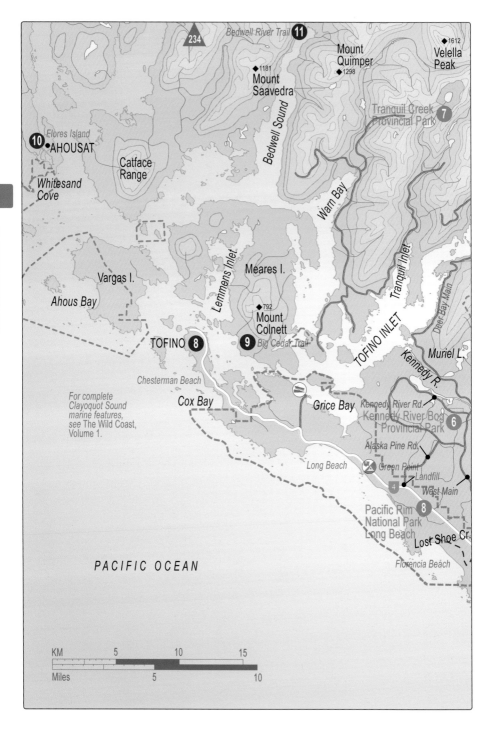

CLAYOQUOT SOUND

234

Bedwell River Trail 11

Mount Quimper
◆1298

◆1612 Velella Peak

◆1181 Mount Saavedra

Bedwell Sound

Tranquil Creek Provincial Park 7

Flores Island
10 •AHOUSAT

Catface Range

Whitesand Cove

Warn Bay

Vargas I.

Lemmens Inlet

Meares I.

Tranquil Inlet

Deer Bay Main

Ahous Bay

◆792 Mount Colnett

TOFINO INLET

Muriel L.

TOFINO 8

9 Big Cedar Trail

Kennedy R.

Chesterman Beach

Cox Bay

Grice Bay

Kennedy River Rd.

Kennedy River Bog Provincial Park 6

For complete Clayoquot Sound marine features, see The Wild Coast, Volume 1.

Alaska Pine Rd.

Long Beach

2 Green Point

Landfill

4

West Main

PACIFIC OCEAN

Pacific Rim National Park Long Beach

8

Lost Shoe Cr.

Florencia Beach

KM   5   10   15

Miles   5   10

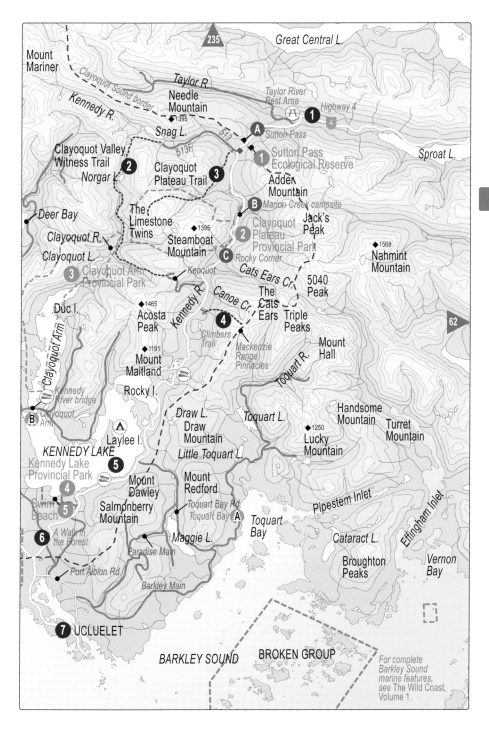

Mount Mariner

Clayoquot Sound border

Taylor R.

Great Central L.

235

Needle Mountain
♦1395

Kennedy R.

Snag L.

513

Taylor River Rest Area

A Sutton Pass

1 Highway 4

4

Clayoquot Valley Witness Trail

2

Norgar L.

Clayoquot Plateau Trail

3

513F

Sutton Pass Ecological Reserve

1

Adder Mountain

Sproat L.

B Marion Creek campsite

Jack's Peak

Clayoquot Plateau Provincial Park

2

Deer Bay

The Limestone Twins

Steamboat Mountain
♦1395

♦1568

Nahmint Mountain

Clayoquot R.

Clayoquot L.

Clayoquot Arm Provincial Park

3

Kenquot

C Rocky Corner

Cats Ears Cr.

5040 Peak

Duc I.

Acosta Peak
♦1465

Kennedy R.

Canoe Cr.

4

The Cats Ears

Triple Peaks

Mount Hall

Mount Maitland
♦1191

Climbers Trail

Mackenzie Range Pinnacles

Toquart R.

Rocky I.

Kennedy River bridge

Clayoquot Arm

B

Draw L.
Draw Mountain

Little Toquart L.

Toquart L.

Handsome Mountain

Turret Mountain

Lucky Mountain
♦1250

Laylee I.

A

KENNEDY LAKE

Kennedy Lake Provincial Park

5

Mount Dawley

4

Mount Redford

Swim Beach

5

Salmonberry Mountain

6 A Walk in the Forest

Port Albion Rd.

Paradise Main

Maggie L.

Toquart Bay Rd.
Toquart Bay **A**

Toquart Bay

Pipestem Inlet

Cataract L.

Broughton Peaks

Effingham Inlet

Vernon Bay

Barkley Main

7 UCLUELET

BARKLEY SOUND

BROKEN GROUP

For complete Barkley Sound marine features, see The Wild Coast, Volume 1.

62

CLAYOQUOT SOUND

One of the trees that helped make Clayoquot Sound famous: the Hanging Garden Tree on Meares Island.

Clayoquot Sound is a name that has earned almost a religious reverence among wilderness lovers. And for good reason. There is something awe-inspiring about seeing an old-growth temperate coastal rainforest in its natural state. Clayoquot moved to the forefront of the environmental movement in 1993 when demonstrations at the Kennedy River bridge to bar logging led to a summer of arrests. It was destined to become Canada's largest case of civil disobedience, and the effort did lead to changes. The province turned most of the Clayoquot Sound's outer shoreline into parks (though that took place before the major protests in 1993), plus a few other key areas. The volume of wood harvesting was reduced. A scientific panel was created to monitor the ecological state of the sound. And, for what it's worth, Clayoquot was made a Unesco biosphere.

It might seem like good news for the preservation of the sound, but the simple truth is that logging is still extensive. Iisaak Forest Resources and International Forest Products are the two main Tree Forest License holders in the sound. Old-growth forest is still being harvested.

As well as Pacific Rim National Park, two other significant portions of the sound are protected as parkland—Clayoquot Plateau and Clayoquot Arm. Both are provincial parks with mainly inaccessible forest. In fact, most of the sound remains off-limits to casual visits, with the best portions accessible by boat. A blue border on the map on page 213 shows the official border for the south end of Clayoquot Sound. Complete information on the marine-accessible portions are detailed in *The Wild Coast, Volume 1*. Limited land access is possible to Bedwell Sound; see page 271. For the rest of the sound, a kayak is strongly recommended.

ℹ **www.clayoquotbiosphere .org**.

TRANSPORTATION

The main route through the region is Highway 4 (also called the Pacific Rim Highway), which continues west for about

Shoreline on the exposed coast of Tofino.

85 km from Port Alberni along a twisting, steep and narrow highway. It is mainly two lanes, making for potentially slow conditions, especially if you have to make a portion of the journey behind a truck or RV. The highway is rich in features, however, many of them described in detail in this chapter.

Highway 4 splits at the Tofino-Ucluelet junction, where it continues north-south in both directions as a mainly two-lane paved route paralleling the ocean. Most of this portion of Highway 4 runs through Pacific Rim National Park, and signs to the various features of the park are clearly marked.

Logging roads dot the area, but they're not ideal for traveling. A few mains are accessible, but deactivated spurs are generally in poor condition and quickly become impassable in the quick-growing temperate rainforest environment. Routes are rarely named by sign, and given the high number of similar logging spurs in close proximity, finding the right one can be difficult. Using GPS waypoints is recommended.

Here are the key auxiliary routes.

WEST MAIN: This is the key artery to west Kennedy Lake and some of its features, beginning at Lost Shoe Creek off Highway 4 near the Tofino-Ucluelet junction immediately northeast of the Walk in the Forest. After the Clayoquot Arm beach and bridge junction it heads northwest as the Deer Bay Main (though don't expect signs indicating names). The Deer Bay Main will take you to the shore of Tofino Inlet at an industrial log dump. A leg continues north from the log dump, but it's rough and poorly maintained; travel will be difficult even by four-wheel drive. These roads are part of the Iisaak Forest Resources' Tree Farm License and most are actively logged, with a high possibility of logging adjacent to the main, so off-hour travel is advised. Auxiliary routes, such as the alternative route from Tofino via the landfill's Alaska Pine Road to Clayoquot Arm, are generally potholed and make for poor travel.

Rocky Corner.

POINTS OF INTEREST

1 **Highway 4** *(map p. 213)*

This is a beautiful stretch of paved road, and for the majority of visitors to Pacific Rim National Park this is the gateway to Clayoquot Sound. West of Sproat Lake the road becomes narrow, twisting, steep in places and prone to erosion. What it lacks in safety is compensated for in numerous pullouts at scenic locations. These are plentiful in large part due to the highway's close proximity to Kennedy River, which cascades down several scenic canyons before dropping into Kennedy Lake. This portion of the text details only the portion of Highway 4 west of Sproat Lake.

A SUTTON PASS: At 250 m elevation, this is the high point for the Highway 4 route between Alberni Valley and the eastern border of Clayoquot Sound. It is about 8 km from the end of Sproat Lake. A good rest area with washrooms is about 4 km to the east—the Taylor River rest stop. A sign marks the high point. In winter carrying chains is required. Access points to the Witness Trail and Clayoquot Plateau Trail are just southwest of the pass.

B MARION CREEK CAMPSITE ●: Look for a rough crescent logging road on the west side of Highway 4 about 8 km past Sutton Pass (40 km from the Pacific Rim Highway junction). Take the south entry option at Marion Creek (the southernmost of the two junctions). At a second junction near the entrance follow the short spur south to a level, clear area adjacent to Kennedy River. This suits one group only, but is probably the best of many roadside wilderness camping options in the region.

C ROCKY CORNER ●: This is a scenic highlight of Highway 4. The highway descends a tight curve to come out alongside a set of small canyons, rapids and overflow rock shelving along the Kennedy. The rock shelving is an ideal place to walk for views of the river and the nearby mountains. The sharp peak across the river is Steamboat Mountain; slightly upriver from Steamboat is Needle Peak. Looking downriver and slightly to the right, the dramatic line of craggy peaks is Mount Maitland. From here the highway is particularly twisty and rolling, with a multitude of pullouts for views of both Kennedy River and Kennedy Lake.

👍 THUMBS UP: If you are mobility impaired, or just quickly passing through, Highway 4 west of Port Alberni is a great way to see a range of scenery from the comfort of a car. With handy roadside pullouts at most viewpoints, this is a fitting introduction to the beauty of Clayoquot Sound, from scenic waterfalls to white-capped peaks, without the need for hiking.

❷ **Clayoquot Valley Witness Trail** *(map p. 213)* 🚶

The Witness Trail was created in 1993 by the Western Canada Wilderness Committee (now just Wilderness Committee or WC) as a massive project that included clearing the 23 km length of the trail and building boardwalks for the first 2.5 km, an endeavor the WC estimates involved 10,000 hours of volunteer time. It was a rugged trail to begin with, and it deteriorated quickly. Add blowdown and overgrowth and the trail is now impassable. It begins in the upper Kennedy River Valley at Upper Solstice Lake southwest of Snag Lake, then parallels the Clayoquot River as far as Delessio Creek, re-entering the Kennedy River valley at the Olympic Creek headwaters. From the north trailhead, a good overnight trip is along the boardwalk to a ridge top and a viewpoint over the Clayoquot River. Anecdotally, the south entrance was in the worst shape, not worth even a day trip at this stage, though a rebuilding of the bridge at the access road bodes well for future improvements.

The old trailhead shanty is now collapsed, and the trailhead almost obscured.

ACCESS: The north trailhead is the second highway TURNOFF ● immediately southwest of Sutton Pass. It quickly becomes too overgrown to allow passage for most vehicles, then is completely impassable after about a kilometre where a bridge is out, requiring a long walk to the collapsed TRAILHEAD SHED ● through logging road with portions overgrown—expect to bushwhack. From there the trail rises quickly to Snag Lake. For the south access, take the logging road across the Canyon Bridge; the turnoff is about 3 km past Rocky Corner.

TRAVEL NOTES: The WC's task in building this trail was monumental, but it was just as large a mistake to

The landslide that created Snag Lake.

spend so much time building boardwalks in an area where nothing lasts without constant maintenance.

Had the trail simply been built on the ground it might have had a better chance of being user-maintained. Instead, as the boardwalks tilted and fell away, they became impediments, requiring difficult bypasses of the trail—hardly what the builders had hoped for. While a great deal of time was spent on the first few kilometres, the rest of the trail was essentially a patch job—so rudimentary it was borderline dangerous, particularly with the numerous log crossings without foot grooves or handrails. This trail was to be a lasting monument to Clayoquot Valley; instead it is a reminder of how quickly ill-advised man-made intrusions can be washed away in the wilds. Visitors may find a hike to the trailhead kiosk now a sufficient day-trip. Otherwise the Clayoquot Plateau Trail is a good nearby alternative.

❸ Clayoquot Plateau Trail *(map p. 213)*

This trail, unlike the Witness Trail, was started quietly by a few volunteers and despite dissimilar manpower it's flourishing nicely. One reason is that volunteers have been working diligently at maintaining the trail, which has improved dramatically since about 2003. From the trailhead it follows an old logging road in danger of becoming overgrown for about 5 km; it then crosses a stream bed and rises steeply as it borders, then crosses another creek up the side of Needle Mountain. Note that there's a difficult crossing about 1 km from the end of the logging road. It requires walking along potentially slippery rock shelving polished smooth by river overflow. The creek must then be crossed over a narrow chasm above rapids. This could be a deal-ender for casual hikers; I rate it as dangerous. From there the trail continues to an area known as Flood Camp at 10 km and 400 m elevation; then to a lookout at 12.5 km and 800 m elevation. The finale, Plateau Camp, is at 15 km from the trailhead and 1,000 m elevation.

The creek alongside the Plateau Trail.

Though some maps indicate it, the trail has never connected on the south with the Witness Trail.

ACCESS: Use the same turnoff for the Clayoquot Valley Witness Trail—the second right west of Sutton Pass. The TRAILHEAD ● is just a few hundred metres

The beach at the Clayoquot Arm recreation site.

down the road. Look for an open area where two logging roads meet. This is suitable for parking. The trail leads southwest from near the clearing and follows the old logging road across a bridge near the trailhead.

TRAVEL NOTES: A new trail is in the works up the side of Steamboat Mountain. Look for the trailhead just north of the Canyon Bridge. An early look showed it to be quite rough. Expect it to be a challenging route.

❹ Climber's Trail *(map p. 213)*

This is a short but steep climb up the side of the Mackenzie Range to the Mackenzie Range Pinnacles, a set of stunning granite spires at about 1,400 m elevation. Reaching the peaks requires technical mountain climbing skills. The TRAILHEAD ● is directly off Highway 4 about 2 km past the Canoe Creek bridge; watch for the signpost for the salmon enhancement project at the trailhead. Money was earmarked in 2006 for trail improvements.

❺ Kennedy Lake *(map p. 213)*

This large lake is the first expanse of water to be seen when driving west on Highway 4 and is regularly mistaken as a view of the ocean. In a way it is like an inland sea, with two distinct arms forming a crescent shape. Fishermen will be drawn to the lake for its cutthroat trout, and also the chinook, coho, peamouth chub, steelhead and threespine stickleback. Paddlers will appreciate the convoluted shoreline and extensive beaches (the best of which tend to be protected in the various parks and recreation sites). While camping is possible just about anywhere, expect the majority of shore to be overgrown to near the water line. Note also that winds can pick up, particularly in the afternoons, creating choppy conditions on the lake. Launching is best at Kennedy Lake Provincial Park or Clayoquot Arm Beach Recreation Site; the latter is the best launch for Clayoquot Arm or Kennedy River.

❻ A Walk in the Forest *(map p. 213)*

This is an easy trail run by Ucluelet and the Ministry of Forests with interpretive signs scattered along its length. The trail leads through a variety of forest ages (though not old-growth). It is located near the Tofino-Ucluelet junction of Highway 4.

❼ Ucluelet *(map p. 213)*

This fishing community has been transformed over the last few decades as it reinvents itself as a rival destination to Tofino. Most activity has traditionally focused on Ucluelet Inlet, a safe haven in good proximity to Barkley Sound. The commercial sector is slowly catching up, with a good (but not great) selection of quaint cafés, restaurants and shops. Resorts dot the coastline, which is more rugged than Tofino's.

🚶 HIKING: A wonderful development in recent years is the Wild Pacific Trail, an 8.5 km route along the Ucluelet shoreline that can be enjoyed in a number of smaller parcels. The starting point is at the junction of Peninsula and Coast Guard roads. From there the trail heads about 1 km along some spectacular shoreline to the Amphitrite Point lighthouse, a beautiful spot

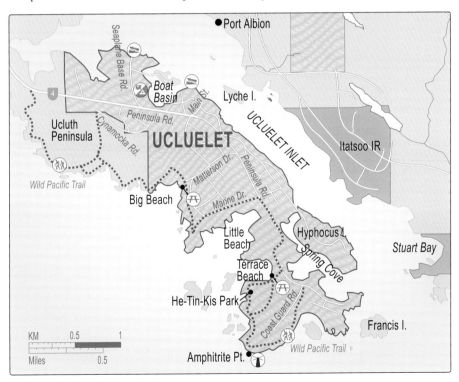

to scramble onto rocks to watch the waves, which can occasionally be quite violent. It then skirts a rough shoreline to join with the He-Tin-His Park boardwalk, with more incredible oceanfront views. The trail then emerges back on Peninsula Road at another parking lot for a short walk back to the original parking area—a loop of just over 2.5 km. A side trail from the second parking area leads to Terrace Beach, one of a number of small beaches along the otherwise rocky shoreline. The next portion of the trail continues along Peninsula Road to Marine Drive. About 4 km from the start of the trail, it follows along the beachfront at Big Beach, a good picnic area. It then continues along a rugged section of shoreline to end at Highway 4, where a bike path follows the highway back into town. Another short access trail joins with Cynamocka Road at just after the 6 km marker. This is a wonderfully scenic trail that offers a good look at some of the most rugged coast of Vancouver Island without having to stray too far from pavement. The 2.5 km loop is an easy walk for most fitness levels, with the reward of some of the island's best ocean scenery for the effort.

8 Tofino *(map p. 212)*

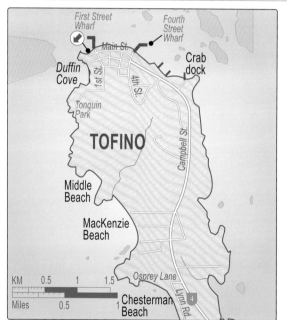

Tofino, set on Esowista Peninsula, has long been the heart of Vancouver Island's west coast. Historically a cultural and wilderness retreat, improvements in road travel and a growth in popularity of Pacific Rim National Park and Clayoquot Sound have turned it from a small fishing and logging community into a burgeoning tourist centre. The west side of the peninsula is dominated by a series of resorts at beaches or rocky bluffs; the village is tucked into the peninsula's north and east end. Everything is easy to find, as there are only about four main roads. There are a variety of restaurants, shops, galleries, tour operators, kayak rentals, surf outfitters and pubs. A personal favourite is the gallery of Henry Roy Vickers—an impressive display of native artistry in the setting of a gallery styled after a longhouse.

- BOAT TOURS: Gray and humpback whales are year-round residents in Clayoquot Sound, making Tofino a good base for a whale watching tour. Nature tours take in attractions such as Cleland Island Ecological Reserve, an important bird nesting sanctuary. Ever popular are day trips to Hot Springs Cove in north Clayoquot Sound.

A quiet evening at Middle Beach.

- SURFING: The main surfing beach in Tofino is Chesterman Beach, which rivals Long Beach for the number of surfers any given day. Surfing tends to be a year-round sport here; during a visit on the kind of bleak winter day when tourism tends to fall off, parking was packed on the nearby streets with surfers.

TRAVEL NOTES: Hot Springs Cove is a unique travel experience, but it's a casualty of overly successful tourism. During summer, the pools are often loaded well beyond their capacity, with Zodiacs and floatplanes dropping off more visitors every few minutes. The Refuge Cove band runs a campground just north of the provincial park, offering campers a chance for a late evening or early morning soak when the crowds die down.

❾ Big Cedar Trail *(map p. 212)*

Meares Island is a landmark from Tofino, distinctive for the peaks of Lone Cone and Mount Colnett (700 m) visible across Browning Passage. The island was declared a Tla-o-qui-aht tribal park in 1984 after a logging controversy that was a precursor to the larger protests that rocked Clayoquot Sound almost a decade later. Water taxis from Tofino are the best way to reach the island and the trailhead for the Big Cedar Trail, a 3 km boardwalk loop created in the 1980s. It passes features such as the Hanging Garden Cedar, a tree estimated to be about 2,000 years old with an 18.3 m circumference.

A rugged portion of the boardwalk on Big Cedar Trail.

⑩ Flores Island *(map p. 212)*

This is one of the largest islands on the west coast of Vancouver Island (second behind Nootka), with a community nestled alongside Matilda Inlet, the best anchorage on the island's southeast side. It is an easy island to reach thanks to a regular passenger shuttle, the *Ahousaht Pride*, which offers transit for a fraction of the cost of a water taxi. This helps make the island an incredible getaway with a range of experiences from simple hikes to multi-day treks. Accommodation is available at the Hummingbird Hostel (visit **www.hummingbird-hostel.com**) or you can camp on the beach at Whitesand Cove or farther afield at Cow Bay.

> **HIKING**: A good day trip is from Ahousat along the trails through Gibson Marine Park to Whitesand Cove, a distance of just a few kilometres. Along the way look for the Ahousaht Warm Spring, a tepid alternative to Hot Springs Cove. The warm spring flows into a concrete basin created for a refreshing soak. Whitesand Cove is the trailhead for the Wild Side Trail to Cow Bay, about 8 km. A rough 4 km extension leads to the peak of Mount Flores (880 m).

⑪ Bedwell River Trail *(map p. 212)*

This trail is the only trail link from Clayoquot Sound into the interior of the island. The trailhead at the top of Bedwell Sound links with the Bedwell Lake trails deep inside Strathcona Provincial Park. It would also be possible to link with Flower Ridge and ultimately cross into Forbidden Plateau, raising the possibility of a cross-island hike. For more information, see page 270–271.

MAJOR PARKS

❶ Sutton Pass Ecological Reserve *(map p. 213)*

This tiny (3.4-hectare) park was created in 1978 to protect a rare adder's tongue fern—one of its few known locations in BC. The fern is found next to shrubs along a pond created by an old rock slide. The pond's seasonal variation in water level helps keep back the growth of shrubs, allowing small herbs like adder's tongue fern that are suited for seasonal flooding to survive.

❷ Clayoquot Plateau Provincial Park *(map p. 213)*

This park protects 3,155 hectares of some of the highest elevations in Clayoquot Sound, including several small lakes that serve as headwaters to the Clayoquot River and some cave systems, all in a pristine condition. Tool marks on 2,600-year-old bones indicate it was a prehistoric site for aboriginal hunting of bear, marten and marmot.

Paddling Clayoquot Arm with Muriel Ridge in the background.

SPELUNKING: The limestone cave system in the park is considered hazardous and sensitive, though it is visited by a handful of diehards each year. Trails lead to the caves, accessible by the Clayoquot Plateau Trail.

ECOLOGY: The park is home to six highly rare plant species found in only a few known locations in BC: alpine anemone, corrupt spleenwort, smooth willowherb, sand-dwelling wallflower, western hedysarum and Olympic mountain asper.

ACCESS: The best access to the park is the Clayoquot Plateau Trail (page 219). Note the trail is not sanctioned by BC Parks.

3 Clayoquot Arm Provincial Park *(map p. 213)*

This park was created in 1995 to protect a portion of the temperate rainforest typical for the west coast of Vancouver Island. Located on the upper shore of Kennedy Lake at its namesake Clayoquot Arm, it includes lower Clayoquot River and Clayoquot Lake. Old-growth Sitka spruce and western red cedar forests, sandy beaches, islets and the Clayoquot River valley compose the park. The Clayoquot River is about the best in Clayoquot Sound for sockeye salmon spawning. Here the salmon do the unusual by spawning in water 20 m deep. Chinook, chum, coho, cutthroat trout, steelhead and numerous other species also use the river. Don't be surprised if you see harbour seals in Clayoquot Lake— they use the tide to enter the brackish water to feed on salmon. Black bear den here, making them year-round residents. A cabin at Clayoquot Lake is used by the Clayoquot Biosphere Trust for research. Evidence of previous First Nations residents includes culturally modified trees and a fish weir. Later uses were a fish cannery and hatchery. The park protects 3,490 hectares.

🔺 CAMPING: Backcountry wilderness camping is allowed.

🚣 PADDLING: The park can be visited by water from boat cartop launches at Clayoquot Arm bridge at the Kennedy River bridge. For a glimpse into an area not normally visited, paddle in to the Clayoquot River, then portage or hike along the rough trails to Clayoquot Lake.

👍 THUMBS UP: Clayoquot Arm has a multitude of islands and some wonderfully rugged shoreline to explore, making it a great place to meander by paddle. Expect beaches to be few and far between, though.

ACCESS: There is no formal road access into the park, though logging roads extend up the spine of Muriel Ridge to the park boundary. The Clayoquot Valley Witness Trail (page 218) skirts the northeast border of the park at the Clayoquot River near Clayoquot Lake. Boat access is your best bet.

---

④ Kennedy Lake Provincial Park (map p. 213)

This park on the south end of Kennedy Lake is divided into two distinct parcels with two very different roles. The parcel adjacent to Highway 4 (the east portion) is meant for recreation, including swimming, paddling, fishing, boating and picnicking, but no camping. The western portion of the park protects sensitive spawning habitat, including spawning streams and a large (154-hectare) foreshore area. The gravel is used for spawning by sockeye salmon—an unusual location, as sockeye don't usually spawn on shore. To protect the habitat, the western beach should be avoided. For those who wish to view sockeye, creeks by the highway are also used for beach spawning in the fall. This creates a double viewing opportunity, as black bears often frequent the area during this time.

🍴 PICNIC AREAS AND DAY USE: The park has a waterside picnic area with toilets, firepits and a boat launch.

ACCESS: The day-use portion of the park is adjacent to Highway 4 just 4.8 km east of the junction to Tofino and Ucluelet.

---

⑤ Pacific Rim National Park (Swim Beach Unit) (map p. 213)

Often overlooked as part of the national park, this 441-hectare parcel is located on the south shore of Kennedy Lake between the two parts of Kennedy Lake Provincial Park. It's a day-use area only, providing a lakeside beach access. Watch for signs for the turnoff just west of Kennedy Lake.

---

⑥ Kennedy River Bog Provincial Park (map p. 212)

This park combines some mature forest, bird habitat and an oxbow in the setting of an acidic bog. The park protects 11 hectares and was created in 1995 as part

CLAYOQUOT SOUND

of the Vancouver Island Land Use Plan. It's probably best visited by small boat, which can be launched from near the east side of the Kennedy River bridge. No formal trails into the park exist. It is located about 10 km along West Main.

⑦ Tranquil Creek Provincial Park *(map p. 212)*

Tranquil Creek Provincial Park is located in the subalpine setting of Paradise Lake (elevation 860 m) and the surrounding meadows. The park is 298 hectares and like many of the other Clayoquot Sound parks was created in 1995.

ACCESS: Paradise Lake is located in a roadless section of Clayoquot Sound about 8 km upstream from Tofino Inlet. This is an exceptionally difficult area to hike into.

⑧ Pacific Rim National Park (Long Beach Unit) *(map p. 212 and below)*

This stretch of shore is the most visited on Vancouver Island, attracting as many as 800,000 visitors a year. The reasons are as diverse as the visitors—from casual sightseeing to hard-core surfing, a year-round pursuit here when tourism lags elsewhere on Vancouver Island. The rugged West Coast shoreline is the unifying attraction for all who visit, with its sweeping sandy beaches, multitude of pocket beaches, volcanic rock bluffs and headlands pounded mercilessly by the surf. Forest settings include old-growth forests and unusual bogs. The main features of

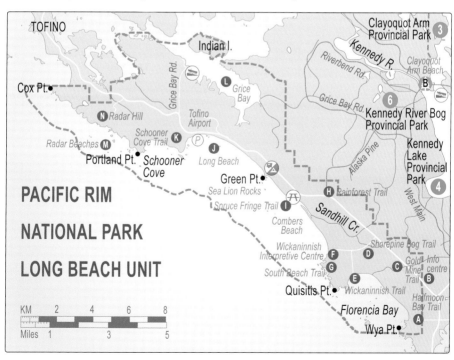

A typical West Coast day at Schooner Cove.

the park are accessible by vehicle, with a choice of nine trails to navigate. Some beach areas are adjacent to the parking lots, an advantage for casual sightseers and for surfboarders and surf kayakers who must carry equipment. There are other beaches that can only be reached by a lengthy hike. Points of interest are covered separately below.

(A) CAMPING: Green Point Campground is located on the middle of Long Beach adjacent to the ocean. The campground features 94 vehicle-accessible campsites, group camping and 20 walk-in campsites in a forest setting. Amenities are washrooms, phones, water, garbage disposal, food caching and a telescope on the point for watching the residents of Sea Lion Rocks, which sit just offshore. Reservations are recommended. Call 1-877-737-3783 or visit **www.pccamping.ca.**

(A) HALFMOON BAY TRAIL: This is the only Pacific Rim National Park trail that begins south of the Highway 4 junction. Two km south of the junction turn west onto Willowbrae Road and park at the lot at the end of the road. The trail leads from the parking lot to Florencia Bay, a sweeping sand beach used mostly by surfers. The bay is named for the Peruvian brigantine that sank here in 1860; occasionally it goes by its old name of Wreck Beach.

(B) PARK INFORMATION CENTRE: The information centre is located 3 km north of the Tofino-Ucluelet junction of Highway 4. It's not to be confused with the tourist visitor centre at the Highway 4 junction. The park information centre offers a full range of maps, guides and parking passes. Call 604-726-4212.

The Shorepine Bog.

● GOLD MINE TRAIL: One km past the park information centre (see above) is the trailhead for the Gold Mine Trail. It roughly follows Lost Shoe Creek to an early-1900s placer gold mine operation. Watch for old mining equipment. There's no beach access from this trail.

● SHOREPINE BOG TRAIL: This interpretive boardwalk loop trail makes its way through an eerie but strangely magical bog, where poor drainage and high rainfall have created moss several metres deep in some areas. Stunted shore pine, under 5 m in height, are perhaps centuries old. Be sure to pick up a brochure at the trailhead or the information centre to interpret numbered attractions along the boardwalk trail.

A pocket beach along the Wickaninnish Trail.

E WICKANINNISH TRAIL: This is the most direct route to the north end of Florencia Bay. The trail follows portions of a pioneer corduroy log road that once connected Tofino and Ucluelet. The trailhead is off the road to the Wickaninnish Interpretive Centre.

F WICKANINNISH INTERPRETIVE CENTRE: At one time a resort, the centre is now a showcase for information about Pacific Rim National Park. Exhibits, programs and a small theatre interpret the Pacific ecosystem. The centre also offers guided tours, great ocean views and a restaurant. It's at the end of Wickaninnish Road.

G SOUTH BEACH TRAIL: A personal favourite, this trail leads from the Wickaninnish Interpretive Centre along a forested boardwalk to a narrow sand beach enclosed by rock headlands and reefs. It's an exceptional place to watch the pounding surf on the rocks. A trail crosses the south headland to a second pebble beach. The beaches here were the summer retreat for Group of Seven artist Arthur Lismer (1885–1969) and the first beach is named Lismer Beach in his honour. Another longer leg of the trail continues to Florencia Bay.

H RAINFOREST TRAIL: This trail offers two short loops through some old-growth rainforest of western red cedar, amabilis fir and western hemlock. The trailhead is 5 km past Wickaninnish Road.

I SPRUCE FRINGE TRAIL: This interpretive boardwalk loop is located off the Combers Beach day-use area. It leads through a Sitka spruce forest that has an unusual ecology due to its close proximity to the ocean. Watch for alder swamps and old-growth trees on a glacial terrace.

LONG BEACH: The name is fitting, as this is the longest beach on Vancouver Island, though the south end is known as Combers Beach. Wind, surf and fog are ordinary features here, making it a cool place to visit even in the height of summer. The parking lot at the north end provides the best access and is a popular staging point for surfers and surf kayakers. Just off the beach in Wickaninnish Bay is a set of remote rocks known as Sea Lion Rocks for the migratory residents—the Steller's sea lions that congregate here each year. You can watch them from the telescope at Green Point.

SCHOONER COVE TRAIL: From the north end of Long Beach a boardwalk trail leads to Schooner Cove Trail. A portion is best passed at low tide; at higher tides a rough trail over the headland must be used. Box Island can also be visited at low tide. Note that camping was once allowed at Schooner Cove but is now prohibited. The cove is patrolled for compliance.

GRICE BAY: This bay becomes an extensive mudflat at low tides, making it key waterbird habitat and a migratory bird feeding area. It can be reached by Grice Bay Road, where a boat launch provides water access to Clayoquot Sound.

RADAR BEACHES: This remote stretch of the national park between Cox Point and Portland Point is difficult to reach. Those who do make it will find a series of pocket beaches bound by rock headlands.

RADAR HILL: This is one of the most accessible vantage points in Pacific Rim National Park. A road twists up the hill (126 m), with a short trail leading to the summit for stunning views across Clayoquot Sound. It was once a radar station site, but the dilapidated buildings have been removed.

THUMBS UP: My choices for visiting are Radar Hill for its easy-access viewpoint; any of the beaches off trails leading from the Wickaninnish Interpretive Centre for their astounding mix of surf, rock and sand; and Shorepine Bog Trail for its otherworldly ecology.

FOREST RECREATION SITES

See the map on page 213 to locate these recreation sites.

Toquart Bay

This ranks as one of the most developed and popular of Vancouver Island's forest recreation sites. It was established as a major gateway for boat and kayak traffic into Barkley Sound and the Broken Group. A boat launch is provided; a fee is charged for overnight parking.

PICNIC AREAS AND DAY USE: The recreation site has a day-use area at the beach with vehicle-accessible picnic tables and an expansive beach area used for swimming.

△ CAMPING: Toquart Bay has 78 vehicle-accessible campsites. Fees apply.

ACCESS: From a JUNCTION ● at Highway 4 adjacent to Kennedy Lake take Toquart Bay Road to the recreation site.

Ⓑ Clayoquot Arm

This recreation site is set on the small peninsula at the border between Kennedy Lake and Clayoquot Arm. From the main parking area a trail leads via boardwalk through a mature forest with two huge old trees—not record-setters, but they look the part—to a sandy beach area. This is meant as the day-use portion, but camping is traditional in a clear area in the forest upland or at several spots along the beach. Continuing on the logging road past the first parking lot brings you to the Clayoquot Arm bridge, with an adjacent boat launch and a large parking area that doubles as vehicle-accessible camping. The long-term plan is apparently to phase out vehicle camping in favour of day-use only, but it may be difficult as the use seems entrenched. As the only no-host recreation area in Clayoquot Sound, expect it to be rowdy.

ACCESS: From Highway 4, 1.5 km northeast of the Tofino-Ucluelet junction or just southwest of the Lost Shoe Creek bridge, take the West Main (not named by signs) northwest for about 11 km. You should reach a junction with the main route continuing west. Keep to the right (east). The road is rutted with potholes. At about 200 m there's a PARKING LOT ● to the left and the boardwalk to the right. To get to the Clayoquot Arm bridge, just continue along the road.

A monster tree on the Clayoquot Arm boardwalk.

CHAPTER FIVE

Nootka-Strathcona

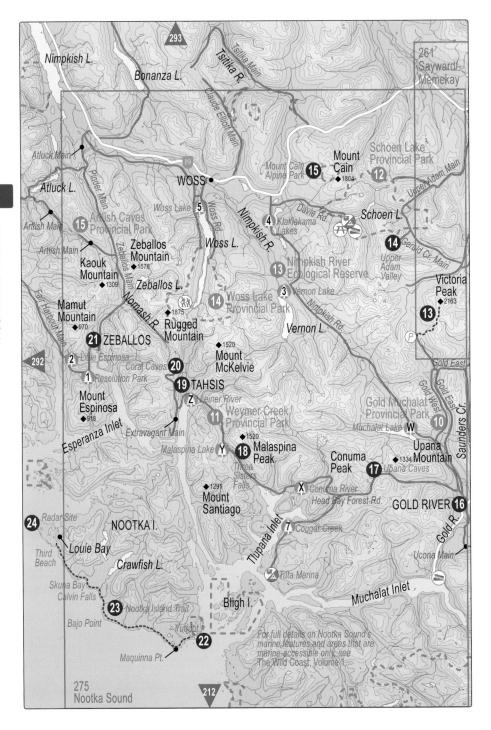

Nimpkish L.

Bonanza L.

Tsitika R.

Tsitika Main

293

261
Sayward/
Memekay

Atluck Main

19

WOSS

Mount Cain
Alpine Park

15

Mount
Cain
◆1804

Schoen Lake
Provincial Park

12

Upper Adam Main

Atluck L.

Artlish Main

Artlish Caves
Provincial Park

15

Pinder Main

Woss Lake

5

Woss Rd.

Woss L.

Nimpkish R.

Davie Rd.

4

Klaklakama
Lakes

Schoen L.

14

Gerald Cr. Main

Artlish Main

Kaouk
Mountain
◆1309

Zeballos
Mountain
◆1578

Zeballos Main

Zeballos L.

Nimpkish River
Ecological Reserve

13

Upper
Adam
Valley

Victoria
Peak
◆2163

Mamut
Mountain
◆970

Earl Harbour Main

Nomash R.

14

◆1875

Woss Lake
Provincial Park

3

Vernon Lake

Nimpkish Rd.

P

13

21 ZEBALLOS

Rugged
Mountain

Vernon L.

Gold East

292

2

Little Espinosa

1 Resolution Park

Coral Caves

20

◆1520

Mount
McKelvie

Gold West

Gold East Cr.

Gold Muchalat
Provincial Park

Gold West

Saunders Cr.

Mount
Espinosa
◆918

19 TAHSIS

Z Leiner River

11 Weymer Creek
Provincial Park

Muchalat Lake W

10

Extravagant Main

Y

Malaspina Lake

18

◆1520

Malaspina
Peak

Upana
Mountain
◆1334

Upana Caves

Esperanza Inlet

Three
Sisters
Falls

Conuma
Peak

17

◆1291

Mount
Santiago

X Conuma River

Head Bay Forest Rd.

GOLD RIVER 16

Gold R.

24 Radar Site

NOOTKA I.

Louie Bay

Third
Beach

Crawfish L.

Tlupana Inlet

7 Cougar Creek

Ucona Main

Skuna Bay
Calvin Falls

23 Nootka Island Trail

Bajo Point

Bligh I.

Tuta Marina

Muchalat Inlet

22

Yuquot

Maquinna Pt.

For full details on Nootka Sound's
marine features and areas that are
marine-accessible only, see
The Wild Coast, Volume 1.

275
Nootka Sound

212

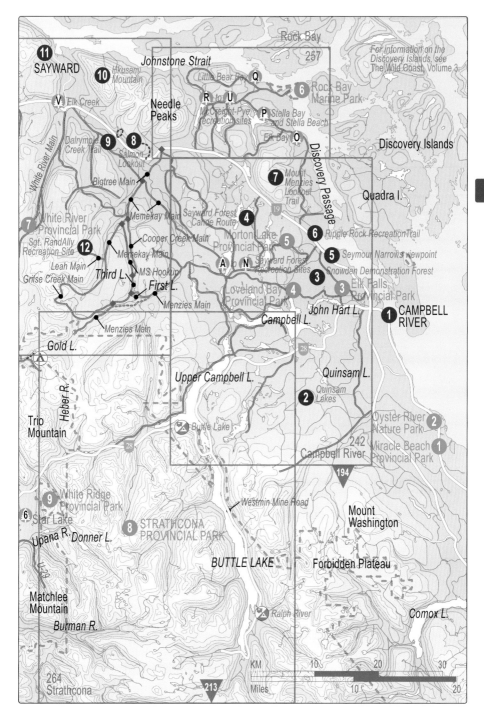

For information on the Discovery Islands, see The Wild Coast, Volume 3.

Rock Bay 257

SAYWARD 11
10 *Itkusam Mountain*

V *Elk Creek*

Johnstone Strait

Little Bear Bay Q

R to U
McCreight-Pye recreation sites

Needle Peaks

6 *Rock Bay Marine Park*

P

O *Stella Bay and Stella Beach*

Elk Bay

Discovery Islands

9 8 *Dalrymple Creek Trail*

Salmon Lookout

White River Main

Bigtree Main

Memekay Main

7 *Mount Menzies Lookout Trail*

Discovery Passage

Quadra I.

7 *White River Provincial Park*

Sgt. Rand Ally Recreation Site

12

Leah Main

Cooper Creek Main

Memekay Main

Third L.

MS Hookup

First L.

Grilse Creek Main

4 *Sayward Forest Canoe Route*

Morton Lake Provincial Park

A N

5 *Sayward Forest Recreation Sites*

Loveland Bay Provincial Park

19

6 *Ripple Rock Recreation Trail*

5 *Seymour Narrows viewpoint*

5 *Snowden Demonstration Forest*

3

3 *Elk Falls Provincial Park*

4

Menzies Main

Menzies Main

Gold L.

Campbell L.

John Hart L.

1 **CAMPBELL RIVER**

Upper Campbell L.

Quinsam L.

2 *Quinsam Lakes*

28

2 *Oyster River Nature Park*

Trio Mountain

Heber R.

Butle Lake

28

242 *Campbell River*

1 *Miracle Beach Provincial Park*

194

9 *White Ridge Provincial Park*

6 *Star Lake*

Upana R. *Donner L.*

8 **STRATHCONA PROVINCIAL PARK**

Westmin Mine Road

Mount Washington

Matchlee Mountain

Burman R.

BUTTLE LAKE

Forbidden Plateau

Comox L.

Ralph River

264 Strathcona

213

KM 10 20 30

Miles 10 20

Mount Cain is the backdrop for much of this region.

My introduction to this vast region involves two memorable experiences. My first visit to Strathcona Provincial Park was a camping trip at Buttle Lake shortly after I moved to BC. It was my first time camping in the midst of an old-growth forest, and a day-trip up to Augerpoint Mountain found me deep in the snow looking out over the tallest peaks of Vancouver Island. This started a love affair with this provincial park that continues today.

My first trip to Nootka Sound was a winter kayaking trip. I took a chance with a favourable forecast and after some initial fog found myself one January in the midst of sunshine and warm weather—rare even in the summer. Returning along the higher elevations of Head Bay Forest Service Road I drove through a sea of hoar frost that created a thick white coating on the evergreens. The whole world seemed to shine.

While logging is always an impediment to the views here, I never fail to marvel at the size and majesty of the peaks in this region. And I'm greatly thankful for the forethought of a previous generation in protecting such a large area of Vancouver Island in Strathcona Provincial Park, one of the province's first parks. Yes, there is a mine in the south end, but it's not difficult to find places in this park where all traces of human interference disappear. It's certainly something to be cherished.

TRANSPORTATION

Two highway routes are the backbone for road transportation in this region. The Island Highway continues north and west along the east side of Vancouver Island, connecting Victoria, Nanaimo, Campbell River and points north. North of Campbell River the highway turns inland, leaving the coast until near Port McNeill far to the northwest. It follows the path of least resistance along a series of low river valleys: Menzies River, Roberts Creek and Salmon River.

The only other highway through this region is Highway 28, an often twisting and steep but paved road between the communities of Campbell River and Gold River.

The following are a few other major routes to consider. The roads with a 👍 thumbs-up icon are exceptional driving routes.

👍 WESTMIN MINE ROAD: This paved route leads south from a JUNCTION ● with the Island Highway along the east side of Buttle Lake deep into Strathcona Provincial Park, ending at the Westmin Resources mine at the south end of the park. It's a scenic wonderland, with vistas changing as

Driving into the Upper Adam Valley.

quickly as the tight curves. Given the narrow, twisting road and industrial mining truck traffic it can be tricky, but it's well worth the drive. Most features of central Strathcona park are reached from this road.

MENZIES MAIN: This is a key route through the Sayward Forest district, leading to areas such as Mohun and Brewster lakes. The TURNOFF ● from the Island Highway is 1.7 km west of the Seymour Narrows viewpoint. It heads west for 47 km, eventually petering out at the remote north end of Strathcona Provincial Park. It connects with GRILSE CREEK MAIN ● and MS HOOKUP ● near the end. Both allow possible circuits of the region via logging road.

SAYWARD FOREST SERVICE ROADS: These roads connect the various lakes in Sayward Forest. Due to the recreational nature and the fact they are government rather than private roads, they tend to be easy to travel and well marked. Most of the minor roads are named for the lakes they pass, making it simple to get around. Well-signed routes also help. A few connector roads between the smaller lakes are slightly overgrown but easy enough to travel and quite scenic as they meander through maturing forests.

BIGTREE MAIN: This is the north link to a series of logging roads through Crown forestry lands north of Strathcona Provincial Park. The TURNOFF ● from the Island Highway is fairly easy to see, about 5 km west of Rock Bay Main. The land it takes you into is all part of Tree Farm License 39, controlled by Western Forest Products, and is being intensely logged. Be prepared for heavy truck traffic during working hours. It's easy to get lost as you cross from Bigtree to MEMEKAY ● to MS HOOKUP ● or COOPER CREEK ● mains (note that the Cooper Creek and MS Hookup mains RECONNECT ● ; see the map on page 261), so it's a good idea to use a GPS. All three mains will eventually take you to Menzies Main, potentially reconnecting to the Sayward Forest service roads for a loop of the region. Probably due to the intense forestry, Bigtree leads through one of the areas of Vancouver Island least developed for recreation.

NIMPKISH ROAD: The official name notwithstanding, if you're traveling from Gold River, it will be the Road to Woss. If you're traveling from Woss, it will be the Road to Gold River. Either way it's a quick route between the two communities. It's wide and generally well maintained but can suffer from storm damage (it was blocked for the summer north of Muchalat Lake in 2007). A few key recreational opportunities extend from here, including Gold Muchalat Provincial Park, approaches to Victoria Peak, plus Vernon and Muchalat lakes. From Gold River, skirt the town by staying on the main route as it swings north past the village. It will cross Gold River (the river, not the village) via a narrow bridge, then come to the HEAD BAY JUNCTION ●. The Head Bay Forest Service Road is left (south then immediately west) and Nimpkish Road is right (north). If traveling from the north, take the turnoff (DAVIE ROAD ●) for Schoen Lake

The distinctive summit of Conuma Peak.

Provincial Park and follow the signs, taking the first option south instead of heading to the park. Other options from the north include a maze of logging road links, including a route directly through Woss. As it is a fairly major route, most roads are well signed, so just about any turnoff between Schoen Lake and Woss is a good bet for reaching Gold River.

HEAD BAY FOREST SERVICE ROAD: This is the official name of the road to Tahsis, heading west from Gold River through some of the most spectacular scenery on Vancouver Island. From stunning viewpoints over the Nootka Sound waterways to massive granite mountain crags such as Conuma Peak to beautiful waterfalls such as Three Sisters to an array of wildlife viewing opportunities from bears to elk, this drive should not be missed if you are traveling to Gold River. It even has an interesting cave group to visit along the way. The route is wide and well maintained, and industrial traffic is generally slow-moving oversized logging trucks, making this a good road to travel during working hours (if you aren't too distracted by all the beautiful scenery). The route begins 2 km north of the town of Gold River; cross the Gold River via the narrow bridge and turn left (south). The road then takes a quick turn uphill to the west.

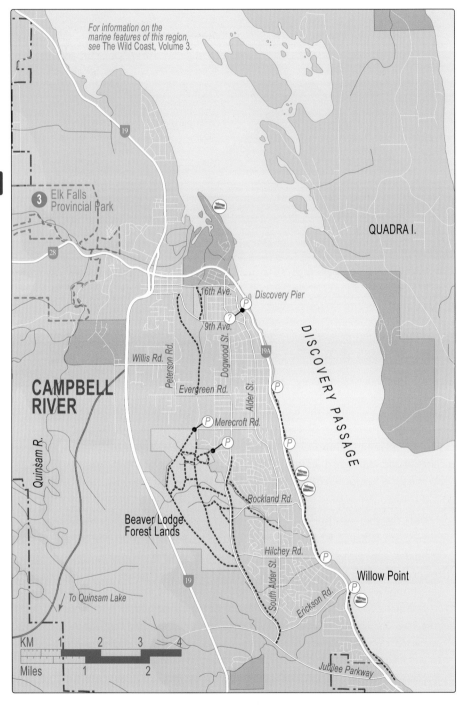

For information on the
marine features of this region,
see The Wild Coast, Volume 3.

19

3 Elk Falls
Provincial Park

28

QUADRA I.

16th Ave.
Discovery Pier

9th Ave.

19A

Willis Rd.

Peterson Rd.

Dogwood St.

Evergreen Rd.

Alder St.

D I S C O V E R Y

CAMPBELL
RIVER

Merecroft Rd.

P A S S A G E

Quinsam R.

Rockland Rd.

Beaver Lodge
Forest Lands

Hilchey Rd.

South Alder St.

19

Willow Point

To Quinsam Lake

Erickson Rd.

KM   1   2   3   4

Miles   1   2

Jubilee Parkway

See pages 234–235 for main chapter map.

👍 ZEBALLOS MAIN: This is a logging route from Highway 19 to Zeballos (sections of the northern arm are often referred to as the Atluck and Pinder mains, but the three legs are essentially indistinct). The TURNOFF ● from the Island Highway is 20 km west of Woss and is well signed from the highway. The drive is exceptional, with viewpoints of a set of tall waterfalls (Mason's Falls) and a river canyon along the way. As a major route it is wide and well maintained. A turnoff at about 35 km leads to Fair Harbour. If you want to travel to Zeballos as well as Fair Harbour, don't backtrack. A short link from Zeballos goes directly west to provide a cross-link to the Fair Harbour Main.

Campbell River region

This is country for lake and salmon lovers. The city of Campbell River is at the seaside edge of the namesake valley, a relatively flat expanse not far from some of the highest peaks on Vancouver Island. A scattering of lakes is dominated by Campbell and Upper Campbell lakes, which are created in part by a dam system. Campbell River as a region is noted for its ocean and river salmon fishing, but trout lovers tend to focus on the Sayward Forest lakes, as do visitors drawn to the many campsites there. While this area lacks the visual impact of the more mountainous areas of Vancouver Island, with the exception of a few scenic corridors, it compensates with a simple charm—something you'll understand when you hear the loons call on a quiet summer's evening.

POINTS OF INTEREST

❶ Campbell River (map p. 240)

This community is growing by leaps and bounds, shedding the last vestiges of a frontier-style roughness for a more polished image of new housing developments and a burgeoning retail sector. A great improvement has been the development of a seawalk trail through most of the city, from the thriving south end at Willow Point to near the downtown core in the north. The downtown features a busy commercial area, including the terminal for ferry service to Quadra Island. Visitors can choose to bypass it all by staying on Highway 19 or can drive the more scenic but slower Highway 19A along the waterfront. As well as the waterfront walkways, Campbell River features a large forest park known as Beaver Lodge Forest Lands, which was gifted to the province by the Elk River Timber Company in 1931 for the development of an experimental forest. It doubles as a large municipal park and includes 13 km of trails, with a main trail along the former Esquimalt and Nanaimo railway right-of-way.

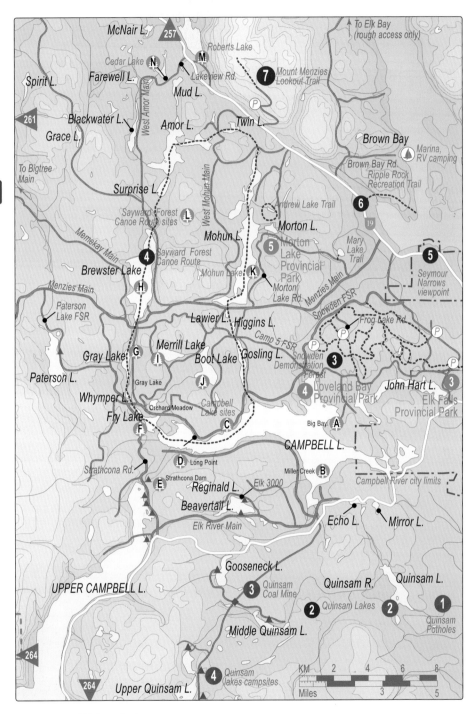

McNair L.

257

Roberts Lake

Cedar Lake   N   M
Farewell L.   Lakeview Rd.
Spirit L.   7   Mount Menzies
                         Mud L.   Lookout Trail
261   P
Blackwater L.   Amor L.   Twin L.
Grace L.   Brown Bay

West Amor Main

To Bigtree   Marina,
Main   RV camping
                                              Brown Bay Rd.
                    Surprise L.   Ripple Rock
                                              Recreation Trail
Memekay Main   Sayward Forest   L   Andrew Lake Trail
                    Canoe Route sites   6
                                 West Mohun Main   19
                                        Morton L.
                    4   Sayward Forest   Mohun L.   Morton   Mary
                         Canoe Route   5   Lake   Lake
Brewster Lake   Provincial   Trail   5
         H   Mohun Lake   K   Park
Menzies Main   Morton   Seymour
     Paterson   Lake Rd.   Narrows
     Lake FSR   Menzies Main   viewpoint
                    Lawier L.   Higgins L.   Snowden FSR
Gray Lake   G   Merrill Lake   Camp 5 FSR   Frog Lake Rd.   P
         I   Boot Lake   Gosling L.   Snowden   P   P
Paterson L.   Demonstration   3
                    Gray Lake   J   Forest   4   Loveland Bay   John Hart L.
Whymper L.   Orchard Meadow   Provincial Park   Elk Falls   3
Fry Lake   Campbell   Big Bay   A   Provincial Park
     F   Lake sites   C   CAMPBELL L.
              D   Long Point
         Strathcona Rd.   Miller Creek   B
              E   Strathcona Dam   Campbell River city limits
                    Reginald L.   Elk 3000
              Beavertail L.
                    Elk River Main   Echo L.   Mirror L.

UPPER CAMPBELL L.   Gooseneck L.
                         3   Quinsam   Quinsam R.   Quinsam L.
                              Coal Mine
                         2   Quinsam Lakes   2   1
264   Middle Quinsam L.   Quinsam
                                                          Potholes
264   4   Quinsam   KM   2   4   6   8
         Upper Quinsam L.   lakes campsites
                                              Miles   3   5

See pages 234–235 for main chapter map.

CAMPBELL RIVER REGION

Quinsam Lake.

❷ **Quinsam Lakes** *(map p. 242)*

A string of lakes south of Campbell River are part of a low-lying range of private forestry lands with the large open-pit Quinsam Coal Mine as the industrial focal point. Other than the mining lands, the forestry roads are generally open to recreation, but viewpoints are slim and the options humdrum compared to the nearby Campbell-Sayward lakes. Ongoing logging tends to reshape accesses and reduce the general appeal. Below are some of the key features of the area.

❶ QUINSAM POTHOLES: If you plan to find something here similar to the Sooke Potholes, you will be yet another victim of an enduring local joke. There are no potholes in the river; the potholes actually refer to the condition of the access road. It is used locally as a watering hole but is not remarkable by Vancouver Island standards. Directions are convoluted; use the waypoint for QUINSAM POTHOLES ● if you're determined.

❷ QUINSAM LAKE: This lake is farther along from the Quinsam Potholes on the same route from Campbell River (Willis Road to the logging road southwest, right at the Y at 3.8 km, right at the junction with the Gilson Main at 7.9 km). The traditional route is to turn right before the gate, but the entire area has been logged, and as of 2007 access to the lake hadn't been readily re-established among the maze of logging roads and slash. If you find a route to the lake you'll likely find a camping area. Don't try to reach this area from Highway 28. Some maps show the Gilson Main continuing through the region, but the ends no longer connect.

③ QUINSAM COAL MINE: This open-pit mine has been riding the prosperity of the rising energy needs of China, rejuvenating an industry that should have died out along with steam engines. The mine produces about 1.2 million tonnes a year from the same coal seam that opened Nanaimo to the trade over a century ago. It is located about 5 km along the Argonaut Main. Watch for heavy industrial truck traffic along this portion.

④ QUINSAM LAKES CAMPSITES: Vehicle-accessible wilderness camping options exist at three lakes: Middle Quinsam, Gooseneck and Upper Quinsam. Just past the coal mine along the Argonaut Main is a FIVE-WAY JUNCTION ●. The second left leads to Middle Quinsam Lake and a CAMPSITE ● with trail access to the lake. Continue past Middle Quinsam Lake and the road becomes restricted mining land. Take the right (north) at the five-way junction, then right after the bridge, then right again after the gate, and you'll reach Gooseneck Lake (a closer route from Highway 28 has been blocked because a bridge was removed). A large GRASSY CLEARING ● adjacent to the lake is used for camping. Continue straight at the five-way junction and you'll reach UPPER QUINSAM LAKE ●. A variety of options for camping are strung along the lake. Two sites are along the Argonaut Main, while another on the north end of the lake is reached by turning west near the A12 marker, then taking the next left to some spacious FORESTED CAMPSITES ●.

❸ Snowden Demonstration Forest *(map p. 242)*

Here's a mouthful: Silviculture Treatment for Ecosystem Management in the Sayward, or STEMS for short. STEMS is an experiment to measure the effectiveness of various tree farm techniques by studying costs, regeneration and forest health. It is open to the public via loop tours with twelve designated stops that include examples and descriptions of clear-cut, patch cut, group selection and other silviculture techniques. To get to the trailhead from Highway 28 take the Snowden Forest Service Road west to Frog Lake Road. Follow that south to a parking lot. Take the trail to the right (north) to begin the tour. For additional information pick up a brochure at the Campbell River visitor centre or visit **www.for.gov.bc.ca/hre/stems**.

MOUNTAIN BIKING: The forest has about 30 km of developed trails that are suitable for hiking but are most popular for mountain biking. For easiest access take Highway 28 to Elk Falls Provincial Park, cross the bridge via the private logging road and park at the water tower. From there a single trail leads to a cluster of trails. Or from Highway 28 take Brewster Lake

Typical lakeshore scenery in the Sayward Forest.

Road across the Elk Falls Dam, parking just to the north of the dam at the trailheads. The map on page 242 shows a rough route of the trails; a more detailed map is available from the Campbell River visitor centre. Note the trails are notoriously hard on bikes. Make sure you have sturdy forks and tires.

❹ Sayward Forest Canoe Route *(map p. 242)*

This canoe route circles various lakes in the Sayward Forest via a number of designated portages. The circle requires about 7.3 km of portaging, with a total distance of about 50 km. Three to four days is recommended to complete it. Watch for orange markers and portage signs to help locate portage trail locations. An anti-clockwise route would be: Campbell Lake, Gosling Lake, Higgins Lake, Lawier Lake, Mohun Lake, Twin Lake, Amor Lake, Surprise Lake, Brewster Lake, Gray Lake, Whymper Lake and Fry Lake. Official campsite locations are covered separately under the forest recreation site listings. Expect casual marine-access-only campsites and beaches along the way, particularly at Amor Lake. Note that lakefront vehicle-accessible campsites will fill up most quickly, and so may not make a good choice for paddlers. One difficulty of this route is the potential for some extensive boggy areas. These can mean muddy walks requiring you to push your canoe.

⑤ Seymour Narrows viewpoint *(map p. 242)*

A turnoff from Highway 19 about 10.8 km north of Campbell River offers a good viewpoint of Seymour Narrows, a major shipping route through one of the most powerful tidal channels in British Columbia. It's a recommended stop for those transiting the region. Signs indicate the TURNOFF ●.

⑥ Ripple Rock Recreation Trail *(map p. 242)*

This trail leads from Highway 19 about 16.7 km north of Campbell River (1.3 km north of the Morton Lake turnoff) to a lookout over Seymour Narrows. The trail is named for a large rock in the middle of the tidal channel that was once a notorious shipping hazard credited with 114 fatalities. The solution in 1958 was to blow it up—the largest non-nuclear human-created explosion in history. The clearance over the rock is now 13 m at low tide (still enough to be a marine hazard—the cruise ship *Sundancer* hit bottom in 1984, narrowly avoiding completely sinking). The 8 km trail to the viewpoint was built in 1983 and passes through mostly immature forest with one section of old growth on the east side of Menzies Creek. Consider it an easy half-day to full-day hike. The turnoff to the parking lot at the TRAILHEAD ● is easily missed when driving the Island Highway north. Watch for the sign of a hiker, then a break in the white line at the roadside. Turn right down a steep road at the break in the white line. As the parking lot is well hidden from the highway, be warned that it makes an easy target for thieves.

⑦ Mount Menzies Lookout Trail *(map p. 242)*

This trail has a reputation for being vehicle-accessible, but that time is quickly coming to an end. The TURNOFF ● is 5.1 km north of the Brown Bay Road intersection. Front-wheel-drive vehicles can probably make the first 2.5 km to a major switchback (marked with a P on the map) at about 600 m elevation, where there's a wide area suitable for PARKING ●. Even four-wheel drives will find it nearly impossible beyond that, as the road is washed out. From there you can walk up to an excellent VIEWPOINT ● at about 900 m elevation. Just keep right at the various logging road junctions along the way. The peak (1,238 m) and other lower viewpoints can be reached by diverging along other old roads, making this an ideal place to explore several times.

👍 THUMBS UP: The lower viewpoint is a strenuous but worthwhile hike taking little more than two hours to complete from the parking lot. The reward is a stunning lookout over the Sayward Forest lakes and the distant peaks of Strathcona Provincial Park.

A view from atop Mount Menzies.

Miracle Beach.

MAJOR PARKS

1 Miracle Beach Provincial Park *(map p. 235)*

This is a popular family campsite overlooking the northern Strait of Georgia.

PICNIC AREAS AND DAY USE: The park has two day-use areas. The south parking lot gives access to a beach with a picnic shelter, barbecues, tables, change rooms and flush toilets. The north parking lot gives access to a trail, the Black Creek estuary and beach. Parking fees apply.

CAMPING: The park has 201 vehicle-accessible campsites; reservations are accepted. There are also 4 walk-in campsites and a 10-unit group campsite.

SHORT WALKS: The park has 2 km of walking trails leading from the campground and north parking lot through forest and then along the

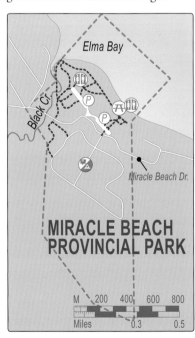

MIRACLE BEACH
PROVINCIAL PARK

Black Creek estuary, with some old-growth forest along the way. There's a designated dog-walking trail.

ACCESS: From Highway 19A approximately 20 km north of Courtenay, take Miracle Beach Drive east to the park entrance. From Highway 19, take exit #144 to Highway 19A, then drive north a short distance to Miracle Beach Drive.

❷ Oyster River Nature Park *(map p. 235)*

This small (5-hectare) regional park features a variety of trails alongside deltas of the Oyster River, located between Comox and Campbell River. A PARKING AREA ● designated for the trails is next to Fishermen's Lodge pub. To reach it, take Regent Road just past the bridge and turn into the pub. From there you'll find a variety of trails, beach access and river accesses. The trails are also suitable for cross-country biking.

FISHING: Oyster River is home to coho, pink, chum and chinook salmon as well as steelhead, cutthroat, Dolly Varden char and rainbow trout.

❸ Elk Falls Provincial Park *(map p. 242)*

Elk Falls Provincial Park is on one of Campbell River's prettiest sections, with cliffs as high as 60 m on the north side of the river. A steep canyon near John Hart Lake has a series of three waterfalls.

PICNIC AREAS AND DAY USE: A day-use area is located 3 km west of the campground at the Elk Falls location. It has picnic tables, toilets and short trails to a viewpoint. Picnicking on the rocks next to the river is a popular family outing, though due to the dam the river level can fluctuate suddenly. Listen for the sirens.

CAMPING: Elk Falls has 122 campsites accessible from the eastern park entrance; 25 are on the Quinsam River and the rest are in a second-growth forest. About half the campsites can be reserved.

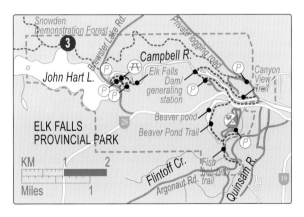

Elk Falls.

SHORT WALKS: Elk Falls park features 6 km of trails off the two main parking areas. One of the longer is the Canyon View Trail, which skirts a portion of Campbell River below Elk Falls. Another trail from the campsite area leads along a beaver pond and marsh. From the day-use area, short trails lead to a portion of old-growth Douglas-fir forest and to a set of three waterfalls—Elk, Moose and Deer falls. The falls are best viewed during the winter months when water volume is high. Viewing platforms provide lookouts into the canyon.

 THUMBS UP: I drove past the provincial park dozens of times before actually taking the time to visit. The short walk from the day-use area to the falls is a worthwhile stop for anyone transiting the area. The view of the waterfall is definitely the most stunning site in the region.

ACCESS: The park is located just west of Campbell River along Highway 28. The day-use area is 3 km past the campground entrance. Both are well marked from the highway.

---

❹ Loveland Bay Provincial Park (map p. 242)

This small (30-hectare) park on the northern arm of Campbell Lake is a gateway for many of the water sports on the lake, such as fishing, paddling, windsurfing or waterskiing, thanks to the park's boat launch and a floating 20 m wharf.

Ⓐ CAMPING: The 31 campsites stretch along the lakefront, with a few simple tent pads. Reservations are accepted, and a few are set aside as first-come, first-served. Group sites are at the far extent of the camping area.

ACCESS: Reaching the PARK ● requires a short drive along active logging roads. From Highway 28, 4 km west of Campbell River, take the road for the Elk Falls viewpoint and continue over the dam. The first logging road on the left over the dam leads 12 km to the park. Note that the road was out in 2007; alternative access is via the Snowden Forest Service Road.

---

❺ Morton Lake Provincial Park (map p. 242)

This park protects all of Morton Lake and part of adjacent Mohun Lake.

🏕 PICNIC AREAS AND DAY USE: The park has a large picnic area on the west end of Morton Lake with a sandy beach noted for the warm water. You'll find tables, change rooms and toilets.

🚶 SHORT WALKS: A 30-minute trail leads north from the campsite area near campsite #7 to Andrew Lake.

🛶 PADDLING: The park is on the Sayward canoe route and is a potential launching point and staging area. A boat ramp gives access to Mohun Lake.

Morton Lake.

FISHING: Rainbow, cutthroat and Dolly Varden trout can be found at Mohun Lake.

CAMPING: The park has 24 campsites near a sandy beach along Morton Lake. It's possible to reserve some sites and others are first-come, first-served.

ACCESS: From the Island Highway turn onto the Menzies Main logging road 1.7 km past the Seymour Narrows viewpoint. Follow the Menzies Main for 12 km to Morton Lake Road, then 7 km to the PARK ●.

FOREST RECREATION SITES

See the map on page 242 to locate these recreation sites.

This area has about two dozen established recreation sites and numerous other casual sites along the various lakefronts. Fishing is good in all the lakes. Expect cutthroat and Dolly Varden trout. ATVs are a secondary feature of the area. As most sites are fundamentally similar—lakefront locations in mature forest settings—variety comes in the number of choices, not necessarily the features you'll find. Considering that most sites are within a few kilometres of one another, it's not difficult to visit a half-dozen to pick one to your liking. Things to consider are whether you want an open or forested site; whether you want evening sun or morning sun; and congestion. A general rule of thumb: the farther it is from the highway, the less congested a site is likely to be. Note that the best sites at non-hosted locations are often commandeered, sometimes for the entire summer. Keep in mind that turn-around space can be limited at some locations—or non-existent when the site is full; RVers may want to walk down to some sites to eyeball the situation before driving down. Individual access roads have not been named on the map as they are generally named after the lake they pass, and the roads are well signed. The campsites are not. Look for generally unmarked turnoffs from the forest service roads. Note that some sites have multiple lake accesses. If in doubt, use the GPS waypoints in the appendix. Trails are surprisingly limited; look to the Snowden Demonstration Forest, Morton Lake Provincial Park, Mary Lake or portage routes for a walk.

Ⓐ Big Bay ●

This is a treed site with 11 campsites and a boat launch. It can be difficult to find. From the CAMP 5–SNOWDEN JUNCTION ● go west for 3 km, then south for 2.5 km. The turnoff to the recreation site is 0.25 km after a sharp turn.

Ⓑ Miller Creek ●

This site is on the south arm of Campbell Lake. It's located 15 km along Highway 28 west of Campbell River off the forest service road that runs parallel to the highway. The second right is Miller Creek Road. Follow it past the hydro lines and take a sharp right turn; the entry to the campsite is a quick left. The campground has 24 drive-in sites plus 2 designated for tents and a boat launch. It is hosted.

Ⓒ Campbell Lake sites (north)

If you travel west from the Camp 5-Snowden junction along the Campbell Lake Forest Service Road you'll pass 7 forest recreation sites. Descriptions are east to west. The first is BURNT BEACH ●, a 4-unit site with no boat launch and limited lake access but private, forested campsites. GOSLING BAY ● is a 6-unit site with a boulder beach and rough launch on the Sayward Forest Canoe Route. PETITE GOSLING ● has a narrow, steep access to a single site on the lakefront—good if you get it. Otherwise pick one of 3 forest sites set back with limited lake access. FIR GROVE ● is another small site best suited for one group at the end of the access road. Other sites up from the lake have limited water access. CAMPBELL LAKE ● (Beer Belly Flats) is a larger 20-unit hosted site that is gated from 10 p.m. to 7 a.m. Good sites face the water. DOGWOOD BAY ● has about 5 sites set on various levels over the bay, with a small beach area and launch. LOON BAY ● is a pretty location with a selection of forested sites and a good sand beach.

Upper Campbell Lake.

Long Point

This site is hidden along obscure logging roads on the southwest side of Campbell Lake. It has about eight campsites and a short trail to a sandy beach. The best access is off Elk River Main that departs Highway 28 just west of Echo Lake. From there follow the road along the south side of Campbell Lake to the recreation site. Easier-to-find sites along the same forest service road connector can be found on Beavertail Lake. From Elk River Main take the Elk 3000 spur north for 0.8 km, where you'll find a treed site with large clear areas next to the lake. An alternative is an open RV-style site on the south side adjacent to the Elk River Main, 1.8 km west of the Elk 3000 junction.

Strathcona Dam Recreation Area ●

This recreation area is more ideally suited to RVers. The sites are in an open area below the dam, and from a wilderness perspective they're not particularly desirable. From Highway 28 take Strathcona Road north. Signs indicating the recreation area are good. Cross the dam then take the next right; it will lead back along the base of the dam to a small peninsula with a mix of industrial hydro fixtures and campsites along the river. Casual sites dot Strathcona Road along the shore of Upper Campbell Lake, north and west past the dam.

ⓕ **Fry Lake** ●

Three official sites are set on the shore of Fry Lake, a western adjunct to Campbell Lake. They are Fry Trestle, Orchard Meadow and Fry Gravel Pit, but because of multiple accesses they more or less blur into one site with various access points along the lakeside. The gravel pit is on the south end, where an open pit is the obvious attraction. Expect noise from motorized off-road vehicles in this area, potentially affecting the Loon Bay campsite. Orchard Meadow is a large site with well-dispersed campsites spread along Fry Lake with good lake access.

ⓖ **Gray Lake** ●

Gray Lake is a small treed site with picnic tables on the south end of the lake. The lake is part of the canoe route, with a portage required here. Brittany Bay, just to the north, is a small site with limited turning space. It would be congested when the three sites are in use. Note that nearby Paterson Lake is off the map so far as the official recreation sites for the area go, but it is accessible. Look for a not particularly pretty open clearing along the east side of the lake just off the Paterson Lake Forest Service Road.

ⓗ **Brewster Lake**

Four sites are set in close proximity on the south end of this lake. BREWSTER CAMP ● is on the narrow southernmost portion with three turnoffs; generally they are grassy lakeside clearings best suited for a single group. Camp 5, just off the Menzies Main on the southwest side of the lake, has sites in a forested clearing. The name refers to the logging camp that was located here. APPLE POINT ●, on the southeast corner of the lake, is named for the apple trees— one of the last reminders of the camp that once hosted 500 workers. The railroad logging camp was started in 1943 and dismantled in 1964 when trucking replaced railroads. Look for the concrete foundations; buildings in the camp included two schools, cook houses, a recreation hall and a library. The BREWSTER LAKE ● site, farther up the southeast end of the lake, has 12 forested campsites with a larger-than-average beach area. It is hosted.

ⓘ **Merrill Lake** ●

This site has three units and a small boat launch. It could be difficult to turn around if full. The drive along the Merrill Lake logging road is particularly pretty.

ⓙ **Boot Lake** ●

This is a small site with a steep, rocky access road that may deter some users. There is a rock boat ramp but no beach to speak of.

(K) Mohun Lake ●

Two open sites are on the south end of Mohun Lake, with a boat ramp and beach access. It's on the canoe route with a portage to Lawier Lake. It's located at the 12 km marker along Menzies Main.

(L) Sayward Forest Canoe Route sites

The northern sites among this group are the most remote, with many accessible only by boat. Seagull Bay is on the northern tip of Mohun Lake, with boat access or possibly walk-in access via the old road. The Twin Lake site is vehicle-accessible; it's in a small but pretty setting with a rough boat launch, small beach, dock and about 2 km of trails through the area. Drive 3.4 km down the Mohun West Main (the turnoff from the Island Highway is 6.5 km past Browns Bay Road). The site is part of the portage route to Twin and Amor lakes. Sterling Beach, Sterling Island and Mr. Canoehead on Amor Lake are accessible by boat only. Sterling Beach has two tent sites, the island has one and Mr. Canoehead has five. The Amor Lake site is vehicle accessible; take the Amor Lake West Main 8.8 km south (with the turnoff 11.7 km past Browns Bay Road; it is marked Lakeview Road) to find sites directly off the main on both sides of the road. There is a small launch area and beach. Note that paddlers will find numerous other undesignated beach sites in these upper lakes.

(M) Roberts Lake ●

This is a small day-use area at a sandy beach on Roberts Lake, northwest of Mount Menzies and north of Highway 19. A short trail leads from the parking area to the lake. Take the Island Highway to the logging road 11.3 km past Browns Bay Road, then follow the logging road north. Turn left immediately after the second bridge and continue, passing all gated roads along the way, to the grassy parking lot and trailhead.

(N) Cedar Lake ●

This is a small site set on a lake north of the Sayward Forest Canoe Route. Take Lakeview Road west 11.7 km after Brown Bay Road. Follow it 2.9 km past Edaus School and keep right at the gated road until you reach the Cedar Lake turnoff.

Rock Bay

Given a choice of the Sayward Forest lakes and those north of the Island Highway in the Rock Bay Main area—well, there really is no comparison. The level Campbell River valley gives way in the north to a mountainous region dotted with lakes and jagged peaks, making the McCreight Lake view over Needle Peaks among the prettiest viewpoints in the area; the southern lakes simply can't match it. Again, a good selection of forest recreation sites can be

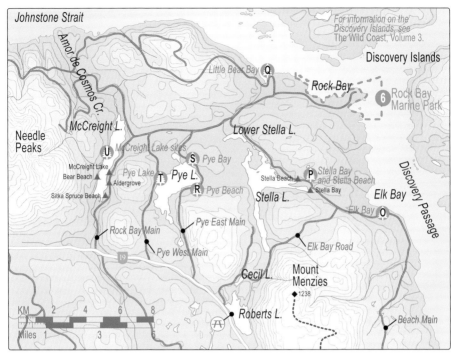

See pages 234–235 for main chapter map.

Map labels:

Johnstone Strait

Amor de Cosmos Cr.

Little Bear Bay Q

For information on the
Discovery Islands, see
The Wild Coast, Volume 3.

Rock Bay

Discovery Islands

6 Rock Bay
Marine Park

McCreight L.

Lower Stella L.

Needle
Peaks

U McCreight Lake sites

S Pye Bay

McCreight Lake
Bear Beach

Pye Lake

Aldergrove

T Pye L.

R Pye Beach

Sitka Spruce Beach

Stella Beach

P Stella Bay
and Stella Beach

Stella Bay

Elk Bay

Stella L.

Elk Bay

O

Discovery Passage

Rock Bay Main

Pye East Main

Pye West Main

19

Elk Bay Road

Cecil L.

Mount
Menzies

1238

KM 2 4 6 8

Roberts L.

Beach Main

Miles 1 3

ROCK BAY

A view over McCreight Lake.

A view from above Elk Bay.

found here, with correspondingly fewer users, given the distance from Campbell River (which, in the scheme of things, is really quite insignificant). It also has the added advantage of access to Discovery Passage, a popular boating area that includes Quadra Island and the other nearby Discovery Islands. For information on those islands, see *The Wild Coast, Volume 3*.

FOREST RECREATION SITES

See the map on page 257 to locate these recreation sites.

Elk Bay ●

The sites at Elk Bay are set along the ocean on the south side of the namesake bay, with some wonderful views over Discovery Passage toward Quadra Island. A variety of access points leads to a mixture of camping locations—open RV clearings or neatly forested sites with picnic tables and firepits. A downside is close proximity to the Elk Bay log sort. Expect a good deal of industrial noise and traffic during business hours. Access is via the Elk Bay Main, with the turnoff at Roberts Lake 0.5 km past the rest area. Note that the road from Brown Bay to Elk Bay is generally impassable.

TRAVEL NOTES: The B movie *The 13th Warrior* was filmed near here. The only vestige of the shoot is three totems on the hilltop north of Elk Bay.

Stella Bay and Stella Beach ●

Stella Bay features one main unit at the end of the access road next to a beach with a simple dock. Another small adjacent site is on a pretty lake. At Stella Beach, about a dozen sites are spread around the forest next to a sandy beach featuring wonderful views. Sites have picnic tables. The campground is hosted.

Q Little Bear Bay ●

Fifteen sites are spread along the east end of this small ocean bay near a fish hatchery, with a trail to a waterfall and some large fir trees. A boat launch makes it a key access point to the south end of Johnstone Strait, and the best public access to Rock Bay Marine Park. Note private facilities, including camping, are closer to Rock Bay.

R Pye Beach ●

Half a dozen sites are located in small clusters along Pye Lake with a shared beach, dock and boat ramp. Other dispersed sites can be found along the lake. Access for Pye Beach and Pye Bay (below) is off Pye East Main, and can be reached from Rock Bay Main.

S Pye Bay ●

About seven units are located in a forest setting sharing a communal gravel beach, small dock and boat launch.

T Pye Lake ●

This is a small site best used by three groups or less with a small gravel launch beach. It is off the Pye Lake West Main, with the turnoff 5 km past Elk Bay Road.

U McCreight Lake sites

Officially three recreation sites are located along the southeast shore of McCreight Lake, but they are in close enough proximity to consider as one. All three have the beautiful scenic backdrop of the craggy peaks to the west. Sitka Spruce Beach, the south campsite, is walk-in or boat-in only, reached by a short trail from a pullout just off the Rock Bay Main. The small site has a good sandy beach. Just up from Sitka Spruce Beach is Aldergrove, a treed site with two units and a trail to a sandy beach. The northern of the three sites is MCCREIGHT LAKE ●, which has two accesses to the lake. The southern access has four sites in a string overlooking the lake atop a short slope. The north access is meant as a boat ramp but is often used for RV camping at the lake level. A fourth campsite on the lake, Bear Beach, is located across the lake in the setting of an old-growth cedar forest. The site is best for two tents, and is accessible by boat only.

MAJOR PARKS

6 Rock Bay Marine Park *(map p. 257)*

This is an unusual park in that it protects the foreshore and marine area only, with all adjacent upland privately owned, including Chatham Point, a lighthouse and marine weather station. A nearby private campground offers camping and a boat launch; it's also possible to launch from the Little Bear Bay recreation site. Strong wind and currents make this a potentially hazardous area, though the island clusters and reefs make for interesting paddling. For the full water-based potential for visiting this region, see *The Wild Coast, Volume 3.*

Sayward-Memekay

This is a region where most of the best features seem to be on the periphery—Victoria Peak and Strathcona Provincial Park to the south, Upper Adam Valley and Schoen Lake to the west and the saltwater attractions in Johnstone Strait to the north, to name just a few. What you will find here is a small community, Sayward, which provides one of the few paved accesses to Johnstone Strait, and a mess of logging roads to the south. Many of these tend to be quite active, so if you decide to scoot down Bigtree Main to the interior of the island one day, be prepared for the dust and noise of logging trucks, which can pass through every few minutes. For your effort you will find a few pretty regions, such as White River Provincial Park, and some wonderful views, such as Victoria Peak, one of the tallest on Vancouver Island. But stunning vistas are otherwise limited along here, just as the recreational opportunities are. This is probably due to a lack of lakes; the only sizeable one is Tlowils, which can be reached by logging road for those who find reason. This limits the main attractions to mountain hikes or rivers. A recommended circuit is the drive along White River and Upper Adams mains, both wild and pretty areas. The access to north Strathcona Provincial Park is covered in the section beginning page 265.

POINTS OF INTEREST

❽ Salmon Lookout *(map p. 261)*

This is a steep, 6 km, two-hour round trip trail to a former forest service lookout. Unfortunately, the lookout is now just a bit of debris, leaving only marginal views through trees at the summit. The TRAILHEAD ● is about 9 km past the Rock Bay Main just past a rest area. Look for the trail at the far (southeast) end of the parking lot.

❾ Dalrymple Creek Trail *(map p. 261)*

This is a short (0.5 km) interpretive walk through various forest features, with limited information provided on signs. A pamphlet is available; ask at the Campbell River tourist information centre. The trail is marked by a small hiking sign at the Island Highway about 55 km north of Campbell River and 10 km past the Bigtree Main; take the short access road to a PARKING AREA ● and two picnic table sites.

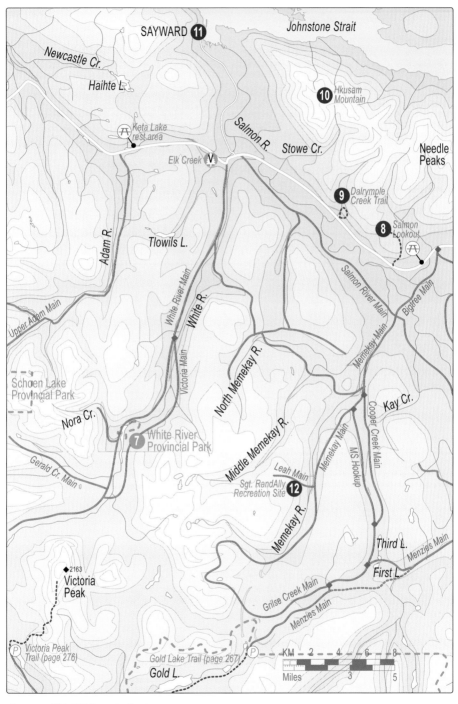

SAYWARD ⓫

Johnstone Strait

Newcastle Cr.

Haihte L.

Hkusam
⓾ Mountain

Salmon R.   Stowe Cr.

Needle
Peaks

🅟 Keta Lake
rest area

Elk Creek Ⓥ

⑨ Dalrymple
Creek Trail

Adam R.

Tlowils L.

⑧ Salmon
Lookout
🅟

Upper Adam Main

White River Main

White R.

Salmon River Main

Bigtree Main

Memekay Main

Schoen Lake
Provincial Park

Victoria Main

North Memekay R.

Kay Cr.

Nora Cr.

⑦ White River
Provincial Park

Middle Memekay R.

Cooper Creek Main

Gerald Cr. Main

Leah Main

Sgt. RandAlly
Recreation Site ⓬

Memekay Main

MS Hookup

Memekay R.

Third L.

Menzies Main

◆2163
Victoria
Peak

First L.

🅟 Victoria Peak
Trail (page 276)

Gold Lake Trail (page 267) 🅟

Grilse Creek Main

Menzies Main

Gold L.

KM   2   4   6   8
Miles   3   5

See pages 234–235 for main chapter map.

SAYWARD-MEMEKAY

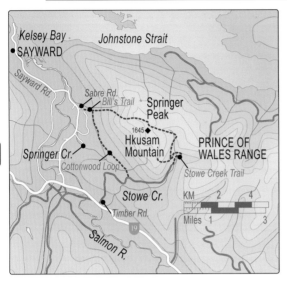

Kelsey Bay
Johnstone Strait
•SAYWARD
Sayward Rd.
Sabre Rd.
Bill's Trail
Springer Peak
1645◆
Hkusam Mountain
Springer Cr.
PRINCE OF WALES RANGE
Cottonwood Loop
Stowe Creek Trail
Stowe Cr.
KM   2   4
Timber Rd.
Miles 1   3
19
Salmon R.

At 1,645 m, Hkusam Mountain is a wonderful viewpoint over the surrounding countryside, particularly across the Strait of Georgia to the mainland mountains. An advantage is good accessibility. The trails have been linked into a loop popularized through the Kusam Klimb, a grueling 23 km race held every June. Visit **www .kusamklimb.ca**. For casual visitors, the prime trail is known as Bill's Trail, named for its creator. It leads up the west ridge near Springer Peak to a small alpine lake, then toward the summit of Hkusam Peak. Side trails are possible to both the Springer and Hkusam summits. Another trail leads up Hkusam's southeast flank along Stowe Creek.

ACCESS: To reach the trailhead for BILL'S TRAIL ●, take Sayward Road north from the Island Highway. At about 4.8 km, turn east onto Sabre Road. Follow it uphill to a sharp right; the trailhead is just off the gravel road to the left at the turn.

⑪ Sayward *(map p. 261)*

This small community is near Johnstone Strait behind Salmon Bay. It's a popular staging ground for trips into the strait, particularly fishing excursions. Full information on the nearby marine features is covered in *The Wild Coast, Volume 3*. Services are limited, but there is a well-stocked store.

Ⓐ CAMPING: The Village Centre Campground is run by the community and is quite central, located next to a pleasant pond. It has washrooms and a sani-station. An RV park, run by the local Community Futures organization, is located next to the dock at the north end of Sayward Road, at the west entrance to Kelsey Bay. The rest of the bay is mainly dominated by marinas, a log sort facility and the intertidal mudflats of Salmon River.

SAYWARD-MEMEKAY

12 Sgt. RandAlly Recreation Site ● *(map p. 261)*

This is an odd little park with numerous signs—at logging road junctions as far away as Woss. For the effort in reaching it you'll be rewarded with a walk in the woods to the world champion yellow cedar, a tree possibly as old as 1,800 years. The tree was found by Ally Gibson and Randall Dayton; the site's name is a combination of their first names (with no explanation of where the sergeant fits in). There's a problem, however, with protecting a stand of old-growth trees on a ridge surrounded by logged areas. Blowdown has obliterated the trail, and in 2007 it was impassable. If you are traveling to Gold Lake in north Strathcona, this can make an interesting diversion—assuming the blowdown is eventually cleared up.

ACCESS: Follow the signs to Leah Main from Memekay Main. The site is a short drive up Lean Main, which is moderately steep.

MAJOR PARKS

7 White River Provincial Park *(map p. 261)*

BC Parks refers to White River Provincial Park as the Cathedral Grove of the North Island due to the old-growth forest. It shares a few features with the other park. One is the diminutive size; White River is just 68 hectares. Within it are some of the same types of massive Douglas-fir and western red cedar trees. The park itself is undeveloped.

FISHING: The White River is home to summer steelhead, summer coho, rainbow trout and Dolly Varden trout.

SHORT WALKS: A short TRAIL ● departs from the Victoria Main about 5.8 km past the Victoria–White River mains junction and leads into the old-growth forest.

ACCESS: The park is flanked by two logging roads. The east side is reached via the Victoria Main. While only a small portion of the park is adjacent to this main, it provides the best forest access. The west side is bordered by the White River Main. For either option take the White River Main from the Island Highway, which heads south from the Sayward Road junction. The VICTORIA–WHITE RIVER MAINS JUNCTION ● is about 17 km south of the Island Highway. Hopefully a clearer trail from the west will develop.

TRAVEL NOTES: According to BC Parks, the stand of firs was impressive enough to prompt the loggers in the area to refuse to cut it. If you see some boardwalks in the park, chances are they were used for the movie *The Scarlet Letter*, filmed here in 1994. The boardwalks were created for the movie's horse-drawn carriages.

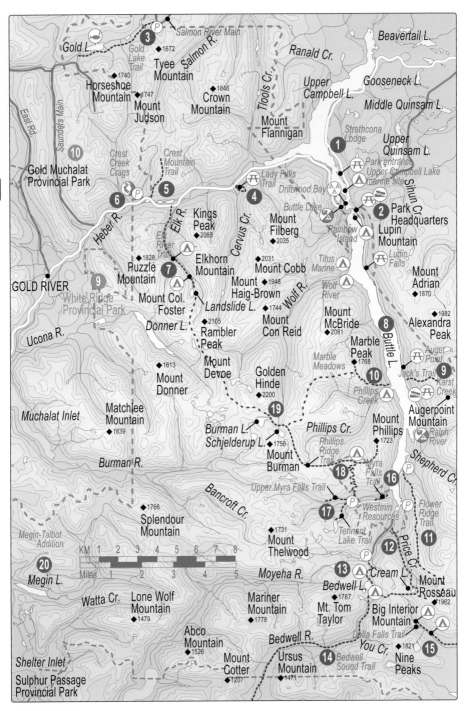

STRATHCONA

Beavertail L.

Gold L.
3
1672
Salmon River Main
Ranald Cr.
Gooseneck L.

Gold Lake Trail
Tyee Mountain
Salmon R.
Upper Campbell L.
Middle Quinsam L.

1740
Horseshoe Mountain
1747
Mount Judson
1846
Crown Mountain
Tlools Cr.
Mount Flannigan
Strathcona Lodge
Upper Quinsam L.

East Rd.

Saunders Main

Crest Creek Crags
Crest Mountain Trail
Gold Muchalat Provincial Park
10
Lady Falls Trail
Driftwood Bay
Buttle Lake
Park entrance
Upper Campbell Lake marine site
1
Sihun Cr.

6
5
Elk R.
Kings Peak
2065
Cervus Cr.
Mount Filberg
2035
Rainbow Island
Park Headquarters
2
Lupin Mountain
Lupin Falls
Mount Adrian
1870

Heber R.
Elk River Trail
1828
Puzzle Mountain
7
Elkhorn Mountain
2031
Mount Cobb
1948
Mount Haig-Brown
Titus Marine
Wolf R.
Wolf River

GOLD RIVER
9
White Ridge Provincial Park
Mount Col. Foster
Landslide L.
1744
Mount Con Reid
Mount McBride
2081
8
Alexandra Peak
1982

Donner L.
2105
Rambler Peak
Marble Peak
1768
Auger Point
Jack's Trail
9
Karst Creek

Ucona R.
1613
Mount Devoe
Marble Meadows
10

Mount Donner
Golden Hinde
2200
Phillips Creek
Augerpoint Mountain

Matchlee Mountain
1839
19
Phillips Cr.
Mount Phillips
1723
Ralph River

Burman L.
Schjelderup L.
1756
Phillips Ridge Trail
Shepherd Cr.

Burman R.
Mount Burman
18
Myra Falls Trail
16
Flower Ridge Trail

Bancroft Cr.
Upper Myra Falls Trail
Westmin Resources

1766
Splendour Mountain
17
P
Tennent Lake Trail
12
Price Cr.
11

Megin-Talbot Addition
1731
Mount Thelwood
P
13
Cream L.
Mount Rosseau

KM 1 2 3 4 5 6 7 8
20
Moyeha R.
Bedwell L.
1962

Megin L.
Miles 1 2 3 4 5
Mariner Mountain
1787
Big Interior Mountain

Watta Cr.
Lone Wolf Mountain
1479
1778
Mt. Tom Taylor
Della Falls Trail

Abco Mountain
1526
Bedwell R.
You Cr.
1821
15

Shelter Inlet
Mount Cotter
1207
Ursus Mountain
1471
14
Bedwell Sound Trail
Nine Peaks

Sulphur Passage Provincial Park

See pages 234–235 for main chapter map.

FOREST RECREATION SITES

Elk Creek *(map p. 257)*

This site can be found off the Island Highway about 300 m west of the Sayward Road turnoff. Look for a wood marker on the south side of the highway. The access road leads to a loop of about six campsites in a treed setting. It would make a convenient overnight stop in a transit of the area.

Strathcona

MAJOR PARKS

8 Strathcona Provincial Park
(map p. 235)

Detailed map page 264

There is simply no mistaking Strathcona Provincial Park as you approach. The snow-capped peaks will loom larger until you are surrounded by many of the most impressive sights on Vancouver Island. Strathcona is Vancouver Island's largest (at 245,800 hectares) and first provincial park. The paved road along Buttle Lake gives access deep into the park, allowing travel by casual visitors, while backcountry routes provide the potential for a lifetime of exploring alpine areas for hardy hikers and climbers.

Casual visitors will enjoy the many picnic areas along Buttle Lake, each with its own spectacular mountain vistas, as well as short trails exploring various features of the park. Highlights include walks to places like Myra Falls, a beautiful waterfall cascading over various tiers before emptying into Buttle Lake.

An odd feature of the park is a working mine just west of the south end of Buttle Lake. Boliden-Westwin Resources mines about 1.4 million tonnes of ore a year for the zinc, copper,

Camping at the alpine level deep in Strathcona Provincial Park.

STRATHCONA

gold and silver. The trucks are a regular feature on the narrow and winding Westmin Mine Road along Buttle Lake.

The Forbidden Plateau portion of Strathcona park is covered beginning page 202. The various day features, trails and main backcountry opportunities in the rest of the park are described separately below.

Ⓐ CAMPING: There are three designated campgrounds in Strathcona, with backcountry potential along many trails and five designated marine camping areas along Buttle Lake. Reservations are accepted at the main campsites.

- BUTTLE LAKE: This family-oriented campground is located on the north end of Buttle Lake in the setting of a young forest. Various short trails lead from the 79-unit campsite and the access road to beach areas or to Darkis Lake, a small fishing lake immediately west of the campground.

- DRIFTWOOD BAY: This is a group camping area adjacent to the lake near the Buttle Lake campsite; it has a covered picnic site, wood stove and wheelchair-accessible pot toilets. It's a reservation-only site.

- RALPH RIVER: This campground features 75 sites, some quite private and dispersed, in the incredible setting of an old-growth forest. Some sites are along Ralph River, while a few locations likely to be snapped up quickly face the lake. Various short trails lead to the lake and to Ralph River. Across the Westmin Mine Road is a choice of trails. The Shepherd Creek Loop Trail begins directly across from the campground and goes 1.8 km through a scenic forested area with moderate elevation gains and drops. Across Ralph River opposite the campsite is the 800 m Wild Ginger Loop Trail. Undesignated trails diverge from the loop and continue along Shepherd Creek and Ralph River, giving access to the backcountry and potentially the Comox Glacier and Mount Albert Edward.

- MARINE CAMPSITES: The park offers a selection of marine-access-only campsites—four on Buttle Lake and one on Upper Campbell Lake. Tent pads and tables are supplied at the sites, called Upper Campbell Lake, Rainbow Island, Titus, Wolf River and Phillips Creek. All are marked on the main map on page 264. Most are limited to five tent pads. Fees apply, with pay stations at the boat ramps and day-use areas.

👍 THUMBS UP: Strathcona Provincial Park has some of the best scenery, camping and hiking on Vancouver Island. Because it is a park most features are clean, supervised and well maintained. The trails give a range of opportunities from short, accessible walks to multi-day alpine hikes and aggressive mountain climbing. There is something for every level of enjoyment here, and for those who fall in love with it, a lifetime of exploring lies ahead.

Hiking into the alpine can mean snow almost any time of year in Strathcona.

Following are the other key locations.

1 STRATHCONA LODGE: This lodge on the shore of Upper Campbell Lake has been a fixture on the outskirts of the park since 1959. It offers accommodation, adventure recreation from horseback riding to mountaineering and education through school programs and its Canadian Outdoor Leadership Training program, a wilderness guide training school. Visit **www .strathcona.bc.ca**.

2 PARK HEADQUARTERS: Those driving into Strathcona park will first see a picnic area on Upper Campbell Lake. Just south of the junction of Westmin Mine Road and Highway 28 is the park headquarters, with a picnic site and boat launch just a bit farther south.

3 GOLD LAKE TRAIL: This is an unusual way to enter Strathcona park, with the reward of an intriguing wilderness trail through some old-growth forest. North of Campbell River, take the Menzies Bay Main west to the end. The TRAIL ● leads through an old cedar forest, then skirts Gold Lake, petering out as it nears the west access off East Road (see Gold Muchalat Provincial Park, page 284).

A creek along the Gold Lake Trail.

4 LADY FALLS TRAIL: This 900 m trail leads from Highway 28 through some old-growth forest to a viewing platform across Elk River into Roosevelt elk habitat.

5 CREST MOUNTAIN TRAIL: This 5 km trail gains 1,250 m in elevation, making it one of the more challenging routes. There are wonderful views at the summit.

6 CREST CREEK CRAGS: The crags offer about 150 climbing routes catering to all skill levels.

7 ELK RIVER TRAIL: The designated portion of this trail leads 11 km south from Highway 28 and gains 600 m in elevation by following the Elk River valley to Landslide Lake. The trail is also the approach for ascents of Mount Colonel Foster, one of Vancouver Island's premier climbing peaks at 2,135 m, as well as Elkhorn Mountain and Rambler Peak. Camping is designated at Butterwort Flats, 6 km along the trail, and at the upper gravel bar at 9 km. There is no camping at Landslide Lake. The lake is the start of the route for the north approach to Golden Hinde, a difficult route with a potential connection to Phillips Ridge.

8 BUTTLE LAKE AND PICNIC SITES: The lake is a popular paddling and fishing destination, with a handful of designated marine camping areas along its length. Fishing is likely to land cutthroat, rainbow and Dolly Varden trout. Visitors driving south along Buttle Lake will have a selection of picnic stops— pleasant, grassy, day-use areas with adjacent short trails. Lupin Falls has an 800 m trail to viewpoints of the falls. Auger Point has a short loop trail through an area recovering nicely from a mid-1980s forest fire. Karst Creek has a 2 km trail through a karst area with a disappearing stream and a waterfall.

TRAVEL NOTES: Buttle Lake was created by the damming of Upper Campbell Lake and many tree stumps now lie submerged. This can make boating hazardous, particularly as the lake level has dropped in recent years. It has the advantage of allowing long walks along the shoreline.

9 AUGERPOINT MOUNTAIN (JACK'S TRAIL): Between the Karst Creek and Auger Point day-use areas is a trailhead for an undesignated trail; you can find it by watching for the arrow painted on the road about 1 km north of Karst Creek. Parking is possible on the nearby roadside. The trail leads steeply up the hillside of Augerpoint Mountain by way of a series of switchbacks. You'll find an excellent viewpoint on a bluff about an hour up the trail. This makes a good picnic site for those who want to hike only a portion of the trail, with about the best views possible in the park for the effort. From there the trail is a difficult climb with one section of steep scree that can be intimidating. It then levels out to an alpine ridge top with incredible views over the surrounding countryside. From

Buttle Lake from the vantage of Flower Ridge's alpine level.

Augerpoint Mountain a route continues east to Mount Albert Edward. This is a backcountry route for experts only.

⑩ MARBLE MEADOWS: The official portion of this trail leads 6.6 km with a 1,250-m elevation gain from the Phillips Creek marine campsite. Because of that, access is by boat only, but that tends to add to the experience of traveling this incredible route to the alpine meadows and its views over the region. An unusual feature of this route is an alpine hut that's available to hikers. Adjacent Marblerock Canyon has some popular climbing walls. Side routes allow ascents of Marble Peak (1,767 m) and Mount McBride (2,081 m). This is also one possible way to reach Golden Hinde, Vancouver Island's tallest peak.

⑪ FLOWER RIDGE TRAIL: This trail is one of the more accessible ways to reach the alpine level in central Strathcona. The trail rises comparatively gently up a north-facing ridge to the alpine level. A downside is the first good viewpoints tend to look over the Westmin industrial mining area. However, the views north along Buttle Lake are wonderful. The designated portion of the trail is 6 km, with an elevation gain of 1,250 m. It's a good full-day hike, and I've seen it completed by children. The trail continues south along the open ridge, with the potential to connect to the Bedwell Lake and Price Creek trails.

⑫ PRICE CREEK TRAIL: This trail leads 8.5 km from the trailhead at the south end of Buttle Lake to Cream Lake, with an elevation gain of 1,200 m. The first portion is along a gravel road, then along the main valley before crossing Price Creek to a tortuously rough and steep scramble to the alpine level. Cream Lake sits under the cover of Mount Septimus (1,850 m) and Mount Rousseau (1,962 m), two distinct and craggy climbing peaks. Reaching Cream Lake is simplest and most popular via the Bedwell Lake route.

⑬ BEDWELL LAKE TRAIL: This trail begins by way of an old gravel road, Jim Mitchell Lake Road, that leads south from Westmin Mine Road at the south end of Buttle Lake to a parking area and the trailhead. The designated portion of the trail is 6 km and gains 600 m in elevation, with designated camping at both Bedwell Lake and Little Bedwell Lake to the north (closer to the trailhead). The trail has some good aids, including metal stairwells up some steep portions, but nature has a habit of destroying these; for instance, in 2006 a winter storm caused a landslide that blocked the access road, effectively closing the trail. Check the park website before setting out. A branch heads east up a ridge to Cream Lake. This is a challenging route but accessible to most fit hikers. It is best reached in two days, though hardy hikers could complete it in one.

TRAVEL NOTES: Some recreation maps may show a link between the trail to Cream Lake and Della Falls via Drinkwater Creek. I have found no evidence of this trail, and a portion of cliff would seem to preclude there ever being a route (though every so often someone tells me it does indeed exist). The connection can be made via Mount Septimus; one fellow who completed that route, a highly accomplished hiker, called it "difficult" and said he would never do it again. (When someone like that considers a route difficult, watch out.)

14 BEDWELL SOUND TRAIL: This trail branches southwest from Bedwell Lake to Bedwell Sound deep in the heart of Clayoquot. This is an unofficial trail that leaves the park by following the Bedwell River valley to its mouth. The waterfront portion at Bedwell Sound is private property owned by the Clayoquot Wilderness Resort, which keeps an upscale tent resort on the property. The resort allows public access from the sound to the trail, which leads up an old mining roadbed in generally good condition. Despite work over the years by the Friends of Strathcona, the trail in 2007 was overgrown and difficult to follow. Bridges were also in poor repair. A proposal by the resort would see them upgrade the trail for use by mountain bikers and horseback riders, with tent pads for public use at You Creek. Access by water taxi or charter boat is possible to the Bedwell Sound trailhead from Tofino.

15 DELLA FALLS TRAIL: This incredible trail is best reached by Great Central Lake and is my vote for the best combined paddling and hiking trip on Vancouver Island. The trail is discussed more completely on page 189.

16 MYRA FALLS TRAIL: A short trail leads from a parking lot off the south end of Buttle Lake near the Westmin Mine; the initial trail leads along an old logging roadbed to a choice of lookouts over the falls, which are best seen in the spring when the snowpack is melting. The 1 km trail may be steep for some fitness levels on the return walk.

17 UPPER MYRA FALLS AND TENNENT LAKE TRAILS: The Tennent Lake Trail begins at the parking lot just past the Westmin mine. It's a challenging 7 km trail with an elevation gain of 1,500 m leading up Mount Myra (1,810 m) to Tennent Lake. The Upper Myra Falls Trail is a far easier trail. It leads 3 km to a viewing platform looking out over the waterfall.

18 PHILLIPS RIDGE TRAIL: This trail leads from a parking lot just west of the Westmin Mine up to Arnica Lake, a formal campsite with tent pads. The official portion of the trail is 6 km with a gain of 800 m. This makes an excellent base for a next-day trip to the cairn at the summit of Mount Phillips (1,723 m) with panoramic views over Strathcona. Another option is to travel westward along the ridge toward Golden Hinde (page 272).

TRAVEL NOTES: There is a viewpoint about a two-day hike along the ridge that looks over Schjelderup Lake. It's a 360-degree view in which there is no evidence of human occupation beyond what little trail skirts the ridge. This is a true wilderness opportunity.

A view of the Golden Hinde from Phillips Ridge.

19 GOLDEN HINDE: This is Vancouver Island's tallest peak, at 2,200 m. It's a favourite ascent, usually scaled in late summer when the snow is at its lowest. The most popular route to get here is along Phillips Ridge. From Arnica Lake it follows a series of alpine ridges generally northwest to Schjelderup Lake. Burman Lake is a good staging area; the most popular ascent is up the southeast ridge, a relatively easy route up some gullies with some loose rock and scrambles to the summit. Other approaches are possible from Elk River and Marble Meadows.

20 MEGIN-TALBOT ADDITION: The 27,390 hectares of the Megin-Talbot watersheds were added to Strathcona park in 1995. The entire addition is essentially wilderness, lacking both road accesses and designated hiking trails. Determined visitors will find old-growth forests and the largest unlogged watershed on the island. Most recreation tends to focus on Megin Lake. Here float planes drop off campers, paddlers and fishermen. A cabin at the lake is available for public use, but should be arranged in advance through Tofino Air (**www.tofinoair.ca**). A good trip would be a drop-in to paddle down the Megin River and through Clayoquot Sound to Tofino. Casual visitors can paddle or boat to the outskirts of the addition through Clayoquot Sound. A wonderful waterfall drops into Shelter Inlet just east of the mouth of Megin River. Bring a fishing rod. Megin River is home to salmon, steelhead and Dolly Varden trout.

TRAVEL NOTES: My attempt to paddle upstream to Megin Lake was cut short by current. We didn't make more than a hundred metres. Some recreation maps mark a trail along the west side of the creek. I have yet to find evidence of the trailhead or trail.

---

9 **White Ridge Provincial Park** *(map p. 264)*

This ridge, named for its limestone, is the eastern backdrop for the village of Gold River. There is no development within the park, though undesignated trails do cross the area. It's notable for its numerous caves and elk habitat.

SPELUNKING: The caves within the park are among Canada's longest and deepest. Seventeen have been recorded. Advanced cavers only should attempt these caves; if they do they can expect to view speleothems, ice deposits, paleontological remnants (the black bear bones found are the oldest discovered since glaciation 9,000 years ago) plus resident bats and unusual insects. As a management plan for the park has not yet been completed, use is not recommended to protect any rare karst features.

TRAVEL NOTES: The traditional access to the area was via Ucona Main leading from the south end of Gold River, then Ucona-7. The route is now essentially impassable. This was also the route for Donner Lake within Strathcona Provincial Park. Access is now limited to only the most determined.

Nootka Sound

Nootka is a word intrinsically linked to the history and geography of Vancouver Island. It was here in 1788 that Capt. James Cook established trade with Chief Maquinna, leading to the otter fur trade that transformed the Pacific coast. It was the location of the only Spanish fort ever built in Canada, in 1789, and the site of a conflict that almost led to war between England and Spain. Modern history has been checkered. Long reliant on logging, the communities of Zeballos, Tahsis

Three Sisters Falls.

and Gold River have all faced mill closures in recent years, which have hurt the vibrancy of the region. Most services are still available, however, and the area's natural appeal is as strong as ever.

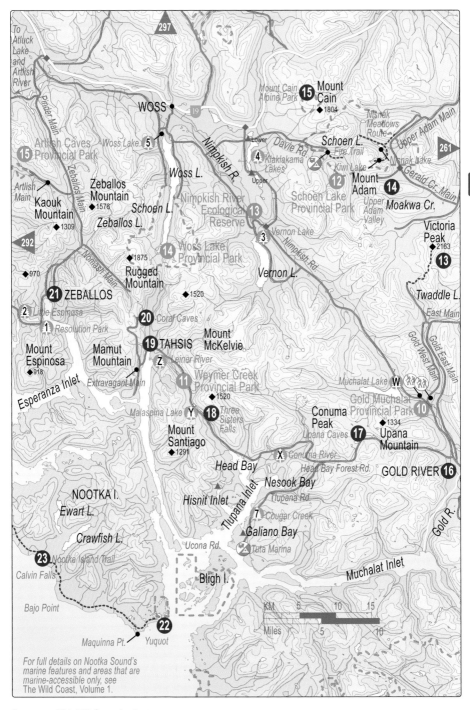

To
Atluck
Lake
and
Artlish
River

297

WOSS

19

15 Mount
Cain
◆1804

Mount Cain
Alpine Park

Nisnak
Meadows
Route

Davie Rd.
Lower

Schoen L.
Fire Trail

Nisnak Lake

Upper Adam Main

261

Artlish Caves
Provincial Park
15

Woss Lake **5**

Kiakiakama
Lakes
4
Upper

Nimpkish R.

Kiwi Lake

12 Mount
Adam
14

Gerald Cr. Main

Woss L.

Nimpkish River
Ecological
Reserve
13

Schoen Lake
Provincial Park

Upper
Adam
Valley

Moakwa Cr.

Artlish
Main

Kaouk
Mountain
◆1309

Zeballos
Mountain
◆1576

Schoen L.

Zeballos L.

Vernon Lake
3
Vernon L.

Nimpkish Rd.

Victoria
Peak
◆2163
13

292

◆1875
Rugged
Mountain
14

Woss Lake
Provincial Park

◆970

Zeballos Main

Nomash Main

Vernon L.

Twaddle L.

East Main

21 ZEBALLOS

◆1520

2 Little Espinosa
1 Resolution Park

20 Coral Caves

Gold West Main

Gold East Main

Mount
Espinosa
◆918

Mamut
Mountain

19 TAHSIS
Z
Leiner River

18 Mount
McKelvie

Weymer Creek
Provincial Park
11
◆1520

Muchalat Lake
W

Gold Muchalat
Provincial Park
10

Esperanza Inlet

Extravagant Main

Malaspina Lake **Y**

Three
Sisters
Falls

Conuma
Peak

Upana Caves
◆1334
17 Upana
Mountain

Mount
Santiago
◆1291

X Conuma River

Head Bay

Head Bay Forest Rd.

GOLD RIVER **16**

NOOTKA I.

Ewart L.

Hisnit Inlet

Nesook Bay

Tlupana Rd.

Gold R.

Crawfish L.

23 Nootka Island Trail

Calvin Falls

Ucona Rd.

Tlupana Inlet

7 Cougar Creek

Galiano Bay
Tata Marina

Muchalat Inlet

Bligh I.

Bajo Point

KM 5 10 15

Maquinna Pt. Yuquot
22

Miles 5 10

For full details on Nootka Sound's
marine features and areas that are
marine-accessible only, see
The Wild Coast, Volume 1.

NOOTKA SOUND

See pages 234–235 for main chapter map.

Victoria Peak.

POINTS OF INTEREST

⑬ Victoria Peak *(map p. 275)* 　　　　　　　　　　　　 ⊛

This is Vancouver Island's third-tallest peak; at 2,163 m it towers above the surrounding countryside but it's not often seen, as it is in a remote area with limited access. The simplest and most common ascent is the south face. While not technical, it will be beyond the capability of most hikers. Mountain climbers will find no end of challenges here.

ACCESS: From Gold Muchalat Provincial Park (page 284) take the Gold East Main north (the Gold West Main is ditched and closed). Continue north as the east and west mains reconnect and pass Twaddle Lake. The road ends at an active logging site, with a BRANCH ● continuing east. It is a steep, four-wheel drive only road for about 6 km to a parking area at the start of the route; watch for the rock cairns marking the trailhead.

The Upper Adam Valley.

⑭ **Upper Adam Valley** (map p. 275)

This is simply one of the most stunning valleys on Vancouver Island. The Moakwa Creek runs through the upper valley, which is ringed with jagged peaks on three sides, the tallest being Mount Adam (1,729 m) in the middle. While hikers and mountain climbers will enjoy pressing up Mount Adam, another possibility is mountain biking up the logging road past where it is ditched—possibly an ideal way to enjoy the incredible scenery.

ACCESS: At the junction with Upper Adam and Gerald Creek mains take the Upper Adam Main southwest into the Upper Adam Valley. The road is ditched shortly after the junction at the UA800 spur at about 600 m elevation.

⑮ **Mount Cain Alpine Park** (map p. 275)

This regional ski hill is operated by a non-profit society, the Mount Cain Alpine Park Society. Because of the remote location it's only open on weekends during the ski season (and Mondays for schools), which is usually mid December to late March or early April. The average annual snowfall is about 300 cm (compared to Mount Washington at 860 cm). The top ski elevation is 1,768 m, though, taller than Mount Washington at 1,588 m. Services include two T-bars up the slopes, a ski shop, lessons, snowshoeing and a restaurant. Cabins are also available, as well as inexpensive and more rustic hostel-style rooms and some chalets. Mattresses

Ski hill service buildings under the cover of Mount Cain.

are provided, but bring your own bedding. Visit **www.mountcain.com**. Call 250-949-7669 in winter for conditions before heading out.

🚶 HIKING: During the summer the park is open to alpine hiking, with mountaineering possible on the pronounced rocky peaks of Mount Cain. Casual visitors will enjoy the drive to the ski area at 1,200 m elevation with its many viewpoints, plus the scenery at the road's summit. An easy walk is up the ski hill; more adventurous hikers could push into the alpine terrain toward Mount Cain. Bring bug spray.

ACCESS: From the Island Highway, 75 km west of Sayward and 8 km east of Woss, take Davie Road east and follow the signs. They are prominent and should be easy to follow. During winter a shuttle bus is available at the base of Mount Cain. See the website for details. For cars, winter restrictions apply, such as uphill traffic only until 1 p.m and downhill after. Chains are mandatory.

16 Gold River *(map p. 275)*

This town's claim to fame in recent years has been Luna, an orphaned killer whale that became stranded in Muchalat Inlet and developed a dangerous affection for boats that eventually claimed its life. Luna brought a flurry of activity to the otherwise sleepy town, which had seen a decline since the closing of its mill, the main employer. It does, however, serve as a great supply and service centre in an area where towns are few and far between. It is also a valuable gateway to many of the recreation opportunities in the area, which run the gamut from whitewater paddling to caving. Boat launching into Nootka Sound (Muchalat Inlet) is possible at the end of Highway 28, 13 km south of the town centre.

- WHITEWATER PADDLING: Gold, Upana and Heber rivers are all popular paddling routes, made accessible by the proximity to the community of Gold River. Central Gold River is the best location for those starting out; the British Columbia White Water rates it a good class 3. The classic put-in is at the bridge north of Gold River on the Gold River Main; the classic take-out is at the local Big Bend Park.

- COMMUNITY TRAILS: Gold River has the advantage of some wonderful scenery that can be enjoyed via a number of local trails. Recommended is a 1 km trail along the Gold River from Peppercorn Park (Dogwood Drive) to the Muchalat Drive bridge. Or follow the Heber River canyon for half a kilometre from the Matchlee Drive bridge.

- GOLD RIVER FORESTRY TRAILS: Western Forest Products has provided some interpretive and recreational trails on the outskirts of the village of Gold River. The forestry walk begins off East Road in a loop that passes through mature and immature (1971) forest with interpretive signs. The Scout Lake Trail meanders for 2 km along Scout Lake through immature forest before heading north to Antler Lake on a 1 km connecting trail. Another trail circles Antler Lake, which is surrounded by mostly mature forest.

🛆 PICNIC AREAS AND DAY USE: Two picnic sites are located at Antler Lake, each with tables, fire rings, toilets and parking. A short trail connects the two sites. The lake is suitable for boating (no motors), swimming or fishing for trout, with regular bullhead derbies held locally. Another picnic site is located south of the town at Big Bend.

🛆 CAMPING: The Lions Campsite is located 4.8 km south of the information centre.

ACCESS: Gold River is at the end of Highway 28, 89 km west of Campbell River. Most services are located along Muchalat Drive, the main route through town. For the Antler Lake picnic sites, take the Tahsis road 2 km to the second bridge. Before crossing it turn right for about a kilometre to the lake entrances. Other trails lead off the access road.

TRAVEL NOTES: Matchlee Mountain, elevation 1,822 m, has historically been a good mountain climbing area, with local routes created through good alpine terrain. It is located southeast of Gold River on the border of Strathcona Provincial Park, with traditional access via the Ucona Main. Deterioration of the road has made the route impassable for all but the most determined; in 2007 the road was closed completely. In the event it reopens, the Ucona Main is reached by the last left (south) turn off Muchalat Drive before crossing the Gold River bridge. A route to Matchlee Mountain trailhead is off Ucona-29 at Quatchka Creek.

⑰ Upana Caves *(map p. 275)*

This small but intriguing selection of caves makes an interesting side trip on the way to Tahsis. While probably not large enough to attract diehard spelunkers, the caves do have a combined length of 450 m, and are honeycombed enough to keep you guessing as to where you'll surface. The caves are joined by a well built trail that includes canyon and waterfall viewpoints. Be warned that some portions of the caves can be wet.

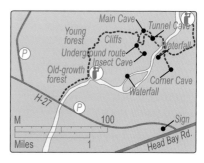

ACCESS: From Gold River follow the Head Bay Forest Road to Tahsis. The TURNOFF ● is about 18 km from Gold River just after Upana Lake.

18 Three Sisters Falls ● (map p. 275)

This waterfall is just one attraction along an exceptionally beautiful stretch of the Head Bay Forest Service Road. The triple falls originate from Malaspina Peak at 1,573 m elevation, and flow into the Sucwoa River. Other viewpoints along the way include the distinctive single summit of Conuma Peak, elevation 1,481 m, and a lookout over the Conuma River valley. Watch for interpretive signs at the roadside.

19 Tahsis (map p. 275)

This small forestry community is tucked into the shelter of the north end of Tahsis Inlet under the cover of some impressive scenery, particularly the multiple peaks of Rugged Mountain. The community has had a tough time in recent years since the closing of its mill, reflected in the sign at the edge of town: "Last one out turn out the lights." Regardless, it remains a full-service community with a store, accommodation, fuel and a marina. A boat ramp provides access to Tahsis Inlet and some exceptional fishing for chinook and coho.

The view from downtown Tahsis.

SHORT WALKS: The 2 km West Bay Trail follows the shoreline at the west head of Tahsis Inlet. The trail is maintained by the community and leased from Western Forest Products. The short Ubedam Creek Trail at the south end of town leads off North Maquinna Road, the main road through town. A worthwhile side trip is the new Leiner River Estuary Trail. It is adjacent to the Leiner River forest recreation site at the entrance to Tahsis. A parking lot and outhouses are provided at the entrance; a loop trail circles through mature forest with views of the estuary and down Tahsis Inlet.

20 Coral Caves (map p. 275)

This is the best known cave in the region, with a length of 1.5 km and an underground stream. As in so many cases, deteriorating roads have made access questionable. To reach the cave, follow Maquinna Road through Tahsis and continue south as it turns into a logging road that heads inland. At the junction with the Extravagant Main you'll see a stop sign and information about the contractor. Look to your right—an old overgrown logging road winds its way uphill. If you can follow that for a few kilometres (four-wheel drive only or mountain bikes) you'll reach the trailhead to the caves. Look for the signs indicating the way.

NOOTKA SOUND

Mason's Falls on the road to Zeballos.

㉑ **Zeballos** *(map p. 275)*

This is a remote community of about 200 on the north end of Zeballos Inlet, with access by logging road only. Its prosperity over the years has waxed and waned with the fortunes of the mining industry. A mini gold rush in the 1930s led to its peak of four mines, mills, 500 workers and a thriving community with a post office, hospital, newspaper and library. After the Second World War and the drop in the price of gold the town dipped to a low of 35 residents. It's now a gateway for trips into Esperanza Inlet and Nootka Island, highlights being the nearby provincial marine parks of Nuchatlitz and Catala Island. Both are enjoyed by kayakers, who traditionally launch from the Little Espinosa recreation site. Zeballos is a full-service community with accommodation, restaurants, a small grocery store and a gas station with some pumps that actually work (but, often, not all). Activity around the waterfront is mainly centred around the boat launch.

Ⓐ CAMPING: The Cevallos Campsite is located near downtown Zeballos, and has 10 sites, outhouses, firepits, firewood, picnic tables and water with a large shared covered picnic area. Fees apply. It is operated by the village of Zeballos; visit **www.zeballos.com** or call 250-761-4229.

SHORT WALKS: The Zeballos River Estuary Trail is a loop trail leading from the south end of the Cevallos Campsite.

HIKING: An old logging road is the route for the Little Zeballos Trail, a 5 km walk to a picnic area and viewpoint. It is part of the old route to the Little Zeballos River estuary.

ACCESS: Zeballos is reached by logging road only. The turnoff, well marked from the Island Highway, is about 22 km west of Woss. Follow the signs or take the Pinder and Zeballos mains south.

22 Yuquot (map p. 275)

This historic little First Nations community is situated on the southeast side of Nootka Island in a small bay, Friendly Cove. It's remarkable for its incredible history, both First Nations and European, particularly as the site of the Spanish trading post Santa Cruz de Nutka and the only Spanish fort in Canada, Fort San Miguel, back in the late 1700s. There's a reminder at the historic little church: depictions on stained glass windows donated by the Spanish government. An interesting side trip is a visit to the First Nations cemetery, where items from the lives of the deceased have been placed on or by the tombstones.

The community is accessible from Gold River by way of the MV *Uchuck III*, a commercial ferry and cargo ship that makes the trip twice a week during the summer. Details are at **www.mvuchuck.com**. The 1.5-hour layover allows a chance to visit the church and walk the start of the Nootka Island Trail or other shorter trails through the area. A fee applies for landing at the dock and accessing the First Nations land. Longer trips are possible by camping or renting one of the six cozy little cabins set between the ocean and Jewitt Lake. They are operated by the Mowachaht First Nation. Call 250-283-2015.

CAMPING: Fee camping is available on the grassy clearing over Friendly Cove on Mowachaht land. Beach camping is possible closer to the lagoon entrance off the reserve.

23 Nootka Island Trail (map p. 275)

This trail is often described as a more desirable and less traveled alternative to the West Coast Trail. The part about fewer hikers is definitely true. The rest is a matter of taste, and the Nootka Island Trail has its advantages and disadvantages. Because the trail is mostly over Crown land, it has no official status. This means no fees, but it also means no maintenance or overseeing of the route. It is user-defined and user-maintained, so consequently it has no handy stairs and handrails across rougher sections. Purists will like this, but it certainly raises the difficulty quotient.

Traveling north to south, the trailhead is at Louie Bay. Here boats or planes can drop off hikers, who then have to cross to Third Beach, a popular camping spot on the first night. From there many portions are rough overland to Skuna

Bay. The beach portions of the trail can be equally difficult—sand or gravel that can give way underfoot, forcing you to work extra hard. The first major reward comes at Calvin Falls, which is in the middle of a sweeping section of sand beach. Here a branch of the trail leads up the side of the falls to a wonderful watering hole. An extension connects to Crawfish Lake, and logging roads lead to the more heavily logged east side of Nootka Island. The falls is sometimes reached via floatplane and a hike from Crawfish Lake.

The trail continues south along the beach to Bajo Point, formerly the site of a native village. The shoreline turns more rugged as the trail shifts eastward toward Yuquot. Portions are private property and First Nations reserve, so stay to the beach. At Maquinna Point look for side trails to sea caves. The last major crossing is a tidal lagoon just outside Yuquot; a crossing at low tide is recommended.

The trail is about 34 km, but don't count on much more than a kilometre per hour while hiking. It could be completed in a day or five days, depending on your fitness level and pack weight; three to four days is probably most realistic.

ACCESS: Because it's an island, and because the trip is usually one way, hikers must make arrangements to be dropped off on one side and picked up on the other. A favourite way is to get to the trailhead at Louie Bay by float plane or water taxi. A return is possible on the *Uchuck III*, though your timing will have to coincide with the twice-weekly departures.

TRAVEL NOTES: Some water taxi operators will equip hikers with marine radios, giving the option for a mid-trail pickup in the event of injury or difficulty. Otherwise hikers should know they are alone. There is no cell service, and there are no checkpoints or trail patrols. It is truly a wilderness trail.

㉔ Radar site

See the main chapter map, page 234, or refer to the BC Coastal Recreation Kayaking and Small Boat Atlas *for a larger scale version.*

This could make an interesting side trip for Nootka Island Trail hikers. An old trail leads from Louie Bay to Ferrer Point, the site of an old radar station. The trailhead is south of Tongue Point at the Esperanza Mission Camp, a campsite where spots can be arranged by marine radio. Watch for the instructions when you arrive.

MAJOR PARKS

⑩ Gold Muchalat Provincial Park *(map p. 275)*

This park, which protects 653 hectares near the confluence of the Gold and Muchalat rivers, includes a few pockets of old-growth forest plus wintering habitat for Roosevelt elk. The park is undeveloped, and walk-in camping is allowed.

HIKING: A rough trail follows along the Muchalat River. For a good trailhead, look for a PARKING AREA ● (one vehicle) at the north boundary of the park off Nimpkish Road. For a trail along the Gold River, take the Gold West Main north; look for the TRAILHEAD ● leading into the mature forest to the right (east) about 200 m past the junction.

FISHING: The Muchalat River is known for its sockeye salmon; summer steelhead, rainbow trout and coho can be found in both the Muchulat and Gold rivers.

ACCESS: The park is on the road to Woss Lake, about 15 km northeast of Gold River. It's intersected by three roads: the Nimpkish Road and the Gold East and Gold West mains. The Gold East Main makes a poor option for entering the park as it is bordered by immature forest only.

⑪ Weymer Creek Provincial Park *(map p. 275)*

This 316-hectare park is known for its limestone and karst geography, with a cave system ranking among the best in Canada.

ECOLOGY: A park resident is the rare Keen's long-eared myotis bat. The park protects the only known limestone cave bat hibernaculum on Vancouver Island. It harbours six bat species, the highest number of any hibernaculum in BC. A hibernaculum is used for roosting, hibernating and raising the young.

SPELUNKING: The Weymer cave system is the second longest and deepest on Vancouver Island, though only a portion is protected by the park. While the caves have been recorded, the park is in its infancy (created in 1996), and use of the caves is not recommended until a management plan is finalized to protect any rare karst features.

ACCESS: The park is 5 km southeast of Tahsis, with no formal access and poor options for using logging roads for access.

⑫ Schoen Lake Provincial Park *(map p. 275)*

Schoen Lake, at 8,430 hectares, is one of Vancouver Island's larger parks, protecting all of Schoen Lake and the surrounding mountainous terrain in a mostly undeveloped wilderness setting. The only amenities are a small camping and day-use area near the park entrance, newly staffed by a Namgis First Nation host. The lake is an ideal paddling location due to the impressive neighbouring mountains. A beach serves as a launching area, and a ramp provides boat access to the lake. This is a recommended way to see the park. Hiking is limited to old logging roads and whatever casual trails might exist.

CAMPING: The designated CAMPING AREA ● has eight sites spread out in two sections near the beach. Wilderness camping is possible elsewhere in the park.

The campground beach at Schoen Lake.

🥾 HIKING: While the park lacks maintained trails, a few routes exist. The simplest is the Fire Trail, which runs from the campsite along the south end of the lake to Schoen Creek. The Nisnak Meadows Hiking Route runs from the east end of the lake along Nisnak Creek to Nisnak Lake. From there a rough route is possible to Kiwi Lake and Nisnak Falls. The route also continues to a logging road off Upper Adam Main through some old-growth forest. Trail conditions depend on how recently the trails have been cleared by users. Flagging is generally good, meaning there's a good chance to bushwhack even if conditions are poor.

ACCESS: Schoen Lake park is about 140 km north of Campbell River, and well signed from the Island Highway. Take Davie Road south, and follow it east at the first junction for about 12 km. Access is possible along the east side of the park (Nisnak Meadows) via the Upper Adam Main. The COMPTON CREEK MAIN ● departs the Upper Adam Main about 15 km from the Island Highway; take the spur that heads southwest and parallels the Adam River. Follow it as far as you can to reach the trailhead at the end.

⑬ Nimpkish River Ecological Reserve *(map p. 275)*

This small (18-hectare) reserve was created in 1988 to preserve a stand of the tallest Douglas-fir trees in Canada. Most are believed to be about 360 years old, but the largest are suspected to be closer to 600 years. The average diameter is 1.3 m and the average height 66 m, with some as tall as 96 m. The reserve is located on a small island created where the river forms a loop and a small channel isolates the grove. While the Douglas-firs are the largest specimens, most trees in the reserve are actually western red cedar. The reserve is a nesting site for northern goshawk.

⑭ Woss Lake Provincial Park (map p. 275)

This park is undeveloped—a pristine gem protecting 6,634 hectares of heavily forested land. It's easiest to explore by paddle, which will take you to a waterfall at the south end of the lake. This is the start of a traditional First Nations trading route to Tahsis Inlet. Look for two native carvings, one facing north and the other south, about 20 m from the lake.

🚶 HIKING: A rough, casual trail follows the low valley between Tahsis and Woss Lake. The low elevation that made it a popular route historically has the drawback of a great amount of vegetation, and so the trail is likely to be overgrown. A popular ascent is up Rugged Mountain, the highest peak in the region at 1,875 m. It can be reached either by the lake or from logging roads to the south.

ACCESS: The best lake access is launching from the Woss Lake recreation site (page 290).

⑮ Artlish Caves Provincial Park (map p. 275)

Old-growth forest along the south fork of the Upper Artlish River and a cave system featuring two of Canada's largest caves are part of this 285-hectare wilderness park. The caves are distinctive for large entrances and an underground

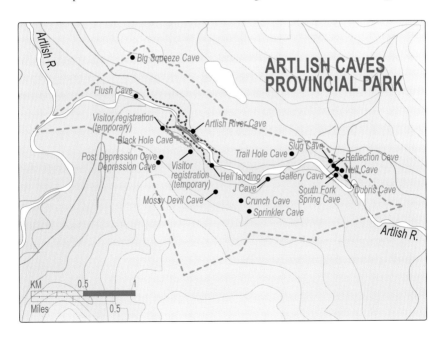

river system; a portion of the Artlish River is completely submerged, making the Artlish River Cave the largest river cave in Canada. About 20 other caves can be found in the area, including sinkholes and springs.

SPELUNKING: This is obviously a popular location for seasoned spelunkers, many of whom arrive by helicopter and land at a sandbar southeast of the caves. While it is possible for casual visitors to enter some of the caves, BC Parks is discouraging visits until a management plan is complete. It's likely the plan will include intense management and possibly restrictions for some of the caves. The two best caves for casual visits are the Artlish River Cave and the lower section of the Black Hole Cave. As with any cave exploration, visitors should be highly sensitive to the possibility of disturbing fragile features as well as the obvious dangers.

FISHING: The Artlish River is home to sockeye, coho, chinook, pink salmon, steelhead and rainbow trout.

ACCESS: This park can be reached from both the east and west sides, though getting here can be an ordeal. Both routes begin by following the Atluck Main. The west entry point is reached by following the route to Artlish River that skirts Atluck Lake. Follow it south about 8 km to a turnoff left (east) at a bridge onto an old logging road. It will quickly split again. One branch is overgrown after a short distance; the other rises and curves east. It is ditched—follow it as far as you can, then walk to the end. From there you can follow a rough trail (or bushwhack) to a small lake, then to the park. For the east entrance, take the route to Zeballos along the Pinder-Zeballos Main. After about 15 km past the Atluck Lake turnoff, take the Artlish Main west, and follow it for about 4.7 km; if you curve south and cross a bridge you've gone too far. Look for an old overgrown logging road heading west at the curve and park near the entrance; the spur is impassable for vehicles beyond here. From there it is 3 km to the park along a route with well established alders, making it a rough trek.

FOREST RECREATION SITES
See the map on page 275 to locate these recreation sites.

Muchalat Lake ●

This is a pretty campground that's arranged much like a provincial park, with camping areas spread around a forested loop. At the far end is a boat launch with a gravel beach and dock. The entrance is well signed off the Nimpkish Main just west of Gold Muchalat Provincial Park.

Conuma River

This is a small site with five campsites and picnic tables on the riverbank. It's considered a good spot to see black bears feeding on salmon in the fall. It's located off the Head Bay Forest Service Road on the descent to Moutcha Bay.

Malaspina Lake ●

This is a small day-use site on the route to Tahsis. A short trail leads to a sandy point on the south side of the lake.

Leiner River ●

This is a pretty camping area alongside a rushing segment of the Leiner River; be sure to watch for the waterfall off Head Bay Forest Service Road opposite the campsite entrance. The site is conveniently located about 3 km outside Tahsis. Eight campsites are set in a line facing the river.

 HIKING AND BOULDERING: A section of the Leiner River upriver from the recreation site is a popular bouldering location. House-sized boulders litter the valley, and the access trail actually follows a cave created by overlying boulders. The trailhead is 30 m east of the Leiner River bridge. The loop is a 30-minute walk, with strenuous rock-climbing segments. The recreation site is also near the Leiner River Estuary Trail (page 281).

Resolution Park

This park features seven semi-open sites near a cobble beach with a boat launch, float and fresh water. It is located just south of the Little Espinosa day-use site but with access to Zeballos Inlet rather than Espinosa Inlet.

Little Espinosa

This day-use site is on the east end of Little Espinosa Inlet along the Fair Harbour Main south of Zeballos. It's a rocky, clear area with a picnic table and a rough shoreline that would be marginal for launching cartop boats. The inlet is notable for the strong tidal rapids at the narrow arm where the Fair Harbour Main crosses via a bridge. The bridge at the tidal rapids is a key kayak launch site for trips down Esperanza Inlet and to the outer coast around Nootka Island, particularly Nuchatlitz and Catala provincial parks. For more information on these areas, see *The Wild Coast, Volume 1.*

Vernon Lake ●

Camping is possible on the north end of Vernon Lake, with a good beach and picnic area in a site provided by Western Forest Products. It's located on the Woss-Gold River route just south and west of the JUNCTION ● that splits the route between Woss and Schoen Lake.

④ Klaklakama Lakes

This series of lakes offers two camping opportunities. The Upper Klaklama Lake site has a few campsites clustered together in an open area by the lake. A short interpretive trail leads through a stand of old-growth forest. The Lower Klaklakama Lake site has four camping areas set around the access road, with one open RV-style site next to the lake with a small shared beach area and boat ramp. These are both Western Forest Products sites and offer garbage collection.

ACCESS: Take the Schoen Lake Provincial Park turnoff (see page 285) from the Island Highway, but instead of turning east into the park at the first junction follow the route south to Gold River, as indicated by signs. The UPPER CAMPSITE ● is 4 km south of the Schoen Lake turnoff. The LOWER CAMPSITE ● is 1 km south.

⑤ Woss Lake ●

This campsite south of Woss has 24 sites, a dock and a boat launch on the north end of Woss Lake. Drive through Woss, following the signs, or from the RONA MAIN JUNCTION ● follow the West Woss Main south to the campsite.

⑥ Star Lake *(map p. 235)*

This is a small day-use site on a lakeside point southeast of Gold River. Expect a rough boat launch, a float and the 1.4 km Star Lake Trail loop for hiking or biking. Access is via Ucona Main, which was closed in 2007.

⑦ Cougar Creek

This key recreation site for Nootka Sound is used as a point of entry for boaters and paddlers. It is hosted and fees apply for camping, overnight parking and wilderness camping. A dock and boat ramp are part of a large beach area that makes this a good day-use site as well. Take Tlupana Road south from the Head Bay Forest Service Road. Following the same route south past the recreation site will take you to Tuta Marina, a private boat launch and camping option.

TRAVEL NOTES: A few bays and inlets along this stretch of Nootka Sound have historically been reachable by logging road. A favourite has been Hisnit Inlet, the head of which can be reached by the Sucwoa Main that passes east of Deserted Lake. The access has been deactivated, however, and is likely to be ditched or otherwise impassable. I don't see this as negative, because the site had been poorly treated; vehicles were regularly driven down the beach and junk was left behind (part of the Nootka Sound land-use plan is to make this inlet inaccessible to vehicle traffic). Galiano Bay is another possibility for wilderness camping. A marina and RV campground are located at Head Bay.

The North Island

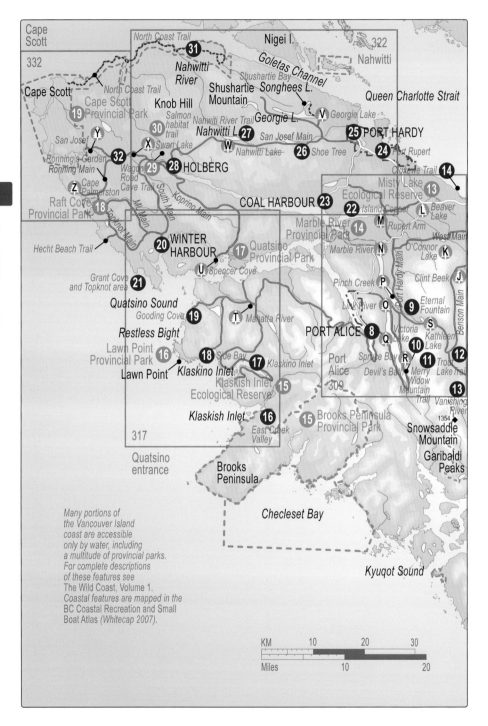

THE NORTH ISLAND

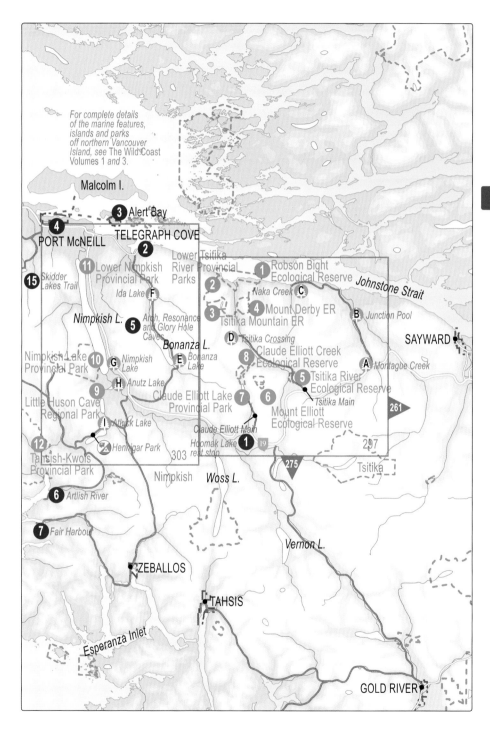

For complete details
of the marine features,
islands and parks
off northern Vancouver
Island, see The Wild Coast
Volumes 1 and 3.

Malcolm I.

3 Alert Bay

4
PORT McNEILL   TELEGRAPH COVE

2

11 Lower Nimpkish   Lower Tsitika
       Provincial Park   River Provincial   **1** Robsón Bight
                          Parks   Ecological Reserve   Johnstone Strait
15 Skidder   **2**
       Lakes Trail   Naka Creek   **C**
                    Ida Lake   **F**   **3**   **4** Mount Derby ER   **B** Junction Pool
Nimpkish L.   Arch, Resonance   Tsitika Mountain ER
                    5   and Glory Hole
                            Caves   **D** Tsitika Crossing   SAYWARD
                    Bonanza L.   **8** Claude Elliott Creek
Nimpkish Lake   Bonanza   Ecological Reserve
Provincial Park **10** **G** Nimpkish **E** Lake   **A** Montague Creek
                         Lake   **5** Tsitika River
          9   **H** Anutz Lake   Ecological Reserve
Little Huson Cave   **7**   **6**   Tsitika Main
Regional Park   Claude Elliott Lake   261
                 I Attuck Lake Provincial Park   Mount Elliott
                                                          Ecological Reserve
         2 Henrigar Park   Claude Elliott Main
12   Hoomak Lake   297
Tahsish-Kwois   rest stop   **1** 19
Provincial Park   Nimpkish   Woss L.   275   Tsitika
                              303
6 Artlish River

7 Fair Harbour   Vernon L.

                    ZEBALLOS

                         TAHSIS

         Esperanza Inlet

                                        GOLD RIVER

The river cave entrance at Little Huson Cave Regional Park.

Northern Vancouver Island has an odd mystique: wild stretches of coast mixed with some of the island's tallest and most dramatic peaks. Topping it all is sprawling Cape Scott Provincial Park, now more accessible due to an extension to the Cape Scott Trail that extends the route almost to Port Hardy (with a land link hopefully only a few years away). Its remoteness tends to keep the north island probably the least visited region on the island; Port Hardy is a four- to five-hour drive northwest from Nanaimo. Once in the region, however, the range of options is endless—from pleasant beach strolls to demanding mountain hikes and from world-class fishing to whitewater rafting on Nimpkish River.

TRANSPORTATION

The Island Highway ends at Port Hardy, with the stretch between Sayward and Port Hardy essentially the only transportation route between the main communities of Woss, Port McNeill and Port Hardy. It is a rambling, two-lane route that twists through some steep areas with only occasional passing lanes. Large vehicles can slow traffic considerably. Other paved roads can be found to Telegraph Cove, Port Alice and Coal Harbour. Beyond that, logging roads are the only options, with the quality and accessibility varying greatly. Here are a few key routes. The waypoints in the appendix pinpoint the location of the junctions.

EVE RIVER MAIN: This is a major link to several of the recreation sites around Robson Bight, particularly Naka Creek. The junction with Highway 19 is about 25 km west of Woss via the EVE CONNECTOR ●. It's easy to find, as a highway rest stop is located at the start of the connector. It then heads roughly north along the Eve River to connect with the ADAM RIVER MAIN ●, an alternative route to the various recreation sites. The Eve Main also continues west from the connector to join with the Muskeg Main just north of the Island Highway.

TSITIKA MAIN: This begins life north of the Island Highway as the MUSKEG MAIN ●, then turns into the TSITIKA MAIN ●. The junction from the Island Highway is about 10 km past the Eve River rest stop, and about 1 km past a compound of strange electrical equipment. At the turnoff keep right and cross the bridge to the Muskeg Creek Main (the Muskeg Main heads left). This route would seem to provide access to a number of areas, as a half-dozen ecological reserves are in this region, but there are remarkably few established areas with recreational potential. A fairly new LOGGING ROAD ● departs the Tsitika Main to link with the Naka Creek Main, providing good alternative access to the Naka Creek Recreation Site.

CLAUDE ELLIOT MAIN ●: This provides a gateway into a pretty valley that is being heavily logged. Spurs are numerous and getting around is difficult; the major feature is Claude Elliot Lake Provincial Park and the wonderful backdrop of Tsitika and Whitilla mountains.

KOKISH MAIN: Identified as K Main by signs, this route departs from Telegraph Cove Road just east of the viewpoint and heads south along the Kokish River to Ida and Bonanza lakes. The south end connects with the Old Steele Main for easy access to the lakes from the Island Highway. The junction is directly opposite the turnoff for the road to Zeballos. Take a sharp right at the turnoff by crossing the river parallel to the highway using the railroad bridge (yes, the railroad bridge). Miss the bridge at your peril; you'll end up in a maze of new logging spurs if you go straight. The bridge is actually made for car traffic as well as rail traffic, and the route continues on to the Kokish Main junction.

ATLUCK MAIN ●: This is the beginning of the route to Zeballos, covered in more detail in Chapter 5 (page 241). The north portion has several possible diversions leading to Atluck and Anutz lakes as well as the NIMPKISH MAIN ● by traveling the south end of the namesake river to Woss. Signs to the various recreational features along this route are generally good.

WEST MAIN ●: This is the first link in the major route between Port McNeill and the many recreational features of the lakes west of Port Alice and southwest of Port McNeill. The second link is Benson Main. Features along the way are well marked, making this an easy area to travel. Traffic is restricted, however; public use is barred during working hours. The exception is roads in the direct vicinity of Alice and Victoria lakes, where movement is unrestricted. Note that limestone mining is now active in the area south of Maynard Lake, blocking road access through that area. A circuit of the area from Port McNeill to Victoria Lake may not be possible. One last possibility is using the Cook Lake connector at the end of J Main to join with the Atluck Main, linking this area with the Atluck Lake region—a bypass, essentially, of a huge chunk of the Island Highway by passing west of Nimpkish Lake.

PORT ALICE HIGHWAY ●: This is a paved route from the Island Highway to Port Alice—a winding, sometimes steep, two-lane road notorious for being dangerous in poor conditions. The pavement ends south of the Neucel pulp mill and the start of Marine Drive.

PORT HARDY MAIN ●: This is a good access road to Rupert Inlet, passing the shoreline at the head of the inlet as it crosses the Port Alice Highway and connects with ALICE LAKE MAIN ● in the south. It links with the Coal Harbour Road in the north.

MARINE DRIVE: This is the main access to the south entrance of Quatsino Sound, leading to Mahatta River and Side Bay. It begins by following the Port Alice Highway south through Port Alice past the Neucel pulp mill around the south end of Neroutsos Inlet. It then has several tight switchbacks at intersections that may lead travelers astray. Keep an eye out for the signs. Marine Drive turns into Teeta Main then K MAIN ●, I MAIN ● and J Main, most of which will be indistinguishable to the average traveler. At the turn for Cleagh Creek it splits into B and J mains that run parallel. At the Mahatta River recreation site the Restless Main continues west and Side Bay Main south. Most logging activity is currently taking place along the south end of this region, particularly along Cayuse Creek and near K Main. On the other end of the spectrum, many of the spurs along the O'Connell Lake and Le Mare Lake areas are impassable due to lack of use, with the Side Bay Main in decline and likely impassable in a year or two.

HOLBERG ROAD: This is the major route to Cape Scott, passing through Holberg. The first portion is forest service road; the last 44 km are private logging road with unrestricted public access, and the final few kilometres into Cape Scott Provincial Park are rutted and in poor condition. Features and junctions along the way are generally well marked, including routes to Raft Cove and Cape Palmerston. Side logging roads tend to be private, with no public access.

KOPRINO MAIN: The routes to Winter Harbour and Koprino Harbour divert from Holberg Road at Holberg. Signs are generally good, but the road is notorious for its rough rocks. Be sure about your spare!

Tsitika region

This area is composed of two major valleys: the Tsitika River and Adam and Eve river valleys. These are bordered by some stunning mountain scenery, with numerous portions of both the valleys and mountain areas protected as parks. Despite the size of this region, very little of the area is available for recreational use, and large portions, particularly the Claude Elliott Creek area, are being heavily logged. Most public use tends to be along the Adam and Eve rivers, popular for fishing, and at Naka Creek, which is a base for kayaking trips and killer whale watching.

MAJOR PARKS

① **Robson Bight Ecological Reserve** *(map below)*

This reserve has the distinction of being the first and only in Canada created specifically as a sanctuary for killer whales. The reserve protects the estuary and surrounding upland of the Tsitika River and a pebble beach with a peculiar attraction for whales: it's ideal for rubbing. The reserve is closed to foot traffic and also boat traffic thanks to a patrolled perimeter within Johnstone Strait. The

See pages 292–293 for main chapter map.

entire marine region, however, is part of the summer migration route for killer whales and supports a healthy whale watching industry based out of Telegraph Cove, Port McNeill and Port Hardy.

ACCESS: The reserve is closed to the public. Whale watching is possible near the reserve by boat or from the shore at places such as Naka Creek (page 301).

❷ Lower Tsitika River Provincial Park *(map p. 297)*

This is an odd park in that it was created essentially to block public access to neighbouring Robson Bight Ecological Reserve. It also protects the lower portion of the Tsitika River, one of the most notable on northern Vancouver Island as home to the last sizeable run of summer steelhead trout on east Vancouver Island. All five species of salmon plus cutthroat trout and Dolly Varden char inhabit the river. Fishing is allowed, as is camping and general public access, though lack of a formal route into the park helps keep the area relatively pristine. There is no access through the park to Robson Bight Ecological Reserve. The park is 3,745 hectares and was created in 1995.

ACCESS: The best option for access is to take the Tsitika Main north past the Tsitika Crossing Recreation Site (page 301) and the Tsitika River bridge. Drive 2.3 km north, keeping right to drive into a large clearing suitable for parking. The road beyond, leading to the park border, is intentionally blocked with large boulders. It would be possible to stroll or mountain bike the former access road toward the park boundary.

❸ Tsitika Mountain Ecological Reserve *(map p. 297)*

Subalpine forest and bog are protected in this reserve adjacent to Lower Tsitika River Provincial Park. The eastern flank of Tsitika Mountain (1,667 m) and small Mudge Lake form the bulk of the reserve, with the lower elevation composed of bog and a scrubby forest. Along the more mountainous portion, high snowfall has created a series of terraces occupied by more bogs and small ponds. The area is home to goldeneye, deer, cougar and wolf. The reserve protects 554 hectares and was created in 1989.

ACCESS: The reserve is open to the public, and as Tsitika Mountain is the highest peak in its range it is a moderately popular ascent, with most hikers entering via Tsitika Main and Mudge Lake. Expect a considerable bushwhack; this would be for experienced backcountry hikers only.

❹ Mount Derby Ecological Reserve *(map p. 297)*

This 557-hectare reserve was created in 1989 to protect a range of forest vegetation across all elevations up to the alpine zone. The steep northwest and southwest slopes of Mount Derby (1,646 m) are within the reserve, with amabilis fir and western red cedar forests at the lower elevations and mountain hemlock and mountain heather at the higher elevations. Public access is allowed, but no formal route exists.

⑤ Tsitika River Ecological Reserve *(map p. 297)*

This reserve protects 110 hectares of boggy wetland in a gently sloping peat flood plain next to the Tsitika River. Trails through the reserve are likely to be created by Roosevelt elk, which are common visitors to the wetland. Deer, beaver, wolf and bear are other occasional residents.

⑥ Mount Elliott Ecological Reserve *(map p. 297)*

Cirques and hanging valleys—terms probably more familiar to alpine explorers than the average explorer—are the reason for protecting Mount Elliott. A cirque is a mountain basin, usually with a lake. A hanging valley is one that is set high above the main valley, with the rift usually caused by glacial erosion. Both these elements are found in the subalpine area of Mount Elliott Ecological Reserve. It differs from nearby Tsitika Mountain and Mount Derby reserves by having igneous rock rather than volcanic rock, though the cirque might appear volcanic, almost like the mouth of an ancient volcano. Tsitika Lake sits within the cirque. Mount Elliott peaks at 1,557 m, but in the cirque the level is below 900 m. The reserve protects 324 hectares and was created in 1989.

ACCESS: There is no designated trail, though logging spurs do approach the south slopes. This would make a fascinating ascent for serious mountain hikers.

⑦ Claude Elliott Lake Provincial Park *(map p. 297)*

This is the southern of two protected parcels adjacent to Claude Elliott Lake. Claude Elliott Lake Provincial Park protects the namesake lake and smaller Fickle Lake to the north.

FISHING: Tsitika River is considered among the most important fish rivers on Vancouver Island. Both lakes within the park are popular for sport fishing of coho salmon and cutthroat, Dolly Varden, kokanee and rainbow trout.

SHORT WALKS: A 10-minute trail leads from the TRAILHEAD ● to the lake. Portages to the lake are possible, but deteriorating conditions of the access road and the trail itself would make this difficult.

CAMPING: The park has no official campsites, but wilderness camping is allowed. An obvious makeshift campsite exists at the end of the deteriorating access road outside the trailhead.

ACCESS: Getting here is a convoluted trip. From the Island Highway take the route left (northwest) at the Claude Elliott Main and drive 1.4 km to a junction, then stay right. After a bridge at 1.3 km, keep left, drive 1.4 km to the Upper

Lukwa Main junction, keep left, drive 2 more km, turn left at a Y-junction (look for a downed CE-12 sign), pass Ski Jump (there'll be a sign), keep right past CE-14, drive 1.5 km farther, turn right onto CE-37, drive 2 km to the park sign and walk down the deteriorating access road to the trailhead. Naturally it sees little traffic, so the trail is not in particularly great shape.

⑧ Claude Elliott Creek Ecological Reserve *(map p. 297)*

Claude Elliott Creek Ecological Reserve was created in 1989 to protect the undisturbed montane forest environment along Claude Elliot Creek. Most of the rest of the island's coastal western hemlock forest has been logged in the Northern Island Mountains, making this one of the few remaining pristine examples. The reserve is also winter habitat for ungulates, and breeding and feeding habitat for the northern goshawk and northern pygmy owl.

FOREST RECREATION SITES
See the map on page 297 to locate these recreation sites.

Ⓐ Montague Creek ●

This small site is set not far from the Island Highway alongside the namesake creek. The access road leads to an open area with a single picnic table, firepit and outhouse. It's best suited to one small group.

ACCESS: From the Island Highway, about 25 km west of the Sayward Road junction, take the Eve River Connector north for a short distance, looking for the access road to your left (west).

The Montague Creek Recreation Site.

B Junction Pool ●

The Junction Pool campsites are set in an open clearing along the access road with minimal water access. This best suits those looking for a base camp for fishing on the Adam or Eve river. Take East Main from the Island Highway for 14 km to the recreation site turnoff.

C Naka Creek ●

This is a popular staging ground for kayakers launching into Johnstone Strait as well as RVers looking for an oceanfront site with the chance of seeing killer whales from the shore. The site is at an old logging camp and is hosted by the camp caretaker. A half-dozen vehicle-accessible tent/RV sites are clustered together in the midst of the empty trailers of the camp. A fee applies for parking on the property but not for using the camping area.

ACCESS: From the Island Highway take the Eve River Connector north to the Naka Creek Main, which leads west up a steep hill with some rough portions to the vacant logging camp. Pass several buildings and empty trailers to the main campsite and rough boat launch.

D Tsitika Crossing ●

This site is in an open, rocky area adjacent to the river. Campsites with picnic tables are set back near the tree line. This best suits two groups but could host more, especially RVs.

POINTS OF INTEREST

① Hoomak Lake rest stop ● *(map p. 297)*

Rest stops don't normally warrant a mention, but this one has a few interesting features. As well as superior washrooms, the grounds have information kiosks on the history of the various communities in the region. Two trails lead from the grounds to the lake. A choice of two loops make for a walk of either 670 m or 1,100 m. Look for it west of the Schoen Lake turnoff.

Nimpkish

Port McNeill and Telegraph Cove are best known as gateways to Johnstone Strait and the Broughton Archipelago, an area known for its fishing, whale watching and exploring by boat or kayak. Nimpkish Lake and Nimpkish River are the two main inland features, providing a good range of freshwater-based adventures, particularly windsurfing on Nimpkish Lake and whitewater sports on Nimpkish River. A smattering of smaller lakes provides other avenues for camping, fishing and paddling. A wonderful feature of this area is the rugged mountain backdrop, dominated by Pinder Peak and the range along the west side of Nimpkish Lake topped by Karmutsen Mountain. Drives along the Island Highway west of Woss can be impressive.

POINTS OF INTEREST

❷ Telegraph Cove *(map p. 303)*

Established first as a telegraph station, this small community then became the site of a sawmill linked by boardwalks. Many of the old buildings still grace the main boardwalk, but tourism has taken its toll on the original charm—including blasting the adjacent headland for a residential development and construction of a large marina out of scale with the quaint boardwalk and historic homes. The cove is a popular staging area for kayakers, and much of the activity focuses on boat and kayak launching and pay parking, as well as whale watching tours. A choice of vehicle-accessible campsites is located at the cove.

ⓘ Tourism information is available at **www.hellobc.com/en-CA/RegionsCities/ TelegraphCove.htm** or **www.vancouverislandtravel/north-island/ telegraph-cove**.

❸ Alert Bay *(map p. 303)*

This island community is a centre for First Nations culture, with a good variety of native arts and crafts shops to choose from. A key feature is the U'mista Cultural Centre and its ceremonial mask display, plus other cultural presentations. Other attractions of note are the totems of the Namgis burial ground and the Alert Bay Ecological Park, which offers a walk through a boggy setting. A ferry from Port McNeill links Vancouver Island with Cormorant Island.

ⓘ Municipal government at **www.alertbay.ca**; tourism information at **www .hellobc.com/en-CA/RegionsCities/AlertBay.htm** or **www.vancouverisland .travel/north-island/alert-bay**; U'mista Cultural Society at **www.umista.org**.

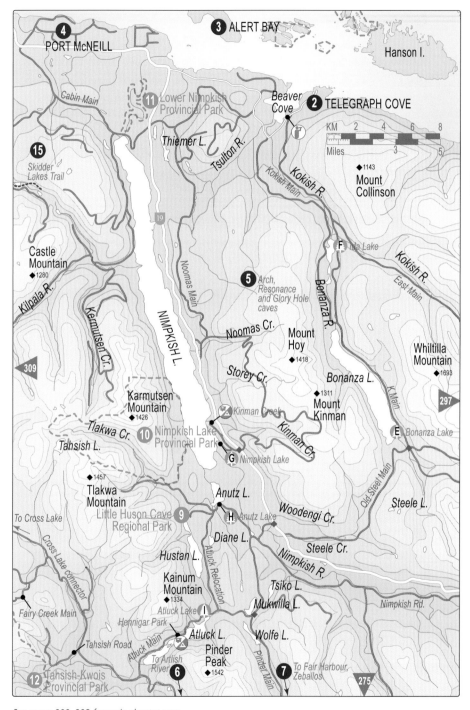

4 PORT McNEILL

3 ALERT BAY

Hanson I.

Cabin Main

11 Lower Nimpkish Provincial Park

Thiemer L.

Tsulton R.

Beaver Cove

2 TELEGRAPH COVE

KM 2 4 6 8

Miles 3 5

◆1143 Mount Collinson

Kokish Main

Kokish R.

15

Skidder Lakes Trail

19

Castle Mountain ◆1280

Kilpala R.

Kermutsen Cr.

NIMPKISH L.

Noomas Main

5 Arch, Resonance and Glory Hole caves

F Ida Lake

Bonanza R.

Kokish R.

East Main

309

Noomas Cr.

Mount Hoy ◆1418

Storey Cr.

Bonanza L.

Whiltilla Mountain ◆1693

Karmutsen Mountain ◆1426

Tlakwa Cr.

Tahsish L.

10 Nimpkish Lake Provincial Park

X Kinman Creek

G Nimpkish Lake

Mount Kinman ◆1311

Kinman Cr.

K Main

E Bonanza Lake

297

◆1457 Tlakwa Mountain

To Cross Lake

Cross Lake connector

Little Huson Cave Regional Park **9**

Anutz L.

H Anutz Lake

Woodengi Cr.

Steele Cr.

Old Steel Main

Steele L.

Diane L.

Hustan L.

Atluck Relocation

Nimpkish R.

Fairy Creek Main

Kainum Mountain ◆1334

Tsiko L.

Mukwilla L.

Nimpkish Rd.

Hennigar Park

Atluck Lake **I**

Tahsish Road

Atluck Main

To Artlish River

X Atluck L.

Pinder Peak ◆1542

6

Wolfe L.

Pinder Main

To Fair Harbour, Zeballos **7**

275

12 Tahsish-Kwois Provincial Park

See pages 292–293 for main chapter map.

❹ Port McNeill *(map p. 303)*

This major fishing, logging and commercial centre has a population of about 2,800 and is second only to Port Hardy for its significance in northern Vancouver Island. Its sheltered harbour is a departure point for boating trips, but it tends to be lacking in cultural attractions. It is a full-service community with groceries, pubs, restaurants and cafés.

ⓘ Municipal government at **www.town.portmcneill.bc.ca**; Chamber of Commerce at **www.portmcneill.net**; tourism information at **www.hellobc .com/en-CA/RegionsCities/PortMcNeill.htm** or **www.vancouverisland .travel/north-island/port-mcneill**.

❺ Arch, Resonance and Glory Hole caves *(map p. 303)*

These three remarkable caves are part of a cluster among the largest caves in Canada. Arch Cave is one of the deepest at 352 m and, according to Caving Canada, the fourth longest, with a length of 8,394 m; Glory Hole measures in at 312 m deep with a length of 2,035 m. Resonance Cave is 95 m with a length of 1,280 m; its name comes from the odd acoustics. Access is through deactivated logging roads in rough condition; for casual visitors the best way to enjoy them is through tour operators, which tend, unfortunately, to come and go. Check tourism resources for a current list of tour providers.

❻ Artlish River *(map p. 293)*

This is a key launch location for Kyuquot Sound, and the closest to the Island Highway—far less circuitous than Fair Harbour, which requires a trip past Zeballos before turning up-island again. Artlish River can be reached from the Island Highway by following the Atluck Main from the Zeballos Road turnoff. The route is well marked, but expect it to be rough on the final leg once south of Atluck Lake.

❼ Fair Harbour *(map p. 293)*

This is a forest recreation site privatized with the addition of a small store and a campground, launch and wharf. The campground is best suited to RVs, with a few sites suitable for tents. The harbour is a gateway for boat trips into Kyuquot Sound. Access is via the Fair Harbour Main that diverges on the route to Zeballos. The route is well marked.

MAJOR PARKS

9 Little Huson Cave Regional Park ● *(map p. 303)*

A short trail from a parking lot leads to two views of a creek entering and exiting a large cave. One view is from a platform overlooking the creek's exit; a stairwell leads to an area of rock platform in front of the same cave entrance. Another nearby cave offers some simple exploring. Bring a good flashlight.

ACCESS: Signs mark the way, but from the Atluck Relocation take R05 for 2.2 km to the parking area. The route becomes rough at the tail end. Note it's also often incorrectly referred to as Little Hustan Cave Regional Park.

10 Nimpkish Lake Provincial Park *(map p. 303)*

This is a 3,950-hectare park on the southwest shore of Nimpkish Lake. It protects the east-facing slopes of the southern Karmutzen Range of the Northern Island Mountains plus the drainage for Tlakwa Creek, known for its prime salmon spawning habitat in the lower reaches. Old-growth forest can be found along the east slopes of Karmutzen Mountain and along Nimpkish Lake. The area along the creek was logged in 1928, and evidence of the railway is still visible along the upper part of the creek. There are no designated trails or camping areas in the park, though Karmutzen Mountain, at 1,433 m elevation, provides views over the region for those hardy enough to make the climb. Wilderness camping is allowed.

ACCESS: Boat access is by far the simplest. You can launch from the Nimpkish Lake recreation site. The park can be reached from the north or south by logging roads near the park boundary, but without designated trails this is an option for experienced backcountry hikers only.

11 Lower Nimpkish Provincial Park *(map p. 303)*

This park is a 300-metre-wide corridor along the lower Nimpkish River south of Port McNeill, extending 6.4 km from the north end of Nimpkish Lake. It's prime eagle nesting habitat, with seven nests inside the park and another eight in the immediate vicinity. This is traditional Namgis territory that plays a role in their mythology and is home to sacred and ceremonial sites. A 16-hectare patch of the 200-hectare park is old-growth forest. The park itself has no facilities or formal trails. A fish hatchery bars access to the east side of the river during all but its open hours, which are limited during the summer. The hatchery is run by the Namgis First Nation, and can raise 2 million chum, 2.5 million chinook, 700,000 coho and 3 million sockeye eggs per year. It's open for tours during summer hours.

FISHING: The Nimpkish is habitat for sockeye, coho, chinook, pink and chum salmon, plus steelhead, cutthroat, Dolly Varden, kokanee and rainbow trout. Watch for black bear along the river's edge during spawning season.

ACCESS: From Highway 19 just west of the Nimpkish River bridge take Nimpkish Heights Road south, following it to the end. This abuts a stand of mature trees where casual local trails can be found into the forest.

⑫ Tahsish-Kwois Provincial Park *(map p. 303)*

At 10,972 hectares, this is one of Vancouver Island's largest parks, but it's also one of the least known, due in part to highly limited access. The park protects the lower river valley of the Tahsish River and all of Kwois Creek— essentially a watershed in its entirety. This makes it a valuable wildlife preserve, notable for the Tahsish River's chinook, coho and chum salmon spawns. It's also home to one of the 36 summer steelhead runs on Vancouver Island. Within the park are substantial portions of old-growth coastal western hemlock forest in a region where logging has made them rare. The park is home to the tallest western hemlock tree in BC, at 76 m. The lower Tahsish River valley is also considered one of Vancouver Island's best Roosevelt elk winter ranges.

At the mouth of Tahsish River is the Tahsish River Ecological Reserve, created to protect the estuary in its pristine form along with a 12-hectare island in the river mouth. It is one of the few estuaries on the island not altered by logging and development, and it's notable for a diverse population of ducks, migrating birds and shore birds and as rearing habitat for a multitude of fish species. The reserve is surrounded by the provincial park; the division is the high tide line. The reserve extends to a depth of 10 fathoms toward Tahsish Inlet.

ACCESS: The park is best visited via paddle up the Tahsish River. Access is possible by adjacent logging road, though no formal trails or points of entry exist. The best foot access is off the Cross Lake connector, which diverts from the Atluck Main south of Atluck Lake. Follow it northwest about 5 km from the Atluck-Cross junction to a deactivated logging road that heads west over the Tahsish River. Take a quick left (south) and follow the unsigned Tahsish Road about 2 km as it turns west and follows the river. The point where it diverges north is about the closest you can get to the park by road, and the logical starting point for a backcountry push into the region. Naturally, paddlers will have the best time in this area.

FOREST RECREATION SITES

See the map on page 303 to locate these recreation sites.

E **Bonanza Lake ●**

This site features about 14 campsites in varying degrees of development set in a row in a mature cedar and hemlock forest. Lake access is available on either end of the campground. Most sites are best suited to tents. A second lake access, slightly north, has two picnic tables, lake access and an outhouse; it would be suitable for RVers. The lake itself is surprisingly large and will be a less busy option than Nimpkish Lake for windsurfers.

ACCESS: The site can be reached directly across from the Zeballos turnoff from the Island Highway. Take the Old Steele Main across the railway bridge (see Kokish Main, page 295). The recreation site is 0.8 km north of the junction with K Main. Or follow the route to Ida Lake and continue south for 16 km.

F **Ida Lake ●**

Nine sites and a boat launch are set along this small lake. To reach it, take the route to Telegraph Cove (page 302). Go past the marked viewpoint overlooking Beaver Cove and take the next sharp right, following the Kokish Main to the recreation site.

G **Nimpkish Lake ●**

This is a busy recreation site due in large part to it being about the only formal and easily accessible access to Nimpkish Lake. On any given summer day it will be a sea of RVs and tent trailers crammed in side by side, most with windsurfing boards and sails leaning against them. Without a doubt Nimpkish Lake is the region's best windsurfing lake. It's possible to launch from here and boat out; limited parking is available in the nooks and crannies of the recreation site. People seeking a quieter camping location may want to seek out the smaller Kinman Creek campsite. It has a few sites but no lake access.

ACCESS: The TURNOFF ● from the Island Highway isn't marked, so look for the logging road on the west side about 5.7 km past the Zeballos turnoff. Keep to the left as you drive through the area; if you reach the Nimpkish logging camp you've missed the left. You can also turn from the highway at the rustic one-pump gas station slightly farther north along the Island Highway, then backtrack through the logging station (if you miss the first highway turnoff). To reach Kinman Creek go north through the logging station to the creekside.

Anutz Lake ●

Several large, clear areas best suited for RVs are set along the lakefront with a few smaller tent sites in the forest. From Highway 19 take the road to Zeballos and the first major right at the junction past the Nimpkish River bridge. The route is signed.

Atluck Lake ●

You'll find open RV-style clearings with picnic tables and firepits, some with lake access. A smaller but potentially more attractive spot for tent campers, called Hennigar Park, is located along the lake farther south from the Atluck Lake recreation site. You'll find a couple of small tent clearings and a pleasant beach area best suited for one group but probably usable by two. Access is via the Atluck Main. The route is well marked. The lake is exceptionally pretty. The Atluck Main skirts the west shoreline for a scenic drive along its length. Paddlers should also enjoy this lake, which includes a large island and wonderful views of jagged Pinder Peak (elevation 1,542 m). Pinder Peak has long been a top mountaineering area; the best access is off the Artlish Main south of Atluck Lake along an old overgrown spur. It heads northeast along a creek into the valley along the peak's southern flank. From there it might require bushwhacking to the bluffs.

Port Alice region

This is an area of lakes and logging, with the advantage of a paved highway to Port Alice, a small mill community set on Neroutsos Inlet. The two major lakes, Alice and Victoria, offer fishing and boating from a variety of recreation sites. The limestone geology of the region offers a few interesting karst features, but accessibility is always an issue; daytime public use of many of the interior logging roads is restricted. A renewal of limestone mining has also barred entry into the area southwest of Alice Lake.

POINTS OF INTEREST

❽ Port Alice *(map p. 309)*

This small town along the shore of Neroutsos Inlet is seeing a resurgence after the purchase of the town's mill in 2005 by Neucel Specialty Cellulose. It ended years of instability and shutdowns that reached a crisis after an abrupt closure of the mill by LaPointe Partners in 2004. Shortly after, much of the town's population

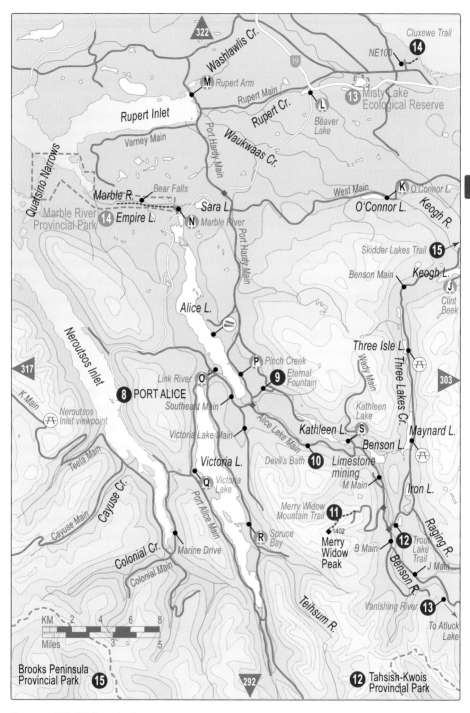

322

Washlawlis Cr.

19

Cluxewe Trail

NE100

14

Rupert Arm
M

Rupert Main

Rupert Cr.

13 Misty Lake
Ecological Reserve

Rupert Inlet

L

Beaver
Lake

Varney Main

Waukwaas Cr.

Quatsino Narrows

Port Hardy Main

Marble R.

Bear Falls

West Main

K

O'Connor L.

O'Connor L.

Keogh R.

Marble River
Provincial Park

14 Empire L.

Sara L.

N

Marble River

Skidder Lakes Trail

15

Benson Main

Keogh L.

J

Clint
Beek

Neroutsos Inlet

Alice L.

Three Isle L.

303

317

K Main

Link River

O

P

Pinch Creek

9

Eternal
Fountain

Wady Main

Three Lakes Cr.

Neroutsos
Inlet viewpoint

8 PORT ALICE

Southeast Main

Kathleen
Lake

Maynard L.

Teeta Main

Victoria Lake Main

Alice Lake Main

Kathleen L.

S

Benson L.

Cayuse Cr.

Victoria L.

Devil's Bath

10

Limestone
mining

Iron L.

Cayuse Main

Q

Victoria
Lake

M Main

Merry Widow
Mountain Trail

11

Raging R.

Colonial Cr.

Port Alice Main

R

Spruce
Bay

1402

Merry
Widow
Peak

B Main

12

Trout
Lake
Trail

Marine Drive

Benson R.

J Main

Colonial Main

Teihsum R.

Vanishing River

13

KM   2   4   6   8

Miles   3   5

292

To Atluck
Lake

Brooks Peninsula
Provincial Park

15

12 Tahsish-Kwois
Provincial Park

See pages 292–293 for main chapter map.

PORT ALICE REGION

The Eternal Fountain.

left. Most services are available in modest proportions, including a store, gas, accommodation, a marina and boat launches, but the core of the town remains industrial.

9 Eternal Fountain ● *(map p. 309)*

Picture a stream running out of an upper cave and falling into a pool below, where it disappears yet again into a hidden cave. Interesting rock formations, hanging moss and exposed root formations add to the appeal. A short trail from the parking lot leads to a viewing platform adjacent to the fountain. From Port Alice take the Southeast Main to the Alice Lake Main junction, then the Alice Lake Main north for a short distance to a marked turnoff east.

⑩ Devil's Bath ● *(map p. 309)*

This is an odd feature to see on a trip through the region—perhaps named more dramatically than is warranted, but an unusual sight nonetheless. A viewing platform adjacent to the parking lot overlooks a sunken lake surrounded by impressive cliffs. From the Port Alice Highway take the Southeast Main, then the Alice Lake Main east; follow the signs.

⑪ Merry Widow Mountain Trail *(map p. 309)*

This is one of the few designated mountain routes in this region, an exception in an area where reaching even the lower levels for an alpine ascent generally requires a great deal of effort. The trail leads from a logging road to the peak at 1,405 m, or to any number of viewpoints along the way. Expect snow at higher elevations most of the year. Though designated, access remains a problem, as the logging road to the trailhead is steep and rocky, making it accessible only by four-wheel drive. Also, watch out if you're navigating by compass. Merry Widow Mountain has one of the strongest magnetic anomalies on Vancouver Island.

ACCESS: Due to limestone mining restrictions the most reliable access is West Main from the Island Highway, then Benson Main to the M Main junction, then west to the B and M mains junction. Follow M Main north for about 1.25 km to a steep left (this should be at the sign for limestone mining access restrictions; driving farther north on M Main may not be possible). Take the SPUR ● (Merry Widow Trail Main by the sign) and follow for this about 2.5 km before a sharp right. It will head north, but you'll want to find your way west; logging near Newt Lake may lure you on new roads in error. The final leg west is deactivated, possibly requiring a hike in to the signposted TRAILHEAD ●.

⑫ Trout Lake Trail ● *(map p. 309)*

This is a modest designated trail rounding a small lake. Like so many non-maintained features it may be overgrown. Access is just northeast of the B-M mains junction.

⑬ Vanishing River ● *(map p. 309)*

This is another odd little designated viewpoint that isn't signed, unlike most other features in this area; the only indication it exists is the Vanishing River Recreation Area sign when you arrive. A short trail leads from the parking area to a viewpoint where the river falls into a dark chasm. There is no indication of how far it falls. Blowdown has obliterated the access to a second lookout point.

ACCESS: Follow the J Main for about 5 km, watching for the sign and parking area on the south side of the road.

⑭ Cluxewe Trail ● *(map p. 309)*

This is a 550 m (20-minute) trail that leads through immature forest (planted 1954 and 1970) down a stairwell to grassy flats and an extensive cobble beach overlooking Broughton Strait. A sign indicates it to be part of the Cluxewe River Salt Marsh Reserve; for the salt marsh, follow the cobble beach east to the river's estuary. This is probably best enjoyed as a route to an otherwise secluded but expansive beach overlooking Pulteney Point on Malcolm Island.

ACCESS: From the Island Highway exit north onto the logging road about 1.3 km west of the Cluxewe River bridge. In a short distance you'll hit a junction (the Rupert Main); follow the route northwest for about 1.6 km to a spur heading north. Follow the spur past its turn east to where it ends at the trailhead.

⑮ Skidder Lakes Trail ● *(map p. 309)*

This is another of those odd little trails that develop with no particular reason or destination—but it's a welcome diversion in an area otherwise short on trails. It begins at the west end of the largest of the Skidder Lakes, continuing along a fairly open section of forest, then past the second Skidder Lake.

ACCESS: Unlike most other features in this area, no signs indicate this trail's existence. Take the West Main and follow the signs for Clint Beek for 8 km, then take the Cluxewe Main for about 0.8 km to a large clearing suitable for parking. A bulldozed path leads to near the lakeside where the trail begins by skirting the south side of the first lake.

MAJOR PARKS

⑬ Misty Lake Ecological Reserve *(map p. 309)*

This reserve south of Port McNeill was created to protect habitat for the giant black stickleback—a rare and vulnerable species. Misty Lake is one of just three places in BC where both stream and lake stickleback species are found. The stickleback found here is thought to be a distinct species from the stickleback found on Queen Charlotte Islands. Also found here are steelhead, cutthroat, coho, Dolly Varden and rainbow trout. Keep an eye open for prickly sculpin as well. The park is 68 hectares and was created in 1996.

⑭ Marble River Provincial Park *(map p. 309)*

This wilderness park is best known for a hiking trail leading along the Marble River. The 4.2 km trail leads to Bear Falls, named for the mammals that can often be found fishing for salmon at the waterfall in season. The trail ends at Emerald

Pools, a popular fly-fishing location. Arguably the best feature of the park is a narrow canyon at the river mouth, accessible by paddle through Varney Bay at higher tides. Launching is possible from nearby Coal Harbour. See *The Wild Coast, Volume 1* for details. The park also protects a portion of the narrow tidal channel Quatsino Narrows.

FISHING: Chinook and coho salmon and steelhead, cutthroat, rainbow and Dolly Varden trout are found in Marble River. It has a reputation for good steelhead fishing.

CAMPING: Walk-in camping is possible, with vehicle-accessible camping in the adjacent Western Forest Products recreation site, a pretty treed area with secluded campsites dotting the area.

ACCESS: The park is reached through the Marble River forest recreation site off the Port Alice Highway. Note that in 2007 it was closed indefinitely due to blowdown.

FOREST RECREATION SITES

See the map on page 309 to locate these recreation sites.

Clint Beek (Keogh Lake) ●

This is one of the more developed and better-used recreation sites in the region, probably because of its proximity to Port McNeill. About a dozen good, forested sites with picnic tables and firepits are set around the access loop, with a dock and beach area for swimming. A separate launch with a dock is located east of the campground. Expect good fishing—Keogh Lake is stocked with trout.

ACCESS: From the West Main follow the Clint Beek signs or drive south for 8 km to the Cluxewe Main junction, turning left then right along the south end of Keogh Lake to the campground, 3.5 km past the turnoff for the Skidder Lakes Trail.

O'Connor Lake ●

This day-use site features picnic tables and a launch for swimming, waterskiing and fishing. It is located off the West Main, about 7.7 km west of the West-Benson mains junction.

Beaver Lake

This small day-use area has picnic tables and a beach with a float ideal for swimming, fishing and canoeing. A short interpretive trail leads through the neighbouring forest. It's located just off the Island Highway at the Alice Lake Highway exit.

Capturing the size of an old-growth spruce on film often requires an unusual perspective.

Ⓜ Rupert Arm ●

This unstructured recreation site is at the head of Rupert Arm at the mouth of Washlawlis Creek. Western Forest Products lists picnic tables, a group picnic shelter, fishing and crabbing, but in reality it tends to be loose RV sites at the end of the various access roads. It would be possible to launch small boats from here. Note the south end of the head of the arm is a private camp. The area is easily reached by taking the Rupert Main from the Island Highway. The intersection is immediately north of the Port Alice Highway junction. Turn north and take any of the accesses to the waterfront.

Ⓝ Marble River ●

This large, 33-unit site is located immediately adjacent to Marble River Provincial Park. It features sites spread out in a mature forest, plus a day-use area and launch to Alice Lake. The recreation site must be entered to reach the trailhead for the Marble River Provincial Park (page 312) trail to Bear Falls. From the Island Highway take the Port Alice Highway approximately 14.5 km to the site entrance.

ⓞ Link River ●

Link River is the local name for the river between Alice and Victoria lakes. This recreation site along the river at the south end of Alice Lake is a well used area with beaches and sheltered barbecue pits. Several nice sites are located near the lake, with 42 sites in total.

ACCESS: From north of Port Alice take the logging road (the Southeast Main) that departs from the south side of the highway and heads east (almost parallel); there is more than one access point, so don't panic and do a dangerous U-turn if you pass your first opportunity. Follow it to the signed recreation site entrance.

ⓟ Pinch Creek ●

Pinch Creek flows into Alice Lake, creating a gravel bar at the mouth. The recreation site is at the gravel bar, with a couple of tent sites set back in the forest along the access road. Boat launching would be possible from the gravel.

ACCESS: Take the Port Alice Highway 10 km from the Island Highway, then the Port Hardy Main south for 14 km. Or from Port Alice take the Southeast Main to Link River and skirt the south end of Alice Lake to the campsite.

ⓠ Victoria Lake

This site features picnic tables, a boat launch, swimming and fishing but no official camping. It's on the west side of Victoria Lake; from the south end of Port Alice just past the Neucel pulp mill take the logging road east to the lakefront.

ⓡ Spruce Bay ●

This site features seven campsites with firepits, swimming, fishing, canoeing, a dock and a forest trail through old-growth forest.

👍 THUMBS UP: The forest trail is an easy 0.5 km loop through a variety of forest types including some impressive old-growth forest. Interpretive signs provide information well above the norm. Even seasoned naturalists are likely to learn something on this charming walk.

ACCESS: From Port Alice take the Southeast Main east to Alice Lake, then the Victoria Lake Main south. Note that the road that appears to loop the lake is gated at the south end, so access to this site is likely from the north only.

ⓢ **Kathleen Lake** ●

This pretty site is located in an out-of-the-way spot east of Victoria Lake. Take the Alice Lake Main about 8.5 km east of the Alice Lake–Southeast mains junction, then head north down the twisting limestone gravel road to the recreation site access. You'll find a pleasant site in mature forest on the lakefront, with dispersed campsites on various levels. Note that in 2007 it was closed indefinitely due to the risk of unstable trees.

Quatsino entrance

This is an exceptional wilderness area with an unfortunate history of extensive logging. Two distinct regions compose this outer portion of Quatsino Sound— the southern shoreline of the sound, which can be reached through Port Alice, and the northern shore, which must be reached through Holberg. It lacks some of the drama of the more mountainous regions of Vancouver Island (Quatsino Sound is characterized by rolling hillsides), but a scattering of beaches, an interesting boardwalk community and some dramatic stretches of remote coast make this an intriguing area to explore.

POINTS OF INTEREST

⓰ **East Creek Valley** *(map p. 317)*

This valley has been a contentious one for environmental groups as it's one of the last great, unlogged valleys on Vancouver Island. The Sierra Club led the fight by forming a Save East Creek campaign, but it fell on deaf ears and the logging trucks have moved in. Oddly, most environmental reports about the activity fell off after about 2003. An exceptional way to see the valley is by paddling in and walking the old-growth forest. Naturally, new logging roads will provide future access to whatever virgin forest remains.

⓱ **Klaskino Inlet** *(map p. 317)*

This inlet has been accessible for a number of years. There's a boat ramp at the head of the inlet; access is by a logging road that skirts both the north and south shores. This followed extensive logging that saw most of the inlet and neighbouring peaks clear-cut. The area is now recovering and logging road access is being maintained. Take B Main, then North Main to Klaskino Main. The launch is rocky at low tide and is best for cartop boats.

⓲ **Side Bay** ● *(map p. 317)*

Hurry if you want to visit this spectacular area. The access road is deactivated and becoming overgrown; I suspect it will be completely impassable in a few years. Take the Side Bay Main from the JUNCTION ● with Restless Main and follow

QUATSINO ENTRANCE

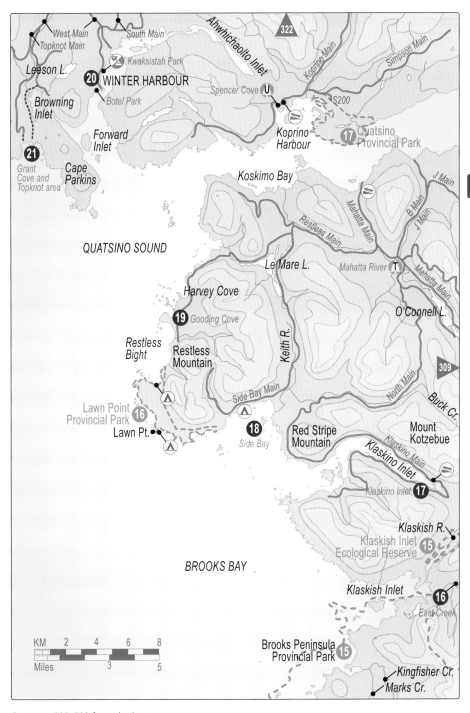

322

West Main
Topknot Main
South Main
Ahwhichaolto Inlet
Koprino Main
Simpson Main
Leeson L.
2 Kwaksistah Park
20 WINTER HARBOUR
Spencer Cove U
S200
Browning
Inlet
Botel Park
Koprino
Harbour
17 Quatsino
Provincial Park
Forward
Inlet
Koskimo Bay
21
Grant
Cove and
Topknot area
Cape
Parkins
QUATSINO SOUND
Restless Main
Mahatta Main
J Main
B Main
J Main
Le Mare L.
Mahatta River T
Mahatta Main
Harvey Cove
O'Connell L.
19 Gooding Cove
Restless
Bight
Restless
Mountain
Keith R.
309
North Main
Buck Cr.
Side Bay Main
Lawn Point
Provincial Park
16
Lawn Pt.
18
Side Bay
Red Stripe
Mountain
Klaskino Main
Mount
Kotzebue
Klaskino Inlet
Klaskino Inlet
17
Klaskish R.
Klaskish Inlet
Ecological Reserve
15
BROOKS BAY
Klaskish Inlet
16
East Creek

KM   2   4   6   8
Miles   3   5

Brooks Peninsula
Provincial Park
15
Kingfisher Cr.
Marks Cr.

See pages 292–293 for main chapter map.

Rough rock outcrops and a beautiful beach dot Side Bay looking toward Klaskino Inlet.

the route as far as the vehicle allows. Should the bushes be held back south of Le Mare Lake, a few washouts follow, but as of 2007 the road was accessible by four-wheel drive. The road eventually leads to a beach access not far from Lawn Point Provincial Park. It would be possible to launch cartop boats from here for trips to the Brooks Peninsula region.

👍 THUMBS UP: This portion of Side Bay has some sweeping sections of sand beach with interesting rock formations, and when the access road becomes overgrown it will still be possible to get in by mountain bike for several years. This will make Side Bay an even more exclusive area to visit, but a highly recommended one.

🔟 Gooding Cove ● *(map p. 317)*

This is an exceptional little beach set on the south entrance to Quatsino Sound. Take the route to Mahatta River, then continue west on the Restless Main. The road first skirts high above Harvey Cove, then descends toward Gooding Cove where a steep turnoff leads to the beach. It is highly advised that you do not drive down; you may not get back up. Walking in gives easy access to a long, sweeping beach that improves in quality (from small rocks to sand) as you walk west. Walk-in wilderness camping is possible, and you could launch cartop boats from here for trips to Restless Bight (again, walking the boats down the sloping access road is probably wisest).

A morning mist rises over Gooding Cove.

⑳ **Winter Harbour** *(map p. 317)*

This is a pretty little community joined in part by an old boardwalk that predates road access. Amenities are minimal—expect rustic accommodation, a post office, a small store and a government wharf. Much of the waterfront activity is for fish processing, which is fitting as the first business here was a crab and clam cannery in 1904. The village has a long early history as a trading post for whaling schooner traffic. Access to the community is by a well-marked but rough logging road from Holberg.

 SHORT WALKS: A trail leads from the west end of town across the headland to Botel Park, a sandy day-use area.

Ⓐ CAMPING: Kwakistah Park is a small regional campground with a half-dozen sites clustered together near the waterfront. Parking could be an issue if it's crowded. This is also a possible boat launch.

㉑ **Grant Cove and Topknot area** *(map p. 317)*

A trail leads to a good stretch of sand beach backed by a grassy berm. The traditional access has been from Browning Inlet, but recent logging has made a closer route possible. Take West Main from South Main; it will eventually head south toward the cove. This is just one of several options for exploring the area west of Winter Harbour. Instead of following the West Main to Grant Cove, you can take the Topknot Main to a viewpoint, then down to Topknot Lake, which has a boat access. A divergence off Topknot Main is possible along the HECHT MAIN ● to the Hecht Beach Trail, a short walk to the rugged coastline along this stretch. (This is not shown on the main map for this section; see the main chapter map for the location.) Or you can take the ML Main North from the West Main to skirt the Macjack River, where canoeists can start a downriver run.

MAJOR PARKS

⑮ Brooks Peninsula Provincial Park and Klaskish Inlet Ecological Reserve *(map p. 317)*

Brooks Peninsula Provincial Park protects a notable peninsula and much of the surrounding geography, while neighouring Klaskish Inlet Ecological Reserve protects the estuary and lower portion of Klaskish River. Logging roads may get you close to this area, but there is no formal land access and the terrain is poor for trekking. This area is most popular as a boating and kayaking destination, though its propensity for wind and storms makes it a formidable place to visit. For full details on this park, Solander Island Ecological Reserve, Checleset Bay Ecological Reserve, Klaskish River Ecological Reserve and Big Bunsby Marine Park, see *The Wild Coast, Volume 1*. None of these provincial parks have land access.

⑯ Lawn Point Provincial Park *(map p. 317)*

This is one of the more remote coastal provincial parks, often visited by boat from nearby Winter Harbour or the boat ramps at Klaskino Inlet or Side Bay, but rarely by foot. Visitors who make it will find one of the more remarkable locations on the Vancouver Island coast—truly a scenic and wild area to explore. Lawn Point itself is unusual for the flat, grassy expanse at the point and two prominent and distinctive mounds for viewpoints across Side Bay toward Brooks Peninsula. Rough trails lead across the tall grass to old-growth forest. On the north side of the park is a wonderful beach facing Restless Bight. Features include intriguing rock formations along the shore and views across to the reefs into Quatsino Sound. The park protects 584 hectares and was created in 1996.

(Ⓐ) CAMPING: Beaches of varying degrees of quality dot the Side Bay area. The best beach is on the southeast side of Lawn Point. Or cross the peninsula to reach Restless Bight. The bight has three main beaches, with a good one within the park boundary facing northwest across the bight.

ACCESS: Formal foot access to the park does not exist. Logging roads reach Side Bay (page 316), but no formal trails lead from that road into the park. Hikers could bushwhack the 400 m from the closest access point at the road to a beach near Lawn Point. The other option is a beach climb from Side Bay, with a tough headland to pass that would entail potentially difficult rock climbing. Paddling would be much simpler.

⑰ Quatsino Provincial Park *(map p. 317)*

This wilderness park on the north shore of Quatsino Sound is billed as a marine-accessible recreation park, but it's not really even that, as it has no formal access of any kind, whether by boat or by road. The shore along Quatsino Sound is generally steep and rugged, thwarting boat visits. Along Koprino Harbour the various bays and coves tend to dry at lower tides, potentially miring boaters. The interior of the park is remarkable for its old-growth forests and for the Koprino River estuary, which is rich in both marine life and waterbirds. Completely protected within the park is Koprino Lake. The park is 654 hectares and was established in 1995.

(A) CAMPING: While backcountry camping is permitted, a lack of formal access and rugged terrain tends to limit options. Formal campsites are at the nearby Spencer Cove recreation site (below).

ACCESS: From Holberg, take the Koprino Bay Main, then Simpson Main immediately outside the park boundary. Turn right onto S200 ● to the park boundary. The trip is about 30 km from Holberg. Note that any trails from the park boundary are informal and may be overgrown.

FOREST RECREATION SITES
See the map on page 317 to locate these recreation sites.

ⓣ Mahatta River ●

This site features a few campsites with rough river access only. It is at the south end of J Main near the J and North mains junction.

ⓤ Spencer Cove ●

This small, 10-campsite recreation area is set in a small cove off Koprino Harbour. The best sites tend to be used on a semi-permanent basis. It is doubly interesting for the old cannery ruins along the waterfront. A rough launch site exists for kayaks and cartop boats, though most boaters use the launch north of the recreation site and immediately north of a log dump. Fishing is possible from a dock within the recreation site. The route is well marked from Holberg. Just follow the Koprino Main to the cove.

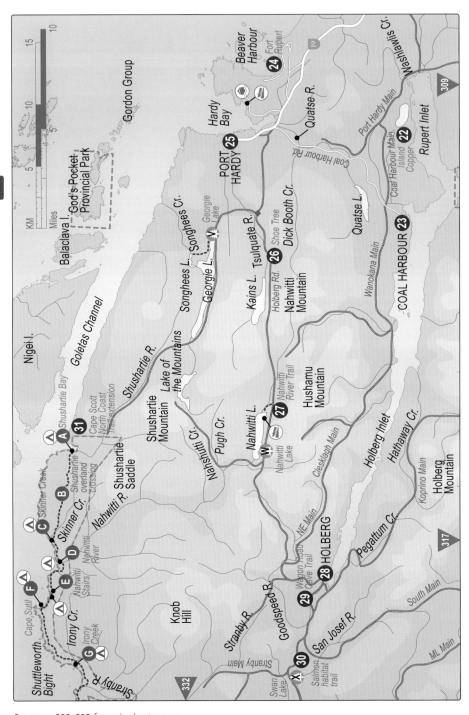

See pages 292–293 for main chapter map.

Nahwitti

North of Quatsino Sound the Northern Island Mountains diminish and a new terrain takes over, the Nahwitti Lowlands, characterized by low, rolling hills, boggy and wet valleys, intertwining river systems and scrubby forest. The main attraction for most visitors is Cape Scott Provincial Park. There is just one route by land in this area—Holberg Road. This forest service road links most of the main features of the region, making it an ideal stretch of road to explore. Much of the northern limits south of the park are inaccessible, either by restricted logging roads or by complete isolation. Those who wish to capture the true spirit will want to try the Cape Scott North Coast Trail extension. This wild and unruly trail is likely to stir interest as it evolves, perhaps growing to rival the West Coast Trail as the main hiking challenge on the island.

POINTS OF INTEREST

㉒ Island Copper *(map p. 322)*

This abandoned copper mine on the shore of Rupert Inlet closed in 1995. Its claim of being the lowest open-air point on earth at 402 m deep ended when the open-pit mine was flooded, creating a deep lake in its place. Since it opened in 1971 it produced 1.2 billion kilograms of copper, making it the third largest copper mine in Canada. While the structures can still be seen from the water on Rupert Inlet, the site is closed.

㉓ Coal Harbour *(map p. 322)*

This is a small residential community set around a cove. The main activity is on the dock, which serves as a gateway to inner Quatsino Sound. The only service is a small store—Lucky Louie's Red and White Store, a throwback to another era. A paved road provides access to the community.

㉔ Fort Rupert *(map p. 322)*

This is one of Vancouver Island's oldest European communities, established in 1849 as a Hudson's Bay Company coal mining town. Two bastions and a stockade protected the fort, which grew to a population of about 100 before a much greater coal discovery in Nanaimo drew interest away. The fort burned in 1889, leaving just a chimney standing that is still in evidence today. The beach surrounding Beaver Harbour is a local park with good picnic sites along the waterside.

The Shoe Tree.

㉕ **Port Hardy** *(map p. 322)*

This is northern Vancouver Island's major community, with a population of about 5,200 and full services, including a busy airport, a hospital and all amenities, such as hotels, stores and restaurants. The waters off Hardy Bay are popular with

NAHWITTI

sports fishermen and kayakers, making this area a staging ground for water-based trips. Launches can be found near the marinas at the south end of Hardy Bay and near the ferry terminal on the east side of the bay. For full information on the coastal features and nearby islands, see *The Wild Coast, Volume 1*.

 A local business directory is available at **www.ph-chamber.bc.ca**; tourism information is available at **www.hellobc.com/en-CA/RegionsCities/ PortHardy.htm** or **www.vancouverisland.travel/north-island/port-hardy**.

26 Shoe Tree *(map p. 322)*

Back in the late 1980s someone had the idea of hanging a shoe on a large tree alongside the Holberg Road. Perhaps a statement on the toll the Cape Scott Trail takes on shoes, perhaps just spontaneous modern art, the Shoe Tree has grown to hundreds of pairs nailed up the tree and placed around the surrounding logs. So if you wear out your shoes on the trail, here's a fitting place to retire them.

27 Nahwitti River Trail ● *(map p. 322)*

A trailhead at a parking lot off Holberg Road leads into mature forest and to the Nahwitti River and Nahwitti Lake. Other routes tend to diverge, making this a worthwhile place to stretch the legs and explore.

28 Holberg *(map p. 322)*

This is a logging camp community of about 100 permanent residents thanks in large part to the Western Forest Products camp here. The community is at the head of Holberg Inlet, making it a possible launch site, with salmon usually the incentive. Amenities are few—just a small store and the Scarlett Ibis Restaurant and Pub on the waterfront. A Canadian Armed Forces base once thrived just west of the village, but it was closed in the 1980s and all traces have been removed. Holberg's main claim to fame was being the largest floating logging camp in the world back in the late 1940s and 1950s. The camp had a population of about 250 and was 0.4 km long, with over 50 buildings.

29 Wagon Road Cave Trail ● *(map p. 322)*

This is a wonderful little trail that leads along a creekside through various types of forest to a small cave suitable for casual (but possibly wet) exploring. A picnic site at the river's edge is obviously rarely used and becoming overgrown. The trail follows the wagon road created by Danish settlers earlier in the last century. The road connected San Josef Bay, Holberg Inlet and the various homesteads along the way. The last remnants are some old discarded cars.

㉚ **Salmon habitat trail** ● *(map p. 322)*

A five-minute trail built by the community of Holberg follows a short boardwalk to a viewpoint over salmon rearing habitat in a small stream. Interpretive signs along the way have faded and become unreadable. The trail seems to have no official name but is marked at the roadside by a small trail sign. Watch for it about 3 km west of Holberg.

㉛ **Cape Scott North Coast Trail extension** *(map p. 322)*

The idea to link Shushartie Bay to Cape Scott has been around for more than a century: at the turn of the last century, the Danish Cape Scott settlers, who lacked a closer all-weather anchorage than Shushartie Bay, created a rough version. The new recreation trail has taken years to develop. Due to open in spring 2008, it will provide access to remote regions of the north coast otherwise inaccessible by land, including some beautiful stretches of beach. When combined with the original Cape Scott Trail, the route will run for 60 km across the entire northernmost end of the island. Expect it to be a rough wilderness trail, however, with parts reminiscent of the West Coast Trail before the trail improvements. Long stretches were created simply by cutting back the brush. Its success will depend in large part on the level of maintenance, the progress of improvements and transportation services at both trailheads.

A cobble beach and impassable headland near Cape Sutil on the North Coast Trail.

TRAVEL NOTES: In 2007 a logging road did reach within about a kilometre of Shushartie Bay, but it was slated to be deactivated. From the logging road there's a descent through a clear-cut. Supporters of the trail are hoping the road will be preserved as land access for the trail.

- WHEN TO VISIT: Any time of the year is likely to be cloudy and quite wet, though less so in the main summer months. There's no guarantee of sunshine, even when the rest of Vancouver Island is basking in fair weather and warmth. The area tends to have its own weather system that's generally bleaker than elsewhere on Vancouver Island.

- HOW LONG IT WILL TAKE: Given the unimproved nature of many stretches and the potentially wet and difficult portions, travel will be slow. An agenda of 15 km per day will likely be aggressive for most people. Until significant trail improvements are made, expect to spend at least five to six nights on the trail. A problem I anticipate is that many of the unimproved sections, particularly those steep portions with only dirt footholds, are going to erode quickly after substantial use. They may erode down to useful roots; they may erode to a slippery mudslide. Either way they are slow going, with a high possibility of injury.

- WHICH DIRECTION TO HIKE: The trailhead at Shushartie Bay can be reached by boat only. Water taxi service will likely be provided by local boat operators rather than BC Parks. Ending your trip at the bay may mean scheduling a pickup in a situation where a definitive timeline to complete the trail is difficult. It may also mean having to wait if storms or adverse conditions make boat travel dangerous. To avoid this you can start at Shushartie Bay, then walk out at the parking lot at Cape Scott. From there

Navigating a steep stretch of the North Coast Trail.

Crossing the bog ridge north of Shushartie Bay.

a vehicle shuttle service will be available back to Port Hardy. Such services will have to evolve; see the Internet resources for information on the latest providers or **www.thewildcoast.ca** for updates. Because of the difficulties involved in completing the trail, many hikers will use the Cape Scott Trail to reach Nissen Bight, then venture eastward in a casual exploration before returning by the same route. This will keep the Shushartie Bay side much less traveled; this is potentially a good thing for those who venture to Cape Sutil, but the downside is the potential for poor trail development.

- IN THE EVENT OF INJURY: The extension is a long wilderness section likely to see few hikers and even fewer park patrols. Cell phones won't work. You are on your own here. An option is a marine radio; the Coast Guard could be alerted to serious injuries by way of the emergency frequencies.

Following are a few key areas.

Ⓐ SHUSHARTIE BAY: The east TRAILHEAD ● begins on the outer rock ridge (it was moved from the estuary late in the planning stage). Shushartie Bay's intertidal area is prime bear feeding habitat. Expect to see several bears here. The bay was the best all-weather anchorage for the Cape Scott settlement, and the ruins of the old dock are still visible on the north shore. Note that a possible secondary route and campsite along Shushartie River was on hold pending the decision on the final location of a dock; this section was in limbo as BC Parks requested a change in the route to avoid using a pocket of private land adjacent to the bay.

Ⓑ SHUSHARTIE OVERLAND CROSSING: From Shushartie Bay the trail leads to the top of a modest ridge. The first portion leads through old-growth to a good viewpoint of the estuary. The trail then opens into a stunted forest in a boggy alpine-like setting where boardwalks reduce the worst risk of mud. Expect many wet portions, but an otherwise easy section of trail.

Ⓒ SKINNER CREEK ●: The trail descends from the overland crossing to a campsite at Skinner Creek, where you'll find an outhouse and bear cache.

Ⓓ NAHWITTI RIVER: The trail between Skinner Creek and Nahwitti River is a fairly easy portion. The river crossing is by a West Coast Trail–style cable car, though the water is generally shallow enough to ford. Just watch your step on the rocks. The trail skirts the river mouth, which is a wide but rather forlorn estuary of rocks heavily modified by a history of poor logging. The beach on the east side of the river is suitable for camping; on the west side are a few ruins of old cabins. Casual trails that predate the North Coast Trail criss-cross the area.

Ⓔ NAHWITTI (LONE TREE HILL) STAIRS: A steep slope halfway between Nahwitti River and Cape Sutil has been made easier by the largest stairwell on the Cape Scott Trail. This marks a transition point for the trail. From the Nahwitti River to the stairs the trail is easy; west of the stairs it becomes quite difficult, alternating between rough, steep sections over headlands and cobble beaches on the way to Cape Sutil. Often the beach accesses are difficult to navigate, requiring scrambles up or down steep rock or dirt embankments. Other portions are notoriously difficult, with ropes added as needed but no ladders or stairs planned as of 2008. One particularly tough section requires an almost vertical climb to a small ledge, then an immediate vertical descent. The next 10 km qualify as the most difficult of the trail.

Cape Sutil.

● CAPE SUTIL: This beautiful and historically rich cape is split into three distinct beaches in a curving arc. The first beach lies below Nahwitti Stairs, and is a long stretch of cobble broken by a few rocky headlands. After a few pocket beaches and rough headland crossings, the trail descends to the main Cape Sutil beach and camping area. Here you'll find a small clearing suitable for upland camping or long stretches of sandy beach. An outhouse is located at the TRAILHEAD ● at the north end of the beach at what appears to be an impassable headland. Almost hidden to the right of the official trailhead is a trail starting with a steep scramble up the headland, then a more gentle crossing to the north beach, an arguably prettier and more sandy beach. This is also an access point for the tip of the cape, which was once a fortified First Nations village. It was abandoned after being shelled by the British Navy in 1850 in retribution for the murder of two British deserters believed to have been killed by members of the Nahwitti tribe. It has never been reoccupied. Trails criss-cross the area, with pocket beaches along the way. It's possible, though some bushwhacking is needed over headlands, to bypass the first overland portion of the trail west of Cape Sutil by instead following the beach.

ⓖ IRONY CREEK: The route between Cape Sutil and Irony Creek, continuous short ascents and descents over unimproved trail, is probably the most difficult portion of the North Coast Trail. Expect scrambles up or down dirt and rock sections. At Irony Creek the trail opens up into Shuttleworth Bight, a long stretch of sandy beach, then a second cable car crossing of the Stranby River. West of the river is an easier portion of the trail, with some good trail aids. This western portion of the North Coast Trail is covered on page 339.

ⓘ The Northern Vancouver Island Trails Society is overseeing the construction of the Cape Scott Trail extension. The official website is **northcoasttrail.com/northcoasttrail.htm**, which includes a list of water taxi providers. Or visit the Port Hardy links (page 325).

FOREST RECREATION SITES

See the map on page 322 to locate these recreation sites.

ⓥ Georgie Lake ●

This site is tucked into the east end of Georgie Lake, one of the largest lakes in the north island, popular for its cutthroat trout. About a half-dozen campsites are scattered throughout a small area in a mature forest with various trails leading from the sites to the lake and a sandy beach area. A charming 3 km trail skirts the east lakeshore to end at Songhees Lake to the north. The turnoff from HOLBERG ROAD ● is about 7 km west of the Island Highway, with the drive north another 5.5 km.

ⓦ Nahwitti Lake ●

Four sites are set in a circle in a forest setting. While it's near the lake, there's no lake access from the campground. For that, look for a turnoff to the lake just east of the campsite.

ⓧ Swan Lake

This small site has five campsites, four picnic tables and firepits but is best suited to just two groups. The setting is a maturing forest with limited access to a lake better suited to ducks than people due to the thick reeds along the shallows near the shore.

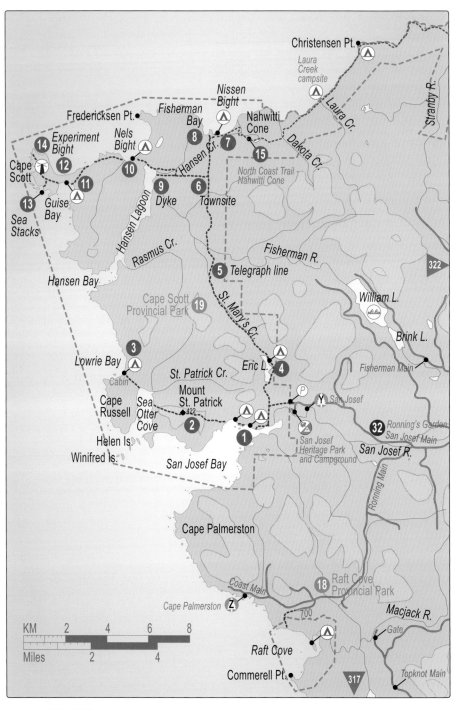

CAPE SCOTT

Christensen Pt.

Laura Creek campsite

Laura Cr.

Stranby R.

Nissen Bight

Fredericksen Pt.

Fisherman Bay

Nahwitti Cone

8

7

Dakota Cr.

Experiment Bight

14

Nels Bight

12

10

15

Cape Scott

Hansen Cr.

North Coast Trail Nahwitti Cone

11

9

6

13

Guise Bay

Dyke

Townsite

Sea Stacks

Hansen Lagoon

Rasmus Cr.

Fisherman R.

5 Telegraph line

William L.

Hansen Bay

Cape Scott Provincial Park **19**

St. Mary's Cr.

Brink L.

322

Lowrie Bay

3

St. Patrick Cr.

Eric L.

4

Fisherman Main

Cabin

Mount St. Patrick

Cape Russell

Sea Otter Cove

422

2

P

Y

San Josef

Helen Is.

1

San Josef Heritage Park and Campground

Ronning's Garden

32

San Josef Main

Winifred Is.

San Josef Bay

San Josef R.

Ronning Main

Cape Palmerston

Raft Cove Provincial Park **18**

Coast Main

Cape Palmerston **Z**

700

Macjack R.

Gate

KM   2   4   6   8

Raft Cove

Topknot Main

Miles   2   4

Commerell Pt.

317

See pages 292–293 for main chapter map.

Cape Scott

Despite its isolation, the northwest shore of Vancouver Island has always had a special allure. Weather-beaten, stormy, windy and forlorn, it dashed two attempts to tame it by idealistic Danish settlers drawn to its elusive potential. Harsh conditions doomed the settlement; today the coast remains largely undeveloped thanks to these same characteristics and the added protection of Cape Scott Provincial Park. Hikers and visitors of a particularly hardy nature make the trip here, populating the sprawling northern beaches for a few months each year, with the occasional straggler during other times. The simplest reward is a quick outing to the wonderful sand beaches of San Josef Bay or Raft Cove, while the traditional prize is a visit to the lighthouse on the point at Cape Scott. It will be interesting to see how the North Coast Trail changes the goals of hikers here.

POINTS OF INTEREST

㉜ Ronning's Garden ● (map p. 332)

An early settler to this region was Bernt Ronning, who in 1910 went to carve out his home at the west end of the Wagon Road. He spent the next 50 years clearing and planting trees and growing plants in the two hectares he cleared, including a pair of rare monkey puzzle trees. After several decades of neglect the garden has been resurrected by the family and is open to the public by way of a 10-minute trail from a parking lot. Another 10-minute trail in the other direction leads to an old cemetery.

Ronning's Garden.

MAJOR PARKS

⑱ Raft Cove Provincial Park (map p. 332)

This pretty park, which can be reached by a trail from the parking lot, gives access to a long sand beach on a spit formed by the Macjack River. Volcanic rock outcrops on the north end of the beach provide an opportunity for visiting tidal pools or watching the exploding surf.

🚶 HIKING: The 2 km path from the trailhead to the beach is one of the muddiest and wettest on Vancouver Island. Good old wellies may not be high enough for some of the puddles and mud you are likely to encounter. You can spend considerable time and effort trying to bypass each mini bog or simply accept the worst and cheerfully wade on through.

PADDLING: The Macjack River is navigable, and hardy paddlers could launch from up the river at the northern limit of the Topknot Main and paddle to Raft Cove. This requires taking West Main just outside of Winter Harbour to Topknot Main. Those who make the trip can look for the old cabin on the south end of the river mouth.

FISHING: The Macjack is home to steelhead, coho and sea-run cutthroat.

CAMPING: Wilderness camping is possible anywhere along the spit on the sandy beach or at one of several clearings that have been created on the upland.

TRAVEL NOTES: A plan dating back to 1993 envisions creating vehicle access to Raft Cove, which would make it the only vehicle-accessible campsite on the northwest coast of Vancouver Island. That plan has been sidelined, however, and is unlikely to occur in the foreseeable future.

ACCESS: From Holberg, follow the San Josef Main 13 km west to the Ronning Main. Follow that south 10 km to a spur. A parking lot and the trailhead are at the end. The route is well marked.

⑲ Cape Scott Provincial Park *(map p. 332)*

This is one of Vancouver Island's wildest and most oddly scenic parks, protecting the entire north coast of Vancouver Island, from San Josef Bay around Cape Scott to Shushartie Bay near Port Hardy. I say it's oddly scenic because it's probably not

The trail to San Josef Bay.

San Josef Bay.

what you would expect of the storm-battered northern limit of the island. It's a charming mixture of expansive sand beaches, swampy forest and unusual features ranging from sea stacks to a desert-like sand tombolo. The most remarkable and accessible features are covered separately below.

1 SAN JOSEF BAY: Less than a kilometre into the Cape Scott Trail a side trail leads through some pretty forest to San Josef Bay, a wide, sandy beach divided in two by a headland broken with sea stacks and caves. Tenting is popular on either

A view of Sea Otter Cove from Mount St. Patrick.

beach, with pit toilets and bear caches provided in the upland. The trail is 2.5 km from the parking lot to the beach. Note the route between the two beaches is blocked at the headland at mid and high tides. A rough bypass goes over the headland.

2 MOUNT ST. PATRICK: Hikers on the San Josef Bay trail can round the beach to the far west extent, then take a rough trail up Mount St. Patrick. A sign states the trail is unsafe, but it's really simply unimproved, meaning exposed roots and mud for the trail. It follows the northern edge of a lower ridge then drops down a valley and rises quickly to the peak, where the heavy forest gives way to a subalpine environment of stunted trees and bog. The peak provides panoramic views over the countryside in all directions. Those who are determined can extend the trip down the west ridge to Sea Otter Cove, a total distance of about 10 km. At low tide the cove can be rounded via the beach to a trailhead leading to Lowrie Bay.

3 LOWRIE BAY: A good sand beach and spectacular surf are the main features of this remote bay, reached only occasionally by kayakers or hardy hikers. A rough cabin offers shelter if needed.

4 ERIC LAKE: This is the first campsite within the park on the Cape Scott Trail, at 3 km. Hikers often arrive late and hike here to spend the first night. Be cautioned: it's not spectacular and it's prone to mosquitoes; you'll probably be happier if you can make it to Nissen or Nels bight in the first day. Remnants of the Danish community can still be seen in a corduroy road built in 1908 south of the lake and a wharf at the south end of the lake. It served the community before a trail was built to bypass the lake. On the northeast side of the lake look for a giant Sitka spruce with a 7.2 m circumference.

5 TELEGRAPH LINE: A telegraph line was built to Cape Scott in 1913; part of the line is still visible here.

6 THE TOWNSITE: At 13.1 km along the trail a junction gives a choice of routes. Continue north along a rough section to Nissen Bight, a popular camping area, or turn west and travel to Nels Bight and the other beaches on the route to Cape Scott. Near the junction are several historic features. Just south of the junction is a set of graves. One is the burial site of an adopted son of the local schoolteacher. William Christiansen died at the age of 12 from an infected cut on his foot in 1906. The pink granite gravestone is just east off the trail. Across the trail are some lesser-known graves. Just west of the junction is the old settlement's townsite. Most indications have disappeared, but look for a wooden cart and a collapsed tool shed at the Spencer farm site north of the trail. A caterpillar tractor between two trees north of the trail was the first motor used at the settlement.

7 NISSEN BIGHT: This beautiful curving sand beach is reached by continuing north along the trail. It's 15 km from the trailhead, the closest beach along the Cape Scott Trail, but visit at the expense of a few extra kilometres of hiking if your goal is the cape. Most campers tend to stay on the more protected west shore, though driftwood wind baffles have been created along the length. Water is from a creek at the far east end of the bight. Toilets and bear caches are just west of the beach.

8 FISHERMAN BAY: This small cove makes a good place to explore if you're camping at Nissen Bight. You can walk a short trail from the main trail or scramble the rocks over the headland to reach the beach. A rusting hulk is a reminder of an ill-fated attempt by the Cape Scott settlement to create a breakwater. The old sailing ship washed up from storms soon after it was put in place.

The sand tombolo at Cape Scott.

9 DYKE: A major feature of the old settlement was fields created by dyking Hansen Lagoon. The first dyke, built in 1899, runs 720 m just east of Fisherman River. The second dyke, along the northwest shore of the lagoon, was built in 1905. The dykes have failed and have since become ditched, but if you feel like making the effort you'll find an old boiler used in 1898 for a milk condensery. It's stuck in the riverbank in the middle arm of the Fisherman River. Be warned: reaching it is not a simple hike.

10 NELS BIGHT: This is the most popular campsite, at 16.8 km from the trailhead. Water is from a creek on the west side of the bight. You'll also find bear caches and toilets here.

11 GUISE BAY: From Nels Bight the trail crosses a headland, then drops to a beach area on the east side of Experiment Bight before crossing to Guise Bay, a camping area at 20.7 km. Look for the evidence of a Second World War military presence here, including a plank road built in 1942, a collapsed building off a short side trail, and a couple of ruined cabins used as barracks. Guise Bay has a bear cache, toilets and water that may be difficult to reach at a small creek. Fencing, farm implements and the N.P. Jensen grave on the beach's west end are reminders of the attempt to farm this inhospitable portion of coast.

⑫ EXPERIMENT BIGHT: Hikers can bypass the main trail by continuing along Experiment Bight instead of crossing immediately to Guise Bay, then crossing at the sand neck. Look for a depression that played a role in Kwakwaka'wakw mythology as a footprint of Kanekelac, a creature that could step from Cape Scott to Triangle Island in a single step. The bight is occasionally used as a campsite, but lacks water or facilities. The sandy neck is an incredible feature of Cape Scott, contributing desert-like dunes to this very wet part of the world. The ecology is unusual due to the introduced species brought in by the Danish to vegetate the sand.

⑬ SEA STACKS: A short side trail west of Guise Bay leads to a small beach with some sea stacks. Portions of the trail here follow an old Second Word War–era plank road for use by the lighthouse.

⑭ CAPE SCOTT: The lighthouse atop the headland of Cape Scott has helped mariners round the notoriously stormy cape since it was built in 1960. The grounds of the lighthouse are open to visitors; sign a guest book or perhaps purchase a drink if your timing is right. A picnic area overlooks the Scott Islands, a string of remote islands as near as 10 km at Cox Island and as distant as 46 km at Triangle Island. The islands are the largest marine bird nesting site in British Columbia, protected in Lanz and Cox Islands Provincial Park and three ecological reserves: Beresford Island, Sardine Island and Anne Vallee (Triangle Island). A trail once led from the lighthouse to a bridge out to a rock, but it has been closed for safety considerations. The lighthouse is now the end of the road.

⑮ NORTH COAST TRAIL–NAHWITTI CONE: The North Coast Trail extension to the Cape Scott Trail heads east from Nissen Bight along a stretch of fairly level and easy terrain aided with boardwalks and bridges. It passes inland to avoid Nahwitti Cone, a low peak east of Nissen Bight. It reaches the shore again near Laura Creek, where a campsite is located. This is an incredible stretch of coast, where some Sitka and hemlock believed to be over 250 years old can be found. Look for the trees, some as high as 37 m, between Laura Creek and 2 km east of Christensen Point. East of Christensen Point the trail is fairly simple until the Stranby River; the remainder of the trail is covered starting page 326.

ACCESS: The CAPE SCOTT TRAIL ● begins at the end of Holberg Road. Simply follow it west to the end. The route is well signed. The trip is about 64 km from Port Hardy, with the final few kilometres potholed and rutted. A moderate-sized parking lot is barely enough to handle the summer traffic. A park host is located in a trailer at the parking lot. Anyone concerned with security can gain an additional watchful eye by paying to park at the San Josef Heritage Park and Campground adjacent to the trailhead.

FOREST RECREATION SITES

See the map on page 332 to locate these recreation sites.

ⓨ San Josef ●

This beautiful campsite in a mature forest adjacent to the San Josef River makes a good base for hikers visiting Cape Scott or San Josef Bay. A boat launch provides a water route to San Josef Bay (best traveled at high tide). A second camping option is at the San Josef Heritage Park and Campground, a private campsite slightly closer to San Josef Bay. There are an assortment of campsites and shelters throughout the property, with rough hostel-style accommodation and a boat ramp. It has the advantage of some measure of supervision for long-term parking.

ACCESS: The campsite is near the trailhead for the Cape Scott Trail. Take Holberg Road to Cape Scott and follow the signs.

ⓩ Cape Palmerston

This is one of the few camping areas on the north coast adjacent to the ocean and easily accessible from a vehicle. Steps and a trail from a small parking area lead to a beach and a scattering of five walk-in tent pads hidden among the trees. A nearby option is a well built cabin. The area is remarkable for the rugged rocky coast and the many offshore reefs that provide a show of breaking waves when the surf is rolling.

ACCESS: From the San Josef Main, take the Ronning Main south approximately 12.6 km west of Holberg. Follow the Ronning Main for 12.7 km past the turn for Raft Cove to the Coast Main, then follow the Coast Main for 2 km to the campsite.

GPS waypoints

Waypoints are given as a backup in helping you get to difficult or confusing locations, particularly where logging road signs are poor. Most GPS units allow you to pre-program waypoints, allowing you to determine the distance and direction of your objective.

Waypoints are also offered for some key locations along routes—either campsites or major features such as summits or landmarks. Use these to ensure you don't get lost or to calculate your distance from your objective.

Every effort has been made to ensure these waypoints are accurate. In the event an inaccuracy does occur, please check the website **www.thewildcoast.ca/ waypoints** for updates and corrections, or to provide a correction.

69 **South Shore Road at Honeymoon Bay**
N48°49.65' W124°12.48'

69 **Carmanah-Nitinat junction**
N48°51.79' W124°38.62'

Sooke region:

72 **Mount Wells parking lot**
N48°26.86' W123°33.29'

72 **Mount Wells summit**
N48°26.74' W123°33.33'

74 **Sooke Mountain Provincial Park parking lot**
N48°23.86' W123°39.94'

74 **Sooke Potholes parks parking lot**
N48°25.70' W123°42.73'

Juan de Fuca:

83 **China Beach trailhead parking area**
N48°26.27' W124°05.53'

84 **Rosemond Creek**
N48°27.00' W124°09.73'

84 **Ledingham Creek**
N48°27.30' W124°11.15'

85 **Chin Beach camping area**
N48°28.35' W124°15.27'

86 **East Sombrio Beach**
N48°29.61' W124°17.66'

87 **West Sombrio Beach**
N48°30.29' W124°18.71'

87 **Little Kuitsche Creek campsite**
N48°30.47' W124°20.29'

87 **Parkinson Creek trailhead**
N48°30.79' W124°22.32'

88 **Payzant Creek camping area**
N48°31.15' W124°23.80'

88 **Botanical Beach trailhead**
N48°31.58' W124°26.60'

90 **Sandbar Trail**
N48°33.90' W124°22.57'

93 **Parkinson Creek access logging road**
N48°32.65' W124°21.84'

93 **Rock cairn at west trailhead**
N48°32.76' W124°20.68'

93 **Bridge over East Sombrio**
N48°32.47' W124°14.56'

93 **Sombrio access**
N48°32.10' W124°13.59'

93 **Noyse Lake**
N48°32.40' W124°12.30'

93 **Jordan River Main**
N48°31.98' W124°10.68'

93 **Gilbert Creek**
N48°31.46' W124°10.10'

94 **Blueberry Hill tent pad**
N48°31.44' W124°08.32'

94 **Squirrel Summit**
N48°31.27' W124°07.94'

94 **Cold Lake**
N48°31.35' W124°07.47'

94 **Elk Lake access**
N48°31.27' W124°07.32'

94 **KOC cabin**
N48°31.46' W124°07.00'

94 **Jordan River access logging road**
N48°26.09' W124°04.54'

94 **Loss Creek bridge**
N48°30.01' W124°04.13'

94 **Another Bridge**
N48°30.89' W124°05.33'

94 **Helipad sign**
N48°31.08' W124°05.22'

94 **Spur north**
N48°31.23' W124°05.43'

94   Kludahk Trail trailhead
     N48°31.68' W124°05.98'

95   Information centre
     N48°33.43' W124°24.01'

96   Harris Creek spruce
     N48°39.65' W124°13.58'

97   San Juan River (Bridge)
     recreation site
     N48°35.28' W124°11.22'

97   Lizard Lake recreation site
     N48°36.41' W124°13.66'

Cowichan Valley region:
100 Kinsol Trestle, south access
     parking lot
     N48°39.32' W123°41.58'

100 Kinsol Trestle, north access
     parking lot
     N48°40.33' W123°41.77'

105 Dogwood Drive
     N48°58.81' W123°48.58'

106 Spectacle Lake Provincial
     Park
     N48°34.55' W123°34.02'

107 West Shawnigan Lake
     Provincial Park
     N48°39.52' W123°39.14'

108 Koksilah River Provincial
     Park parking area
     N48°38.63' W123°44.27'

109 Bright Angel Provincial Park
     N48°44.17' W123°40.75'

110 Sandy Pool Regional
     District Park
     N38°45.40' W123°50.07'

110 Stoltz Pool
     N48°46.31' W123°53.56'

114 South side of Chemainus
     River Provincial Park
     N48°50.34' W123°49.50'

114 Eves Provincial Park entrance
     N48°51.72' W123°41.92'

Cowichan Lake region:
116 Gordon Bay Provincial Park
     N48°50.21' W124°11.85'

117 Bald Mountain
     N48°50.07' W124°10.37'

117 Pine Point
     N48°53.27' W124°15.69'

118 Maple Grove
     N48°53.78' W124°17.12'

118 Little Shaw
     N48°55.30' W124°25.45'

118 Heather Creek
     N48°55.31' W124°27.62'

118 Nixon Creek
     N48°53.96' W124°23.26'

118 Caycuse Creek
     N48°52.21' W124°18.39'

118 Kissinger Lake
     N48°55.35' W124°28.95'

120 Summit Trail east trailhead
     N48°50.56' W124°09.22'

120 First junction
     N48°50.23' W124°08.38'

121 Bald Mountain parking area
     N48°50.14' W124°07.58'

Carmanah-Walbran:
122 Haddon-Wabran Junction
     N48°44.53' W124°34.87'

122 Old overgrown spur
     N48°42.86' W124°36.72'

124 West Walbran Trail trailhead
     N48°42.06' W124°36.80'

124 Bridge Over Troubled Walbran
     N48°39.43' W124°35.45'

124 South trailhead
     N48°39.07' W124°35.62'

GPS WAYPOINTS: CHAPTER 3

CHAPTER 6

295 **Logging Road**
N50°19.87' W126°25.31'

295 **Claude Elliot Main**
N50°13.93' W126°32.65'

295 **Atluck Main**
N50°16.65' W126°51.51'

295 **Nimpkish Main**
N50°16.45' W126°52.90'

295 **West Main**
N50°34.34' W127°07.28'

296 **Port Alice Highway**
N50°36.20' W127°18.52'

296 **Port Hardy Main**
N50°32.42' W127°23.41'

296 **Alice Lake Main**
N50°25.02' W127°21.63'

296 **K Main**
N50°25.54'W127°36.85'

296 **I Main**
N50°27.22' W127°40.50'

Tsitika region:
299 **Claude Elliott Lake Provincial Park trailhead**
N50°18.52' W126°33.83'

300 **Montague Creek**
N50°20.51' W126°12.00'

301 **Junction Pool**
N50°26.33' W126°15.12'

301 **Naka Creek**
N50°28.67' W126°25.63'

301 **Tsitika Crossing**
N50°24.28' W126°33.84'

301 **Hoomak Lake rest stop**
N50°11.49' W126°31.59'

Nimpkish:
305 **Little Huson Cave Regional Park**
N50°17.05' W126°56.98'

307 **Bonanza Lake**
N50°20.32' W126°44.58'

307 **Ida Lake**
N50°27.60' W126°48.55'

307 **Nimpkish Lake**
N50°20.06' W126°55.30'

307 **Nimpkish Lake turnoff**
N50°19.53' W126°53.78'

308 **Anutz Lake**
N50°17.80' W126°55.00'

308 **Atluck Lake**
N50°13.67' W126°55.74'

Port Alice region:
310 **Eternal Fountain**
N50°25.45' W127°20.42'

311 **Devil's Bath**
N50°28.71' W127°18.37'

311 **Merry Widow Mountain Trail spur**
N50°21.27' W127°13.99'

311 **Merry Widow Mountain Trail trailhead**
N50°21.43' W127°15.43'

311 **Trout Lake Trail**
N50°20.75' W127°13.50'

311 **Vanishing River**
N50°18.18' W127°10.14'

312 **Cluxewe Trail**
N50°37.08' W127°12.66'

312 **Skidder Lakes Trail**
N50°29.21' W127°07.65'

313 **Clint Beek (Keogh Lake)**
N50°29.62' W127°10.25'

313 **O'Connor Lake**
N50°32.36' W127°14.27'

314 **Rupert Arm**
N50°35.38' W127°24.90'

314 **Marble River**
N50°31.58' W127°26.09'

315 **Link River**
N50°26.32' W127°23.55'

315 **Pinch Creek**
N50°25.78' W127°22.21'

315 **Spruce Bay**
N50°20.90' W127°21.80'

316 **Kathleen Lake**
N50°23.67' W127°15.83'

Quatsino entrance:

316 **Side Bay**
N50°20.08' W127°54.66'

316 **Side Bay junction**
N50°26.11' W127°51.50'

318 **Gooding Cove**
N50°24.04' W127°56.84'

320 **Hecht Main**
N50°32.83' W128°08.05'

321 **Quatsino Provincial Park S200**
N50°30.70' W127°50.00'

321 **Mahatta River**
N50°25.36' W127°46.29'

321 **Spencer Cove**
N50°30.05' W127°52.43'

Nahwitti:

325 **Nahwitti River Trail**
N50°41.88' W127°48.73'

325 **Wagon Road Cave Trail**
N50°39.84' W128°01.67'

326 **Salmon habitat trail**
N50°40.06' W128°04.35'

329 **Shushartie Bay trailhead**
N50°51.21' W127°52.04'

329 **Skinner Creek**
N50°51.86' W127°58.49'

330 **Cape Sutil trailhead**
N50°52.21' W128°03.28'

331 **Georgie Lake**
N50°44.69' W127°36.84'

331 **Holberg Road**
N50°42.76' W127°34.97'

331 **Nahwitti Lake**
N50°42.21' W127°51.71'

Cape Scott region:

333 **Ronning's Garden**
N50°40.27' W128°10.73'

339 **Cape Scott Trail**
N50°41.13' W128°15.08'

340 **San Josef**
N50°41.05' W128°14.44'

Bibliography

This work represents a new but growing form of book research done almost exclusively in front of a computer instead of in a library (when not in an alpine meadow somewhere, of course). Many obscure government documents that once required a lengthy process to acquire are now available online. This presents a change in the traditional bibliography, which replaces book references with website references. In some cases multiple pages were used from the listed website; in that instance the parent page only is listed. I recommend all the following websites for additional research and information on Vancouver Island. Unfortunately due to the changing nature of this type of information, links are only presented as they were accessible at the time of compilation; for updates watch the links website at **www.thewildcoast.ca**. Note that many of these sites were referred to but information from these websites was not necessarily used in this book.

BC FERRIES
www.bcferries.com

BC GEOGRAPHICAL NAMES INFORMATION SERVICE
ilmbwww.gov.bc.ca

BC HYDRO
www.bchydro.com/recreation

BC MINISTRY OF ENERGY, MINES AND PETROLEUM RESOURCES
www.em.gov.bc.ca/mining/geolsurv/mapplace/default.htm

BC MINISTRY OF FORESTS AND RANGE
www.for.gov.bc.ca/dcr/rec/recmap.htm

BC MINISTRY OF TOURISM, SPORT AND THE ARTS RECREATION SITES
www.tsa.gov.bc.ca/sites_trails

BC PARKS
www.env.gov.bc.ca/bcparks
Documents used within this website included the applicable management plans or draft management statements for all the provincial parks on Vancouver Island.

BRITISH COLUMBIA WHITE WATER
www.bc-ww.com

CANADIAN MOUNTAIN ENCYCLOPEDIA
www.bivouac.com

CAPITAL REGIONAL DISTRICT
www.crd.bc.ca

CAVING CANADA
www.cancaver.ca

CITY OF CAMPBELL RIVER
www.campbellriver.ca

CITY OF COURTENAY
www.city.courtenay.bc.ca

CITY OF DUNCAN
www.city.duncan.bc.ca

CITY OF NANAIMO
www.nanaimo.ca

CITY OF VICTORIA
www.victoria.ca/visitors/leisure_parks.shtml

COWICHAN VALLEY REGIONAL DISTRICT
www.cvrd.bc.ca

DISTRICT OF CENTRAL SAANICH
www.centralsaanich.ca

DISTRICT OF METCHOSIN
www.district.metchosin.bc.ca/parkmaps.htm

DISTRICT OF NORTH SAANICH
www.northsaanich.ca

DISTRICT OF SAANICH
www.gov.saanich.bc.ca/resident/parks

DISTRICT OF SOOKE
www.sooke.ca

FRESHWATER FISH SOCIETY OF BC
www.gofishbc.com/fishstocking.htm

INTEGRATED LAND MANAGEMENT BUREAU
VANCOUVER ISLAND LAND USE PLAN
ilmbwww.gov.bc.ca/lup/lrmp/coast/vanisle

PARKS CANADA
www.pc.gc.ca

REGIONAL DISTRICT OF COMOX/STRATHCONA
www.rdcs.bc.ca

REGIONAL DISTRICT OF MOUNT WADDINGTON
www.rdmw.bc.ca

REGIONAL DISTRICT OF NANAIMO
www.rdn.bc.ca/cms.asp?wpid=848#regionpark

SIERRA CLUB
www.sierraclub.org/specialplace/yourplaces/eastcreek.asp

SOUTH ISLAND FOREST DISTRICT
www.for.gov.bc.ca/dsi/stewardship/objectives_for_recreation.htm

SOUTH ISLAND MOUNTAIN BIKING SOCIETY
www.simbs.com

TIMBERWEST
www.timberwest.com

TOWN OF COMOX
http://comox.ca

TOWN OF LADYSMITH
www.ladysmith.ca

TOWN OF LAKE COWICHAN
www.town.lakecowichan.bc.ca

TOWN OF PORT MCNEILL
www.town.portmcneill.bc.ca

TOWN OF SIDNEY
www.sidney.ca

VILLAGE OF SAYWARD
www.village.sayward.bc.ca

VILLAGE OF ZEBALLOS
www.zeballos.com/outdoor_recreation.html

WESTERN FOREST PRODUCTS
www.westernforest.com/nature/areamaps.html

WILDERNESS COMMITTEE
www.wildernesscommitteevictoria.org

Metric-to-Imperial Conversion

METRES TO FEET:
1 metre = 3.28 feet

KILOMETRES TO MILES:
1 kilo metre = 0.62 miles

HECTARES TO ACRES:
1 hectare = 2.47 acres

Index

Notes